Atlantic France

North Biscay to the Spanish border

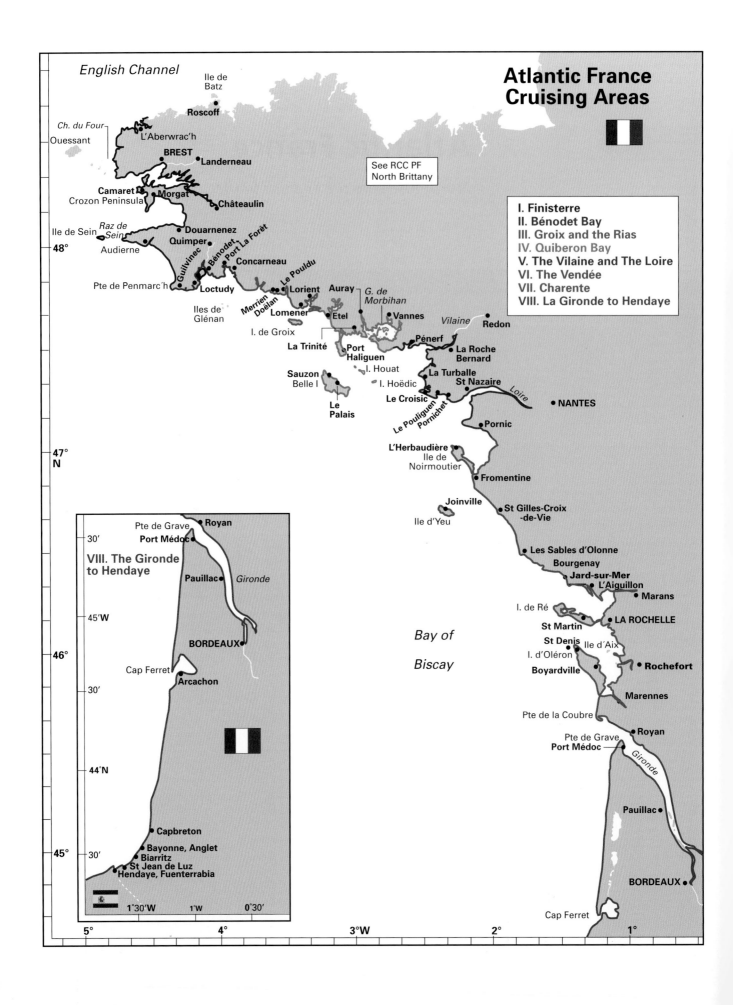

Atlantic France Cruising Areas

English Channel

Ile de Batz

Roscoff

Ch. du Four
Ouessant

L'Aberwrac'h

BREST

Landerneau

Camaret
Crozon Peninsula
Morgat

Châteaulin

Ile de Sein
Raz de Sein

48°

Audierne

Douarnenez

Quimper

Guilvinec

Bénodet

Port La Forêt

Concarneau

Pte de Penmarc'h

Loctudy

Iles de Glénan

Merrien
Doëlan

Lomener

I. de Groix

Lorient

Le Pouldu

Auray

G. de Morbihan

Etel

Vannes

La Trinité

Port Haliguen

I. Houat

Vilaine

Redon

Pénerf

La Roche Bernard

Sauzon
Belle I

I. Hoëdic

La Turballe
St Nazaire

Loire

Le Croisic

NANTES

Le Palais

Le Pouliguen
Pornichet

Pornic

L'Herbaudière
Ile de Noirmoutier

Fromentine

Joinville

Ile d'Yeu

St Gilles-Croix-de-Vie

See RCC PF
North Brittany

I. Finisterre
II. Bénodet Bay
III. Groix and the Rias
IV. Quiberon Bay
V. The Vilaine and The Loire
VI. The Vendée
VII. Charente
VIII. La Gironde to Hendaye

Les Sables d'Olonne

Bourgenay

Jard-sur-Mer
L'Aiguillon

Marans

I. de Ré

St Martin

LA ROCHELLE

Bay of

Biscay

St Denis
Ile d'Aix

I. d'Oléron

Boyardville

Rochefort

Marennes

Pte de la Coubre

Royan

Pte de Grave
Port Médoc

Gironde

Pauillac

BORDEAUX

Cap Ferret

VIII. The Gironde to Hendaye

Pte de Grave
Royan

30'

Port Médoc

45'W

Pauillac

Gironde

46°

BORDEAUX

30'

Cap Ferret

Arcachon

44°N

30'

Capbreton

45°

30'

Bayonne, Anglet
Biarritz
St Jean de Luz
Hendaye, Fuenterrabia

1°30'W   1°W   0°30'

5°   4°   3°W   2°   1°

Atlantic France

North Biscay to the Spanish border

 RCC PILOTAGE FOUNDATION

Jeremy Parkinson

Imray Laurie Norie & Wilson Ltd

Published by
Imray Laurie Norie & Wilson Ltd
Wych House The Broadway St Ives Cambridgeshire PE27
5BT England
✆ +44 (0)1480 462114 Fax +44 (0) 1480 496109
Email ilnw@imray.com
www.imray.com
2010

Partly based on *Harbours and Anchorages of North
Biscay Vols I* and *II* by K Adlard Coles, first published in
1959 and 1960 as *North Biscay Pilot* published by Adlard
Coles Ltd

Revised by Professor A N Black
Second edition 1977
Reprinted with amendments 1978
Third edition 1982
Revised by the RCC Pilotage Foundation
Reprinted with amendments 1985
Reprinted with amendments 1987
Fourth edition 1990
Sixth edition 2000
Seventh edition 2005

As *Atlantic France*
First edition 2010

ISBN 978 184623 280 0

British Library Cataloguing in Publication Data.
A catalogue record for this title is available from the
British Library.

The last input of technical information was August 2010

Printed in Singapore by Star Standard Industries PTE Ltd

CORRECTIONAL SUPPLEMENTS

This pilot book may be amended at intervals by the issue
of correctional supplements. These are published on the
internet at our web site www.imray.com (and also via
www.rccpf.org.uk) and may be downloaded free of
charge. Printed copies are also available on request from
the publishers at the above address. Like this pilot,
supplements are selective. Navigators requiring the latest
definitive information are advised to refer to official
hydrographic office data.

ADDITIONAL INFORMATION

Additional information may be found under the
Publications page at www.rccpf.org.uk. This includes a
downloadable waypoint list, links to Google maps,
additional photographs and mid season updates when
appropriate. Passage planning information may also be
found on that website.

CAUTION

Whilst the RCC Pilotage Foundation, the authors and the
publishers have used reasonable endeavours to ensure the
accuracy of the content of this book, it contains selected
information and thus is not definitive. It does not contain all
known information on the subject in hand and should not be
relied on alone for navigational use: it should only be used in
conjunction with official hydrographic data. This is particularly
relevant to the plans, which should not be used for navigation.

The RCC Pilotage Foundation, the authors and the publishers
believe that the information which they have included is a useful
aid to prudent navigation, but the safety of a vessel depends
ultimately on the judgment of the skipper, who should assess all
information, published or unpublished.

The information provided in this pilot book may be out of date
and may be changed or updated without notice. The RCC
Pilotage Foundation cannot accept any liability for any error,
omission or failure to update such information.

To the extent permitted by law, the RCC Pilotage Foundation,
the authors and the publishers do not accept liability for any
loss and/or damage howsoever caused that may arise from
reliance on information contained in these pages.

POSITIONS

All positions in the text are to WGS 84 datum. They are
supplied as aids to help orientation and to assist in locating and
maintaining transits referred to in the book. As always, care
must be exercised to work to the datum of the chart in use.

WAYPOINTS

The RCC Pilotage Foundation considers a waypoint to be a
position likely to be helpful for navigation if entered into some
form of electronic navigation system for use in conjunction with

GPS. In this pilot they have been derived from electronic charts.
They must be used with caution. All waypoints are given to
datum WGS 84 and every effort has been made to ensure their
accuracy. Nevertheless, for each individual vessel, the standard
of onboard equipment, aerial position, datum setting, correct
entry of data and operator skill all play a part in their
effectiveness. In particular it is vital for the navigator to note the
datum of the chart in use and apply the necessary correction if
plotting a GPS position on the chart.

Our use of the term 'waypoint' does not imply that all vessels
can safely sail directly over those positions at all times. Some –
as in this pilot – may be linked to form recommended routes
under appropriate conditions. However, skippers should be
aware of the risk of collision with another vessel, which is
plying the exact reciprocal course. Verification by observation,
or use of radar to check the accuracy of a waypoint, may
sometimes be advisable and reassuring.

We emphasise that we regard waypoints as an aid to navigation
for use as the navigator or skipper decides. We hope that the
waypoints in this pilot will help ease that navigational load.

PLANS

The plans in this guide are not to be used for navigation – they
are designed to support the text and should always be used
together with navigational charts.

It should be borne in mind that the characteristics of lights may
be changed during the life of the book, and that in any case
notification of such changes is unlikely to be reported
immediately. Users should consult the *Admiralty List of Lights*.

All bearings are given from seaward and refer to true north.
Symbols are based on those used by the British Admiralty –
users are referred to *Symbols and Abbreviations (NP 5011)*.

Contents

THE RCC PILOTAGE FOUNDATION

In 1976 an American member of the Royal Cruising Club, Dr Fred Ellis, indicated that he wished to make a gift to the Club in memory of his father, the late Robert E Ellis, of his friends Peter Pye and John Ives and as a mark of esteem for Roger Pinckney. An independent charity known as the RCC Pilotage Foundation was formed and Dr Ellis added his house to his already generous gift of money to form the Foundation's permanent endowment. The Foundation's charitable objective is 'to advance the education of the public in the science and practice of navigation', which is at present achieved through the writing and updating of pilot books covering many diffent parts of the world.

The Foundation is extremely grateful and privileged to have been given the copyrights to books written by a number of distinguished authors and yachtsmen including the late Adlard Coles, Robin Brandon and Malcolm Robson. In return the Foundation has willingly accepted the task of keeping the original books up to date and many yachtsmen and women have helped (and are helping) the Foundation fulfil this commitment. In addition to the titles donated to the Foundation, several new books have been created and developed under the auspices of the Foundation. The Foundation works in close collaboration with three publishers – Imray Laurie Norie and Wilson, Adlard Coles Nautical and On Board Publications – and in addition publishes in its own name short run guides and pilot books for areas where limited demand does not justify large print runs. Several of the Foundation's books have been translated into French, German and Italian.

The Foundation runs its own website at www.rccpf.org.uk which not only lists all the publications but also contains free downloadable pilotage information.

The overall management of the Foundation is entrusted to trustees appointed by the Royal Cruising Club, with day-to-day operations being controlled by the Director. All these appointments are unpaid. In line with its charitable status, the Foundation distributes no profits; any surpluses are used to finance new books and developments and to subsidise those covering areas of low demand.

PUBLICATIONS OF THE RCC PILOTAGE FOUNDATION

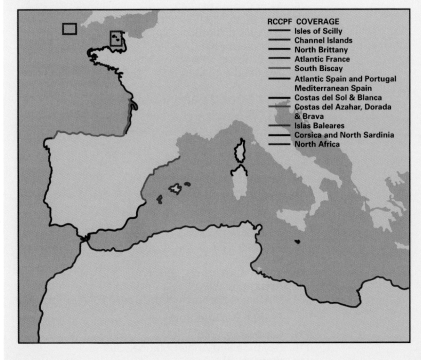

RCCPF COVERAGE
— Isles of Scilly
— Channel Islands
— North Brittany
— Atlantic France
— South Biscay
— Atlantic Spain and Portugal
Mediterranean Spain
— Costas del Sol & Blanca
— Costas del Azahar, Dorada & Brava
— Islas Baleares
— Corsica and North Sardinia
— North Africa

Imray
The Baltic Sea
Norway
North Brittany and the Channel Islands
Faroe, Iceland and Greenland
Isles of Scilly
The Channel Islands
South Biscay
Atlantic France
Atlantic Islands
Atlantic Spain & Portugal
Mediterranean Spain
    Costas del Azahar, Dorada & Brava
Mediterranean Spain
    Costas del Sol & Blanca
Islas Baleares
North Africa
Corsica and North
    Sardinia
Chile

Adlard Coles Nautical
Atlantic Crossing Guide
Pacific Crossing Guide

On Board Publications
South Atlantic Circuit
Havens and Anchorages for the South
    American Coast

The RCC Pilotage Foundation
Supplement to Falkland Island Shores
Cruising Guide to West Africa
Argentina

RCC PF Website www.rccpf.org.uk
Cruising Guide to West Africa
Supplements
Passage Planning Guides

Foreword

The origins of this pilotage book go back many years. The first publication to cover these waters was *Sailing Tours: Falmouth to the Loire* by Frank Cowper at the end of the nineteenth century; this present book is the eighth in line from Adlard Coles' 1959 *Biscay Harbours and Anchorages*, the copyright of which was donated to the Pilotage Foundation.

In this latest edition we have added the pilotage information from L'Aberwrach to Le Four and a major chapter covering from the Gironde to the Spanish border (Part 1 of *South Biscay*) and have therefore re-titled the book *Atlantic France*. In the Seventh edition, Mike and Gill Barron not only made full use of their extensive knowledge of this area but led the modernisation of our books with careful attention to presentation, and the use of GPS positions, in addition to retaining traditional navigational information; now Jeremy Parkinson has taken on authorship covering this extended, and complicated coastline and has spent considerable time cruising the area in his yacht *Feanor* to update the book.

This has been a major task and the Pilotage Foundation is grateful to him for his months of dedication necessary to revise this pilot guide. This work is supported by additional files and links available through www.rccpf.org.uk. These include mid season updates so that important changes that take place do not have to await the annual supplement. All yachtsmen are asked to contribute to keeping the book up to date by sending in their comments and observations as they find them – either to Imray or to the author via the Pilotage Foundation website system.

As always this book would not have been possible without the painstaking efforts of the team at Imray and we are grateful to them for their continuing support.

Martin Walker
Hon Director
RCC Pilotage Foundation
August 2010

Preface

'If, O hardy Corinthians, you have never found your way across the Channel before, I envy you your sensations as you come on deck for the first time in such a harbour as Brest.'

So wrote William Cowper in the first yachtsman's pilot book for North Biscay published in 1894, *Sailing Tours, Part 3; Falmouth to the Loire*.

How cruising under sail has changed since those days! GPS, GRP, dacron, auxiliary engines, marinas to name but a few of the wonderful advances that have been made. Jack-all-alone Cowper as he called himself would hardly recognise today's pastime as being the same as the one he enjoyed. He referred to his 29 ton engineless gaff yawl, *Lady Harvey*, as 'the old tub', yet he completed wonderful cruises in her, often single-handed. He wrote that his time in French waters during his cruise from Falmouth to the Loire was the most 'enjoyable and satisfactory cruise' that he had made and that he had 'no narrow escapes, no accidents and no difficulties of any kind'.

And, although our yachts and aids are so different, we too can come on deck in the morning at some anchorage or harbour on the Atlantic coast of France and enjoy the same sights and sounds and scents of La Belle France that Cowper did a century ago. And later there will be fresh croissants for breakfast, *paté de campagne* with a baguette for lunch under sail, and in the evening perhaps *fruits de mer* accompanied by a bottle of Muscadet at some delightful restaurant on another attractive harbourside.

How I, too, envy younger generations of yachtsmen and women the opportunities they have to discover for themselves, as I have done, these enchanting coasts. My hope is that this 1st edition of *Atlantic France*, (previously published under the title of *North Biscay*) now enlarged to include the whole of the Atlantic coast of France, will help to make many dreams come true.

Jeremy Parkinson,
Weymouth, July 2010

ACKNOWLEDGEMENTS

Perhaps the most important acknowledgement in this new edition is to the authors of the previous editions of *North Biscay*. I should particularly like to thank Gavin McLaren, author of the 6th edition and Mike and Gill Barron joint authors of the 7th edition, for providing me with such an excellent starting point.

An equally important acknowledgement is due to the late John Lawson, author of the companion volumes *North Brittany* and *South Biscay*. John's superb pilots overlap *Atlantic France* by a short distance in the north and by a much greater distance in the south. Big thank-yous are due to Peter Taylor and Robin Rundle who visited by land some of the harbours I was unable to sail to myself notably those in the Rade de Brest, the Bassin d'Arcachon and the French Basque ports and also to Patrick Roach who took the aerial photographs that are such an important feature of the book. The editor took many of the sea-level photos but I must thank Mike Barron for allowing me to use many of his excellent photos from the 7th edition. Other suppliers of pictures are acknowledged in the captions.

While compiling this volume, I have been given help and advice by so many yachtsmen, harbourmasters, marina staff and local people that I am unable to thank them all individually. Thus I must simply thank all the friendly, helpful people who cruise and live in North Biscay and Atlantic France who make cruising there such a pleasure.

Many users of the 7th edition have taken the trouble to contact the RCC Pilotage Foundation at www.rcc.org.uk or to email Imrays at ilnw@imray.com with information about updates they have come across in the course of their own cruises and as editor I would like to thank them all for their contributions which have been vital for producing the annual supplements and updating the new edition. Please keep them coming!

Some people have given me so much help and local knowledge that their contributions need to be recognised individually. These include Jake Backus (*Caper*), Tony Boas (*Ione*), David Darbyshire (*Eleanor Mary*), Stuart Naylor (*Laykin*), Wilfried Krusekopf (*Gueneval*) and Jonathan Virden (*Twayblade*).

David and Annette Ridout took on the vital but tedious task of proof-reading. In the process they made many valuable contributions that have helped to make this book clearer and more accurate.

Last but not least we must thank the unsung heroes at Imray and the RCC Pilotage Foundation who turned my notes and sketches into a book.

Jeremy Parkinson, July 2010

Introduction

OVERVIEW OF ATLANTIC FRANCE

The coast from Brest to Hendaye is over 300 miles long with more than 120 ports and a similar number of anchorages. It comprises seven fairly distinct areas. Each has its own character and is big enough and interesting enough to be a cruising area in its own right.

In previous editions the Gironde, the Arcachon basin and the French Basque harbours have been considered beyond the scope of *North Biscay* but our French publishers have requested that these areas be included, hence the name change from *North Biscay* to *Atlantic France*. And in this edition L'Abervrac'h at the west end of the North Brittany coast has also been included in deference to all those British yachtsmen who make it their first port of call in Brittany on their way from the UK to the Bay of Biscay or the Golfe de Gascoigne as the French call it.

Finisterre

The Chenal du Four and the Raz de Sein are two of Europe's nastier tidal races. As a result, many skippers like to pass through this region as quickly as possible. This is a pity because it is a splendid cruising ground with lots of attractive places to visit.

Camaret is a favourite first or last stop. Brest is a perfect spot in bad weather either at the excellent new Marina du Château in the commercial port or at the older Moulin Blanc Marina which is handy for a day at the magnificent Oceanopolis aquarium. However, the Aulne is the real treasure of the Rade de Brest and a trip to Port Launay and Châteaulin will be a high point in any cruise. Outside the Rade, there is excellent sailing round the high cliffs of the Crozon peninsula and the spectacular beaches of Douarnenez bay. If weather permits, a visit to Île de Sein offers challenging pilotage and a unique unspoilt island.

Bénodet Bay

Bénodet Bay is classic South Brittany. Bénodet and Loctudy are both delightful and somehow just right for messing about in boats. The Odet river from Bénodet to Quimper is possibly the most attractive river in North Biscay and has a number of peaceful anchorages. The Îles de Glénan, on a sunny day, could be mistaken for the Caribbean. Then there is the fascinating Ville Close at Concarneau, right next to the visitors' pontoon. Those who need a marina, will like the large modern one at Port-La-Forêt.

Groix and the Rias

The mainland opposite Groix has a series of flooded valleys that make interesting and attractive ports. Shallow draught boats can visit Pont Aven, where Gauguin worked, and see the fine art gallery and masses of artists' studios. The Belon River, home of the famous Belon oyster, is a pretty river where it is possible to combine peace and quiet with good walking and serious gastronomy.

Lorient is a big city with several marinas. There is plenty to do and a good waterbus for getting about. Etel is famous, or infamous, for having a very dangerous bar. It is necessary to call the pilot for entry instructions, which of course makes entry very easy. Once inside there is a nice town, a spectacular beach and an inland sea not much smaller than the Morbihan.

Quiberon Bay

Quiberon Bay is one of Europe's prime yacht racing centres. There are three large marinas – Haliguen, Trinité and Crouesty – and a dinghy-racing centre at Carnac. In addition, the Morbihan inland sea, which opens into Quiberon Bay, offers yet more good cruising.

It is said that the Morbihan has an island for every day of the year and the tides run so fast they can strip the galvanizing from an anchor chain. Neither statement is true, but there certainly are a lot of islands and the tide does run extremely fast, which makes the pilotage great fun but quite challenging. The Morbihan also has two very attractive medieval towns, Vannes and Auray. Vannes is particularly popular because it has a marina in the heart of town.

The chain of islands that protects Quiberon Bay also offers good cruising. Belle-Île, the 'beautiful island', is the largest with a couple of proper harbours and lots of anchorages; one of these has been described as the most beautiful in all France. The little islands of Houat and Hoëdic are also very attractive and perfect spots to anchor in good weather.

The Vilaine and the Loire

Brittany is generally considered to end at the Loire but some towns south of the Loire, such as Pornic, consider themselves to be Breton. However, well before the Loire the character of the ports and the coastline becomes much softer and more southern than true Brittany.

The jewel in this area is the Vilaine which was turned into a huge boating lake when a barrage was built near its mouth. It has 20 miles of non-tidal water, dozens of riverside anchorages and two delightful historic towns, La Roche Bernard and Redon.

South of the Vilaine, the granite hills of Brittany give way to the flat salt country around Guérande.

There are several attractive places to stay. Piriac is a pretty holiday town with a new marina; Le Croisic is a fascinating old salt and sardine port that is still surrounded by active salt ponds. La Baule has two marinas for those who need a spectacular beach, some posh shopping and a visit to the casino.

Vendée

South of the Loire, the smart holiday resort of Pornic is well worth visiting, as are the two lovely islands of Noirmoutier and Yeu. The former is flat and sandy with lots of salt ponds. The latter is rocky with good walking, a modern marina and the best tuna steaks in France.

On the mainland are the attractive fishing port and beach resort of Saint-Gilles and France's premier yachting port, Les Sables d'Olonne. It is at the latter that the Vendée Globe round-the-world race, the pinnacle of single-handed racing, starts and finishes every four years.

Charente

The Charente feels like the real south. There are sunflowers everywhere and the crew start complaining about sunburn and heatstroke instead of frostbite and mildew.

The area is centred on the two holiday islands of Île d'Oleron and Île de Ré. Both have north coast harbours that make good bases for biking and walking. On the mainland, the historic city of La Rochelle is a must and a trip up the River Charente to Rochefort is likely to be the high point of a cruise in this area. Both La Rochelle and Rochefort have good marinas.

The more adventurous can take the canal to Marans and visit the marshes of the Marais Poitevin or perhaps visit the River Seudre to see industrial scale oyster farming around Marennes. The oysters themselves can be sampled almost anywhere.

The Gironde

This river is much used by North European yachtsmen with yachts of moderate draft as a short-cut to the Mediterranean via the Canal du Midi but it is an interesting cruising area in its own right. The currents are fast and the water is silt-laden but for connoisseurs of fine wine it could be a mecca.

The Arcachon Basin

This is a useful stop-over between North Biscay and the Basque ports of France always assuming that there is not too much swell to make entry impossible. Once inside a shoal-draft yacht or a boat that can sit on the mud at low tide has a big advantage as there are very few harbours for fin-keelers. Oyster culture is a major industry and many of the small harbours are given over to it entirely.

The French Basque ports

These four small harbours are holiday resorts with the main emphasis being on their splendid beaches. But they are all interesting and quite different from one another so that they are all worth a visit.

GETTING THERE

Short hops or a long leg?

From the Solent, it is about 210 miles to Camaret, 260 to Bénodet, 310 to Crouesty and 410 to La Rochelle. In a modern cruising yacht, in good weather, that means about 36 hours to Camaret, less than two days to Bénodet and not much more to Crouesty. Even La Rochelle should take less than three days.

In summer, it is not hard to find a weather window of a couple of days but much harder to guarantee any more, at least in the English Channel. Hence there is a lot to be said for going as far south as possible as quickly as possible.

Both the tide and the wind usually make West Brittany and the English Channel easier on the way back. On the other hand, the passage home through North Biscay will usually be against the wind.

The best route

The best route obviously depends on the starting point and personal preference. From the Solent there are essentially two choices: the French route and the English route. The straight-line route is not an option because it cuts diagonally through the traffic separation zone near Alderney.

The shortest route is to head towards Alderney, cross the shipping lanes east of the separation zone and approach the Four along the French coast. This has the great attraction of meeting almost no shipping after Alderney and having no tidal gates until the Four. There are also plenty of ports of refuge.

The alternative is to go north of the separation zone, perhaps with a stop at Dartmouth, and then cross to the Four. This is only 20 miles further but will require long hours in the shipping lanes and must take account of the tide gates at Portland and Start Point.

The route via Falmouth is 50 miles further than the Alderney route. It has some tidal advantages and provides the option of going outside Ushant and Île de Sein. However, from the Solent, it only makes sense if the boat can be delivered to Falmouth in advance of the cruise.

Keeping the boat in France

An increasingly popular option is to keep the boat in a French marina. There are many excellent ones where a boat can be kept or over-wintered. Most are significantly cheaper than UK marinas.

TIDES

Tide times

Tide times for the majority of North Biscay are based on Brest. Those in the Charente are based on Pointe de Grave (PdG), which is only about 10 minutes later than Brest at springs and about 20 minutes later at neaps. Brest HW is at about 0600 and 1800 BST at springs and about 1200 and 2400

BST at neaps. Except in the Morbihan and some rivers, local HW is usually within 30 minutes of Brest. Thus, for planning purposes, the whole coast can be assumed to have midday highs at neaps and midday lows at springs.

Unfortunately, the exact differences from Brest vary quite a bit between springs and neaps and in this book have been averaged. French lock-keepers and French tidal atlases use Concarneau, Port Tudy, Port Navalo, St-Nazaire, Les Sables d'Olonne and La Rochelle as additional standard ports. Tide tables for these places are published in French almanacs and are frequently given away free in marinas. It is best to use them where possible, particularly for lock opening times. In fact it is well worthwhile buying a *Bloc Marine Almanac* (which is in French and English) at the first French chandler you are able to visit.

Official tidal predictions for French ports, in this area, are based on UTC +1. This means they are already adjusted to British Summer Time (BST) but need to have an hour added to convert them to French Summer Time (FST). Free tide tables and lock opening times must be checked carefully because they may be in BST, FST or even UTC.

Tidal heights

Mean tidal heights are given in the data box for each chapter. Accurate calculations of depth of water should be made whenever it matters. However, the sequence 12345 works moderately well for most of the coast. This says there will be roughly 1m of water at MLWS, 2m at MLWN, 3m at half tide, 4m at MHWN and 5m at MHWS. Unfortunately the MLWS figure of 1m is often a bit optimistic and 0.7m is closer to the average.

In Finisterre and the Charente, above half tide, there is more water than the simple rule would suggest. Perhaps it needs to be stressed that the 12345 rule is useful for planning purposes but must never be used when the exact depth of water matters.

All depths and drying heights in this book relate to Lowest Astronomical Tide (LAT) chart datum. Above water rocks, clearances under bridges and the height of lighthouses or hills relate to MHWS unless otherwise stated.

French tide tables and therefore French harbourmasters use a tidal co-efficient to quantify the changing tidal range between springs and neaps. An average tide has a co-efficient of 70, mean springs have a co-efficient of 95 and mean neaps a co-efficient of 45. Knowing the tidal coefficient for a particular tide is useful for gauging the strength of the tidal stream that one is likely to encounter as well as for assessing whether one is likely to be able to use a particular anchorage especially in the shallower areas near the mouth of the Loire and in the Charente region.

In French HW is Pleine mer (PM) or Haute mer (HM) and LW is Basse mer (BM). Springs is Vive-eau (VE) and neaps is Morte-eau (ME).

Tidal streams

Tidal streams in North Biscay are less intuitive than those in the English Channel. They flow towards and away from the coast as much as they flow along it. They are also unpredictable in direction and significantly influenced by the wind. However, in some places, such as the Raz de Sein or the Teignouse passage, they are strong enough to be potentially dangerous. In most rivers and harbour mouths they are also very strong and sometimes dangerous. Thus, it is important to take tidal streams seriously.

Tidal stream information is available from many sources. This book provides a number of simplified tidal charts and there is a summary of key tidal stream data for those ports where it matters. More detail is provided in the tidal stream atlas NP 265 *France West Coast* published by the UK Hydrographic Office and the SHOM tidal atlases, *560-UJA Goulven to Penmarc'h*, *558-UJA Penmarc'h to Noirmoutier*, *559-UJA St-Nazaire–Royan* and *565-UJA Goye de Gascoigne*. The latter are very detailed and highly recommended. However, note that French tidal atlases for La Rochelle are based on the time of low water not high water.

WINDS AND WEATHER

Winds

North Biscay is frequently under the influence of either the Azores high or lows passing along the English Channel. This causes the prevailing winds in summer to be west in the northern part and northwest in the southern part. However, other pressure systems are common and changeable Atlantic weather is the norm.

In addition to winds driven by large-scale weather systems, local sea breeze effects are very important. Atlantic France is well supplied with all the features necessary to generate a big sea breeze during the day. As a rule of thumb, a clear sky and a line of fluffy clouds along the line of the coast indicates that a sea breeze is developing and the afternoon wind will blow freshly onto the shore from the southwest gradually veering to the west. Quiberon Bay and Pertuis d'Antioch are both famous for the strength and complexity of their sea breezes.

There is a reverse phenomenon that is particularly important when anchoring for the night. A land breeze, known by the French as a *brise de terre*, can develop at about midnight starting gently and increasing to a fresh breeze from the northeast. This breeze can be particularly strong if it blows down cliffs or along rivers. Île de Groix is a good example. A night breeze blowing down the valleys and rivers in Lorient will blow directly from the northeast into the harbour at Port Tudy with very uncomfortable results.

Sunshine and rain

The weather in the southern part of the area is quite a bit better than the north. On average, there is less rain, about two hours a day more sunshine, temperatures are about 5°C higher and humidity is 10% lower.

However, when fronts cross southern Brittany or further south they can result in a few days of unsettled weather. One of the attractions of North Biscay as a cruising area is that there is always a protected inland waterway close at hand. The Rade de Brest, Lorient, the Morbihan, the Vilaine, the Charente and the Gironde are all protected and each has interesting towns so it is possible to get away from any unpleasant sea conditions. Further South however between the Gironde and the Basque ports there is no port of refuge and a reliable long-range forecast is needed before embarking on the passage.

Visibility

Fog, mist or haze can be frequent in the summer. On average, visibility is less than five miles on one day in five. Real fog, with visibility of less than 0.5M, averages one day in twenty. The coast is so well marked by beacons and towers that navigation in poor visibility is possible, particularly with the help of GPS and radar. However, fog can be particularly unpleasant in narrow tidal waters and rivers.

Swell

Swell is generated by storms and winds of Force 6 and above. With persistent winds of Force 8 or more, large waves are created that can take a few days to die down and will radiate out into areas that were never affected by the strong winds.

A large swell will break heavily on bars and in shallow water and can make some entrances, such as Belon, Etel and the Vilaine, dangerous even in fine weather. If swell enters a narrowing inlet, it tends to increase in height and steepness and funnel up the entrance to make anchorages uncomfortable or even untenable. In open water it can break intermittently and dangerously on rocks that rise from deep water, even if the depth over them is apparently safe.

In North Biscay swell occurs mainly on the northwest and west coasts of Brittany, particularly in the vicinity of Ouessant and northeast of Le Four. It is less frequent in the Bay of Biscay. However, any anchorages that are open to the Atlantic, such as those on the west and south side of Île de Groix, Belle-Île and Île d'Yeu should only be used in settled weather. Before using such an anchorage, it is worth checking that there have been no recent disturbances in the Atlantic that could generate a sudden swell. French weather forecasts include predictions of the height of the swell (*la houle*).

Weather forecasts

North Biscay is very well served for weather forecasts. The many available sources are summarised in an excellent, 30 page booklet called *Le Guide Marine* from Météo France. This is available free in every port office. It also contains an invaluable lexicon of meteorological terms in French and English.

Navtex forecasts are available from CROSS Corsen on 518kHz (A) and 490kHZ (E). The latter provides more local detail but in French. In the northern part of the area, less detailed forecasts can also be received from Niton on 518kHz (E) and in the southern part from La Coruña on 518KHz (D).

CROSS Corsen and CROSS Etel transmit area forecasts on VHF several times a day. These are detailed and generally accurate. They are in French but, with the aid of the Météo France lexicon mentioned above, even non-French speakers should be able to understand them. The times and frequencies vary from place to place and are shown in the table below.

Area	Ch	Local times
Le Stiff	79	0503, 0715, 1115[1], 1545, 1915
Pte du Raz	79	0445, 0703, 1103[1], 1533, 1903
Penmarc'h	80	0703, 1533, 1903
Île de Groix	80	0715, 1545, 1915
Belle-Île	80	0733, 1603, 1933
St-Nazaire	80	0745, 1615, 1945
Île d'Yeu	80	0803, 1633, 2003
Sables	80	0815, 1645, 2015
Chassiron	79	0703, 1533, 1903
Soulac	79	0715, 1545, 1915

[1] 1 May to 30 September

There is also a continuous forecast for shipping on VHF Ch 63. Again it is in French but the terms used are quite simple and after a little practice, and a basic knowledge of French, one can understand it fairly well.

Most marinas display a daily forecast and quite detailed forecasts are published in the local newspapers.

Mobile phone coverage is excellent throughout the area and Wi-Fi is becoming commonplace in marinas so that phone and internet forecasts can also be used.

SEAMANSHIP

North Biscay harbours

North Biscay is a splendid cruising ground for yachts and powerboats of all types. However, smaller marinas and most local harbours are designed around the needs of local boats. These are typically quite small and many dry out on every tide: small fishing boats are ubiquitous and shallow draught sailing boats under 9m are very common. As a result, the room to manoeuvre and berth a 12m deep-keeled yacht will often be quite limited. There are plenty of deep-water ports and anchorages that can handle larger boats but a 10m bilge-keeler will certainly get to places that larger boats cannot reach.

Berthing space is scarce so rafting is very common. This may be on a visitors' pontoon or using bow and stern buoys or in a daisy round a central buoy. In all cases, long warps and plenty of fenders are needed. Mooring buoys rarely have a pick-up rope so a threading boat-hook is a great help.

Many former anchorages are now full of local moorings and sometimes it is possible to borrow one rather than anchor. In general, visitors' buoys are a distinctive colour or are labelled with a 'V', 'PL' or the word *Visiteur*. In popular harbours, such as the Morbihan, it is possible to phone the harbourmaster and officially borrow a private buoy. Otherwise it may be necessary to borrow one unofficially. This is always tricky because it is hard to tell whether the mooring is strong enough and whether the owner is about to return. There is no simple advice except to check the ground tackle as well as possible, never leave a boat unattended on a private mooring and be prepared to leave immediately if the owner returns.

Search and rescue

Search and rescue and navigational surveillance are handled by the Centres Régionaux Opérationnels de Surveillance et de Sauvetage (CROSS). CROSS Corsen covers the coast from Mont St-Michel to Pointe de Penmarc'h; CROSS Etel from Pointe de Penmarc'h to the Spanish border.

Either station can be contacted on VHF Ch 16 or VHF Ch 70 (DSC). Their telephone numbers are:

CROSS Corsen ☎ 02 98 89 31 31
CROSS Etel ☎ 02 97 55 35 35.

CROSS Etel also provides urgent medical advice. The relevant telephone number depends on the area, as follows:

Brest ☎ 02 98 46 11 33
Vannes ☎ 02 97 54 22 11
Nantes ☎ 02 40 08 37 77
La Rochelle ☎ 05 46 27 32 15
Bordeaux ☎ 05 56 96 70 70

Fishing hazards

There are many fishermen's buoys round the coast and sometimes well out to sea. They present a hazard, especially under power at night, and a constant lookout is necessary. The buoys are often laid in pairs, each with a flag. If the pair can be identified, it is advisable not to pass between them.

South of Lorient a different method of fishing is used and a line of very small floats is often run between the larger buoys. It is particularly important not to pass between these buoys.

Much of the area is used for shellfish farming. Mussels are grown on ropes attached to stout stakes driven into the seabed. They are extremely dangerous because the stakes cover at high water. Oysters are grown in metal baskets supported on racks. They also cover at high water and are dangerous. Shellfish beds are usually shown on large-scale charts and are usually marked with buoys or withies. However, the marks are sometimes a bit patchy, particularly in areas that do not get many visitors.

Some fishing harbours do not wish to receive visiting yachtsmen. These harbours have not been covered in this book and should not be visited except in an emergency. With the decline of fishing, attitudes are changing and some of these harbours are becoming more welcoming. If planning to visit a non-yacht harbour, seek local advice.

Port signals

The French authorities use two systems of signals to control the traffic into harbours. These are best explained by means of the diagram above.

By day and night three green lights one above the other signify that the port is open but that there are obstructions in the channel and vessels must navigate with caution. The traffic signals are not usually hoisted for yachts, and they should be regarded more as a signal to keep out of the way of large vessels.

PORT TRAFFIC SIGNALS

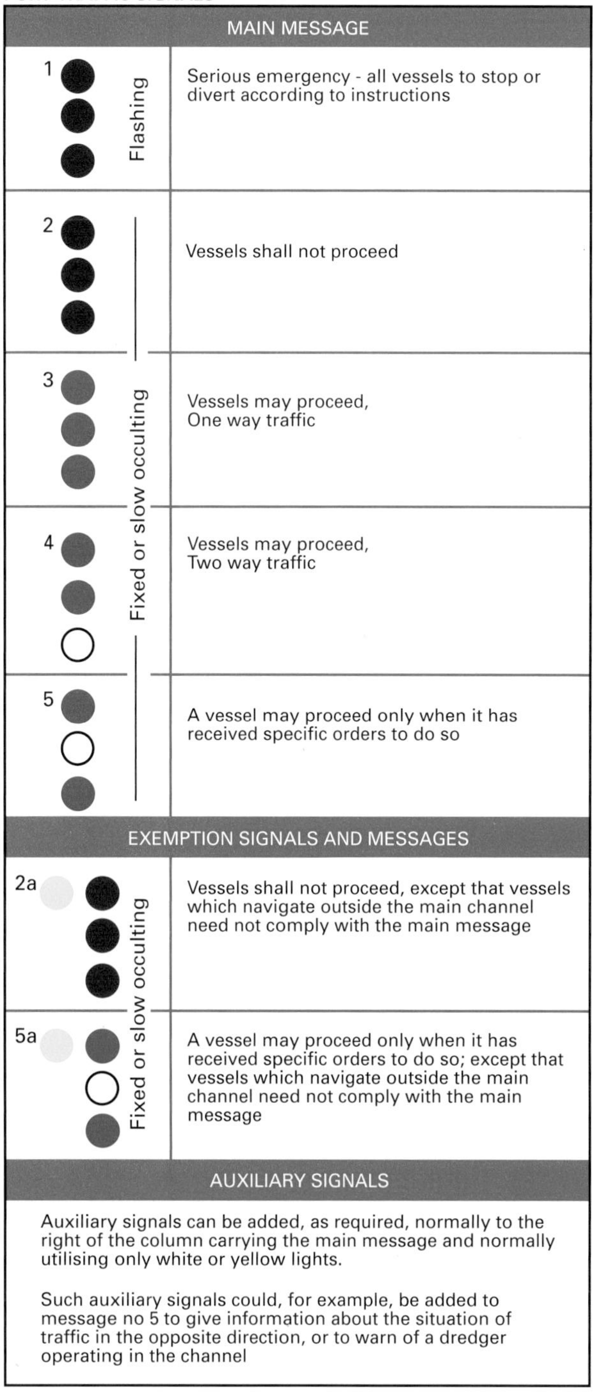

	MAIN MESSAGE	
1 (Flashing)	Serious emergency - all vessels to stop or divert according to instructions	
2	Vessels shall not proceed	
3	Vessels may proceed, One way traffic	
4	Vessels may proceed, Two way traffic	
5	A vessel may proceed only when it has received specific orders to do so	
EXEMPTION SIGNALS AND MESSAGES		
2a	Vessels shall not proceed, except that vessels which navigate outside the main channel need not comply with the main message	
5a	A vessel may proceed only when it has received specific orders to do so; except that vessels which navigate outside the main channel need not comply with the main message	
AUXILIARY SIGNALS		

Auxiliary signals can be added, as required, normally to the right of the column carrying the main message and normally utilising only white or yellow lights.

Such auxiliary signals could, for example, be added to message no 5 to give information about the situation of traffic in the opposite direction, or to warn of a dredger operating in the channel

NAVIGATION

BA and SHOM Charts

See Appendix I on page 318.

British Admiralty charts of the area at 1:50,000 or larger scale are copies of French SHOM charts. The SHOM originals use the same international symbols as British charts and the recent ones have explanatory text in English as well as French. The 'L' series are on good quality thin paper and folded to A4. They are convenient to use, good value and very widely available in chandlers, book stores and even newsagents. They are not updated by the retailer, so watch out for old stock.

Most navigation will be done using the 1:50,000 series but larger scale charts are necessary for some areas such as the Îles de Glénan and the Morbihan. In most cases, identical large-scale charts are available from the British Admiralty and SHOM but there are some important gaps in the Admiralty coverage. Thus it makes sense to stick to SHOM large-scale charts and buy them in France as needed. But beware that many SHOM charts and their BA equivalents are in ED50 and **not** WGS84 and positions obtained from a GPS working in WGS84 will need to be converted before being plotted on such a chart. See below under GPS Warning.

The most useful British Admiralty (BA) and SHOM charts are listed in the Appendix. They are classified into three groups: planning charts (1:200,000), passage charts (1:50,000) and large-scale charts. In each list, the charts are sorted from north to south. Where no exactly equivalent chart exists, NA replaces the number.

Imray charts provide an excellent and much cheaper alternative, particularly to supplement a chart plotter. They provide a passage chart, at a scale between 1:77,000 and 1:350,000, plus large-scale plans of most harbours. Another advantage is that all the Imray charts are in WGS84.

In addition to the list in the Appendix, the textbox for each chapter includes the relevant chart numbers. In the textboxes, the scale is abbreviated by omitting the thousands; thus 1:50,000 is shown as (50).

GPS warning

GPS is a wonderful aid to navigation with one serious shortcoming. Unlike all other forms of navigation, it uses invisible satellites and mathematics to produce a position. There is no link to the real world; hence not much to trigger the navigator's common sense when something goes wrong. Fortunately, modern GPS sets are accurate and reliable and, at least in Atlantic France, the charts are accurate, so what could go wrong? The answer is three types of human error, the wrong datum setting being the most common.

An enormous amount of care has gone into checking the waypoints in this book. Nevertheless, it would be naïve to imagine that there are no errors. Firstly, every waypoint must be treated as suspect until it has been plotted on a paper chart or chart plotter and the bearing and distance to the next waypoint in a route has been checked. That should deal with the authors' human error.

The second human error comes when waypoints are entered into the GPS or plotter. It is easy to type wrong numbers, easy to miss a crucial waypoint from a route and, on a plotter, easy to click a waypoint into a position relative to the wrong headland. Again double-checking is essential as well as a careful look at the resulting track on the chart to ensure that it does not pass over or close to dangers.

The third and most common human error is failure to set the GPS datum correctly. Paper charts for the area are particularly confusing because some use the French datum ED50 while others use the International datum WGS84. All waypoints in this book are based on WGS84. If these are used on an ED50 chart, without adjustment, they could be very dangerous. The difference is about 150m, which in several places could be a large enough error to be serious.

Chart plotters normally work in WGS84 and expect waypoints in WGS84. Thus the waypoints in this book need no adjustment for chart plotters and the visual position of waypoints on the charts and plans in the book should match the plotter.

The problem arises when paper charts are used. Most, particularly older ones, are based on ED50, so WGS84 waypoints must be converted to ED50 before they can be plotted. On the Atlantic coast of France, this requires adding 0'·06 to the latitude and subtracting about 0'·08 from the longitude. Many GPS sets can handle the conversion automatically by separately specifying the datum of the waypoint and the datum of the chart.

The very real risk of human error makes it vital to regularly check the position on the chart against the actual position. Formally plotting the position on a paper chart at regular intervals is good practice. But so is taking every opportunity to confirm the position with informal fixes such as the depth of water, buoys, objects in line, the distance and bearing to radar targets and so forth.

In several chapters, waypoints are provided to supplement intricate visual pilotage. It is obviously essential not to use the GPS as a substitute for visual pilotage but using the two in parallel can work very well.

Navigation and pilotage with GPS

There are three main ways to use GPS to keep off the rocks. First and most obvious is to enter a series of waypoints as a route and monitor the GPS off-track error to remain close to the route. It is often necessary to be a long way off track, particularly going to windward or in tidal waters, so it is always important to know how far off-track either side of the route is safe.

Most GPS sets can display the bearing to the next waypoint and this can often be used as a clearing bearing. In other words, off-track error is considered safe until the bearing to the next waypoint reaches a certain critical value.

All GPS sets display latitude and longitude. This can often be used directly to set horizontal and vertical clearing lines. For example, the dangerous rocks off the southwest side of Douarnenez Bay are all safely south of 48°06′.00N.

In this book, dangers close to routes are often mentioned. In these cases, it is particularly important to monitor the cross-track error near the danger. Not all dangers are mentioned, so it is necessary to check every route.

A good technique is to have a deck slate showing a list of waypoints, a summary of any dangers between them and a note of any clearing lines or clearing bearings. Since most GPS sets display the distance to the next waypoint, this can be used to specify the start and end of the danger zone.

Waypoints in this book

In this book, all waypoints are based on the WGS84 datum. They are shown on area charts and harbour plans using the waypoint symbol ($\oplus$) followed by the waypoint's number. At the back of the book there is an appendix containing a complete list of all waypoints. In the text and the *Appendix*, waypoints are referred to by both a name and a number. To maintain the clarity of the plans, some waypoints have been plotted slightly out of position. Their exact position is shown in the waypoint list and in the waypoint Appendix.

The pilotage section of almost all chapters contains a section headed *By GPS*. This provides one or more routes based on the waypoints. Where relevant, dangers close to the route are mentioned.

Passage waypoints and port approach waypoints are shown on the area chart at the beginning of each section of the book. Entrance waypoints are shown on the harbour plans. However, note that for a number of ports the approach waypoint is too far away to show on the harbour plan.

Navigating among rocks

Rocky areas are rarely as bad as they look on the chart. At any moment, many rocks are either below the keel or showing above water; only those in between are dangerous. Suppose a boat with a 2.5m draught (including 0.5m for safety) is entering the Îles de Glénan at half tide in a calm sea. The height of tide will be about 2.9m so all rocks drying more than 2.9m will be visible above the surface. The boat only needs 2.5m so rocks drying 0.4m or less will be safely below the keel. Therefore, only rocks drying between 0.4m and 2.9m are dangerous. In the Îles de Glénan, there are surprisingly few.

In swell or bad weather, rocks much deeper than the keel of the boat can cause unpleasant or even dangerous seas and are best given a wide berth.

Bearings

All bearings are expressed in degrees true and measured from the boat. In 2009, variation was approximately 3°W in the north and 1.5°W in the south of the area.

Lights

The height of lights is given in metres (m), and the range of visibility is given in nautical miles (M). Where a light has sectors, the limits of the sectors are usually shown on the plan.

The distance at which a light may be seen depends on its brightness and its height. Although its loom may be visible from a very long way off, a light itself cannot be seen when it is below the observer's horizon. Tables at which lights of various heights can be seen from different heights of eye are given in most almanacs.

The distance at which a light is visible also depends on the clarity of the atmosphere at the time. A 'nominal' range can be calculated for each light; this is the range its rays will reach if the meteorological visibility is 10M. It is this nominal range (given in *Admiralty Light Lists*) that is quoted in this book. On a clear night it may shine further and on a hazy night less far. Lights with a range of less than 10M will often merge into other lights on the shore.

The characteristics referred to in the text are for 2010, and are liable to alterations. These will be shown on chart corrections and in the current *Admiralty List of Lights Volumes A* and *D*.

The general practice is for coloured sectors to indicate dangers and white sectors safe passages. However, this is not universal and should not be assumed. Generally, if a light shows a white safe sector with red and green sectors on each side, the green sector is to starboard and the red to port, at least in the principal channel. This rule is not universal and should be checked for each light. Narrow intensified sectors usually, but not always, fall within the safe width of the channel.

Lights are often 'directional'; that is, they show brightly over a very narrow sector and sometimes faintly outside the sector.

Beacons

In bad weather, the offshore marks on the Atlantic France coast suffer damage that may not be repaired for some months. Beacons and beacon towers can lose their topmarks or even be totally destroyed. In this case, they may be replaced by a small buoy, with the appropriate marking, until they are repaired.

Beacons are commonly painted to conform with the cardinal or lateral buoyage systems and often have the appropriate topmarks. The heads of breakwaters, forming a harbour entrance, are often marked with white paint, and may have a green triangle or red square indicating the side on which to pass them. Bridges often have similar marks to indicate the appropriate channel.

ASHORE

Formalities

EU countries, including the UK but not the Channel Islands, no longer require yachts travelling from one EU country to another to report their departure or arrival, unless dutiable or prohibited goods are carried, or non-EU nationals are on board. Only boats arriving from non-EU countries or the Channel Islands should fly a Q flag and report to customs on arrival.

It is essential to carry on board evidence that VAT has been paid on the vessel, and all yachts visiting France must carry a Certificate of Registry. Either full or small ships registration is acceptable. Documents must be originals and not photocopies. Heavy, on the spot, fines are imposed on defaulters.

All members of the ship's company should carry personal passports. In practice they are likely to be required only for identification, for independent return to the UK by public transport and, in the case of the owner, for dealing with the Customs.

It is not unusual to be boarded by customs even when underway. During a visit ask for *une fiche*; if the officers are satisfied, you will be given one to show that the vessel has been cleared. Should you be approached at a later date, it may only be necessary to show *la fiche* to satisfy the officials.

It is no longer forbidden for one skipper to hand over to another in French waters, but owners must be aware of, and abide by, European VAT regulations and the French regulations for chartering.

Provisions

Before setting out to buy stores it is important to remember that many shops including some supermarkets close at 1200LT and do not open again until 1500 or later. (This also applies to many harbour and marina offices).

It is convenient to think about on board provisions in three categories. There are foods with a long-shelf life, those items that keep a few days like meat, cheese or fresh vegetables, and those required on a daily basis, like fish and bread. Fresh milk is not always available in France but UHT milk is much more convenient and seems to be more palatable than it used to be especially in the semi-skimmed form.

Provisions with a long shelf life can be stowed on board before departure or can be purchased from a French supermarket. These wonderful big shops with their wide range of useful long-life provisions have mostly moved to the outskirts of towns, close to the resident population, and are rarely convenient for marinas. Chateaulin and Crouesty both have excellent supermarkets close by but in most cases a special expedition will be required.

Larger towns like Audierne, Vannes, Pornic and Rochefort have specialist shops selling cheese, meat or vegetables and will often have a daily covered market. Smaller towns make use of the touring markets. These move to a different village each day and serve the vast temporary population of holidaymakers. Piriac has a market three times a week, in Pornic and Vannes the market stalls are set up in the old winding streets and at La Rochelle and Rochefort the quality of the food on sale is second to none. Where possible market days have been included in the chapters.

Most small holiday villages have bread shops and many have fishmongers selling the local catch. These are often closed from lunchtime until late afternoon and invariably there are long queues just before lunch.

When the text refers to 'all shops' it implies at least bread, grocer, butcher and cooked meats.

Telephones

Most public telephones require cards that can be bought in tobacconists, bars and post offices as well as other shops. GSM mobile phone coverage is generally excellent but sometimes patchy on the islands, particularly when screened by cliffs.

Wi-Fi

Pronounced *'wee-fee'* in French this is becoming readily available in more and more marinas. However reception is very variable and is better the closer one is berthed to the Capitainerie. A parabolic aerial which can be mounted on deck is a great help as down below one is often screened by various obstructions. In difficult situations most Harbourmasters allow laptops to be operated in the harbour office and some offices have a computer for the use of visitors free of charge.

Charges for the use of the system vary widely and in 2009 ranged from €4 for two hours to €1 for 24 hours. It is often cheaper to go to an internet café. (McDonalds burger bars are well known for supplying free Wi-Fi connection and an aerial may enable one to find other free access sites). In Brittany many of the marinas supplying Wi-Fi use Netabord and in 2009 60 days use could be bought for €14. This could be used in Brittany and also in the Vendée where Vendée Wi-Fi is available.

Water

Water is generally available on marina or pontoon berths. At other places, water may only be available in cans. On a harbour wall, the water supply may be of a size more suitable for a large fishing boat than for a yacht.

If water is not for drinking, it will be labelled *'non potable'*. Water taps rarely have hoses so it is best to carry one, along with a set of threaded adapters obtainable from British garden centres. If piped water is available it can be assumed that it is safe to drink, but it should be left to run for a while as there may be stagnant water in the pipes. As dogs often frequent French marinas it is as well to give the tap a good wash before use.

Fuel

Diesel and petrol are available at the waterside in most places. In France, it is illegal to use duty-free diesel for leisure craft and occasionally there will only be a duty-free pump for fishermen.

Marina diesel pumps are often 24-hour self-service, operated by a 'chip and pin' credit card. UK 'chip and pin' cards work usually but not always. (In which case it will be necessary to find a marina attendant or a friendly local who can be persuaded to operate the pump for cash).

Yacht clubs

There are yacht clubs and sailing schools in most French harbours; they are invariably hospitable to visitors. Assistance or advice is always given readily, and showers are often available.

Facilities

Not all facilities are listed for every harbour and common sense must be used. 'All shops' in a city like Brest clearly means something different from 'All shops' in a small fishing port. In both cases, it means all the shops that would be expected in a town of that type. If there is a marina it may be assumed to have water and electricity available on the pontoons, showers and toilets and a displayed weather forecast. Only the absence of these facilities is normally mentioned. The official number of visitors' berths is not given because these are frequently allocated to long-term visitors and are not available for short-term visitors. The few ports where space is a real problem are mentioned in the text.

Bicycles

Many long-term cruisers in North Biscay carry bicycles. In places, the best shops and particularly the big supermarkets are beyond easy walking distance. Some marinas have bicycles which can be borrowed free of charge.

All the islands are perfect for biking. They are fairly flat, have lots of bike tracks and are too big to explore on foot but perfect on a bike. The mainland is slightly less bike-friendly but there are still a great many places that can be explored on a bike but would be too far on foot.

On the islands, bike hire is easy and it is usually possible to hire a decent bike. On the mainland, bike hire is possible but often requires a long walk to pick up and return the bike and the quality of bikes is a bit variable.

REFERENCE FOR USING THIS PILOT

Using the port chapters

The description of each port is set out in a standard form. At the start of the chapter is a box containing the key data that a skipper is likely to need. Some abbreviations are used and these are explained below under abbreviations.

The body of the chapter provides a brief description of the port followed by pilotage notes and finally a description of the facilities ashore. The aerial and sea-level photographs are an integral part of the chapter and information is often provided in the captions that is not provided elsewhere in the chapter.

In pilotage information a draught of 3m or less is assumed and depths greater than this are either not mentioned or described as deep. Where depths or drying heights are given, they are always related to LAT. Also air draught is considered to be that of a masted yacht. Motorboats will often be able to go beyond bridges that are described as the limit of

navigation. In most cases, passage speed should not make too much difference but the author must confess that he cruises in a sailing yacht with a fin keel and may sometimes overlook the special needs of high-speed navigation and for that matter those of a yacht that can take the ground.

Abbreviations

BA	British Admiralty
ECM	East cardinal mark
HW	high water
HW+0230	two and a half hours after HW
HWN	high water at neaps
HWS	high water at springs
IDM	isolated danger mark
IGN	Institut Geographic National
kts	knots
LF	landfall
LW	low water
LWN	low water at neaps
LWS	low water at springs
m	metres
M	nautical miles
NCM	North cardinal mark
PdG	Pointe de Grave
PHM	Port-hand mark
SCM	South cardinal mark
SHM	starboard-hand mark
SHOM	French hydrographic office
SWM	safe water mark
WCM	West cardinal mark
WRG	White, Red, Green sector light

Key to plans

Where possible, the plans follow the international conventions used on British Admiralty and SHOM charts.

Most plans have been subdivided along the left-hand and bottom margins into tenths of a minute of latitude and longitude. The use of identical units in each plan should give an immediate indication of the scale. Alternatively, in some large-scale plans, a scale of metres is shown on the plan.

Ports of registration

The following letters identify the port of registration of fishing vessels and pleasure boats:

AD	Audierne
AY	Auray
BR	Brest
BX	Bordeaux
CC	Concarneau
CM	Camaret
DZ	Douarnenez
GV	Le Guilvinec
IO	Île d'Oléron
LO	Lorient
LS	Les Sables d'Olonne
MN	Marennes
NA	Nantes
NO	Noirmoutier
SN	Saint Nazaire
VA	Vannes
YE	Île d'Yeu

THE BRETON LANGUAGE

To those unused to Celtic languages, Breton place names seem strange and hard to remember. Many can be translated quite easily and once understood become entirely appropriate and much easier to remember. The wonderfully named Kareg Kreiz, for example, simply means middle rock.

Breton pronunciation is more like English than French, with the final consonants sounded. The letters c'h represent the final sound of Scottish loch or Irish lough (but not English lock); there is indeed a word *loc'h*, meaning a lake or pool; ch is pronounced as sh in shall. The French books and charts do not always distinguish between these, and there may be some errors in this book in consequence. In France, as in England, mobility and the radio/TV are killing regional differences. Thus Raz is now usually pronounced Rah; Penmarc'h, pronounced Penmargh a generation ago, is now often Painmar, and Bénodet has gone from Benodette to Bainoday and collected an accent in the process. The most misleading example is *porz*, which means an open anchorage but is often wrongly changed to the French word port.

A Breton glossary is hard to use because initial letters are often mutated into others, following complicated rules and depending on the preceding word. To cope with this, likely mutations are given after certain letters. For example, I. er Gazek is a common name for a small island. There is no word *gazek* in the glossary, but under G it says 'try K'; *kazek* means 'mare' and mutates into *gazek* after er. Mutations of final letters also occur, but these do not usually cause any difficulty.

Breton	English	Breton	English	Breton	English
aber	estuary	ell	rock, shallow	kleuz(iou)	hollow, deep
anaon	the dead	enez	island	koad, goad	wood
al, an, ar	the	er a, an	the	kornog	shoal
arvor	seaside	Breton	English	koz	old
aven	river	fank	mud	kreiz	middle
B (try P)		froud, fred	strong current	kriben	crest
balan, banal	broom	freu	river	Breton	English
bann, benn	hilltop	G (try K)		lan, lann	monastery
barr	summit, top	garo, garv	rough	marc'h	horse
baz	shoal	gavr	goat	melen	yellow
beg	point, cape	glas	green	men	rock
beniget	cut, slit	goban	shallow	mor, vor	sea, seawater
benven, bosven	above-water rock	gromell, gromilli	roaring	nevez	new
		gwenn	white, pure	penn	head, point
bian, bihan	small	hir	long	plou, plo	parish
bili, vili	shingle	hoc'h, houc'h	pig	porz, porzig	anchorage
bir, vir	needle, point	iliz	church	poul	pool, anchorage
bran	crow	izel	shallow	raz	strait, tide race
bras, braz	large	inis	island	roc'h	rock
bre, brenn	small hill	kan(iou), kanal	channel	ros	wooded knoll
breiz	Brittany	karn	cairn	ruz	red
bri, brienn	cliff	kareg	rock	ster	river, inlet
C (try K)		kastel	castle	stiv, stiff	fountain, spring
D (try T)		kazek	mare	teven, tevenneg	cliff, dune
daou	two	kein	shoal	toull	hole, deep place
don, doun	deep	kel(ou)	large rock	trez, treaz	sand, beach
dour	water	ker	house, hamlet	V (try B, M)	
du	black	kern	summit, sharp peak	W (try Gw)	
				yoc'h	group of rocks

I. Finisterre

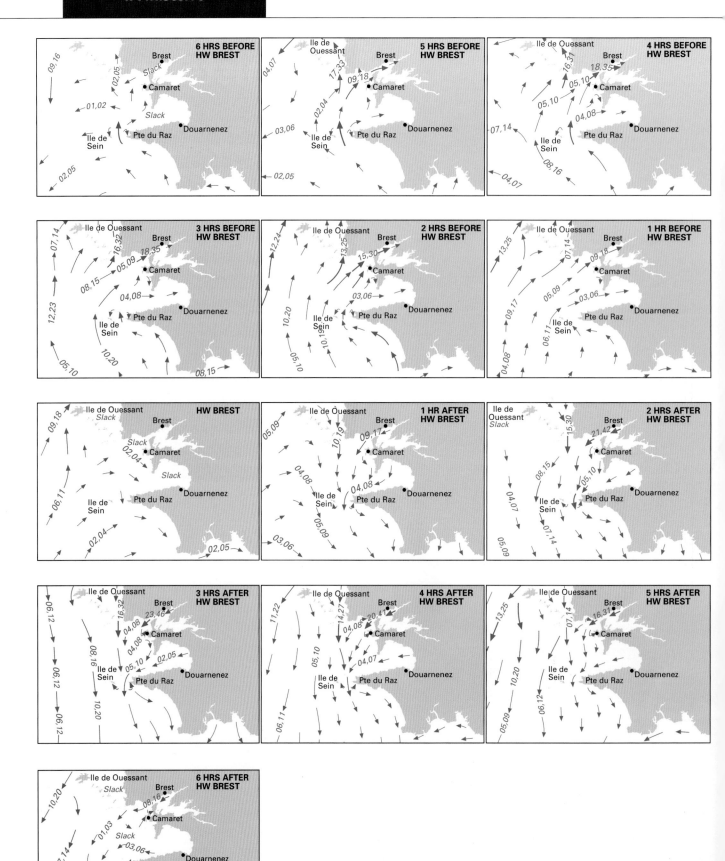

FINISTERRE TIDAL STREAMS

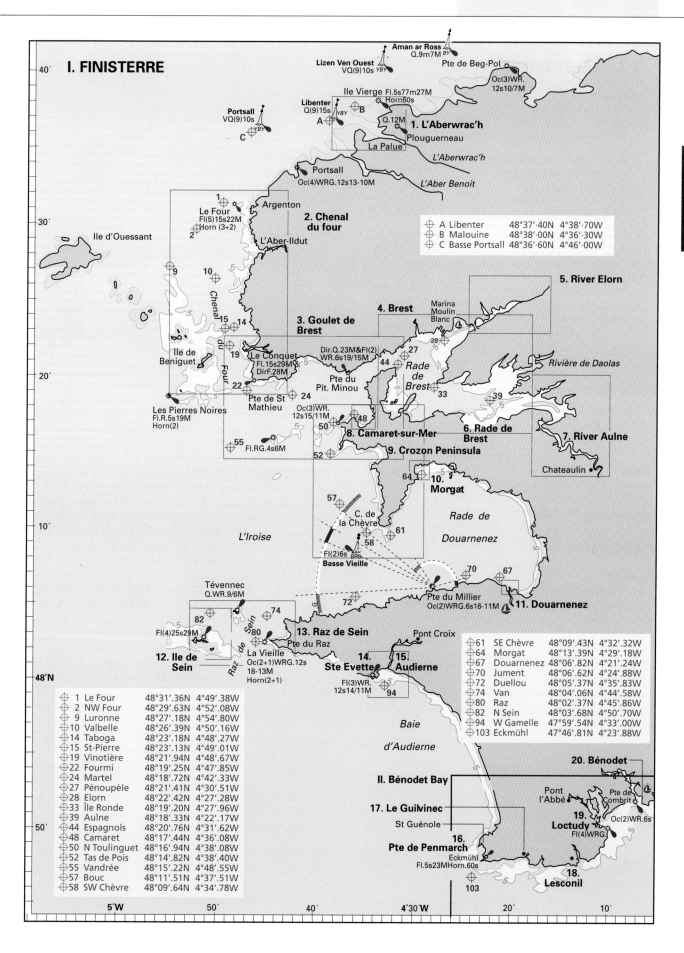

I. FINISTERRE

I. FINISTERRE

Aman ar Ross Q.9m7M *BY*

Lizen Ven Ouest VQ(9)10s *YBY*

Pte de Beg-Pol

Oc(3)WR. 12s10/7M

Ile Vierge Fl.5s77m27M Horn60s

Libenter Q(9)15s *YBY*

A   B

Q.12M

1. L'Aberwrac'h

Plouguerneau

Portsall VQ(9)10s

C *BY*

La Palue

L'Aberwrac'h

L'Aber Benoit

Portsall Oc(4)WRG.12s13-10M

⊕	A Libenter	48°37'·40N	4°38'·70W
⊕	B Malouine	48°38'·00N	4°36'·30W
⊕	C Basse Portsall	48°36'·60N	4°46'·00W

Ile d'Ouessant

1

Le Four Fl(5)15s22M Horn (3+2)

2

Argenton

2. Chenal du four

L'Aber-Ildut

9   10

5. River Elorn

4. Brest

Marina Moulin Blanc

3. Goulet de Brest

15   14

19   **Le Conquet** Fl.15s29M DirF.28M

Dir.Q.23M&Fl(2) WR.6s19/15M

Ile de Beniguet

22

Pte du Pit. Minou

27

44

Rade de Brest

33   39

Rivière de Daolas

24

Pte de St Mathieu

Oc(3)WR. 12s15/11M

48

50

8. Camaret-sur-Mer

52

6. Rade de Brest

7. River Aulne

Chateaulin

Les Pierres Noires Fl.R.5s19M Horn(2)

55   Fl.RG.4s6M

9. Crozon Peninsula

64

10. Morgat

57

C. de la Chèvre

61

58

Rade de Douarnenez

Fl(2)6s *BRB* **Basse Vieille**

70   67

Tévennec Q.WR.9/6M

82

74

Pte du Millier Oc(2)WRG.6s16-11M

11. Douarnenez

Fl(4)25s29M

80

72

13. Raz de Sein

Pont Croix

Pte du Raz

La Vieille Oc(2+1)WRG.12s 18-13M Horn(2+1)

14. Ste Evette

15. Audierne

12. Ile de Sein

Fl(3)WR. 12s14/11M

94

⊕	61 SE Chèvre	48°09'·43N	4°32'·32W
⊕	64 Morgat	48°13'·39N	4°29'·18W
⊕	67 Douarnenez	48°06'·82N	4°21'·24W
⊕	70 Jument	48°06'·62N	4°24'·88W
⊕	72 Duellou	48°05'·37N	4°35'·83W
⊕	74 Van	48°04'·06N	4°44'·58W
⊕	80 Raz	48°02'·37N	4°45'·86W
⊕	82 N Sein	48°03'·68N	4°50'·70W
⊕	94 W Gamelle	47°59'·54N	4°33'·00W
⊕	103 Eckmühl	47°46'·81N	4°23'·88W

Baie d'Audierne

20. Bénodet

II. Bénodet Bay

Pont l'Abbé

Pte de Combrit

17. Le Guilvinec

St Guénole

19. Loctudy Fl(4)WRG.

Oc(2)WR.6s

16. Pte de Penmarch

Eckmühl Fl.5s23MHorn.60s

103

18. Lesconil

⊕	1 Le Four	48°31'.36N	4°49'.38W
⊕	2 NW Four	48°29'.63N	4°52'.08W
⊕	9 Luronne	48°27'.18N	4°54'.80W
⊕	10 Valbelle	48°26'.39N	4°50'.16W
⊕	14 Taboga	48°23'.18N	4°48'.27W
⊕	15 St-Pierre	48°23'.13N	4°49'.01W
⊕	19 Vinotière	48°21'.94N	4°48'.67W
⊕	22 Fourmi	48°19'.25N	4°47'.85W
⊕	24 Martel	48°18'.72N	4°42'.33W
⊕	27 Pénoupèle	48°21'.41N	4°30'.51W
⊕	28 Elorn	48°22'.42N	4°27'.28W
⊕	33 Île Ronde	48°19'.20N	4°27'.96W
⊕	39 Aulne	48°18'.33N	4°22'.17W
⊕	44 Espagnols	48°20'.76N	4°31'.62W
⊕	48 Camaret	48°17'.44N	4°36'.08W
⊕	50 N Toulinguet	48°16'.94N	4°38'.08W
⊕	52 Tas de Pois	48°14'.82N	4°38'.40W
⊕	55 Vandrée	48°15'.22N	4°48'.55W
⊕	57 Bouc	48°11'.51N	4°37'.51W
⊕	58 SW Chèvre	48°09'.64N	4°34'.78W

L'Iroise

5°W   50'   40'   4°30'W   20'   10'

1 L'Aberwrac'h

Location
48°35'·94N 4°33'·64W

Shelter
All weather entry. Excellent shelter in marina.
Rather exposed from NW on wavebreaker and moorings

Depth Restrictions
1 and 2m in marina. Beware rocks SE of marina entrance marked by Y buoys and beacons inside and outside the wavebreaker.

Night Entry Yes, via Grand Chenal but 5M visibility needed to see Ldg Lts

Tidal Information
HW Brest +0030, LW +0037

Mean Height of tide (m)

MHWS	MHWN	MLWN	MLWS
7.7	6.1	2.8	1.0

Tidal Streams (off the entrance)
ENE-going stream starts HW Brest -0400
WSW-going stream starts Brest +0200.
Rate 3kns at springs 1.5kns at neaps

Berthing
In marina or on mooring outside marina or at anchor

Facilities
All including fuel berth but shops 2km uphill.

Charts
BA 1432 (25)
SHOM 7094 (25)
Imray C35

Radio
VHF Ch 09

Telephone
HM ☏ 02 98 04 91 62

Good staging post

L'Aberwrac'h itself is no more than a small village with a large sailing school and a yachtyard in a beautiful estuary but it is a useful stop to enable one to get the tide right for going down the Le Four channel. In 2007 a new and capacious marina was opened. There are bars and restaurants but if stores are needed it is a 2km walk up the hill to the village of Landéda although there is a bus in season.

PILOTAGE

By day

The easiest approach is by the Grand Chenal which begins 400m southwest of the Libenter WCM buoy which marks the extensive Libenter reef. In good visibility the Ldg Marks on Île Wrac'h and at Lanvaon on the hill 1.5M behind Île Wrac'h may be seen on 100° but from Libenter, Lanvaon is 4.5M away. If the Ldg Line cannot be identified steer on 100° to pass south of the conspicuous BYB ECM beacon tower Petit Pot de Beurre and leaving the Trépied PHM buoy and the Grand Pot de Beurre PHM beacon to port. Once past the Petit Pot de Beurre and the Basse de la Croix SHM buoy alter course to 128° up the marked channel towards the marina.

The alternative approach from the north and east is the Malouine Channel which provides a short-cut of 2–3M. However it should only be used in daylight and in good conditions and preferably above half-tide. The channel is named after the large rock La Malouine which is left close to port half way down. Start from a position 1.5M west of Île Vierge and identify the large La Malouine rock with the red PHM tower beacon behind it. Next identify the conspicuous BYB ECM tower beacon Petit Pot de Beurre which is the front Ldg Mk and steer 176° towards it when the rear Ldg Mk which is a white obelisk on Petite Île will be seen. There may be a strong cross-tide. Beware of the shallow patch (0.7m) close to starboard of the Ldg Line at the entrance to the channel and the drying rock on the port side a little further on. In any swell seas will be breaking on the starboard side. Once La Malouine

L'Aberwrac'h estuary looking west

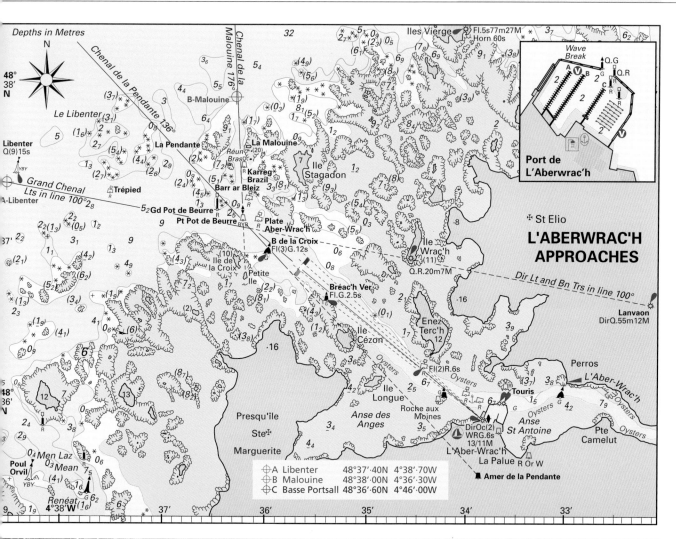

L'Aberwrac'h Marina from the north. The yellow buoys and perches marking the shallow
rocky area at the west end of the east wavebreaker can just be seen

I. FINISTERRE

L'Aberwrac'h estuary looking east with the lifeboat slip and the marina on the right

Rock and the PHM beacon tower are passed, course should be altered to port to leave two PHM buoys to port and the Petit Pot de Beurre to starboard and the main channel will then be joined.

The third approach channel from the northwest is the Chenal de la Pendante but it is narrow, has a strong set across it and the leading line is difficult to identify from seaward. For a first time it should only be used on departure with a large scale chart, above half-tide and then only in good conditions. It will not be described further here.

By night

Grand Chenal. Reach a position 400m southwest of Libenter WCM buoy Q(9)15s when the Leading Lights on Île Wrac'h (front) QR20m7M and at Lanvaon (rear) QW55m12M(intens) will be in line on 100°. Follow this course leaving the unlit Trépied PHM buoy to port until the first SHM buoy Fl.G 2.5s is nearly abeam when the second Leading Line Light Dir.Oc(2)WRG6s5m13/11M will be picked up on 128°. This leads past several PH and SH beacons and buoys, some lit and some unlit towards the marina and the moorings.

The Chenal de la Malouine and the Chenal de la Pendante are both unlit and unsuitable for entry at night.

By GPS

For the Grand Chenal use:
⊕A-Libenter 48°37'·4N 4°38'·7W

for Chenal de la Malouine use:
⊕B-Malouine 48°38'N 4°36'·3W)

BERTH

Either in the marina or on visitors moorings north of the marina. There is also an anchorage rather exposed to the northwest in 12–17m between Roches aux Moines SHM tower beacon and the lifeboat slip but beware oyster beds on either side. Anchoring is not permitted east of the lifeboat slip because of moorings. Yachts that can take the ground can anchor in the Anse des Anges clear of the oyster beds. Visiting vessels up to 15m moor to the wave-breaker pontoon on the west side of the marina where there is 2.3m. The inside of the wavebreaker is more sheltered. Inside the marina are pontoon berths in 1m and 2m for vessels up to 12m. Beware of rocks marked by yellow buoys and beacons both inside and outside the western end of the eastern wave-breaker. (See aerial photo on page 15).

The visitors' moorings are in 5–7m and can take vessels up to 18m. The fee charged is 80% of that charged in the marina. There are also visitors' moorings 3M further up the river at Paluden where it is beautifully sheltered in a blow. But there is not much water at LW springs. And there are no facilities. Anchoring in the river above the lifeboat slip is forbidden because of oyster beds.

ASHORE AT L'ABERWRAC'H

There is a yachtyard, chandler, sailmaker, bars and restaurants but if stores are required the shops and supermarket are 2kms up the hill at Landéda. A shuttle bus operates in season. There is a fuel berth at the base of C pontoon and Wi-Fi in the marina.

L'Aberwrac'h. The marina looking north

L'Aberwrac'h estuary at dusk *J Robbins*

2 Chenal du Four

Location
48°22'N 4°49'W

Hazards
Strong tide over uneven seabed;
complex tidal streams; well marked
rocks and shallow patches; fog

Night passage Well lit

HW time
Brest HW

Mean height of tide (m) Le Conquet

HWS	HWN	LWN	LWS
6.8	5.3	2.5	1.0

Tidal stream Le Four light
N – Brest HW–0530 to +0130 (2.2kns)
S – Brest HW+0130 to –0530 (1.6 kns)

Tidal stream Chenal du Four
N – Brest HW–0600 to –0030 (3.4kns)
S – Brest HW–0030 to +0600 (4.0kns)

Charts
BA 2356 (50), 3345 (30)
SHOM 7149 (50), 7122 (25)
Imray C36 (80)

Radio
CROSS Corsen VHF 16, 70 (DSC),
79 (MSI)
Le Conquet VHF 16, 12
Direction finding VHF 16, 11, 67

Telephone
CROSS Corsen ☎ 02 98 89 31 31
St-Mathieu ☎ 02 98 89 01 59
Le Conquet HM ☎ 02 98 89 16 98
or 06 30 36 89 56

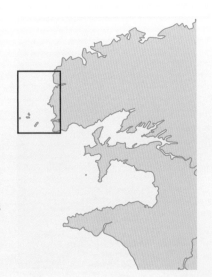

Exposed northwest corner of Brittany

The Chenal du Four is the shortest route between the English Channel and the Biscay ports. It avoids the larger seas and heavy traffic outside Ouessant. The channel is wide and deep and the navigation is not difficult. However, the strong tides and exposure to the Atlantic swell often result in steep seas, and the visibility is sometimes poor.

PILOTAGE

Tidal strategy

The roughest seas occur in the north approaches, not in the Chenal du Four itself. Northerly winds can bring a considerable swell to the area north of Le Four and wind against tide conditions produce steep seas. These reduce as soon as the tide turns. Also, Ouessant and the inner islands provide some shelter from west winds in the Chenal du Four.

With a fair wind, aim to go through the Four when the tide is favourable. If the wind is ahead, go through the narrow part, off St-Mathieu, at slack water because the stream there runs very hard.

The tide turns at St-Mathieu earlier than it does north of Le Four. Southbound, this is a nuisance because several hours of south stream run to waste. However, south of St-Mathieu the stream is much less strong and will have turned fair by the time the Raz de Sein is reached. Northbound, the tidal lag is a benefit and provides a few extra hours of fair tide.

Navigating in poor visibility requires special care. Once the narrows are reached, it is difficult to turn back. Speed over the ground is likely to be high so the buoys themselves become a hazard. In very bad visibility it may be better to avoid the area altogether.

The Chenal de la Helle is W of the Chenal du Four and is preferable in rough weather.

Chenal du Four

By day

From the northeast keep clear of the rocks and shallows of the Roches de Portsall by passing close to the Grande Basse Portsall WCM buoy and then at least 0.25M west of Le Four lighthouse. Then take care to avoid Les Linioux and especially the Plateau des Fourches. Enter the Chenal du Four northeast of Les Plâtresses which are now marked by two SBH buoys, the former beacon tower having been washed away. Valbelle PHM buoy marks the east side of the entrance to the channel. The lighthouses of St-Mathieu and Kermorvan should be in transit, bearing 158°. Continue on this course until Pointe de Corsen bears 012°.

Turn onto 192° and use Pointe de Corsen 012° as a back-bearing to pass between Rouget SHB buoy and Grand Vinotière PHM tower beacon. About 0.5M S of Grande Vinotière turn onto 160° to leave Tournon et Lochrist buoy and Les Vieux Moines to port.

Arriving late on the tide, the worst of the foul stream can be avoided by standing into the bay towards the Anse des Blancs Sablons, and the bay south of Le Conquet, but care must be taken to avoid the dangers.

By night

From the northeast, the channel is well lit and in good weather the navigation is easy. Steer with Kermorvan and St-Mathieu in transit, bearing 158°. St-Mathieu shows a fixed white directional light in a narrow sector each side of this transit, as well as the flashing light that shows all round.

When Corsen turns white steer in this sector, with the light astern. As soon as the auxiliary light on St-Mathieu becomes red, make good 174°, and enter the red sector of Corsen.

When Tournant et Lochrist buoy is abeam, the auxiliary light on St-Mathieu will turn white and the red light on Les Vieux Moines will open. Make good

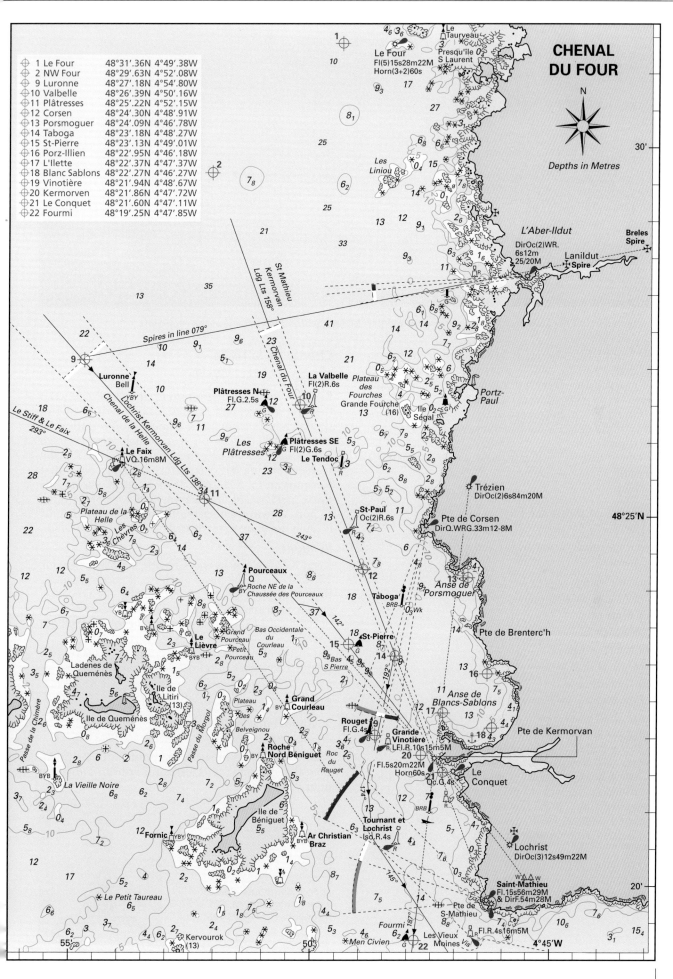

CHENAL DU FOUR

Depths in Metres

⊕	1	Le Four	48°31'.36N	4°49'.38W
⊕	2	NW Four	48°29'.63N	4°52'.08W
⊕	9	Luronne	48°27'.18N	4°54'.80W
⊕	10	Valbelle	48°26'.39N	4°50'.16W
⊕	11	Plâtresses	48°25'.22N	4°52'.15W
⊕	12	Corsen	48°24'.30N	4°48'.91W
⊕	13	Porsmoguer	48°24'.09N	4°46'.78W
⊕	14	Taboga	48°23'.18N	4°48'.27W
⊕	15	St-Pierre	48°23'.13N	4°49'.01W
⊕	16	Porz-Illien	48°22'.95N	4°46'.18W
⊕	17	L'Ilette	48°22'.37N	4°47'.37W
⊕	18	Blanc Sablons	48°22'.27N	4°46'.27W
⊕	19	Vinotière	48°21'.94N	4°48'.67W
⊕	20	Kermorven	48°21'.86N	4°47'.72W
⊕	21	Le Conquet	48°21'.60N	4°47'.11W
⊕	22	Fourmi	48°19'.25N	4°47'.85W

Le Four
Fl(5)15s28m22M
Horn(3+2)60s

Le Taurveau

Presqu'île
S Laurent

L'Aber-Ildut
DirOc(2)WR.
6s12m
25/20M

Lanildut
Spire

Breles
Spire

St Mathieu
Kermorvan
Ldg Lts 158°

Chenal du Four

Spires in line 079°

Luronne
Bell

Lochrist Kermorvan Ldg Lts 138°

La Valbelle
Fl(2)R.6s

Plâtresses N
Fl.G.2.5s

Plateau
des
Fourches
Grande Fourche
(16)

Portz-
Paul

Ile de
Ségal

Le Stiff & Le Faix
293°

Le Faix
VQ.16m8M

Chenal de la Helle

Plateau de la
Helle

Les
Chèvres

Les
Plâtresses

Plâtresses SE
Fl(2)G.6s

Le Tendoc

St-Paul
Oc(2)R.6s

Trézien
DirOc(2)6s84m20M

Pte de Corsen
DirQ.WRG.33m12-8M

Pourceaux
Q
Roche NE de la
Chaussée des Pourceaux

Taboga
BRB

Anse de
Porsmoguer

Pte de Brenterc'h

Grand
Pourceau

Le Lièvre

Petit
Pourceau

Bas Occidentale
du
Courleau

St-Pierre

Bas
S Pierre

192°

Anse de
Blancs-Sablons

Pte de Kermorvan

Ladenes de
Quéménès

Ile de
Litiri
(13)

Plateau
des
Belveignou

Grand
Courleau

Ile de Quéménès

Passe de la Chimère

Passe du Morgol

Rouget
Fl.G.4s

Grande
Vinotière
LFl.R.10s15m5M

Fl.5s20m22M
Horn60s

Qc.G.4s

Le Conquet

Roc
du
Rouget

Roche
Nord Béniguet

La Vieille Noire

Ile de
Béniguet

Tournant et
Lochrist
Isd.R.4s

BRB

Fornic

Ar Christian
Braz

Lochrist
DirOc(3)12s49m22M

145°

187°

Le Petit Taureau

Fourmi

Saint-Mathieu
Fl.15s56m29M
& DirF.54m28M

Pte de
S-Mathieu

Fl.R.4s16m5M

Kervourok
(13)

Men Civien

Les Vieux
Moines

ATLANTIC FRANCE 19

Southern part of Chenal du Four looking north with Les Vieux Moines beacon tower visible at the centre left

145° until Kermorvan is brought in transit with Trézien, bearing 007° astern. Be sure to get Kermorvan and Trézien in transit before leaving the green sector of St-Mathieu auxiliary.

Going south, keep east of the 007° transit until clear of the unlit La Fourmi buoy, which lies close to the transit.

Going east or southeast, leave Les Vieux Moines to port.

By GPS

From the northeast aim for:

⊕1-Le Four

From the north or northwest aim for:

⊕2-NW Four

continue using:

⊕10-Valbelle, ⊕14-Taboga, ⊕19-Vinotière

For Brest use:

⊕23-St-Mathieu, ⊕24-Martel

For the Raz use

⊕22-Fourmi, ⊕55-Vandrée

For Camaret use:

⊕23-St-Mathieu, ⊕48-Camaret

Note that ⊕22-Fourmi is close to the unlit Fourmi buoy so care is required at night.

It is possible to omit ⊕14-Taboga but this short-cut passes very close to the unlit Saint-Pierre buoy.

The Chenal du Four is wide and deep. In good weather, it is possible to deviate a long way from the suggested route, providing care is taken to avoid the isolated dangers. In bad weather it is best to stay close to the recommended route.

Chenal de la Helle

By day

Bring Kermorvan lighthouse to bear 138°, between the first and second houses from the right of five similar houses forming Le Conquet radio station. In good weather steer on this transit until Corsen lighthouse bears 012°, then make good 192° using Corsen bearing 012° as a stern bearing. Note that Kermorvan/Le Conquet transit leads across the Basse St-Pierre (4.5m) leaving St-Pierre SHM buoy to port. In bad weather the shoal can be avoided, by leaving the buoy to starboard.

By night

Keep Kermorvan in transit with Lochrist, bearing 138°. To avoid the Basse St-Pierre, if necessary, leave this alignment when Le Stiff light on Ouessant comes in transit with Le Faix, bearing 293°, and make good 113° on this stern transit to join the Four channel.

Northbound, take care not to leave the Lochrist/Kermorvan transit before the unlit Luronne buoy has been passed.

By GPS

Southbound, use:

⊕9-Luronne, ⊕15-St-Pierre, ⊕19-Vinotière

then continue as in the Chenal du Four. At night, note that Luronne, St-Pierre and Fourmi buoys are unlit.

Le Four lighthouse marks the extent of the Roches d'Argenton *M&G Barron*

ANCHORAGES

Ouessant and the inner islands are well worth exploring in settled weather. They are covered in the companion volume RCCPF *North Brittany* and require a detailed chart.

The following anchorages on the mainland are available under suitable conditions:

⚓ L'Aber-Ildut

This attractive little harbour is described in RCCPF *North Brittany* and not in this volume. It should not be entered without a detailed chart as there are rocks in the approach.

⊕4-Aber Ildut 48°28'·09N 4°48'·14W

⚓ Porspaul

Sheltered from northeast to southeast and slightly sheltered from other directions by the Plateau des Fourches. Porspaul is a drying harbour with an outer anchorage that can be used in fine weather and no swell. The entrance through the Plateau des Fourches requires a large-scale chart.

Identify Grande Fourche, about 1.25M east of La Valbelle, and approach it above half tide from the direction of Valbelle. Avoid the dangers of Plateau des Fourches, which are about 0.25M northwest of Grande Fourche. Pass about 200–300m north of Grande Fourche (⊕7-Porspaul). Steer towards Basse de Porspaul green beacon tower on 095° and round it by about 200m (⊕8-Porspaul 1). Anchor in about 200m east-northeast of the beacon. Boats that can take the ground can dry out in the harbour on firm sand clear of local moorings.

⊕7-Porspaul 48°26'·58N 4°48'·08W

The fishing town of Le Conquet looking north.
Pointe Ste-Barbe at the foot of the breakwater in Le Conquet has superb views at sunset when the lights from all the lighthouses from Le Four to Île de Sein can be seen.
To the north is the anchorage of Anse des Blancs Sablons and, beyond that, the next sandy bay and anchorage is Anse de Porsmoguer

⚓ Anse de Porsmoguer

Sheltered from north through east, this pretty bay is about 1M south of Pointe de Corsen. There is good holding in sand with depths shoaling from 6m.

The beach is popular for bathing and there is a village, without shops, about 0.5M to the north.

⊕13-Porsmoguer 48°24'·09N 4°46'·78W

⚓ Anse des Blancs Sablons

Sheltered from the southeast through southwest, this wide sandy bay is 3M south of Pointe de Corsen. It is free from dangers except off the headlands on each side. The anchorage is anywhere, in from 9m to 1m on a sandy shelving bottom. The bay dries out nearly 0.25M from the shore, except on the west side, where there is 3m close to the rocks off Kermorvan. There is often some swell.

This is a good place to wait out a foul tide. Slip round L'Ilette (the small islet just north of Kermorvan) when the stream becomes fair but watch out for the rock, awash at datum, that lies 200m east of L'Ilette.

⊕18-Blancs Sablons 48°22'·27N 4°46'·27W

⚓ Porz-Illien

When the wind is from the north or east, better shelter may be found in this little bay in the northeast corner of Anse des Blancs Sablons.

⊕16-Porz-Illien 48°22'·95N 4°46'·18W

⚓ Le Conquet

Sheltered from northwest through southeast, there is a good, though often crowded, anchorage in the inlet south of Pointe de Kermorvan. Leave the red La Louve tower to port and go in as far as depth permits. For a full description see RCCPF *North Brittany*.

⊕21-Le Conquet 48°21'·60N 4°47'·11W

I. FINISTERRE

3 Goulet de Brest

Location
48°20'N 4°34'W

Hazards
Strong tide in the narrows; well marked rocks in mid-channel

Night passage Well lit

HW time
Brest HW

Mean height of tide (m)

	HWS	HWN	LWN	LWS
Brest	6.9	5.4	2.6	1.0

Tidal streams Goulet de Brest (Chart 1c)
NE – Brest HW–0530 to –0030 (3.9kns)
Slack – Brest HW–0030 to +0030
SW – Brest HW+0030 to –0530 (4.0kns)
South side stream is weaker
Counter current in S side +0530 to –0530

Charts
BA 2356 (50)
SHOM 7149 (50)
Imray C36 (77)

Radio
CROSS Corsen VHF Ch 16, 70 (DSC), 79 (MSI)
Le Conquet VHF Ch 16, 12

Telephone
CROSS Corsen ☏ 02 98 89 31 31
St-Mathieu ☏ 02 98 89 01 59

Entrance to the Rade de Brest

The Goulet de Brest is the passage between the Avant-Goulet de Brest and the Rade de Brest. At the narrowest point, it is 1M wide and the tide in the narrows is fierce.

There are cliffs on either side but they are steep to. In mid-channel there is a chain of well-marked rocks called Plateau des Fillettes. The navigation is not difficult.

PILOTAGE

Rade de Brest approaches

By day

From the Chenal du Four, round Pointe de St-Mathieu and leave Les Vieux Moines PHM tower beacon, Le Coq PHM buoy and Charles Martel PHM buoy all to port. The transit for the Goulet is the twin white towers of Le Petit Minou in line with Pointe du Portzic grey octagonal tower on 068°.

The rocky Plateau des Fillettes is in mid-channel. Fillettes WCM marks the west end and Roche Mengam BRB beacon tower, 0.25M to the northeast, marks the east end. A line between them marks the south edge of the north channel.

The plateau extends well south of the line between Fillettes and Roche Mengam and two additional PHM buoys mark the limit of the danger.

The south passage is useful if the tide is ebbing because there is a counter-current on the south side of the Goulet in the last hour and a half of the ebb.

When using the south passage, take care to avoid La Cormorandière just off Pointe des Espagnols.

By night

From the Chenal du Four or west, round Pointe de St-Mathieu and identify the leading lights (068°) of Le Petit Minou and Portzic and steer on this transit. Once past Charles Martel PHM buoy bear to starboard to pass between Pte du Petit Minou light and Fillettes WCM buoy.

Pointe de St-Mathieu looking north.
Apart from the lighthouse, the buildings on the headland include those of a large Benedictine abbey church that was founded in the 6th century. It has been abandoned since the French revolution. The red beacon (inset) is Les Vieux Moines which should be left to port when approaching the Goulet de Brest *M&G Barron*

Leave Roche Mengam tower to starboard, steer about 070° towards Pénoupèle buoy. Beware that Kerviniou PHM buoy and Goudron PHM buoy are port-hand marks for the southern passage.

Coming from Camaret, steer N to enter the intense white sector of Portzic (Q(6)+LFl.15s). Alter to starboard and keep in this sector on about 047° until Roche Mengam beacon tower is abaft the beam to port, then turn onto 065° towards Pénoupèle PHM buoy as above.

By GPS

From the Chenal du Four use:

⊕23-St-Mathieu, ⊕24-Martel

From the Chenal du Toulinget use:

⊕50-N Toulinguet, ⊕46-Kerviniou, ⊕45-Robert

From Camaret use:

⊕47-Capucins, ⊕46-Kerviniou, ⊕45-Robert

Then for Brest and the Elorn use ⊕27-Pénoupèle

for the Aulne use ⊕44-Espagnols

The channel is wide and the dangers well marked so there is no need to stick slavishly to a GPS track.

Lighthouses at Pointe de Petit Minou
M&G Barron

ANCHORAGES

⚓ Anse de Bertheaume

Sheltered from north and west, but exposed to the south and east, this convenient bay is about 3M east of Pointe de St-Mathieu. Fort de Bertheaume, on the southwest corner of the bay, should be given a good berth to avoid Le Chat rocks. These are particularly hazardous when they are covered near HW springs. Anchor in one of the two bays immediately north of Le Chat, going in as far as possible for shelter. There are some visitors' moorings. Further north and east the bottom is foul with rocks.

⊕25-Bertheaume 48°20'·38N 4°41'·58W

⚓ Sainte-Anne de Portzic

Sheltered from the north and east and with a mole that provides some protection from the west, this is a small local harbour just west of Pte de Portzic. There are no dangers in the approach but there is an isolated rock marked by a beacon on the east side of the harbour.

The pier is used by survey vessels from the nearby Oceanographic research centre and must not be used by visiting yachts. However, it may be possible to borrow a mooring or to anchor outside the moorings.

⊕26-St-Anne 48°21'·53N 4°32'·88W

The Goulet de Brest looking east.
The Goulet is only 1M wide at its narrowest point, between Pointe de Portzic and Pointe des Espagnols. The Goulet marks the entrance to the Rade de Brest with its many anchorages and rivers and the sprawling city of Brest at the north of the Rade

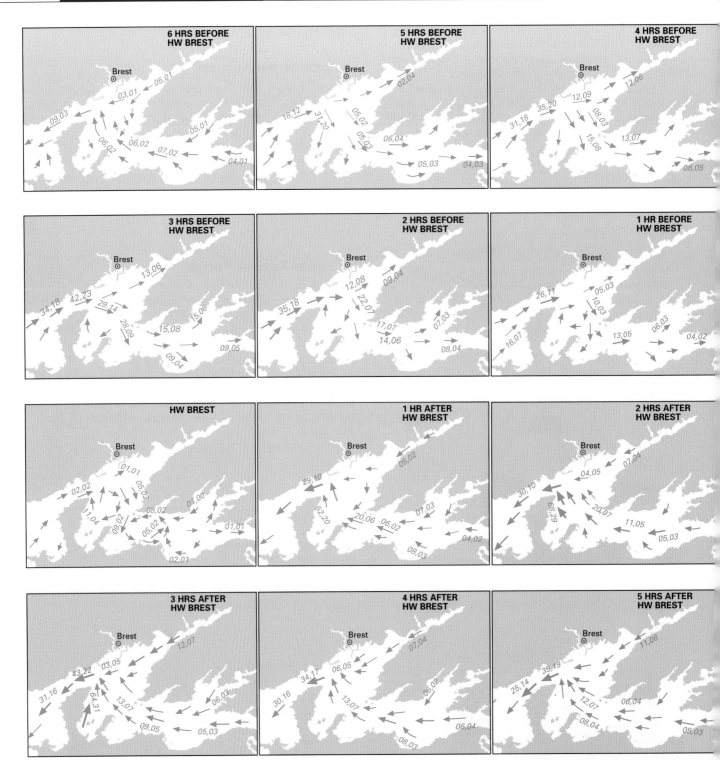

GOULET DE BREST TIDAL STREAM

GOULET DE BREST

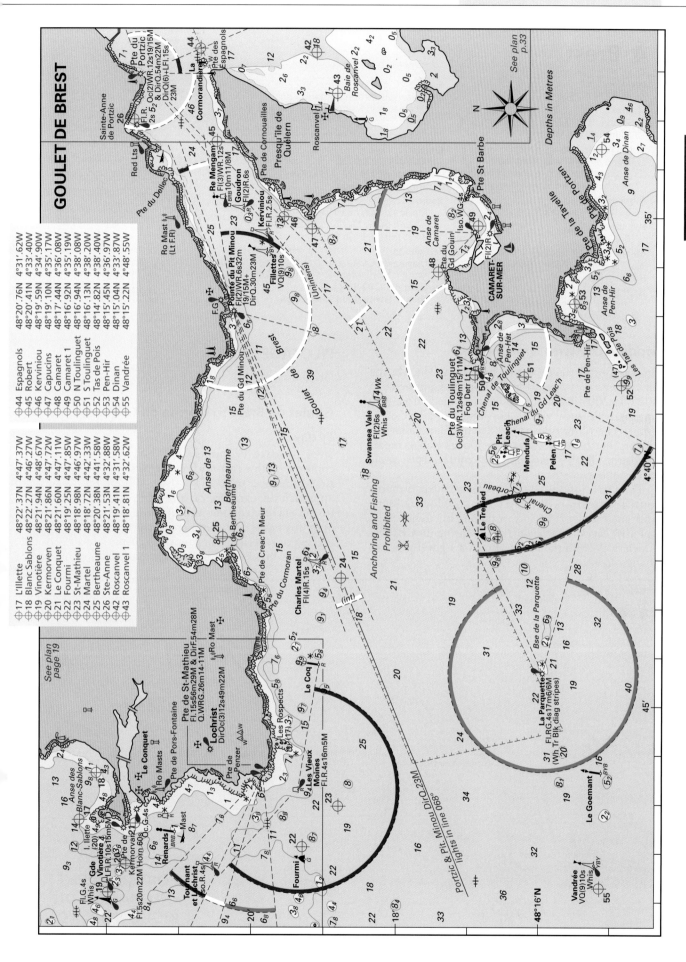

⊕17	L'Illette	48°22'.37N	4°47'.37W
⊕18	Blanc Sablons	48°22'.27N	4°46'.27W
⊕19	Vinotière	48°21'.94N	4°48'.67W
⊕20	Kermorven	48°21'.86N	4°47'.72W
⊕21	Le Conquet	48°21'.60N	4°47'.11W
⊕22	Fourmi	48°19'.25N	4°47'.85W
⊕23	St-Mathieu	48°18'.98N	4°46'.97W
⊕24	Martel	48°18'.72N	4°42'.33W
⊕25	Bertheaume	48°20'.38N	4°41'.58W
⊕26	Ste-Anne	48°21'.53N	4°31'.58W
⊕42	Roscanvel	48°19'.41N	4°31'.87W
⊕43	Roscanvel 1	48°18'.81N	4°32'.62W

⊕44	Espagnols	48°20'.76N	4°31'.62W
⊕45	Robert	48°20'.41N	4°33'.40W
⊕46	Keriviniou	48°19'.59N	4°34'.90W
⊕47	Capucins	48°19'.10N	4°35'.17W
⊕48	Camaret	48°17'.44N	4°36'.08W
⊕49	Camaret 1	48°16'.92N	4°35'.19W
⊕50	N Toulinguet	48°16'.94N	4°38'.08W
⊕51	S Toulinguet	48°16'.13N	4°38'.20W
⊕52	Tas de Pois	48°15'.45N	4°38'.40W
⊕53	Pen-Hir	48°15'.04N	4°33'.87W
⊕54	Dinan	48°15'.22N	4°48'.55W

I. FINISTERRE

4 Brest

Location
48°23′N 4°26′W

Shelter
Excellent in Marina du Château and Moulin Blanc Marinas

Depth restrictions
None at Marina du Château
1.5m in approach to and 1.4m at fuel berth in Moulin Blanc Marina

Night entry
Both marinas well lit

HW time
Brest HW

Mean height of tide (m)

	HWS	HWN	LWN	LWS
Brest	6.9	5.4	2.6	1.0

Berthing
Visitors' pontoons and on wavebreakers

Fuel
Visitors' pontoon at Marina du Château and S side of Moulin Blanc N basin

Marina facilities All services

Charts
BA 3429 (22.5)
SHOM 7400 (22.5), 7397, 7398 (12.5)
Imray C36 (Various)

Radio
Marina du Château VHF Ch 09
Moulin Blanc Marina VHF Ch 09
Brest port VHF Ch 08, 16

Telephone
Marina du Château ① 02 98 33 12 50
Moulin Blanc Marina ① 02 98 02 20 02
Customs ① 02 98 44 35 20
Tourist Office ① 02 98 44 24 96

Modern city with large marina

Brest is a modern city with a busy port. The Marina du Château was opened in the Port du Commerce in 2008. In 2009 it was still being developed into a very fine marina with visitor berthing for all sizes of yacht. The older marina at Moulin Blanc also has visitors' berths for vessels up to 30m as well as repair facilities. Both marinas are under the same management.

The Océanopolis oceanographic centre, a major tourist attraction, is very close to Moulin Blanc Marina. Transport by bus, train and air (twice daily to Paris) is good particularly for Marina du Château which is close to the centre. Brest is a good place to change crews.

PILOTAGE

(See plan page 33)

Goulet de Brest to Marina du Château

By day

Steer to leave Pénoupèle PHM buoy to port and continue on this east-northeast course to open up the first entrance to the Port de Commerce. Then approach the entrance on a bearing of 344° keeping to the starboard side and keeping a watchful eye open for naval and commercial ships which may be leaving or entering. They must be given right of way. The outer breakwater of the marima will be seen fine

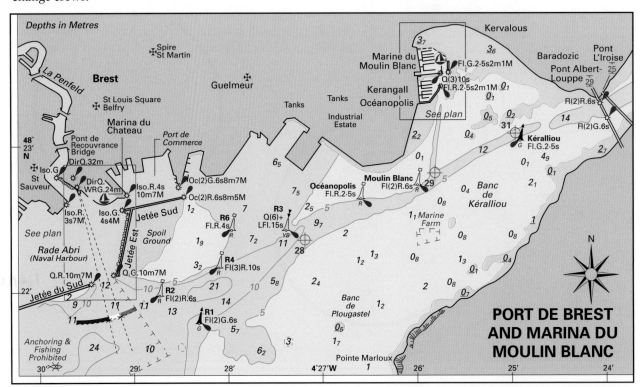

PORT DE BREST AND MARINA DU MOULIN BLANC

Brest, Marina du Château entrance from the northeast

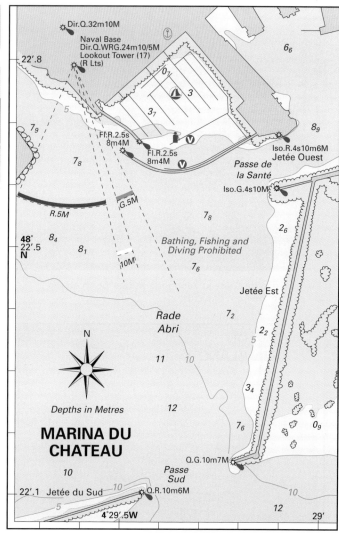

on the starboard bow. The marina entrance faces northwest and the outer breakwater end must be rounded to enter the marina. Entry to the naval and commercial parts of the port is prohibited.

By night

Steer an east-northeast course from the Goulet de Brest to leave the Pénoupèle PHM buoy to port and continue on this course until the first entrance of the Port de Commerce is opened up and the Ldg Lts will come into line on 344°. The front Ldg Lt is a WRG sector light. They lead to the west of the marina enrance when the southern breakwater head can be rounded.

By GPS

From ⊕27-Pénoupèle continue towards ⊕28-Elorn until the entrance is opened up.

Brest, Marina du Château from south

I. FINISTERRE

Brest, Marina du Château. Alongside visitors' berth on the left and on the right of picture

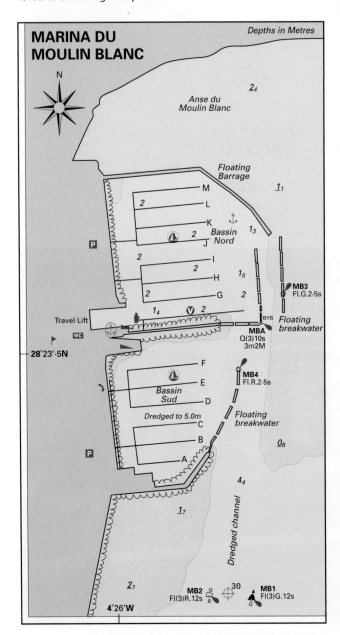

MARINA DU MOULIN BLANC

Depths in Metres

N

Anse du Moulin Blanc

2_4

Floating Barrage

1_1

M
L
2
K
J   Bassin Nord 1_3
2
P
I
2
H 1_5
G   2
2

Travel Lift
1_4 V   2
WC
28°23'·5N

MB3
FI.G.2·5s

BYB
MBA
Q(3)10s
3m2M

Floating breakwater

F
E
Bassin Sud
D
C
B
A

MB4
FI.R.2·5s

Floating breakwater

Dredged to 5.0m

0_6

P

4_4

1_7

Dredged channel

2_1

MB2
FI(3)R.12s
R
30

MB1
FI(3)G.12s
G

4°26'W

Brest, Marina du Château fuel berth

Goulet de Brest to Moulin Blanc marina

By day

From Pointe du Portzic steer about 065° and look for the curved arches of the Albert-Louppe Bridge (with the new motorway bridge behind it) over the River Elorn. In the foreground a line of PHM channel buoys lead past the breakwater of the commercial port. Beyond is the conspicuous white roof of the Océanopolis centre. To its right is the breakwater of Moulin Blanc marina.

Leave Moulin Blanc buoy 200m astern before turning into the dredged marina channel, which is marked by small, lateral buoys.

Enter the marina between MB4 and MB3. Then leave MBA ECM beacon, marking the extremity of the central pier, to port. The central pier has been extended northwards by a floating breakwater the northern end of which must be rounded to port to reach the visitors' pontoon.

By night

Leaving Pénoupèle close to port, steer 065° to follow the buoyed channel to Moulin Blanc buoy. Leave it to port and continue for about 200m before altering to about 005° to locate the lights marking the narrow dredged channel. When MB1 and MB2 have been identified, steer between them on 007° to the

Brest. Moulin Blanc marina

marina entrance between floating breakwaters which have been extended northwards.

By GPS:

⊕7-Pénoupèle, ⊕28-Elorn, ⊕29-Moulin Blanc, ⊕30-Moulin Blanc 1

Berths

Marina du Château

The visitors' pontoons are in the southern part of the marina either along the southern breakwater or on the southern side of the pontoon with the fuel berh on its western end. There is 4.5m depth and the largest of yachts can be accommodated.

Moulin Blanc Marina

the visitors' pontoon lies along the southern side of the northern basin. Visiting yachts also berth on both sides of the western floating breakwaters. yachts with a draft greater than 2m may be berthed on the southern wavebreaker at spring tides.

Facilities

The marinas are both well equipped and the staff are helpful. In 2009 the Marina du Château was still being developed and facilities were not yet complete. At present facilities for repairs and storage are better at Moulin Blanc where there are chandlers, sailmakers, engineers and a newly installed 50-ton boatlift. Fuel at both but the one at Marina du Château has an easily operated 24 hour self-service with a credit card. Wi-Fi at Marina du Château and free use of computers is available at Moulin Blanc.

Ashore in Brest

A supermarket in Rue de Verdun, northwest of Moulin Blanc marina, will return you and your shopping to either marina free of charge with orders over €50. Sunday morning market near St-Louis

Church. Marina du Château is close to the town centre and very convenient and from Moulin Blanc the bus service into Brest is frequent.

A spectacular Festival of Sail is held every four years. In fact the Marina du Château was temporarily opened early especially for the last one in 2008. The next will be in 2012.

At Marina du Château the maritime museum in the castle is worth a visit. There are good views from there. At Moulin Blanc Océanopolis is a marine scientific centre. The distinctive white concrete and glass building is shaped in the form of a crab and has a large amount of exhibition space and three big aquaria. One aquarium houses the grey seal collection.

The Conservatoire Botanique National is in the Stang Alar valley one mile north of Moulin Blanc. It is dedicated to the preservation of endangered plant species many of which come from the Brittany peninsula. The gardens cover 40 acres and contain plants native to five continents.

Brest. Commercial premises at Moulin Blanc marina with the oceanarium behind *M&G Barron*

5 River Elorn

Location
   48°22'N 4°20'W
Depth restrictions
   Dries above St-Jean
   2m to Landerneau at MHWN
Height Restriction 25m
Night passage
   Lit to St-Jean but not recommended
HW time
   Brest HW
Mean height of tide (m)

	HWS	HWN	LWN	LWS
Brest	6.9	5.4	2.6	1.0

Tidal stream Elorn River
   Slack – Brest HW–0530 to –0500
   Flood – Brest HW–0500 to –0030
   Slack – Brest HW–0030 to +0030
   Ebb – Brest HW+0030 to –0530

Berthing
   Anchorages
   Drying quay at Landerneau
Charts
   BA 3429 (22.5) (to St-Jean)
   SHOM 7400 (22.5) (to St-Jean)
   Imray C36 (large scale)
Telephone
   Lifting bridge ① 06 11 03 31 20

Tidal river to historic town

The Elorn is an attractive tidal river with several peaceful anchorages. At all states of the tide, it is navigable to St-Jean, which is about 4M beyond Moulin Blanc marina. The remainder of the river dries but it is possible to visit the historic town of Landerneau on the tide.

PILOTAGE

Moulin Blanc to Landerneau

By day

The River Elorn leads 8M to the attractive old town of Landerneau. For deep-draught yachts it is navigable at all states of tide as far as St-Jean. Above St-Jean the river dries but is navigable, near high water, for boats drawing up to 2m.

From Moulin Blanc buoy (*see plan on page 26*), pass under Albert-Louppe Bridge (clearance 29m) and the Pont de l'Iroise motorway bridge (clearance 25m). Follow the channel markers and the deep-water moorings. It is possible to anchor on either side of the river or find a vacant mooring as far up as St-Jean.

At Kerhuon there is a slip, marked by a beacon with an orange top. A wharf marks the eastern end of Kerhuon where the river curves north and then east for the last stretch before St-Jean.

Above St-Jean, rather small and widely spaced green and red buoys and the yacht moorings mark the channel. 3.5M above St-Jean there is a lifting bridge which will be opened on request by telephoning a little while in advance (①06 11 03 31 20).

The River Elorn

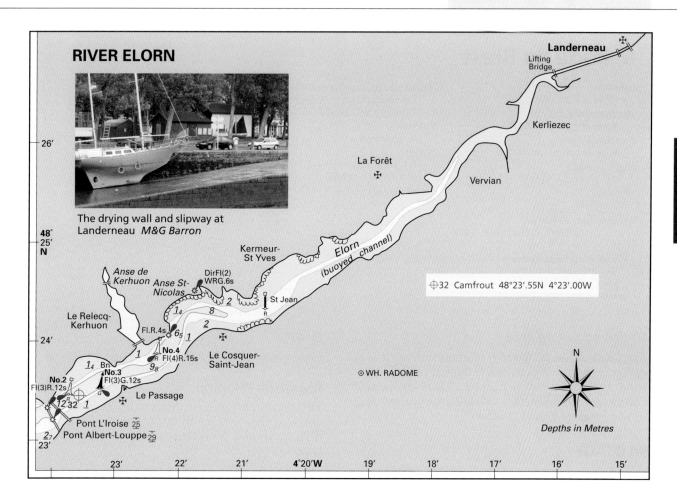

RIVER ELORN

The drying wall and slipway at
Landerneau *M&G Barron*

⊕32 Camfrout 48°23'.55N 4°23'.00W

Depths in Metres

I. FINISTERRE

Follow the canal to Landerneau, pass the large sand-barge wharf, and tie up against the wall on the port side before the fixed bridge just above the slip.

By night

The Elorn is only lit as far as Anse Saint-Nicolas and night passage is not recommended.

By GPS

This route requires visual pilotage. The following waypoints may be of assistance in the first section

⊕29-Moulin Blanc, ⊕31-Kéraliou, ⊕32-Camfrout

BERTHS AND ANCHORAGES

Landerneau

Landerneau is attractive and has all the facilities of a fair-sized town. Market days are Monday, Tuesdays, Fridays and Saturdays. It is on the Morlaix-Brest railway line.

It may be possible to dry out on the port side against a short length of wall with a slipway and where there are ladders. But it has recently been reported that the bottom has silted against the wall making it difficult to avoid leaning inward uncomfortably. There is 3m at HW neaps. There is electricity on the quay on the port side and water at the toilet block 100m upstream.

⚓ Le Passage

Although somewhat exposed to the southwest, there is an attractive anchorage about 0.75M above the Albert-Louppe Bridge on the south side of the river near Le Passage. The bottom may be foul so buoy the anchor.

⊕32-Camfrout 48°23'.55N 4°23'.00W

⚓ Anse Saint-Nicolas

Anse Saint-Nicolas is better sheltered from the southwest than Le Passage. It is in a bay on the north side of the river, about 1.75M above Albert-Louppe Bridge.

⚓ Kerhuon

Good shelter from all directions can be found in the stretch of river between Anse de Kerhuon and about 0.25M northeast of Saint Jean beacon tower.

Landerneau looking downstream *R Rundle*

6 Rade de Brest

Location
48°19'N 4°25'W

Depth restrictions
None in main channel

Prohibited area
Near Île Longue in SW

Night passage
Not recommended

HW time
Brest HW

Mean height of tide (m)

	HWS	HWN	LWN	LWS
Brest	6.9	5.4	2.6	1.0

Tidal streams Rade de Brest
Flood – Brest HW–0500 to –0030 (1.5kns)
Slack – Brest HW–0030 to +0030
Ebb – Brest HW+0030 to –0530 (1.0kns)

Flood stream counter-currents
Espagnols Brest HW –0430 to –0030
Armorique Brest HW –0230 to –0030

Berthing
Anchorages

Charts
BA 3429 (22.5)
SHOM 7400 (22.5)
Imray C36 (77)

Sheltered sailing area

The Rade de Brest offers very good sailing. It has shelter from the Atlantic but is large enough for the wind not to be too disturbed. There are many anchorages for boats that can take the ground and several for deep draught yachts.

PILOTAGE

The restricted areas

There is a restricted area in the southwest of the Rade. Roscanvel on the west of Île Longue Military Port and Le Fret on the E can be visited. However, there are areas where navigation is restricted and anchoring prohibited. In particular, entry is prohibited within 500m of the shore around Île Longue.

The Naval College beyond Pen-ar-Vir has a restricted zone marked by the NCM buoys and yellow buoys. Anchoring is not allowed in this area and entry may also be prohibited without warning. Boats may also be refused access to a rectangular area north of the Naval College marked by yellow buoys.

Goulet de Brest to Traverse de l'Hôpital

By day

From the Goulet de Brest steer 120° to Le Renard WCM buoy. Leave Île Ronde and the two rectangular concrete dolphins 300m to port.

A course of 104° will lead to the outer PHM buoy No.4, about 1M west of the Île du Bindy.

The succeeding channel buoys No.6 and No.8 are also red. After No.8 the numbered buoys are closer together and easier to see. Note that PHM buoys are conical although painted red.

By night

Night passage is not recommended.

By GPS

⊕44-Espagnols, ⊕33-Île Ronde, ⊕39-Aulne, ⊕40-Hôpital

Rivière de l'Hôpital

The pretty entrance of this small river lies to the north of the entrance to the Aulne. Since the river dries it can only be visited around HW (*see plan on page 35*).

Rivière du Faou

Upstream of the entrance to the Rivière de l'Hôpital, the Aulne turns south into a large double bend. The mouth of the Rivière du Faou is on the east bank of the curve. The bar dries 0.6m and lies between Île de Tibidy and the charming little islet of Arun. North of this islet is a pool with 0.4m. Beyond the pool the river dries but, at springs, it is possible to go up to the substantial village of Le Faou (*see plan on page 35*).

ANCHORAGES

⚓ Roscanvel

Sheltered from north through west to southeast, the east coast of Presqu'île de Quélern offers good protection. Between Pte des Espagnols and the village of Roscanvel there are several small bays with yacht moorings. There is a welcoming yacht club at Roscanvel, which may loan a mooring on request.

Roscanvel is a small holiday village. It has a double slipway, one running out east and the other south. Anchor off the slips clear of the moorings. The east slip dries at LW and there are obstructions outside it. If landing at the south slip towards LW approach from the south and use the inside only.

Watch out for the stream in the Baie de Roscanvel. There is a counter-current on the flood from about Brest HW-3 to HW but no counter-current on the ebb. This means the stream only runs south for a couple of hours after LW.

⊕43-Roscanvel 1 48°18'·81N 04°32'·62W

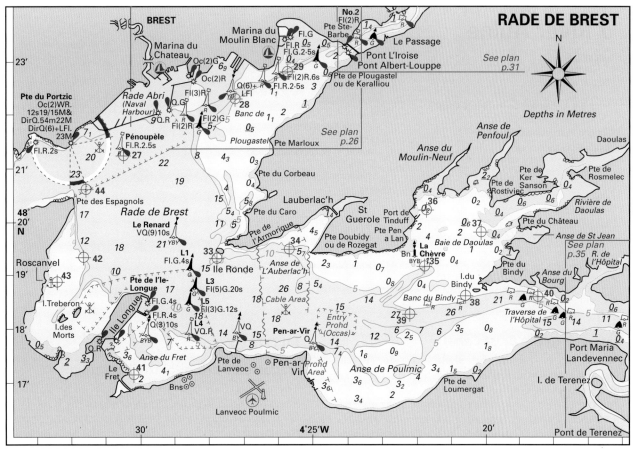

RADE DE BREST

Depths in Metres

⊕27	Pénoupèle	48°21′.41N	4°30′.51W	⊕38 Bindy	48°18′.69N 4°20′.64W
⊕28	Elorn	48°22′.42N	4°27′.28W	⊕39 Aulne	48°18′.33N 4°22′.17W
⊕29	Moulin Blanc	48°22′.79N	4°25′.86W	⊕40 Hôpital	48°18′.63N 4°18′.72W
⊕33	Île Ronde	48°19′.21N	4°27′.96W	⊕41 Le Fret	48°17′.12N 4°30′.17W
⊕34	Auberlac'h	48°19′.55N	4°25′.48W	⊕42 Roscanvel	48°19′.41N 4°31′.58W
⊕35	La Chèvre	48°19′.41N	4°21′.89W	⊕43 Roscanvel 1	48°18′.81N 4°32′.62W
⊕36	Tinduff	48°20′.27N	4°21′.85W	⊕44 Espagnols	48°20′.76N 4°31′.62W
⊕37	Daoulas	48°19′.99N	4°19′.57W		

⚓ Anse de l'Auberlac'h

Sheltered from all directions except southwest, the picturesque hamlet of L'Auberlach lies at the head of a bay running northeast from Île Ronde. It is rather crowded with moorings, but there are three or four white visitors' buoys. There may be space to anchor but beyond the pier the bay shoals rapidly.

⊕34-Auberlac'h 48°19′.55N 4°25′.48W

⚓ Le Fret

Sheltered from all directions except northwest, the Anse du Fret provides a pleasant anchorage southeast of Île Longue. A course of 215° from Île Ronde will lead into the anchorage clear of the exclusion zone. There is space to anchor with good holding on sand/mud. From the pier, fast ferries go to Brest and buses go to Camaret.

⊕41-Le Fret 48°17′.12N 4°30′.17W

⚓ Tinduff

Sheltered from west and north, Tinduff is a small drying harbour on the west side of the shallow Baie de Daoulas, 0.5M to the north of Pointe de Pen a Lan. Keep at least 0.25M from the point to avoid the shoals and La Chèvre rock (dries 4.7m), which is marked by an ECM beacon. There is another rock (drying 4.2m) closer inshore and a third unmarked isolated rock, drying 0.7m, about 300m west-southwest of the beacon.

The bay is shallow and can only be entered with sufficient rise of tide but there is a 2m pool off the end of the pier. There are many moorings but there is room to anchor, with good holding. At neaps, it is possible to go further into the bay where there is better shelter. Keep clear of the fish farm, marked by small, unlit yellow buoys.

⊕36-Tinduff 48°20′.27N 4°21′.85W

⚓ Rivière de Daoulas

Sheltered from all directions, this shallow river runs into the northeast corner of the Baie de Daoulas. The bay can only be entered with sufficient rise of tide as there is a bar at the entrance. The deepest water is found by keeping Pte du Château on a bearing of 070°. The Pointe is not easy to distinguish against the land but can be identified by the conspicuous large grey shed with houses above and to the right. Almost the entire river is taken up with moorings and there is little space left to anchor. There may be space about 0.75M upriver off the second slip, in 1.8m (mud). The river to Daoulas dries 4.5m.

⊕37-Daoulas 48°19′.99N 4°19′.57W

7 River Aulne

Location
48°18'N 4°16'W

Depth restrictions
6m to Pte de Térénez
2.5m at MHWN to the Guily Glaz
2.7m beyond the lock

Height restrictions 23m

Guily Glaz lock opens
Brest HW -0200 to +0200 (0730 to 2100
April–September)
(0800 to 1900 October–March)

HW time
Brest HW

Mean height of tide (m)

	HWS	HWN	LWN	LWS
Brest	6.9	5.4	2.6	1.0

Tidal streams Landevennec
Flood – Brest HW–0530 to –0030
Slack – Brest HW–0030 to +0030
Ebb – Brest HW+0030 to –0530

Berthing
Quay at Port Launay
Visitors' pontoon at Châteaulin
Anchorages

Fuel
Châteaulin hypermarket

Facilities
Water at Port Launay and
Châteaulin
Hypermarket at Châteaulin

Charts
BA 3429 (22.5)
SHOM 7400 (22.5)
Imray C36 (large scale)
IGN TOP25 sheet 0518

Telephone
Guily Glaz lock ☎ 02 98 86 03 21

Gateway to the Brest Canal

The Aulne is a beautiful sheltered river in the southern part of the Rade de Brest. It it navigable on the tide to Guily Glaz lock where the Aulne joins the old Nantes-Brest canal. Beyond Guily Glaz there is the pretty canal village of Port Launay and the market town of Châteaulin. Perhaps surprisingly, Châteaulin is a good place for provisioning because the visitors' pontoon is very close to a hypermarket.

The River Aulne with the naval graveyard in the right

PILOTAGE

Traverse de l'Hôpital to Châteaulin

There is no chart of the river above Pont de Térénez. Sheet 0518 *Châteaulin-Douarnenez* in the IGN TOP 25 series of maps is the best alternative and shows the line of deepest water. However, the plan on page 35 provides sufficient detail for the passage.

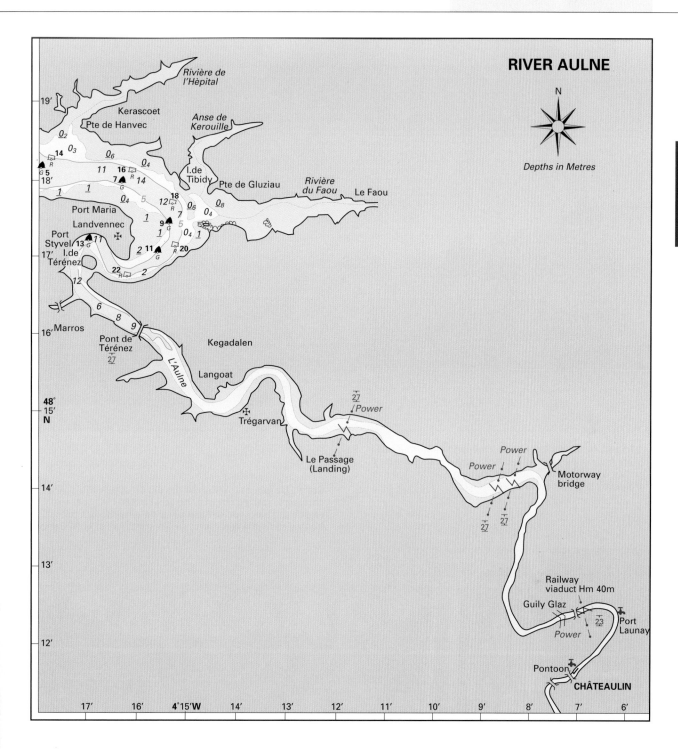

Apart from a 6m patch at Traverse de l'Hôpital there is 10m as far as Pont de Térénez. From there to within about a mile of the lock, there is at least 4m at half tide. In the last mile to the lock, depth is reduced in some places to 2.5m at MHWN. Vessels may enter the lock if the seaward gate is open. In the upper reaches the bottom is generally very soft mud. Beyond the lock at Guily Glaz there is between 2.7m and 3m. The overhead clearance below bridges and power lines is 27m or more. The power line above the viaduct at Guily Glaz is 23m.

From Traverse de l'Hôpital to Port Styvel there are mud banks on both sides of the river and it is

best to keep to the buoyed channel. At Port Styvel numerous small warships are laid up in the river and the channel marker buoys end. Continue to the bridge, keeping to the outside of bends and to the middle where the river narrows. From the bridge it is 12M to the lock at Guily Glaz.

At Trégarvan, about two miles above Pont de Térénez, the river bends north and then south and the banks become lower. With luck you may see kingfishers and egret in the reed beds. The river passes very close to the dual carriageway just before turning south again. This is the shallowest part of the trip and the deepest water is close in to the north bank.

At Trégarvan the banks become lower and kingfishers and egrets may be seen in the reed beds. Just ahead is the dual carriageway that briefly disturbs the peace before the river turns away to starboard *M&G Barron*

Guily Glaz lock at the start of the old Brest to Nantes canal. Bonaparte started to build the canal in 1804 in order to escape the blockade of Brest by using canals to get to Nantes; sadly the canal is no longer continuous *M&G Barron*

The flower-covered lock is a surprise after the peace of the river. It evokes an earlier age when barges travelled from Brest to Nantes and pleasure boats from Camaret came up to Port Launay for the day.

Beautiful Port Launay is 1M above the lock. The village has a long curve of grass-covered quays backed by old houses under high tree-covered hills.

To carry on to Châteaulin, leave Port Launay and pass the hotel De Bon Accueil on the port side. (You can tie up if you are staying for supper). Opposite the hotel there are two green markers that indicate a rocky patch on the starboard side. Generally, the deepest water from this point to Châteaulin is on the southeast side of the river. At the town there is a visitors' pontoon on the north bank.

BERTHS AND ANCHORAGES

Port Launay

Port Launay has a long stone quay that runs alongside the main street. Once it must have been full of barges waiting for the tide but today there is plenty of room for visiting yachts. Lie alongside the quay on the east side. Water and electricity is neatly concealed in the shrubs. There are toilets but no showers (key from the town hall), a few small food shops, a restaurant and a number of cafés.

Port Launay looking upstream *R Rundle*

Port Launay from downstream *R Rundle*

Châteaulin

Châteaulin has a visitors' pontoon with 2.6m alongside. Water and one outlet for electricity on the pontoon. There are basic toilets and showers at the north end of the quay. The shower key is obtainable on deposit from the tourist office by the road bridge. Modest berthing fees are also payable at the tourist office.

Ashore it has a visitor centre dedicated to salmon. It has all the facilities of a medium-sized town with markets on Thursdays and Sundays. The hypermarket and fuel station is a short walk from the visitors' pontoon.

Châteaulin *R Rundle*

⚓ Port Maria at Landevennec

Sheltered from the southwest and southeast, Port Maria is a drying jetty on the south bank just inside SHM buoy No.7. From here you can walk to the attractive village of Landevennec.

⚓ Île de Térénez to Pont de Térénez

There are several, well-sheltered, anchorages between Port Styvel and Pont de Térénez.

The bottom is rocky away from the banks but it is possible to anchor at Port Styvel (buoy the anchor because this used to be a ships' graveyard). From here it is possible to land and follow a path through the woods to Landevennec, where there are shops, a hotel and the famous Abbaye de Saint-Guénolé.

Anchoring may be possible at the mouth of either of the drying creeks southwest of Île de Térénez or

on the east side of the river southwest of Île de Térénez. On the starboard side between Port Styvel and Pont de Térénez there are several very small inlets where it may be possible to anchor but buoy the anchor in any of these places as there may have been fishfarms in the past.

⚓ Trégarvan

Trégarvan, 2M upstream of Pont de Térénez, provides a reasonable anchorage; there are several moorings and a slip. There is another landing at Le Passage about 2M further up.

Châteaulin visitors' pontoon *R Rundle*

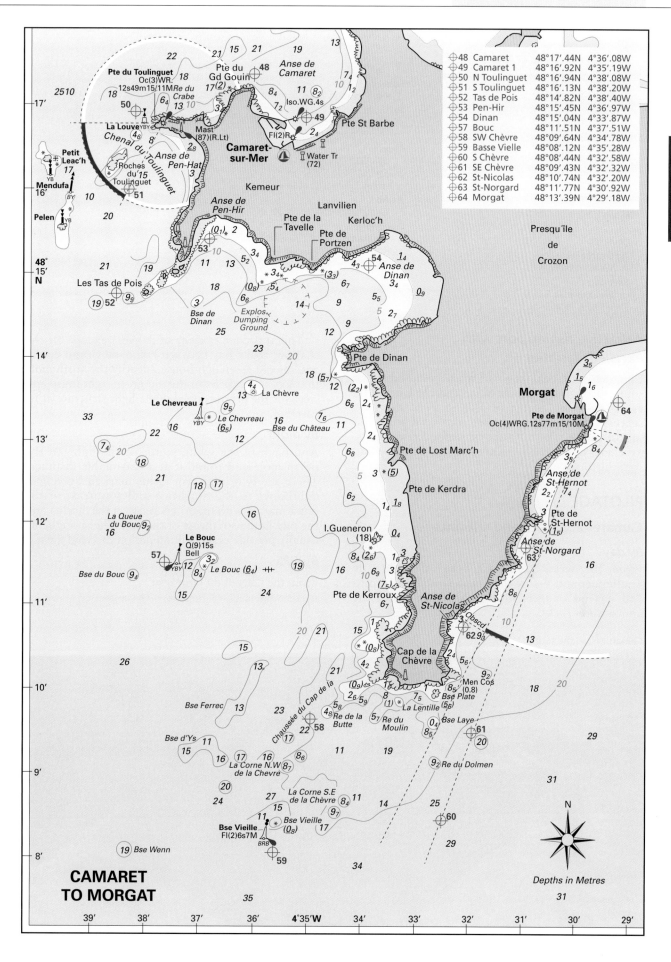

I. FINISTERRE

⊕ 48	Camaret	48°17'.44N	4°36'.08W
⊕ 49	Camaret 1	48°16'.92N	4°35'.19W
⊕ 50	N Toulinguet	48°16'.94N	4°38'.08W
⊕ 51	S Toulinguet	48°16'.13N	4°38'.20W
⊕ 52	Tas de Pois	48°14'.82N	4°38'.40W
⊕ 53	Pen-Hir	48°15'.45N	4°36'.97W
⊕ 54	Dinan	48°15'.04N	4°33'.87W
⊕ 57	Bouc	48°11'.51N	4°37'.51W
⊕ 58	SW Chèvre	48°09'.64N	4°34'.78W
⊕ 59	Basse Vielle	48°08'.12N	4°35'.28W
⊕ 60	S Chèvre	48°08'.44N	4°32'.58W
⊕ 61	SE Chèvre	48°09'.43N	4°32'.32W
⊕ 62	St-Nicolas	48°10'.74N	4°32'.20W
⊕ 63	St-Norgard	48°11'.77N	4°30'.92W
⊕ 64	Morgat	48°13'.39N	4°29'.18W

**CAMARET
TO MORGAT**

Depths in Metres

8 Camaret-sur-Mer

Location
48°17'N 4°35'W

Shelter
Good except from NE

Depth restrictions
3m in outer harbour
2m shoaling to 0.4m in inner harbour

Night entry Well lit

HW time
Brest HW–0010

Mean height of tide (m)

	HWS	HWN	LWN	LWS
Camaret	6.6	5.1	2.5	1.0

Tidal streams
Weak in the bay

Berthing
Two marinas
Visitors' moorings

Fuel
Port Vauban wave breaker

Facilities
Some repair facilities, many shops, bars and restaurants

Charts
BA 2350 (50), 3427 (22.5)
SHOM 7401 (22.5)
Imray C36 (large scale)

Radio
Camaret port VHF Ch 09

Telephone
Capitainerie ① 02 98 27 89 31
Tourist Office ① 02 98 27 93 60

Attractive fishing port with excellent facilities

Camaret is an ideal stopover when bound north or south through the Raz de Seine and the Chenal du Four. It is an attractive fishing port that has successfully transformed itself into a yachting and tourist centre. There are shops, seafood restaurants, excellent coast path walking, good beaches and some history.

PILOTAGE *(See plan page 39)*

Camaret approach and entrance

By day

From the west, the coast between Pointe de Toulinguet and Pointe de Grand Gouin is steep-to and has no dangers more than 200m from the above-water rocks.

The approach is clear of dangers except for the shallow, rocky bay between Pointe de Grand Gouin and the old green lighthouse. Identify the north mole that extends east from the old green lighthouse and steer for the green-topped white light structure at its east end.

By night

Approach in the white sector of the light on the north mole and round it at a reasonable distance. There are two large fish farms marked by yellow lightbuoys to the northeast and southeast of the outer marina with moorings between the marina and the one in the southeast of the bay. The shore lights usually provide enough illumination to avoid them.

By GPS

From the Chenal du Four use:
⊕23-St-Mathieu, ⊕48-Camaret, ⊕49-Camaret 1

Camaret from the south

From Brest use:

⊕47-Capucins, ⊕49-Camaret 1

From the Chenal du Toulinguet use:

⊕50-N Toulinguet, ⊕48-Camaret,⊕49-Camaret 1

BERTHS

Port Vauban

Visitors with larger boats are expected to use the outer marina which has pontoons connected to the south side of the north mole. This is exposed to the northeast and, in the past, has been uncomfortable or even dangerous in strong winds between north and east. A new wave breaker, installed in 2004, has improved the protection. The outside of the wave breaker is for ferries and for the fuel dock; visitors go inside.

The Port Vauban harbour office is by the old green lighthouse but is frequently not manned. When closed walk to the main harbour office opposite the gangway to the Port du Notic pontoons. Open 0900–1200 and 1500–1900 in season. Showers and toilets are by the Vauban tower.

Port du Notic

Port du Notic marina has visitors' berths for smaller boats and is in the inner harbour much closer to the town. Depth 1.8m at outer pontoon. Anchoring is forbidden in the inner harbour. The Capitainerie and the showers and toilets are on the quay opposite the entrance to the marina.

Visitors' moorings

In the bay southeast of the north mole there are moorings in 3m or more, including some white ones for visitors. Anchoring is not allowed in the harbour or the approach channel.

Port du Styvel

This marina, just north of Port du Notic, has no places for visitors.

Camaret inner harbour marinas

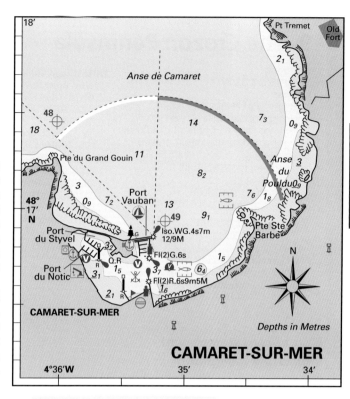

| 48 Camaret | 48°17 .44N | 4°36 .08W |
| 49 Camaret 1 | 48°16 .92N | 4°35 .19W |

ASHORE IN CAMARET

Facilities

Camaret has a fuel berth (24 hours with credit card), chandlers, a shipbuilder, a sailmaker, supermarkets, launderettes, restaurants, bars and a wide variety of leisure shops.

There is a bus service to Le Fret, from where there is a fast ferry to Brest but for a crew-change it would be better to take the boat to the Marina du Château.

Leisure

A walk in Camaret is likely to take you along the breakwater to or from Sillon Point.

The rotting fishing boats are much photographed but the more enduring buildings are also interesting. The church with the broken tower is Notre-Dame de Rocamadour. It is so called because pilgrims from Ireland and Britain used to disembark at Camaret and set out overland to Rocamadour. The church has some fine wooden statues as well as a collection of votive offerings. Sailors brought these, in thanks for narrow escapes at sea.

The rugged Vauban Tower was built just in time to successfully repulse an Anglo-Dutch landing attempt at the end of the 17th Century. It is now an interesting maritime museum. There are another two forts near Camaret, one at the Pointe de Toulinguet and the other at Pointe du Grand Gouin. They are not accessible but on a fine day the walking is wonderful and choughs can be seen on the cliffs.

I. FINISTERRE

9 The Crozon Peninsula

Location
48°15'N 4°38'W

Hazards
Rocks W of Pte du Toulinguet
Rocks S of Cap de la Chèvre
Isolated marked and unmarked rocks
Strong and complex tidal streams

Night passage
Toulinguet is partially lit
S Chèvre is lit

HW time
Brest HW -0015

Mean height of tide (m)

	HWS	HWN	LWN	LWS
Camaret	6.6	5.1	2.5	1.0

Tidal stream Toulinguet
N – Brest HW–0530 to +0030 (1.7kns)
S – Brest HW+0030 to +0530 (1.7kns)
Slack – Brest HW+0530 to -0530

Tidal stream 5M W Cap de la Chèvre
NE – Brest HW–0530 to -0130 (0.7kns)
Slack – Brest HW–0130 to +0030
SW – Brest HW+0030 to +0330
(0.3kns)
W – Brest HW+0330 to +0530 (0.4kns)
Slack – Brest HW+0530 to -0530

Tidal stream 2M E of Cap de la Chèvre
NE – Brest HW–0530 to -0030 (0.4kns)
Slack – Brest HW–0030 to +0030
SW – Brest HW+0030 to +0530
(0.3kns)
Slack – Brest HW+0530 to -0530

Charts
BA 2350 (50), 2349 (30)
SHOM 7172 (50), 7121 (30)
Imray C36 (77)

Magnificent scenery and interesting navigation

The Crozon peninsula separates the Rade de Brest from the Bay of Douarnenez. Its granite cliffs rise from 50m in the north at Camaret to 100m in the south at Cap de la Chèvre. There are many off lying rocks. Some like the Rochers du Toulinguet and Les Tas de Pois are more than 30m high; others are less spectacular but more dangerous. Careful navigation is required but it is well rewarded by the magnificent scenery.

There are two main dangers. In the north, rocks extend west from Point du Toulinguet for nearly four miles. There are several passages through the rocks. The Chenal du Toulinguet is the innermost and saves a good many miles when going between the Rade de Brest and the Bay of Douarnenez or the Raz de Sein.

The second danger is the southern tip of the Crozon Peninsula where several lines of rocks extend like fangs from the Cap de la Chèvre.

PILOTAGE

Chenal du Toulinguet

By day

The west side of the channel is marked by the Roches du Toulinguet, which rise to 30m. Le Pohen (height 8m) is nearest to the channel and is steep-to. La Louve WCM beacon tower marks the east side of the channel.

Keep to the middle of the channel. The depth is at least 4.9m and the channel is 0.25M wide.

By night

The passage is partially lit. From the south use Le Toulinguet light and Petit Minou light; from the north use Le Portzic light. However, night passage without GPS is not recommended.

By GPS

Southbound for the Raz de Sein use:
⊕50-N Toulinguet, ⊕51-S Toulinguet, ⊕80-Raz

Southbound for Cap de la Chèvre use:
⊕50-N Toulinguet, ⊕52-Tas de Pois

These routes need not be followed precisely. The only danger is a 4.9m shallow patch near La Louve beacon (unlit).

Chenal du Petit Leac'h

By day or night

From the southwest, leave Petit Leac'h SCM beacon (unlit) to the west and Pelen SCM beacon and Basse Mendufa NCM buoy (both unlit) to the east.

At night Le Portzic light can be held on a constant bearing of 043°.

The channel is 600m wide with a depth of more than 10m. The tide sets strongly.

By GPS

From the southwest use:
⊕56-Basse du Lis, ⊕50-N Toulinguet

Les Tas de Pois

Les Tas de Pois are five magnificent rocks extending out to sea from the Pointe de Pen-Hir. On a calm day you may feel tempted to pass between them.

Numbering from seaward, the rocks are:

1. Tas de Pois Ouest, height 47m.
2. La Fourche, height 10m.
3. Le Dentelé, height 35m.
4. Le Grand Tas de Pois, height 64m.
5. Le Tas de Pois de Terre, height 58m.

Between Rocks 1 and 2, the channel is about 200m wide. There is a rock, drying 0.5m, about 50m northeast of Rock 1 and another drying rock close to Rock 2. Near LW keep to mid-channel, if anything closer to Rock 2.

Chenal du Toulinguet and Camaret-sur-Mer looking east. In the foreground the Roches du Toulinguet rise to 30m and mark the west side of the channel.
The inset is La Louve (unlit) beacon on the east side of the channel at the Pointe du Toulinguet *M&G Barron*

Between Rocks 2 and 3 the channel is about 100m and clean.

Between Rocks 3 and 4 keep closer to Rock 3; there is a rock drying 0.6m close northwest of Rock 4.

Between Rocks 4 and 5 passage is only possible near HW as the channel dries almost right across.

Between Rock 5 and the land there is no passage.

Cap de la Chèvre

By day

Southbound, pass west of Le Chevreau. The beacon has been partially destroyed and a WCM buoy now marks the rock.

Le Bouc rocks are marked by a WCM buoy but the associated shallow patch extends nearly half a mile east of the buoy.

There are dangers up to half a mile offshore around Cap de la Chèvre. At low water, take particular care to avoid Basse Laye 0.4m shallow patch 0.5M south-southeast of the cape.

By night

The dangers off Cap de la Chèvre are lit by sectored lights at Pointe du Millier and Morgat. See Morgat for details.

By GPS

Southbound for Douarnenez use:

⊕52-Tas de Pois, ⊕57-Bouc, ⊕58-SW Chèvre

For Morgat, continue to:

⊕61-SE Chèvre

ANCHORAGES

⚓ Anse de Pen-Hir

Sheltered from all directions except south and southeast but sometimes subject to swell. This snug anchorage is in the sandy Anse de Pen-Hir, just inside Les Tas de Pois. In the centre of the bay, there is a rocky patch just within the 5m line.

⊕53-Pen-Hir 48°15'·45N 4°36'·97W

Les Tas de Pois looking north.
The boat is passing between No.4 (64m high) and No.3 (35m high). Keep closer to No.3 as there is a rock drying 0.6m close northwest of No.4   *M&G Barron*

⚓ Anse de Dinan

Sheltered from the north and east but exposed to wind or swell from the west and southwest. This wide, shallow bay is 3M east of Les Tas de Pois. Enter from southwest taking care to avoid the rock 400m south of Pointe de la Tavelle and the rock 200m east of Pointe de Portzen. The best anchorage is in the northeast corner of the bay.

⊕54-Dinan 48°15'·04N 4°33'·87W

⚓ Anse de Saint-Nicolas

Sheltered from the northwest, this is a rugged but attractive anchorage about 1M north of Cap de la Chèvre on its east side. Approach from the southeast to avoid the dangers of Cap de la Chèvre.

⊕62-St-Nicholas 48°10'·74N 4°32'·20W

⚓ Anse de Saint-Norgard

Sheltered from the west and northwest, this rocky bay is about 2M south of Morgat. Approach from the southeast to avoid the drying rocks off Pointe de Saint-Hernot.

⊕63-St-Norgard 48°11'·77N 4°30'·92W

Cap de la Chèvre *M&G Barron*

Les Rochers du Toulinguet looking north *M&G Barron*

Les Tas de Pois looking south *M&G Barron*

10 Morgat

Location
48°13'N 4°32'W

Shelter
Reasonable except from N and W
Swell sometimes enters the marina

Depth restrictions
1.5m in dredged channel
0.6m to 1.8m in the marina

Yachts >12m Must anchor

Night entry
Lit but care is required

HW time
Brest HW −¼

Mean height of tide (m)

	HWS	HWN	LWN	LWS
Morgat	6.5	5.0	2.4	0.9

Tidal streams
Weak in the bay

Berthing
Marina
Anchorage and some mooring buoys

Fuel
Base of visitors' pontoon

Facilities
Limited facilities, more shops in
Crozon

Charts
BA 2349 (30)
SHOM 7121 (30)
Imray C36 (large scale)

Radio
Marina VHF Ch 09

Telephone
Marina & HM ☎ 02 98 27 01 97

Nineteenth century seaside resort

Morgat is a pretty seaside resort in the northwest corner of Douarnenez Bay.

The marina is not piled and can be uncomfortable but it is well protected by submerged concrete wave breakers and a rocky breakwater. Beyond the breakwater is a small sandy beach, protected from the southwest by the Pointe de Morgat. There is another larger beach a short walk from the marina in Morgat village.

Yachts greater than 12m LOA are officially required to use the moorings or anchor but this rule does not appear to be enforced.

Morgat from the south

PILOTAGE

Morgat approach and entrance

By day

Pointe de Morgat is a bold headland with a red and white square tower lighthouse in the trees at the top of the cliff. Two conspicuous above-water rocks at the foot of the headland are steep-to and can be passed within 50m.

The breakwater of the new harbour lies just to the north of the two rocks, but watch out for the concrete obstruction in the intervening bay. Continue north to the end of the breakwater where Morgat PHM buoy marks the safe ground. Leave this to port before entering the harbour between the port and starboard beacons marking the ends of the submerged wavebreakers or going to the anchorage.

Approaching from Douarnenez, or the beautiful beaches in the east of the bay, there is a rocky patch 0.75M south-southwest of Rocher L'Aber and 2M east-southeast of Morgat. It consists of three groups of rocks. The largest is Les Verrès with a partially drying wreck to its northeast. Southwest of Les Verrès is La Pierre Profonde with Le Taureau, the third group, to the north.

By night

The dangers south of Cap de la Chèvre can be cleared by keeping in one of the two white sectors of Pointe du Millier light until Pointe de Morgat light turns from red to white. Steer towards Pointe de Morgat light, keeping in the white sector until the 10m depth contour is reached. Turn to run along the coast on a course of about 035° crossing the green sector of Pointe de Morgat light. When Morgat PHM buoy off the harbour entrance (Fl.R.4s) is seen alter course to leave it to port and then into the entrance. Keep a lookout for unlit mooring buoys. There are flashing green and red lights marking the entrance between the wave breakers.

The red and white lighthouse on the top of the cliff at Pointe de Morgat *M&G Barron*

By GPS

From the northwest use:

⊕58-SW Chèvre, ⊕61-SE Chèvre, ⊕64-Morgat

There are dangers off Cap de la Chèvre, Pointe de Saint-Hernot and Point de Morgat.

From Douarnenez use:

⊕67-Douarnenez, ⊕64-Morgat

The rocks near La Pierre Profonde, are unlit and less than 0.5M east off this route.

From the Raz de Sein use:

⊕80-Raz, ⊕74-Van, ⊕73-Basse Jaune, ⊕59-Basse Vieille, ⊕61-SE Chèvre, ⊕64-Morgat

There are dangers close to ⊕74-Van, ⊕73-Basse Jaune and ⊕59-Basse Vieille and northwest of the leg between ⊕61-SE Chèvre and ⊕64-Morgat. The track from ⊕74-Van to ⊕61-SE Chèvre is a straight line but the additional waypoints make it easier to identify the dangers.

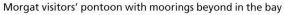

Morgat visitors' pontoon with moorings beyond in the bay

The visitors' pontoon at Morgat is on the west side of the harbour near the fishing boats *M&G Barron*

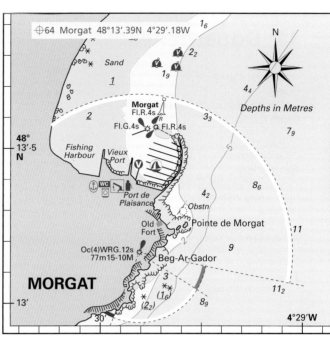

BERTHS AND ANCHORAGES

Morgat marina and anchorage

Visitors' berth alongside the pontoon with the large *Visiteurs* sign in the southwest corner of the harbour. Harbour dues are exceptionally moderate.

There are many mooring buoys (some of which are for visitors) in the bay north of the harbour. Yachts may anchor in 2m in the bay clear of the moorings. Anchoring is not permitted in the area enclosed by the breakwater and the wave breakers.

⚓ Île de l'Aber

Sheltered from the northwest to the northeast, this attractive anchorage behind Île de l'Aber is about 2M east of Morgat.

Coming from Morgat, leave Rocher de l'Aber close to port and turn north-northeast into the anchorage.

Coming from Cap de la Chèvre or Douarnenez, approach from the south to pass east of Les Vèrres and the nearby drying wreck.

⊕65-Île de l'Aber 48°13'·42N 4°25'·81W

ASHORE IN MORGAT

The marina has all the facilities of a substantial marina and fishing port.

Morgat was originally developed by the founder of the Peugeot car company as a place to send his executives for their holidays; consequently there are some fine hotels and villas. There are modest shops, bars and restaurants on the beachfront but the nearest large town is Crozon, which is 1.5M away and a steep climb.

In calm weather it is great fun to take a dinghy trip into the caves at the foot of Pointe de Morgat. The largest cave is like a cathedral and is 300 feet long and 33 feet high with brightly coloured walls.

For walkers, the cliff path starts close to the lighthouse and leads all the way to Cap de la Chèvre. In the summer there is a daily ferry to Ouessant.

Morgat harbour from northwest

11 Douarnenez

Location
48°06′N 4°20′W

Shelter
Good except in strong NW winds

Depth restrictions
1.5m on visitors' pontoon
Port Rhu sill dries 1.1m
3m in Port Rhu

Port Rhu lock
Opens HW−0100 Closes HW+0100

Night entry Well lit

HW time
Brest HW −0010

Mean height of tide (m)

	HWS	HWN	LWN	LWS
Douarnenez	6.4	4.9	2.3	0.9

Tidal streams
Weak in the bay

Berthing
Visitors' pontoon and moorings
Port Rhu marina and anchorages

Fuel
NW side of Tréboul marina

Facilities
Some repair facilities, good shops
and restaurants

Charts
BA 2349 (30)
SHOM 7121 (30)
Imray C36 (large scale)

Radio
Marina VHF Ch 09

Telephone
Port Rhu ① 02 98 92 00 67

Fishing port and maritime heritage

Douarnenez, in the sheltered southwest corner of Douarnenez Bay, is really two towns. The River Pouldavid, with Île Tristan at its mouth, splits the fishing port of Douarnenez from the beach resort of Tréboul.

Visiting yachts use the pontoons and buoys near the river entrance or go further upstream. At Port Rhu a barrage with a lock has been built across the river to form a basin. This contains a visitors' pontoon, a large floating maritime museum and a marina for local boats.

Treboul and Douarnenez from south

PILOTAGE

Douarnenez approach and entrance

By day

From Pointe de la Jument (3M west of Douarnenez) there is a safe route clear of the rocky coast by keeping Pointe du Millier lighthouse open of Pointe de la Jument.

Douarnenez is easy to locate from seaward and easy to enter. Île Tristan, with its lighthouse, is in the foreground with Rosmeur harbour mole east of the island and the Grande Passe and Tréboul marina to the west.

Leave Île Tristan to port to enter the river or to starboard to approach the anchorage.

A clearing transit that clears any shallow patches in the entrance is Douarnenez belfry and Ploaré church, at the back of town, both in line with Île Tristan lighthouse. Keep Ploaré church to the right of Île Tristan for Tréboul or to the left for the anchorage at Rade du Gouet.

By night

Île Tristan light has a red sector covering Basse Veur and Basse Neuve so keep in the white sector until the inner lights are picked up. For the anchorage at Port de Rosmeur, round the breakwaters a reasonable distance off, keeping a good lookout for the numerous unlit mooring buoys. For the visitors' pontoon in the Grande Passe, or Tréboul Marina, leave Pointe Biron light close to starboard. The sectored light at the head of the basin at Port Rhu leads into the Grande Passe and on to the gate in the barrage.

Douarnenez. Tréboul entrance *R Rundle*

By GPS

From the Cap de la Chèvre use:

⊕58-SW Chèvre, ⊕67-Douarnenez

From Morgat use:

⊕64-Morgat, ⊕67-Douarnenez

La Pierre Profonde and its adjacent rocks lie less than 0.5M northeast of this track.

I. FINISTERRE

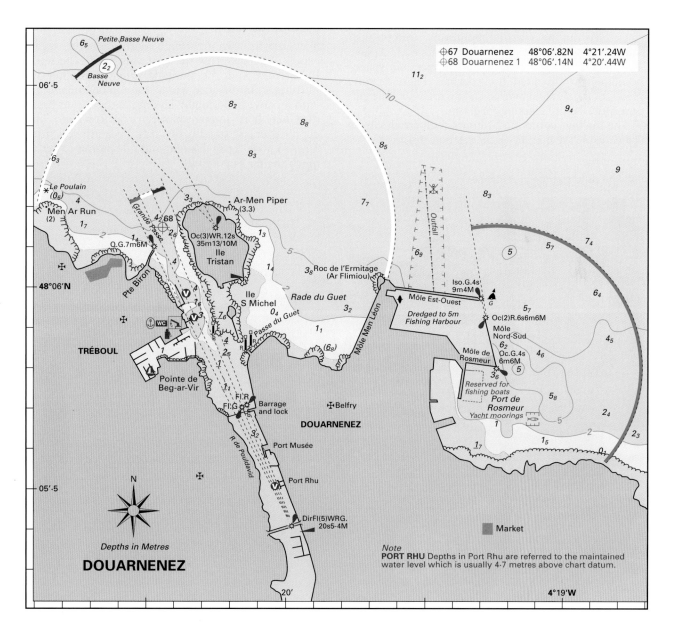

From the Raz de Sein use:

⊕80-Raz, ⊕74-Van, ⊕72-Duellou, ⊕70-Jument, ⊕67-Douarnenez

There are dangers off Pointe de Van, Basse Jaune and near ⊕72-Duellou.

For the final approach to Tréboul use:

⊕67-Douarnenez, ⊕68-Douarnenez 1

This route leaves Basse Neuve 2.2m shallow patch just to port.

BERTHS AND ANCHORAGES

Tréboul

There is a long visitors' pontoon on the west side of the river and a second, smaller, visitors' pontoon with finger berths in the channel just before the turn to starboard into the marina. There are also two large white mooring buoys in the harbour entrance which may be available by arrangement with the harbour office. These berths are all exposed to the northwest and in rough weather the harbourmaster may be able to arrange a berth elsewhere. Water and electricity on the visitors' pontoons, toilets and showers on shore. Tréboul basin is dredged to 1.5m. The marina is crowded and no longer has space permanently allocated for visitors. There is not much room to manoeuvre so call by radio or visit the port office before entering the basin.

The fuelling pontoon (24 hours with credit card) is just inside the marina on the starboard side.

Port Rhu

This was once the drying commercial port. In 1992 a barrage was built across the river to create a large wet basin for the Maritime Museum. Additional vessels are housed in the museum building on the east bank. In front of the barrage the bottom dries 3m (mud and sand). The lock is open from HW-0130 to HW+0130 at springs and HW-0100 to HW+0100 at neaps between the hours of 0700 and 2200 in summer. There is a long visitors' pontoon on the port side above the museum area. Water and electricity on pontoon, toilets, showers and laundry on adjacent quay. Before going through the lock a call to the harbour office on VHF Ch 09 is appreciated.

In summer, Port Rhu is the venue for open-air concerts and similar tourist events. A major Classic Boat Rally is held in Douarnenez every two years (see www.tempsfete-dz.com). The next will be in 2012 when it will combine with Brest's Festival of Sail.

⚓ Rade du Guet

Sheltered from west through south to southeast but exposed to swell from the west, this bay lies between Île Tristan and the mole leading to Rocher de l'Ermitage. In offshore winds it is a good anchorage, with a convenient dinghy landing at the slip in Passe du Guet. It is quieter than Port de Rosmeur. The depths decrease steadily towards the southwest from 3m. Go in as far as draught and tide permit to get as much shelter as possible.

Port Rhu visitors' pontoon *R Rundle*

Tréboul visitors' pontoon *R Rundle*

The Passe du Guet, leading from the anchorage to the river, dries 3.5m, the best water is on the south side near the PHM beacons marking the slip. When the base of the first beacon is just covered there should be 1.5m in the Passe.

Fishing harbour
Visitors may not use this harbour.

⚓ Port de Rosmeur
Protected by the land and the breakwater from all directions except the east, Port de Rosmeur lies to the east of Douarnenez. The northwest half of the harbour is for fishing boats and there are many yacht moorings and a fish farm in the remainder of the bay. Anchor in around 5m outside the moorings but buoy the anchor. There is good holding in mud. Inshore the depths vary irregularly and once the 3m line is crossed they shoal quickly in places.

In settled weather at neaps it is possible to anchor just beyond Port de Rosmeur on the west side of Anse du Ris. This is reasonably sheltered from west through south to east.

⚓ Rocher le Coulinec
Sheltered from the south, there is a fine-weather anchorage off Plage des Sables Blanc about 300m southeast of Rocher le Coulinec.
⊕69-Coulinec 48°06′·32N 4°21′·05W

⚓ Porz Péron
Sheltered from the southwest through south to east, this rocky little bay is about 1.25M west of Pointe de Milier. Approach from the north, leaving the 9m rock Karreg Toull to starboard.
⊕71-Porz Péron 48°05′·38N 4°29′·05W

ASHORE IN DOUARNENEZ
At Tréboul there is a fuel berth, repair facilities, a 6-ton fixed crane, 32-ton mobile crane, 15-ton travelift, chandlers, launderette, cafés, restaurants and shops. Market day is Wednesday.

Douarnenez has all the usual facilities of a substantial town including a daily covered market. The Maritime Museum, which has 40 vessels afloat as well as the covered exhibition, is well worth a visit.

Rosmeur anchorage from Douarnenez Old Port

Douarnenez. Marine Museum *R Rundle*

I. FINISTERRE

12 Île de Sein

Location
48°02'N 4°51'W

Shelter
Fair from S or SW but may be swell

Hazards
Many marked and unmarked rocks

Depth restrictions
0.8m beyond Nerroth
1.8m in anchorage

Night entry
Lit but not recommended

HW time
Brest HW –0005

Mean height of tide (m)

	HWS	HWN	LWN	LWS
Île de Sein	6.2	4.8	2.4	0.9

Tidal streams N approach
SE – Brest HW –0530 to +0330 (0.6kns)
Slack – Brest HW +0330 to +0400
NW – Brest HW –0600 to –0530

Berthing
Limited room to anchor

Facilities
Bars and restaurants but very limited shopping

Charts
BA 2819 (50), 2348 (20, 10)
SHOM 7147 (50), 7423 (20, 10)
Imray C37 (large scale)

Radio
Pte du Raz VHF Ch 16

Tiny island surrounded by rocks

Île de Sein is tiny but well worth a visit. The only town, Port de Sein, is a mass of painted houses and narrow streets. The island itself is so low-lying that the sea has occasionally covered it. There are no trees, or even bushes; just old fields surrounded by dry stone walls. However, the real attraction is the ever-present Atlantic and the huge Breton sky.

PILOTAGE

Warning

A large-scale chart is essential.

The navigation is intricate so slack tide at neaps is best for a first visit. Neap tides have the additional benefit of increasing the available anchoring space.

Navigating in the area around Île de Sein is not as difficult as it appears from the chart. The entrance channels are clearly marked. The tidal streams are not nearly as strong as in the Raz. Also the plateau is compact on the northeast and east sides and the fringes are clearly marked.

Identifying Nerroth is the key. It forms the east side of the entrance to the harbour and looks like a flattish, rocky island at low water and three very large flat rocks at high water. Two white masonry beacons on the north and south ends of Nerroth are important day marks.

The north channel

This is the principal channel and the easiest for a stranger.

By day

From the north, approach the Cornoc-An-Ar-Braden SHM pillar buoy.

Île de Sein anchorage *D Lomax*

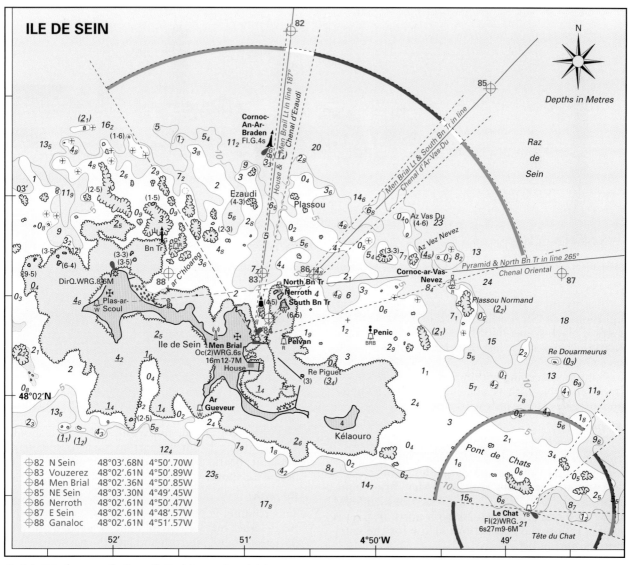

ILE DE SEIN

Depths in Metres

Raz
de
Sein

Cornoc-
An-Ar-
Braden
Fl.G.4s

Ezaudi
(4·3)

Plassou

Az Vas Du
(4·6) 23

Az Vez Nevez

Cornoc-ar-Vas-
Nevez

Plassou Normand
(2₂)

Re Douarmeurus
(0₃)

North Bn Tr
Nerroth
South Bn Tr
(6·5)

DirQ.WRG.8·6M

Plas-ar-
w Scoul

Bn Tr

ar C'hloareg

Ile de Sein
Men Brial
Oc(2)WRG.6s
16m12·7M
House

Penic
BRB

Pelvan

Re Piguet
(3)

Ar
Gueveur

Kélaouro

Pont de Chats

Le Chat
Fl(2)WRG.
6s27m9-6M

Tête du Chat

⊕82 N Sein	48°03'.68N	4°50'.70W
⊕83 Vouzerez	48°02'.61N	4°50'.89W
⊕84 Men Brial	48°02'.36N	4°50'.85W
⊕85 NE Sein	48°03'.30N	4°49'.45W
⊕86 Nerroth	48°02'.61N	4°50'.47W
⊕87 E Sein	48°02'.61N	4°48'.57W
⊕88 Ganaloc	48°02'.61N	4°51'.57W

I. FINISTERRE

Port de Sein from south. Nerroth Rock is seen top right

Men Brial Lighthouse with the black-striped house just open to the left of it for the northern approach

Identify the green and white tower of Men Brial lighthouse and beyond it the white house with the vertical black stripe, third from the left by the quay. Keep the black stripe just open left of the lighthouse on 187°.

Continue, keeping within 50m either side of the track until Nerroth is abeam. Continue into the anchorage using the instructions below.

By night

There must be enough light to make out Nerroth and Guernic SHM concrete beacon and tide must be high enough to allow some margin for error.

Enter in the white sector of Men Brial light, bearing 187° and leave Cornoc-An-Ar-Braden SHM buoy to starboard. When Nerroth north beacon is abeam follow the instructions below for the entry into the anchorage.

By GPS

This passage requires careful visual pilotage but:
⊕82-N Sein, ⊕83-Vouzerez, ⊕84-Men Brial

may provide some assistance.

Nerroth to the anchorage

By day

With Nerroth abeam, enter the harbour using Pelvan red concrete beacon in line with the east end of the east breakwater on 155°. At low water the breakwater is obscured so just steer 155° for Pelvan.

After passing Guernic SHM tower beacon, nudge a bit to starboard of the transit to avoid a shoal patch.

When Men Brial lighthouse bears 220° alter course to the southwest and aim for the anchorage.

By night

When Nerroth north beacon is abeam, alter course to 160° and enter the red sector of Men Brial, leaving Guernic SHM tower beacon 60m to starboard. When the other white sector of Men Brial is entered it is safe to steer for the anchorage.

The northeast channel

Coming from the east or northeast this channel is easier than the east channel.

By day

Start from about 300m northwest of Ar-Vas-Du rock (⊕85-NE Sein). Approach Nerroth using Men Brial lighthouse in line with the white beacon on the south of Nerroth on 224°.

The beacon on the north end of Nerroth should be left about 100m to port so turn to starboard when it bears 265° to enter the anchorage as described above.

By night

This channel is covered by a white sector of Men Brial light, but sufficient light is needed for the deviation round Nerroth and into the harbour.

By GPS

This passage requires careful visual pilotage but

⊕85-NE Sein, ⊕86-Nerroth and ⊕83-Vouzerez

may provide some assistance.

The east channel

By day

From the Raz de Sein, keep the Cornoc-ar-Vas-Nevez beacon bearing less than 290° to avoid the rocks to the south.

Start from a position 100m north of the beacon. Approach Nerroth using the north end of Nerroth in line with the pyramid tower with a fluorescent top just south of the Île de Sein main lighthouse on 265° (*see opposite*). Carreg ar C'hloareg above-water rock and the Cross of Lorraine monument are on virtually the same line. This transit must be held closely because Ar Vas Nevez (dries 5.0m) is close to the north of the line and another rock (dries 1.0m) is close to the south.

The beacon on the north end of Nerroth should be left about 100m to port and when it is abeam start turning to port to enter the anchorage as described above.

By night

Pick up the QFl.WRG Directional light from Île de Seine main lighthouse and keep in the white sector on 270° until Neroth is abeam and course can be altered as in the section above, Neroth to the anchorage at night.

By GPS

This passage requires careful visual pilotage but:

⊕87-E Sein, ⊕83-Vouzerez, ⊕84-Men Brial

may provide some assistance.

ANCHORAGES

⚓ Port de Sein

Sheltered from the south and west but exposed to the east above half tide, the anchorage is immediately off the lifeboat slip, southeast of the Men Brial lighthouse. There is 1.8m off the lifeboat slip and 1m further to the southeast. The bottom is mud over rock. Weed can be a problem.

The whole harbour dries near the quays and south of them. The fishing fleet enters the harbour in the evening, and is often there by day. Its position indicates the best water. The round red buoys belong to the fishermen and there is not much room to anchor between them and the slip so it may be necessary to anchor east of them. Permission can sometimes be obtained to use a buoy.

Swell enters if the wind goes into the north and the anchorage would be dangerous in strong winds from any northerly direction.

Yachts that can take the ground may use the bay south of the slips and can find 1.5m in places at LW neaps. The bottom is mainly sand but there are some weed-covered stony patches.

⚓ Île de Sein lighthouse

Sheltered from the south and southwest, there is a small bay about 400m east-southeast of Île de Sein lighthouse. Approach it from a point just north of Nerroth (⊕83-Vouzerez). Bring the lighthouse onto 270° and hold this course until due south of Roche Ganaloc red beacon tower (⊕88-Ganaloc). Now come round onto 230° and edge in carefully towards the beach as far as draught permits.

⊕88-Ganoloc 48°02′·61N 4°51′·57W

ASHORE ON ÎLE DE SEIN

Facilities

Ship and engine repairs can be arranged and chandlery can be obtained from the fishermen's co-op. There are several small shops, bars and restaurants. Water is scarce but bread is delivered from the mainland although it must be ordered the night before.

History

Île de Sein is an island of heroes. The entire male population left to join the Free French during the Second World War and their exploits are commemorated in an interesting little museum. When General De Gaulle was first reviewing these troops, a quarter of whom were from the island, he is reported to have said 'Where is this Île de Sein? It seems to be a quarter of France'. Nowadays a large number of the lifeboat men of West Brittany come from Île de Sein.

The East Channel approach. Identify the white beacon on the north end of Nerroth (*inset top right*) and a pyramid tower with a fluorescent top just south of the Île de Sein main lighthouse (*inset top left*). Bring these in line on 265°. If the pyramid is hard to identify, look for the Cross of Lorraine monument which is just south of a large rock, Karreg ar C'hloareg, which never covers *M&G Barron*

13 Raz de Sein

Location
48°03'N 4°46'W

Hazards
Dangerous tide race; unmarked rocks SW of Tévennec and W of Pte du Van

Night passage Well lit

Charts
BA 2819 (50), 2348 (20)
SHOM 7147 (50), 7423 (20)
Imray C36 (77)

Radio
Pte du Raz VHF Ch 16, 70 (DSC)

HW time
Brest HW

Mean height of tide (m)

	HWS	HWN	LWN	LWS
Île de Sein	6.2	4.8	2.4	0.9

Tidal stream Raz de Sein
N-going: Brest HW +0545 to –0100
(Sp 5.2 kns, Np 3.0 kns)
Slack: Brest HW –0100 to –0030
S-going: Brest HW –0030 to +0515
(Sp 4.2 kns, Np 2.4 kns)
Slack: Brest HW +0515 to +0545

Koummoudog counter current
E – Brest HW–0230 to -0030 (1.0kns)
W – Brest HW +0030 to +0430
(1.0 kns)

Rocky southwest corner of Brittany

The Raz de Sein is the short passage between the Pointe du Raz on the mainland and the Île de Sein. It has a justifiably bad reputation but under reasonable conditions, it presents no great difficulties.

PILOTAGE

Tidal strategy

Timing is important and when possible, the Raz should be taken at slack water. Even in moderate conditions, with wind and tide, it can be rough. With light winds, neap tides and no swell, it is passable at any time.

The Raz is temperamental and the seas vary considerably but, with strong wind against tide, the overfalls are dangerous.

The Raz de Sein from the north

A yacht leaving the Chenal du Four at the end of the fair tide can punch the tide in the Iroise where it is weak and usually arrive at the Raz in time to take advantage of the stream turning south again.

By day

From the north make for La Vieille lighthouse on 180°, which puts La Vieille midway between Pointe du Van and Tévennec.

When 0.5M off La Vieille, bear to starboard to pass west of La Plate WCM yellow and black tower beacon. There may be overfalls west of La Plate but the sea will moderate once it is passed.

Going south keep Pointe du Van in transit with Gorle Greiz, (the large rock between Pointe du Raz and La Vieille), bearing 041°. This leads between the shallow patches Kornog Bras and Masklou Greiz which can be rough in bad weather.

Going southeast towards Penmarc'h, steer with Tévennec bearing 324° astern, open to the left of La Plate.

By night

Make good 180° in the white sector of Tévennec. When Le Chat turns from green to white, steer 115° until the directional flashing light on Tévennec opens. Then steer 150° past La Vieille and Le Chat.

Going south use the white sector of La Vieille, on 205°.

Going southeast towards Penmarc'h use the directional sector of Tévennec until clear. The southern dangers are clear as soon as Le Chat turns from green to red, bearing 286°.

By GPS

From the Chenal du Four use:
⊕55-Vandrée, ⊕80-Raz

This route is safe but goes slightly outside the area marked by the safe sectors of the lights.

By night this may be preferred:
⊕55-Vandrée, ⊕75-E Tévennec, ⊕78-NE Raz, ⊕80-Raz

From the Chenal du Toulinguet use:
⊕51-S Toulinguet, ⊕80-Raz

By night:
⊕51-S Toulinguet, ⊕78-NE Raz, ⊕80-Raz

remains in the safe sectors of the lights.

From Morgat or Douarnenez use:
⊕74-Van, ⊕80-Raz

Or by night:
⊕74-Van, ⊕78-NE Raz, ⊕80-Raz

The Raz de Sein from the northwest

By day

Avoid the dangers of Basse Plate, 0.5M to the southwest of Tévennec by keeping La Vieille in transit with the southern limit of the cliffs southeast of the Pointe du Raz, on 112°. When 0.5M off La Vieille alter course to leave La Plate to port.

By night

Make good 190° in the white sector of Men Brial light on Île de Sein. When La Vieille turns from red to white, steer 120° until the directional isophase light on Tévennec opens. Then proceed as from the north.

By GPS

⊕81-W Tévennec, ⊕80-Raz

Basse Plate is 0.5M north of this track.

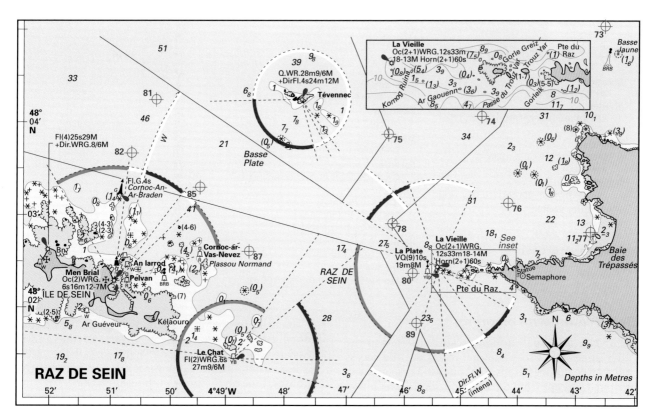

RAZ DE SEIN

I. FINISTERRE

⊕73	Basse Jaune	48°05 .01N	4°42 .44W
⊕74	Van	48°04 .06N	4°44 .58W
⊕75	E Tévennec	48°03 .90N	4°46 .25W
⊕76	Trépassés	48°03 .07N	4°44 .19W
⊕77	Trépassés 1	48°02 .87N	4°42 .78W
⊕78	NE Raz	48°02 .91N	4°46 .26W
⊕80	Raz	48°02 .37N	4°45 .86W
⊕81	W Tévennec	**48°04 .29N**	**4°50 .47W**
⊕82	N Sein	48°03 .68N	4°50 .70W
⊕85	NE Sein	48°03 .30N	4°49 .45W
⊕87	E Sein	48°02 .61N	4°48 .57W
⊕89	SE Raz	48°01 .83N	4°45 .78W

The Raz de Sein from the south

By day

From the south or southwest keep the steep island of Tévennec open to the west of La Plate on a bearing of 327°. Pass La Plate leaving it 0.5M to starboard.

Going north keep the back-bearing on La Vieille between 160° and 200° to clear the dangers off Pte du Van and Tévennec.

Going northwest make 295° from La Plate keeping in the middle of the channel between Tévennec and Île de Sein.

By night

Keep in the directional Fl.4s sector of Tévennec light until it bears 330° and La Plate bears 110°. A track of 020° will then lead north clear of the Raz. A track of 295° leads northwest between Tévennec and Île de Sein.

The Pointe du Raz looking west towards Île de Sein

By GPS

From Audierne use:

⊕90-Koummoudog, ⊕80-Raz

From the Pointe de Penmarc'h use:

⊕103-Eckmühl, ⊕80-Raz

From the southwest use

⊕89-SE Raz, ⊕80-Raz

to ensure an approach in the white sector of La Vieille. There is rough water in 3.6m and 8m about 0.5M south of ⊕89-SE Raz.

At night, these are cleared using the white sector of La Vieille.

ANCHORAGE

⚓ Baie des Trépassés

Sheltered between northeast and southeast but exposed to swell from the west, there is a fair-weather anchorage in the Baie des Trépassés, east-northeast of the Pointe de Raz. To avoid the dangers southwest of Pointe du Van, approach from due west. The bay is sandy and shelving so anchor in the most suitable depth. The best position is either in the centre, facing the valley or in the northeast corner about 200m southeast of Gravendeileg. Expect some swell.

⊕77-Trépassés 48°02'·87N 4°42'·78W

14 Sainte Evette

Location
48°00'N 4°33'W

Shelter
Reasonable except from strong E or SE wind

Hazards
Marked wrecks and rocks in approach

Depth restrictions
2.2m patch in approach to moorings

Night entry Well lit

HW time
Brest HW –0030

Mean height of tide (m)

	HWS	HWN	LWN	LWS
Audierne	5.2	4.1	2.0	0.8

Tidal streams
Weak in the bay

Berthing
Visitors' buoys

Fuel
Diesel Berth

Facilities
Good facilities in Audierne

Charts
BA 2819 (50,12.5), 3640 (24)
SHOM 7147 (50,12.5)
Imray C37 (large scale)

Radio
Ste-Evette VHF Ch 9

Telephone
Ste-Evette HM ① 02 98 70 00 28

Beach resort with moorings

Ste-Evette is a small holiday resort situated in the outer approaches to Audierne. It has all-tide access and a large number of visitors' buoys. These are well sheltered, except from the east and south. The buoys are rather close together but a few can accommodate 12m LOA maximum. They are often crowded but they provide a convenient overnight stop. There is some room to anchor.

Ste-Evette has few facilities but it is a pleasant walk along the river bank to Audierne.

PILOTAGE (*See plan on page 61*)

Ste-Evette from the west and south

By day

From the Raz de Sein, the entrance to Sainte Evette is 0.5M west of Gamelle West WCM buoy (⊕94-W Gamelle).

Identify two white, red-topped lighthouses to the north of the bay. Kergadec is on the skyline and is easy to spot. Below it, the old lighthouse of Trescadec is less easy to locate. Look for it in a gap between the houses. Line up the two lighthouses on 006°.

There are rocky patches either side of the channel, one at Le Sillon to the southwest of the harbour and the other is La Gamelle to the east of the channel. If there is a swell the seas break on La Gamelle. At low water, also note the shoal patch depth 2.2m on the leading line east of Ste-Evette.

For Ste-Evette moorings, leave the leading line and steer for the mole head when it bears 315°. Take care to avoid the rocks on the north edge of the mole.

By night

Enter the narrow white sector of Kergadec quick flashing light (006°). When the light on the Ste-Evette mole head bears northwest alter course for the Ste-Evette anchorage.

The moorings at Ste-Evette looking northeast. The long breakwater protects the bay from the southwest but not from strong winds from the east or south. There are two slipways just north of the breakwater. One is for the lifeboat while the more northerly of the two is marked by an inconspicuous E Cardinal at its end (*see inset, M&G Barron*)

The moorings at Ste-Evette *M&G Barron*

By GPS

From the Raz de Sein use:

⊕80-Raz, ⊕90-Koummoudog, ⊕94-W Gamelle,
⊕95-St-Evette

La Gamelle shallow patch (dries 0.8m) is about
0.25M E of the track a little N of ⊕94-W Gamelle
(*See plan on page 61*).

From the southwest or south:

⊕94-W Gamelle or ⊕98-E Gamelle can be approached
directly. The continuation from ⊕94-W Gamelle
is described above. The continuation from
⊕98-E Gamelle is described below in approaches from
the southeast.

Ste-Evette from the southeast

By day

From the southeast the channel between La Gamelle
to the west and the land to the east is wide and the
least depth on the leading line is 2.5m. Gamelle East
SCM buoy should be left well to port.

The transit is Kergadec lighthouse, white with a
red top on the skyline, with the Raoulic Jetty light
tower on 331°. When Ste-Evette breakwater head
bears 293° it is safe to steer for the moorings.

By night

Approach with Raoulic light and Kergadec light in
line on 331°. Pte de Lervily light has a red sector
covering La Gamelle. When this light turns from red
to white, it is safe to steer for Ste-Evette.

By GPS

From the Pointe de Penmarc'h use:

⊕103-Eckmühl, ⊕98-E Gamelle, ⊕97-NE Gamelle,
⊕95-St-Evette

There is a wreck (dries 1.5m) on the east side of La
Gamelle shallow patch about 400m west of the track
between ⊕98-E Gamelle and ⊕97-NE Gamelle.

BERTHS AND ANCHORAGES

Ste-Evette moorings and anchorage

The Ste-Evette anchorage is sheltered from west and
north by the land and from the south by the
breakwater. Some swell enters if there is south in the
wind and this may be considerable if the wind is
strong. The depths are 2.5m or more north of the
end of the mole, decreasing steadily towards the
shore. The moorings are tightly packed and some are
not suitable for boats over 10m and others over
12m. A charge is collected for their use.

There may be room to anchor east of the
moorings, with less shelter from the south. The
holding is not very good and there are a few rocky
patches. Buoy the anchor. It is best to tuck in behind
the breakwater as far as depth allows to get out of
the swell.

The bay contains two hazards. First, the more
northerly of the two slips extends a long way and
has an inconspicuous ECM at its end (*see opposite*).
Second, there is a rock ledge, La Petite Gamelle
marked by a SCM beacon, in the northern part of
the anchorage. The bay is shallow N of this beacon.

⚓ Anse du Loc'h

Sheltered from all directions except southeast to
southwest, this sandy bay is 3M west of Pointe de
Lervily. Enter it on 030° to avoid the rocks on the
east side.

⊕92-Anse de Loc'h 48°01'·44N 4°38'·29W

⚓ Anse du Cabestan

Sheltered from north through east, this wide sandy
bay is 3M west of Audierne. Approach from the
southwest to avoid two rocks. Basse du Loc'h (dries
1.9m) between Anse du Loc'h and Anse du Cabestan
and Roche de Porz-Tarz at the northwest end of
Anse du Cabestan.

⊕93-Cabestan 48°00'·56N 4°35'·91W

⚓ Pors-Poulhan

Protected from the northeast, this tiny harbour is
3M southeast of Audierne. The harbour itself is very
small and dries but there is an outside anchorage
that can be used in settled weather.

⊕99-Pors-Poulan 47°59'·00N 4°27'·80W

ASHORE IN STE-EVETTE

Facilities

Land at the ferry slip, or at Raoulic jetty or the little
pier in the northwest corner of the bay. Both the
latter dry at LW. There is a diesel berth on the
northern side of the root of the northern slip but
watch the depth as there can be less than 1m at LW.
There is a launderette and a few shops at the ferry
pier. Audierne has all facilities and is only about a
mile away.

A ferry goes to Île de Sein from Ste-Evette. The
tourist ferry takes a rock-hopping route and is
recommended.

I. FINISTERRE

15 Audierne

Location
48°01'N 4°32'W

Shelter
Good in marina

Hazards
Audierne channel in strong S wind
Marked wrecks and rocks in approach

Depth restrictions
Audierne channel dredged 1m
Marina 2m on pontoons D-G

Night entry
Lit but not recommended

HW time
Brest HW-0030

Mean height of tide (m)

	HWS	HWN	LWN	LWS
Audierne	5.2	4.1	2.0	0.8

Tidal streams
Weak in the bay but strong in the
river and marina

Berthing
Marina

Facilities
Some repair facilities, good shops,
market and restaurants

Charts
BA 2819 (50,12.5), 3640 (24)
SHOM 7147 (50,12.5)
Imray C37 (large scale)

Radio
Audierne Marina VHF Ch 09, 16

Telephone
Audierne Marina ☎ 02 98 75 04 93

Attractive fishing port with marina

Audierne is an attractive port. It is 1M inland,
accessed by a dredged channel (1m) which is subject
to silting. The small marina has some space for
visitors on the hammerheads.

PILOTAGE

Warning

The mouth of the Audierne channel is dangerous in
strong south winds.

Audierne from west or south

By day

From the Raz de Sein, arrive at a point about 0.5M
west of Gamelle West WCM buoy(⊕94-W Gamelle).

Line up Kergadec and Trescadec red-topped
lighthouses on 006° to avoid the rocky patches
either side of the channel. Deep draught vessels
should also note the shoal patch of 2.2m on the
leading line east of Ste-Evette.

Continue on 006°,then head for the end of
Raoulic Jetty when it bears 034°.

Pilotage from the end of the jetty is given below.

By night

Partially lit but not recommended.

By GPS

From the Raz de Sein use:

⊕80-Raz, ⊕90-Koummoudog, ⊕94-W Gamelle,
⊕96-Audierne

La Gamelle is about 0.25 M east of the track a little
north of ⊕94-W Gamelle.

From the southwest or south use:

⊕94-W Gamelle

or ⊕98-E Gamelle can be approached directly.

Audierne from southeast

By day

Leave Gamelle East SCM buoy well to port and
come in using Kergadec red-topped lighthouse in
line with the Raoulic Jetty light tower on 331°.

By night

Partially lit but not recommended.

By GPS

From the Pointe de Penmarc'h use:

⊕103-Eckmühl, ⊕98-E Gamelle, ⊕96-Audierne.

There is a wreck (dries 1.5m) on the east side of La
Gamelle shallow patch two cables west of the track
between ⊕98-E Gamelle and ⊕96-Audierne.

The dredged channel to Audierne

By day

The channel is maintained at between 1m and 2m
but is subject to silting. In the first section it is
narrow and close to the pier and at low water there
is not much room for error so it is best to make a
first visit above half tide. There is a new PHM
beacon halfway along the pier and close to it.

There are two leading lines marked with pairs of
red and white chevron boards and they are not easy
to see. The first is on the Raoulic Jetty on 359°. The
second is on 043° alongside a white patch on the fish
market. This lines up with a grey cottage on the hill
behind on the same bearing (*see photos opposite*).
This second bearing takes one very close to the end
of the Vieux Mole and below half-tide it is better to
follow the junction of the rocks at the base of the
jetty with the sand which can easily be seen.

At the fish market the channel turns on to 303°
and runs along the quays to the marina.

By night

Partially lit but not recommended.

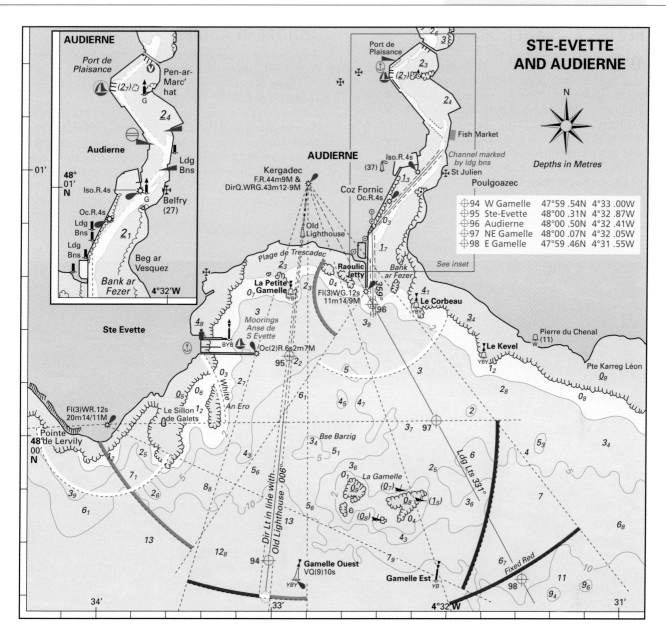

STE-EVETTE AND AUDIERNE

AUDIERNE

Port de Plaisance

Pen-ar-Marc'hat

(2₇)

G

2₄

Audierne

48° 01' N

Iso.R.4s

G

Oc.R.4s

Ldg Bns

Ldg Bns

Belfry (27)

2₁

Beg ar Vesquez

Bank ar Fezer

4°32'W

N

Depths in Metres

Port de Plaisance

(2₇)

2₄

Fish Market

Iso.R.4s

(37)

Channel marked by ldg bns

St Julien

Poulgoazec

1₃

0₃

⊕ 94	W Gamelle	47°59 .54N	4°33 .00W
⊕ 95	Ste-Evette	48°00 .31N	4°32 .87W
⊕ 96	Audierne	48°00 .50N	4°32 .41W
⊕ 97	NE Gamelle	48°00 .07N	4°32 .05W
⊕ 98	E Gamelle	47°59 .46N	4°31 .55W

AUDIERNE

Kergadec
F.R.44m9M &
DirQ.WRG.43m12-9M

Coz Fornic
Oc.R.4s

Old Lighthouse

Plage de Trescadec

2₃

Ste Evette

Raoulic Jetty

La Petite Gamelle
YBY

0₇

2₃

0₄

Fl(3)WG.12s
11m14/9M

359°

96

Bank ar Fezer

4₁

Le Corbeau
YBY

3₄

Pierre du Chenal
(11)
W

Le Kevel
YBY

1₂

Pte Karreg Léon

0₉

4₈

Moorings Anse de S Evette

BYB

/Oc(2)R.6s2m7M

95

2₂

5

3₉

3

2₈

0₈

White

0₃

0₅

0₆

An Ero

2₇

6₁

4₅

4₇

3₇

97

2

Fl(3)WR.12s
20m14/11M

Le Sillon de Galets

1₂

Ldg Lts 331°

6

5₃

4

3₄

Pointe de Lervily

48° 00' N

1₂

2₅

7₁

2₆

8₈

Bse Barzig

3₄

5₁

5

4₃

5₆

3₆

0₁

La Gamelle
(0₇)

2₅

3₆

7

6₈

3₉

6₁

10

5₆

0₉

0₈

(1₅)

0₄

4₃

13

12₈

Dir Lt in line with Old Lighthouse - 006°

13

94

Gamelle Ouest
VQ(9)10s
YBY

0₉

0₈

7₉

Gamelle Est
YB

6₇

Fixed Red

98

9₄

9₆

11

10

6₈

34'

33'

4°32'W

31'

Audierne. Kergadec light and Raoulic Jetty light in line for the southeast approach

Audierne southern-most harbour leading marks

Audierne fishmarket leading marks

I. FINISTERRE

BERTHS AND ANCHORAGE

Audierne marina

The marina has been extended and there is now some space for visitors on the hammerheads. Pontoons A–C have been dredged 2m on the hammerheads, D–G are reported to have 2m throughout. If possible, avoid F and G because the tide sets across them.

The channel to the yacht berths is marked with green starboard posts.

ASHORE IN AUDIERNE

Audierne is a pleasant town that has successfully combined fishing with tourism.

There is a shipyard as well as mechanical and electrical engineers. Diesel at St-Evette.

The market square and shopping area are close to the pontoons and there is a wide range of shops and restaurants. The showers are next to the supermarket in the north of the square with a code from the harbourmaster's office in the middle of the square but if he is not there it is obtainable (in office hours) from the Mairie along the waterfront to the south.

The river to Audierne with the deeper water showing clearly in the channel. At the fish market on the right-hand side of the picture, the channel turns through 90° and continues past the quays to the marina

Audierne approach to marine pontoons

II. Bénodet Bay

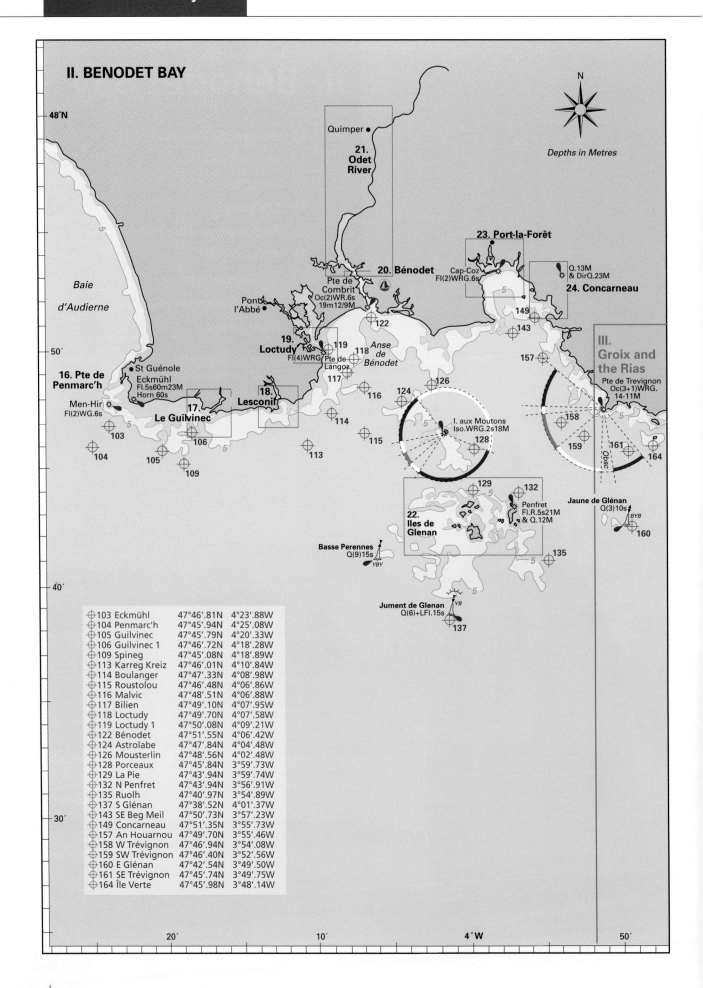

II. BENODET BAY

48°N

N

Depths in Metres

Baie d'Audierne

Quimper ●

21. Odet River

23. Port-la-Forêt

Cap-Coz
Fl(2)WRG.6s

20. Bénodet

Q.13M
& DirQ.23M

24. Concarneau

Pte de Combrit
Oc(2)WR.6s
19m12/9M

149

143

III.
Groix and the Rias

50′

Pont l'Abbé ●

⊕ 122

19. Loctudy
Fl(4)WRG

119
118
Pte de Langoz

157

Pte de Trevignon
Oc(3+1)WRG.
14-11M

16. Pte de Penmarc'h

St Guénole ●
Eckmühl
Fl.5s60m23M
Horn 60s

117

Anse de Bénodet

158

Men-Hir ☼
Fl(2)WG.6s

18. Lesconil

116

126

124

159

161

164

⊕ 103

17. Le Guilvinec

114

115

I. aux Moutons
Iso.WRG.2s18M

128

Obsc

⊕ 104

106

⊕ 113

129

132

Jaune de Glénan
Q(3)10s

105

109

Penfret
Fl.R.5s21M
& Q.12M

BYB

160

22. Iles de Glenan

135

40′

Basse Perennes
Q(9)15s

YBY

Jument de Glenan
Q(6)+LFl.15s

YB

137

⊕103	Eckmühl	47°46′.81N	4°23′.88W
⊕104	Penmarc'h	47°45′.94N	4°25′.08W
⊕105	Guilvinec	47°45′.79N	4°20′.33W
⊕106	Guilvinec 1	47°46′.72N	4°18′.28W
⊕109	Spineg	47°45′.08N	4°18′.89W
⊕113	Karreg Kreiz	47°46′.01N	4°10′.84W
⊕114	Boulanger	47°47′.33N	4°08′.98W
⊕115	Roustolou	47°46′.48N	4°06′.86W
⊕116	Malvic	47°48′.51N	4°06′.88W
⊕117	Bilien	47°49′.10N	4°07′.95W
⊕118	Loctudy	47°49′.70N	4°07′.58W
⊕119	Loctudy 1	47°50′.08N	4°09′.21W
⊕122	Bénodet	47°51′.55N	4°06′.42W
⊕124	Astrolabe	47°47′.84N	4°04′.48W
⊕126	Mousterlin	47°48′.56N	4°02′.48W
⊕128	Porceaux	47°45′.84N	3°59′.73W
⊕129	La Pie	47°43′.94N	3°59′.74W
⊕132	N Penfret	47°43′.94N	3°56′.91W
⊕135	Ruolh	47°40′.97N	3°54′.89W
⊕137	S Glénan	47°38′.52N	4°01′.37W
⊕143	SE Beg Meil	47°50′.73N	3°57′.23W
⊕149	Concarneau	47°51′.35N	3°55′.73W
⊕157	An Houarnou	47°49′.70N	3°55′.46W
⊕158	W Trévignon	47°46′.94N	3°54′.08W
⊕159	SW Trévignon	47°46′.40N	3°52′.56W
⊕160	E Glénan	47°42′.54N	3°49′.50W
⊕161	SE Trévignon	47°45′.74N	3°49′.75W
⊕164	Île Verte	47°45′.98N	3°48′.14W

30′

20′   10′   4°W   50′

16 Pointe de Penmarc'h

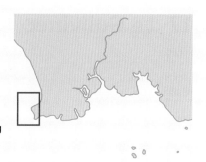

Location
47°48'N 4°23'W

Hazards
Well marked rocks
Complex tidal streams that are much
affected by the wind

Night passage Well lit

HW time
Brest HW–0025₄ neaps, –0030 springs

Mean height of tide (m)

	HWS	HWN	LWN	LWS
Guilvinec	5.1	4.0	2.0	0.9

Tidal streams Pte de Penmarc'h
SE-going: Brest HW–0230 to
+0230 (1.0kns)
NW-going: Brest HW+0230 to
–0230 (1.0kns)

St-Guénole
St-Guénole is a commercial fishing
port that does not welcome
yachtsmen. Entry is hazardous
except in very good conditions

Charts
BA 2819 (50), 2820 (50)
SHOM 7147 (50), 7146 (50)
Imray C37 (77)

Gateway to the sun

Eckmühl lighthouse marks the start of South Brittany so passing it eastbound is always a pleasure. In good weather at sunrise or sunset it is a magical place.

The Pointe de Penmarc'h is a low headland with a very high octagonal lighthouse, Eckmühl (named after the Prince d'Eckmühl, a heroic marshall in Napoleon's army). Reefs extend, in all directions from the headland. These are well marked and, in good weather, it is possible to round close, using the various beacon towers. In poor weather or on passage south it is better to stay a few miles offshore.

PILOTAGE

Rounding Penmarc'h

By day

Give Men-Hir Lt Bn a good berth as the reef on which it stands extends over 200m to the west. Otherwise there are no hazards outside the lines joining the buoys. However, there is often a heavy swell in the vicinity of Pointe de Penmarc'h and in these circumstances, or in poor visibility, it is best to stay at least 3M off shore.

By night

Use the white sector of Men-Hir to keep clear of the rocks off the Pointe of Penmarc'h. After that the principal buoys are lit although care should be taken to keep well south of the unlit Ar Guisty which is south of Le Guilvinec.

By GPS

For Loctudy or Bénodet use:

⊕103-Eckmühl, ⊕109-Spineg, ⊕113-Karreg Kreiz, ⊕115-Roustolou, ⊕116-Malvic

This route can be used at all states of the tide but it passes close to a number of well marked dangers so care is required. ⊕116-Malvic lies directly between two unlit buoys, which is a bit scary at night. The shortcut:

⊕113-Karreg Kreiz, ⊕114-Boulanger, ⊕117-Bilien

has a least depth of 2.2m but keeps well away from unlit buoys.

For Port-La-Forêt or Concarneau, use:

⊕103-Eckmühl, ⊕109-Spineg, ⊕113-Karreg Kreiz, ⊕115-Roustolou, ⊕124-Astrolabe

The last leg has a least depth of 2.3m and passes between two unlit beacon towers.

For the southeast use:

⊕104-Penmarc'h, ⊕137-S Glénan

In good weather, ⊕193-Eckmühl can be substituted for ⊕104-Penmarc'h. This shortcut passes close south of Men-Hir and Spineg; both are lit.

Pointe of Penmarc'h Men-Hir light beacon and Eckmühl light

II. BENODET BAY

17 Le Guilvinec

Location
47°48'N 4°17'W
Shelter Good
Hazards
1.8m shallow patch on leading line
Depth restrictions
3m in harbour
Night entry Well lit
Other restrictions
Total priority to fishing vessels
No entry or exit 1600–1830
HW time
Brest HW–0010 neaps, –0025 springs
Mean height of tide (m)

	HWS	HWN	LWN	LWS
Guilvinec	5.1	4.0	2.0	0.9

Berthing
Two small visitors' pontoons
Facilities
As of a busy fishing port
Charts
BA 2820 (50), 3640 (15)
SHOM 7146 (50), 6646 (15)
Imray C37 (large scale)
Radio
Harbourmaster VHF Ch 12
Telephone
Fishing Harbourmaster
② 02 98 58 05 67
Pleasure Craft Office
② 02 98 58 14 47

Colourful fishing port

Le Guilvinec is a commercial fishing port 4M east of Penmarc'h. The harbour is sheltered and the entrance is straightforward, providing care is taken to avoid outlying rocks. Le Guilvinec has recently made an effort to be more welcoming to visitors. There is not much room but there used to be two small visitors' pontoons, one on the northwest side of the harbour and one on the southeast. However in 2010 major construction work was taking place in the harbour and it is reported that it will be closed to visiting yachts until the work is finished in 2012 or 2013.

Le Guilvinec from the southeast showing new construction in the centre

PILOTAGE

Guilvinec main channel

By day

From the west keep well clear of Les Etocs above-water and drying rocks and make for Névez SHM buoy, 900m south of Raguen SCM tower beacon.

Le Guilvinec is difficult to see among all the white houses with grey roofs. Look for the long white fish market, a red-topped lighthouse on the north mole and the massive blue travel-lift. The conspicuous leading marks, two large red cylinders on orange-red columns, will be in transit on 053°.

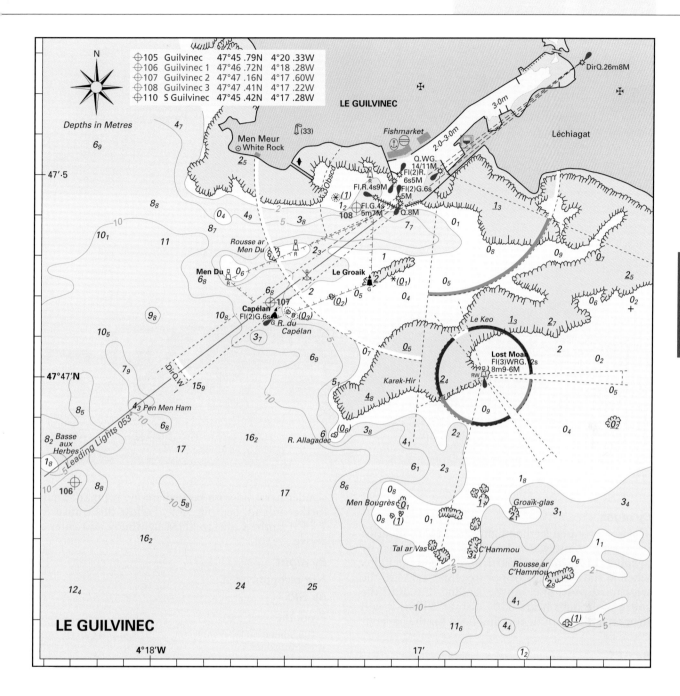

⊕105 Guilvinec	47°45.79N	4°20.33W
⊕106 Guilvinec 1	47°46.72N	4°18.28W
⊕107 Guilvinec 2	47°47.16N	4°17.60W
⊕108 Guilvinec 3	47°47.41N	4°17.22W
⊕110 S Guilvinec	47°45.42N	4°17.28W

LE GUILVINEC

II. BENODET BAY

Le Guilvinec rear leading mark and visitors' pontoon

The leading line crosses a 1.8m shallow patch, Basse aux Herbes. Near low water, especially in rough weather, it is best to move 150m to starboard when the Eckmühl light tower is in line with Locarec beacon (292°).

Follow the leading line and pass Men Du PHM beacon tower, Capelan SHM lightbuoy, Rousse ar Men Du PHM beacon tower and Le Groaik SHM beacon tower.

Enter the harbour between the outer south mole and the north mole head and spur.

From the east leave Basse Spineg SCM buoy to starboard to make for the Névez SHM buoy and enter as above.

Le Guilvinec harbour with the rear leading mark framed by the conspicuous blue boat hoist

Le Guilvinec fish quay

By night

The synchronised leading lights are easy to identify. If entering at low water, avoid Basse aux Herbes by keeping 150m to starboard of the leading lights when in the red sector of Locarec light 1.5M to the west-northwest. Stay on the leading line until the south mole light bears 030° distant 200m; it will then be safe to turn to port and head for the harbour entrance.

By GPS

From the west use:

⊕103-Eckmühl, ⊕105-Guilvinec, ⊕106-Guilvinec 1, ⊕107-Guilvinec 2, ⊕108-Guilvinec 3

There is a 1.8m shallow patch on the leading line, which ⊕106-Guilvinec 1 avoids. With enough rise of tide and calm conditions, this waypoint can be omitted.

From the east use:

⊕109-Spineg, ⊕105-Guilvinec

Guilvinec south channel

By day

This route should only be used if the marks can be identified with certainty. Start near ⊕110-S Guilvinec, between Ar Guisty south cardinal tower beacon and Spinec SCM buoy. Les Fourches rocks 800m northeast of this position never cover. Identify the Men Meur white-painted rock, at the west end of the Guilvinec waterfront, and bring it into transit with a slender pyramid with large diamond topmark a mile further inland, bearing 352°. Follow this transit for 1.75M to the Capelan SHM lightbuoy and enter as above.

By night

Not recommended.

By GPS

From the west use:

⊕109-Spineg, ⊕110-S Guilvinec, ⊕107-Guilvinec 2, ⊕108-Guilvinec 3

From the east use:

⊕113-Karreg Kreiz, ⊕110-S Guilvinec

BERTHS AND ANCHORAGES

Le Guilvinec harbour

Le Guilvinec is very busy and visitors must not secure to a quay or a fishing boat except in an emergency.

Yachting facilities have been improved and there is a small visitors' pontoon in the northwest side of the inner harbour.

ASHORE IN LE GUILVINEC

The harbour is packed with brightly painted fishing boats and busy with fishing activity. The main part of town is on the north side of harbour. Water and electricity on the pontoon but no showers. Many seafood restaurants. Market day is Tuesday.

18 Lesconil

Location
47°47'N 4°12'W
Shelter
Good in harbour; anchorage sheltered from W through N to E
Hazards
Do not enter in strong S wind
Depth restrictions
2.6m in approach
1.5m in harbour entrance
Night entry Well lit
HW time
Brest HW-0010 neaps,-0030 springs
Mean height of tide (m)

	HWS	HWN	LWN	LWS
Lesconil	5.0	4.0	2.0	0.9

Berthing
Three fore-and-aft visitors' moorings in harbour or anchorage outside harbour
Facilities
As of a fishing port
Charts
BA 2820 (50), 3640 (15)
SHOM 7146 (50), 6646 (15)
Imray C37 (large scale)
Radio
Harbourmaster VHF Ch 12
Telephone
Harbourmaster ① 02 98 82 22 97

Small fishing port with limited facilities for visitors

Lesconil is an attractive fishing port that is less crowded and more attractive than Le Guilvinec. The harbour has very limited room for visiting boats but there is an anchorage outside. Access is easy except in strong southerly winds.

PILOTAGE

Lesconil approach and entrance

By day

Identify the Men-ar-Groas light from a position 600m north of Kareg Kreiz ECM buoy. The light has a slender white tower with a green top and is on the east side of the harbour. It is not easy to see but is to the right of a conspicuous white gable end with a large diamond shaped window and to the left of a long grey roof. The belfry of Lesconil church will be just open to the left when the light bears 325°.

Follow 325° passing the white mark on Enizan 400m to starboard and Men-Caës PHM beacon tower to port. Turn to port to enter the harbour between the breakwater lights. There is 1.5m minimum depth in the entrance and 3m in most of the northern basin.

Within the harbour red and green unlit buoys mark the deep water.

By night

From Kareg Kreiz ECM buoy steer 325° for Men-ar-Groas remaining in the white sector.

By GPS

⊕113-Kareg Kreiz, ⊕111-Lesconil

Routes to and from ⊕113-Kareg Kreiz are given in *Chapter 16, Pointe de Penmarc'h.*

Lesconil from the south

II. BENODET BAY

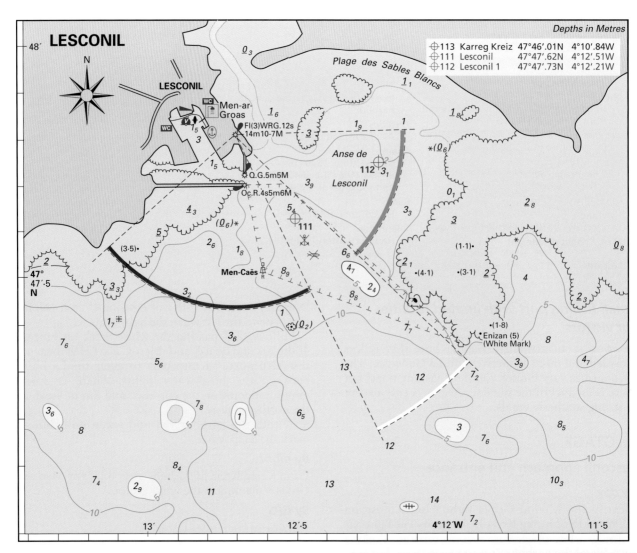

⊕113	Karreg Kreiz	47°46'.01N 4°10'.84W
⊕111	Lesconil	47°47'.62N 4°12'.51W
⊕112	Lesconil 1	47°47'.73N 4°12'.21W

Depths in Metres

BERTHS AND ANCHORAGE

Lesconil harbour

Yachts used not to be welcome but with the decline in fishing three fore-and-aft moorings for visiting yachts have recently been laid in the northern basin in 1·5m and in 2010 it was reported that pontoons for yachts are planned. Water on the quay but no electricity. Public toilets on the quay and showers in the Centre Nautic.

Yachts may not lie alongside the quays but there is a small pontoon on the western wall for temporary mooring while embarking stores or water and for tenders.

Visitors' fore and aft moorings *P Taylor*

⚓ Anse de Lesconil

Sheltered from the west through north to northeast, there is a fair weather anchorage in the Anse de Lesconil immediately to the east of the harbour entrance. Enter from the southwest to avoid the extensive rocks on the east side of the bay.

⊕112-Lesconil 1 47°47'·73N 4°12'·21W

ASHORE IN LESCONIL

Fuel is available in cans. There is a launderette, a few modest shops and some bars.

A ketch is alongside the west wall in the short-stay berth *P Taylor*

19 Loctudy

Location
47°50'N 4°10'W

Shelter
Excellent except in strong ESE

Hazards
Bar and unmarked shallow patches
Strong tide in harbour

Depth restrictions
0.9m in the approach; 1.5m in marina

Night entry Partially lit

HW time
Brest HW–0010 neaps, –0030 springs

Mean height of tide (m)

	HWS	HWN	LWN	LWS
Loctudy	5.0	3.9	1.9	0.8

Tidal stream Loctudy entrance
Flood – Brest HW –0500 to –0230 (3.0kns)
Slack – Brest HW –0230 to +0230
Ebb – Brest HW +0230 to +0430 (3.0kns)
Slack – Brest HW +0430 to –0500

Berthing
Marina, visitors' buoys and
anchorages

Fuel
Marina wave breaker

Facilities
All facilities

Charts
BA 2820 (50), 3641 (20)
SHOM 7146 (50), 6649 (15)
Imray C37 (large scale)

Radio
Harbourmaster VHF Ch 9

Telephone
Marina ① 02 98 87 51 36

Pretty Breton estuary

Loctudy is a happy combination of fishing port and yachting centre. Île Tudy on the opposite side of the river is a picture postcard Breton village. The approach is sheltered from the prevailing westerly winds but should be avoided in strong east-southeast winds. The harbour is attractive and secure.

Loctudy

PILOTAGE

Loctudy from north and west

By day

From Bilien ECM buoy proceed northwest until Les Perdrix BW chequered beacon tower is in line with the white Château Durumain on 289°. This transit crosses a shallow patch (1.3m) and leaves Karek Croisic PHM buoy marking it to starboard. Below

half-tide leave the transit to pass the PHM buoy correctly. Once the buoyed channel is entered follow it into the river towards the marina being careful to leave the unmarked drying patch to the east of the marina to starboard.

By night

From Bilien ECM buoy steer northwest to enter the white sector of Langoz. Follow this until Karek-Saoz PHM light-beacon and Karek Croisic PHM lightbuoy are identified. Leave these to port and then enter the river leaving the two SHM lightbuoys to starboard. The approach to the marina is not lit but there are three lit green buoys which lead into the fishing harbour. Note that Les Perdrix BW beacon tower is no longer lit.

By GPS

From Penmarc'h follow the route to:

⊕116-Malvic or ⊕117-Bilien

as described in Chapter 16 Pointe de Penmarc'h. Then use:

⊕118-Loctudy, ⊕119-Loctudy 1, ⊕120-Loctudy 2

It is possible to omit ⊕118-Loctudy at high water.

From Bénodet use:

⊕122-Bénodet, ⊕118-Loctudy, ⊕119-Loctudy 1, ⊕120-Loctudy 2, ⊕121-Loctudy 3

Loctudy entrance with Les Perdrix beacon

Pont L'Abbé *P Taylor*

Pont L'Abbé *P Taylor*

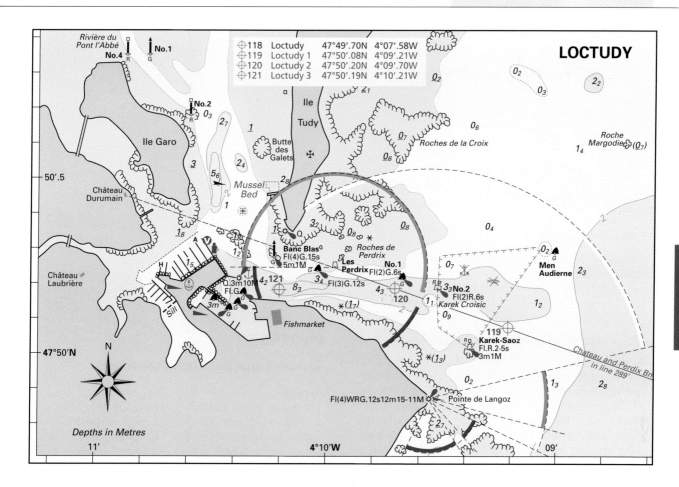

⊕118	Loctudy	47°49'.70N	4°07'.58W
⊕119	Loctudy 1	47°50'.08N	4°09'.21W
⊕120	Loctudy 2	47°50'.20N	4°09'.70W
⊕121	Loctudy 3	47°50'.19N	4°10'.21W

LOCTUDY

II. BENODET BAY

Loctudy from east

By day

From the east and southeast leave Île aux Moutons to port and steer northwest, leaving Les Poulains NCM beacon tower and Men Dehou ECM beacon tower to port. To avoid the rock (depth 2.1m) northwest of Men Dehou, keep Île aux Moutons lighthouse midway between Les Poulains and Men Dehou. Continue to Bilien ECM buoy and enter Loctudy as from the north and west.

By night

Leave Île aux Moutons light to port and steer north to get into the white sector of Pointe de Langoz light. Stay in the white sector until Bilien ECM lightbuoy is abeam to port. Then proceed as above.

By GPS

From the Baie de la Forêt use:
⊕126-Mousterlin, ⊕118-Loctudy, ⊕119-Loctudy 1, ⊕120-Loctudy 2, ⊕121-Loctudy 3

From the southeast use:
⊕160-E Glénan, ⊕118-Loctudy, ⊕119-Loctudy 1, ⊕20-Loctudy 2, ⊕121-Loctudy 3

Rivière de Pont l'Abbé

The channel is reported to have silted and a visit to Pont l'Abbé is best made by dinghy.

BERTHS AND ANCHORAGES

Loctudy Marina

Visitors should berth on pontoon A but beware of tidal currents. Larger boats should use the inside of the wave breaker. There are some white visitors' buoys northeast of the marina. The marina is well managed, modern and has all facilities. It would be a good place to leave a boat.

⚓ Île Chevalier

Sheltered from all directions, there is a useful neap tide anchorage at the southeast end of Île Chevalier (north of Rivière du Pont l'Abbé) but beware of mussel beds on either side.

⚓ Île Tudy

It may be possible to find space to anchor beyond the moorings west of Île Tudy.

ASHORE IN LOCTUDY

Loctudy has a full range of shops, bars and restaurants plus a good vegetable market on Tuesdays and excellent fish shops at the fishing port. The marina office has bicycles for the use of visitors.

Île Tudy is a pretty holiday village. It has only basic facilities but it does have a magnificent beach and good walking.

20 Bénodet and Sainte-Marine

Location
47°53'N 4°07'W

Shelter
Excellent except in strong S wind

Hazards
Shallow patches in approach
Strong tide in marinas

Night entry Lit but care required

HW time
Brest HW neaps, –0020 springs

Mean height of tide (m)

	HWS	HWN	LWN	LWS
Bénodet	5.2	4.1	2.1	0.9

Tidal stream
In the marinas, spring rates reach 2.5 knots

Berthing
Marinas and visitors' buoys

Fuel
Penfoul marina, base of E pontoon

Facilities
All facilities

Charts
BA 2820 (50), 3641 (20)
SHOM 7146 (50), 6679 (20)
Imray C37 (large scale)

Radio
Marinas VHF Ch 9

Telephone
Penfoul Marina ☏ 02 98 57 05 78
Ste-Marine HM ☏ 02 98 56 38 72

Major yachting centre in a beautiful river

Bénodet is one of South Brittany's principal yachting centres. There are two marinas, many visitors' buoys, a beautiful river and good facilities ashore. The location, in the centre of the Anse de Bénodet, is a good base for day sailing and there is also the beautiful River Odet to explore. Bénodet gets busy in high season but there is usually space to squeeze in somewhere.

Bénodet town occupies the E bank of the Odet. It is a busy holiday resort with beaches, hotels, shops, a casino and a large supermarket. Sainte-Marine, on the west bank, is a quiet holiday village with a few shops and restaurants.

Bénodet, Sainte-Marine and the river Odet looking northwest. Sainte-Marine is on the west bank and Bénodet on the east. Beyond the bridge the Odet turns to the north and continues for about 14M to Quimper. The long inlet on the west side of the river above the bridge is the anchorage of Anse de Combrit

PILOTAGE

Bénodet approach from southwest

By day

There are many hazards between Île aux Moutons and the mainland but they are well marked and the approach is not difficult. The usual route, which relies on the buoys, passes between Boulanger SCM buoy and Roche Hélou WCM buoy, then between Chenal du Bénodet ECM buoy and Basse Malvic WCM buoy. If the buoys are hard to identify, Pyramide lighthouse at Bénodet (white tower with green top) in line with Pte de Combrit Light (white square tower, grey corners) bearing 001° leads safely in from the south. Once within a mile of Pte de Combrit, alter course to starboard for the entrance. The Pyramide/Pte de Combrit transit of 001° ultimately leads onto the shore, not into the river.

In good conditions and with sufficient tide there are several other routes through the shallow patches.

By night

Stay outside the lit buoys marking the hazards south of Pte de Penmarc'h. After passing Spinec SCM buoy, continue southeast until Île aux Moutons light turns from red to white. Keep within this white sector, until Pte de Combrit and Bénodet Pyramide lights come into line bearing 001°. Turn onto this transit and maintain it watching the Pte de Langoz light; it will change colour as one progresses north. When it changes from green to white bearing 257°, the way is clear to turn to starboard to bring the Bénodet leading lights in line on 346° and enter the river. Many other lights will also be seen.

By GPS

From Penmarc'h follow the route to:
⊕116-Malvic or ⊕117-Bilien

as described in *Chapter 16 Pointe de Penmarc'h*. Then use:
⊕122-Bénodet, ⊕123-Bénodet 1

Bénodet approach from south and southeast

By day

The easiest entrance is north of Plateau de la Basse Jaune, leaving Les Porceaux, Île aux Moutons, Les Poulains NCM tower beacon and Men Dehou ECM tower beacon all to port. La Voleuse SCM buoy marks the limit of the dangers off Pte de Mousterlin and must be left to starboard. Once past Men Dehou it is safe to turn towards the harbour entrance leaving Le Taro tower WCM tower beacon 0.5M to starboard.

By night

Approach within or just south of the intensified sector of Île aux Moutons light, leaving Jaune de Glénan ECM buoy to port. Continue in this sector until Pte de Langoz light is identified and Trévignon light has turned from white to green bearing more than 051°.

Steer to starboard to get into the white sector of Pte de Langoz light, bearing about 295° and keep within it until Pte de Combrit light opens white bearing 325°. Then steer for this light, crossing the green sector of Pte de Langoz light, and bring the Bénodet leading lights in transit on 346°. Many lights other than those described will be seen.

By GPS

From Glénan use:
⊕128-Pourceaux, ⊕122-Bénodet, ⊕123-Bénodet 1

From the southeast use:
⊕126-Mousterlin, ⊕122-Bénodet, ⊕123-Bénodet 1

From the Baie de la Forêt use:
⊕143-SE Beg Meil, ⊕126-Mousterlin, ⊕122-Bénodet, ⊕123-Bénodet 1

In good weather and with enough rise of tide use:
⊕144-Laouen Pod, ⊕127-Men Vras, ⊕125-La Voleuse, ⊕122-Bénodet, ⊕123-Bénodet 1

This shortcut has a least depth of 2.2m but passs very close to several shallow patches which would be very dangerous at low water.

Entrance to the river Odet

By day

During the season and particularly at weekends the entrance to Bénodet is so busy that speed is limited to 3kns above the Pte de Coq beacon.

The leading line is the tower of Pyramide light in transit with Le Coq light (346°). However, the dangers in the entrance are marked and it is not necessary to keep strictly to the transit. Pyramide light is conspicuous, but Le Coq is less easy to identify. It will be seen to the left of the conspicuous letters YCO on the grassy bank in front of the old yacht club.

When within 400m of Le Coq, alter to port and steer up the middle of the river.

By night

Entrance is straightforward, but the river is congested with moorings, and anchoring is prohibited in the channel until well beyond the bridge. The leading lights lead clear of all unlit buoys and beacons. When within 400m of Le Coq, turn to port to pass halfway between Le Coq and Pte du Toulgoët flashing red light. Fixed red and green lights will be seen on the bridge and the shore lights may give some guidance.

BERTHS AND ANCHORAGES

Ste-Marine visitors' pontoon

Sainte-Marine visitors' pontoon is on the west side of the river 0.25M beyond Pte du Toulgoët. It is a long pontoon where yachts can lie alongside and raft if necessary. Afterwards, move into the marina or use a river mooring.

The tidal stream is roughly parallel to the pontoon so, unlike Bénodet marina, manoeuvring in a strong tide is feasible.

Bénodet marina

Bénodet marina is on the east side of the river about 0.25M beyond Ste-Marine at the entrance to the Anse de Penfoul. There are long outer pontoons that may be used by visitors. One of these pontoons lies across the tide and manoeuvring is difficult except at slack water. Another wavebreaker pontoon lies along the current and manoeuvring alongside it from the outside is less problematic. The current can press a yacht hard against the pontoons so plenty of fenders are needed. Finger berths inside the marina are sometimes available from the harbourmaster. The current inside is less than on the outer pontoons but it is best to enter only at slack water.

Short stays are free in the morning for shopping.

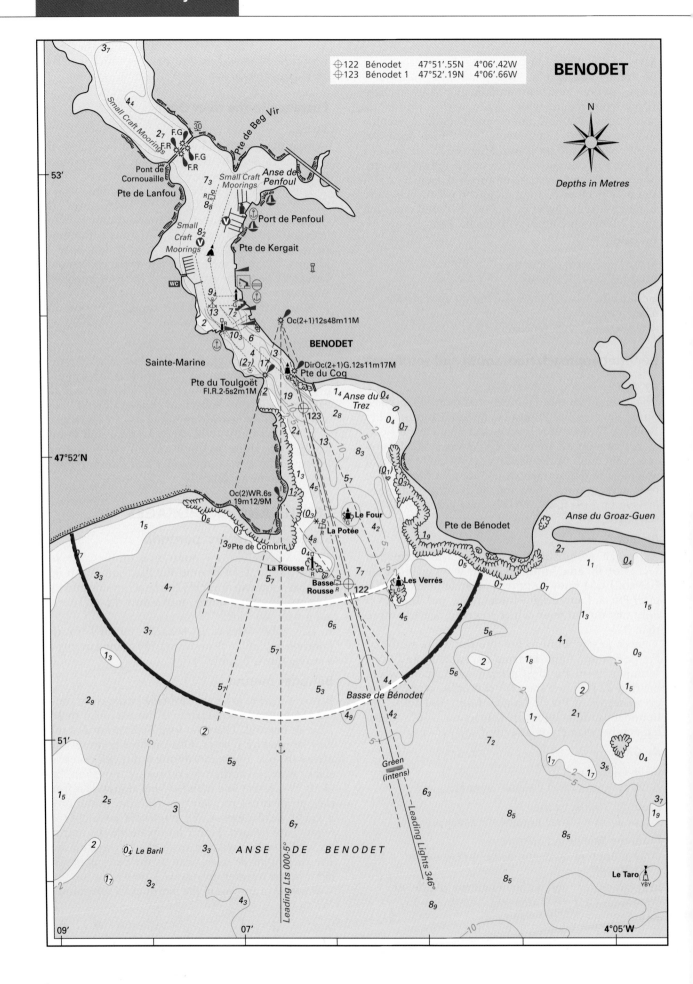

Bénodet looking northwest.
Sainte-Marine is on the far bank of the river and the visitors'
pontoon is just visible downstream of the marina. Bénodet
Marina, on the near side, has two parts. Large boats use the
downstream marina and visitors moor on the outer pontoon

II. BENODET BAY

Visitors' moorings

Both Bénodet and Sainte-Marine provide river
moorings which are usually marked with a V. On
the Sainte-Marine side, the harbourmasters buzz
around in dorys and will often direct visiting yachts
to a free mooring. On the Bénodet side, the
harbourmasters are less active and it is necessary to
look around for available buoys.

⚓ Anse du Trez

Sheltered from west through north to east, Anse du
Trez is an attractive sandy bay just inside the mouth
of the Odet on the east side. During the day, the bay
is a centre for Optimist and sailboard sailing but it is
peaceful at night.

⚓ Plage du Treven

Sheltered from north and west, the long sandy beach
west of Pointe de Combrit makes a pleasant lunchtime stop.

ASHORE IN BENODET AND STE-MARINE

Facilities in Bénodet

Bénodet has all the facilities of a major yachting
centre and holiday resort. Most repairs can be
carried out either at Bénodet or Sainte-Marine.
Chandlery is available at Bénodet marina.

Fuel is available at the Anse de Penfoul marina,
but the berth lies across the current so that slack
water is the best time to fill up.

There is a full range of shops and a good
supermarket on the road to Quimper. The attractive
footpath along the south side of the Anse de Penfoul
is the shortest route to the latter from the Benodet
Marina. Buses run to the RER rail station in
Quimper so Bénodet is a convenient place to change
crews.

Facilities in Sainte-Marine

Sainte-Marine is a pleasant holiday resort with a
small supermarket, a few shops and delightful bars
and restaurants.

There is a pleasant walk to Pointe de Combrit
from where the energetic can continue along the
magnificent three mile Plage du Treven to Île Tudy.

21 River Odet

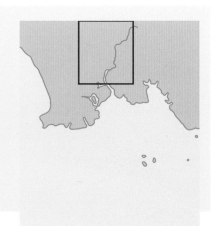

Location
47°53'N 4°07'W

Shelter Excellent

Depth restrictions
2.6m to Lanroz, 0.5m to Quimper

Night passage Not recommended

HW time
Brest HW+0015

Mean height of tide (m)

	HWS	HWN	LWN	LWS
Corniguel	4.9	3.8	1.6	0.3

Tidal stream
Spring rates can reach 2.5 knots

Berthing
Anchorages

Fuel
Penfoul marina, base of E pontoon

Charts
SHOM 6649 (15)
Imray C37 (large scale)

Beautiful river to Quimper

The Odet is a beautiful river with steep, tree-covered banks. Unfortunately there is a bridge (height 5.8m) about 0.5M from the town of Quimper so masted boats must anchor and use a dinghy for the last leg. Even without a visit to Quimper, the river is well worth exploring. As far as Lanroz there is plenty of water at all states of the tide and there are several attractive anchorages.

PILOTAGE

Bénodet to Quimper

Leave Bénodet and pass under the Pont de Cornouaille (height 30m). After about 1M the Anse du Combrit opens out on the W side. This is an attractive creek and a pleasant anchorage.

The river then narrows as it runs between steep wooded banks. After about 2M it narrows dramatically and makes a sharp turn to starboard. Port and starboard beacons mark this turn but care should be taken because the shallows extend beyond the starboard mark.

The next stretch is narrow, winding and very attractive. After about 2M there is a little fjord that forms the Anse de St-Cadou (*see Anchorages*).

About 0.5M beyond this, at Lanroz, the river opens out quite suddenly into a broad lake from where there is a good view of Quimper.

The route across the lake is well marked by beacons but the river shallows rapidly to a least depth of 0.5m. At the far end of the lake is a sharp turn to port at the commercial jetties of Corniguel used mainly by sand barges.

Above Corniguel the river nearly dries and the beacons are further apart. A bridge (with a clearance of only 5.8m) prevents masted yachts from reaching Quimper, but boats that can take the ground may anchor or borrow a mooring below the bridge and visit Quimper by dinghy. Motor yachts can carry a depth of drying 1.5m up to the first quays in Quimper. The bottom here is hard and rather uneven for drying out.

There is also a regular ferry service from Bénodet to Quimper.

Frank Cowper's *Sailing Tours* written in 1894 described Château Kérouzien as a 'comfortable-looking white house'.

Château Keraudren was less favoured and was described as 'a new and rather stuck-up looking château'.

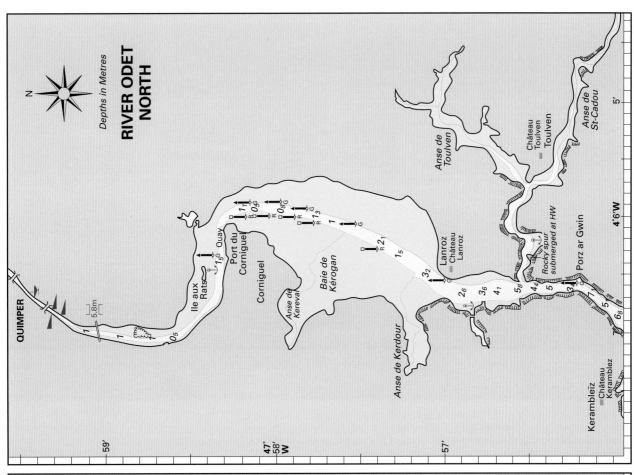

RIVER ODET NORTH

Depths in Metres

QUIMPER

Ile aux Rats · Quay · Port du Corniguel

Corniguel

Anse de Kereval

Baie de Kérogan

Anse de Kerdour

Lanroz · Château Lanroz

Rocky spur submerged at HW

Porz ar Gwin

Keramblëiz · Château Keramblez

Anse de Toulven

Château Toulven · Toulven

Anse de St-Cadou

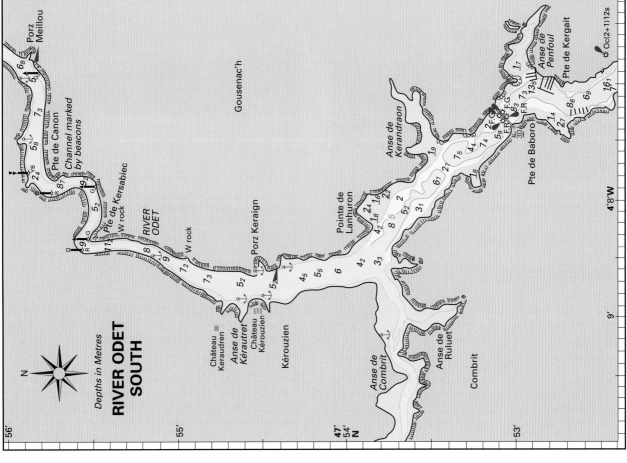

RIVER ODET SOUTH

Depths in Metres

Porz Meillou

Pte de Canon

Channel marked by beacons

Pte de Kersabiec

W rock

RIVER ODET

Château Keraudren

Anse de Kérautret

Château Kérouzien

Kérouzien

W rock

Porz Keraign

Gousenac'h

Pointe de Lanhuron

Anse de Kerandraon

Anse de Combrit

Anse de Ruluet

Combrit

Pte de Baboro

Pte de Kergait

Anse de Penfoul

Oc(2+1)12s

II. BENODET BAY

The River Odet looking south. The two sharp bends downriver are in a very steep, wooded section called Les Vire-Court. The first bend is so sharp that the Spanish fleet, approaching to attack Quimper, did not dare to continue and turned back

The narrow entrance to Anse de St-Cadou. Keep to the far bank to avoid a rocky plateau on the starboard side *M&G Barron*

The first small pool in Anse de St-Cadou with just enough room for two boats to anchor. The second pool is a little larger *M&G Barron*

ANCHORAGES

Anchoring is forbidden near the Pont de Cornouaille, but elsewhere it is possible to anchor anywhere out of the stream. The bottom is rock in the main channel so the holding is poor.

⚓ Anse de Combrit

Sheltered except from the east, the Anse de Combrit is an inlet on the west side of the Odet about 1M above Pont dé Cornouaille. It is possible to go in quite a long way with a large-scale chart.

⚓ Porz Keraign

Sheltered except from due north or due south, this is a small inlet on the east side of the Odet between the Châteaux of Kérouzien and Keraudren.

⚓ Porz Meilou

Sheltered from all directions, Porz Meilou is on the east side about 1.5M above the sharp turn at Pointe de Kersabiec. There is not much of an inlet but there is a shallow area at the edge of the river, marked by a starboard beacon. Tuck in as far as possible to get out of the tide.

Kerogan Bay and Quimper looking north.
At Lanroz the river opens out into a broad lake. The route across the lake is marked by beacons and the deeper water is close to the port-hand side. At the far end is a sharp turn to port at the commercial jetties of Corniguel

⚓ Anse de St-Cadou

Sheltered from all directions, this delightful little fjord is on the east side of the Odet about 0.5M before the river widens out at Lanroz. It is hard to spot at first because the entrance is quite narrow. Once identified, keep close to the north bank to avoid the drying rocky plateau on the south side. In this pool a large area has 1m depth and 2m can be found in which to swing on short scope. At the end of the first pool there is a rock with 1m or less, on the inside corner of the sharp turn to the north.

⚓ Lanroz

Sheltered from all directions except north, there is a shallow bay on the west side of the river just south of Lanroz.

⚓ Port du Corniguel

It is possible to anchor just above Corniguel in 1.5m and even to go alongside at Corniguel but beware of the sand barges.

Ashore in Quimper

There are no facilities in the river beyond Bénodet but Quimper has everything. It is the regional capital of West Brittany and is an attractive city with many half-timbered buildings and a fine cathedral. At the heart of the city is an area known as the Quays where flower-decked footbridges criss-cross the Odet.

Quimper cathedral

Quimper has three fine museums for those with time to spare. The Fine Arts Museum has one of the best collections of Breton 19th-century art. The Brittany Museum covers regional history and the Museum of the Faience has displays that explain the development of the famous Quimper painted pottery.

22 Îles de Glénan

Location
47°43'N 3°57'W

Shelter
Limited particularly at high water

Hazards
Many unmarked rocks
Difficult to leave anchorages at night

Depth restrictions
1m or more in most anchorages but much less in some channels

Night entry Not recommended

HW time
Brest HW neaps, –0030 springs

Mean height of tide (m)

	HWS	HWN	LWN	LWS
Île Penfret	5.0	3.9	1.9	0.8

Tidal stream N approach
Slack: – Brest HW–0600 to –0400
E-going: Brest HW–0400 to +0100 (0.5kns)
Slack: – Brest HW+0100 to +0300
W-going: Brest HW+0300 to –0600 (0.6kns)

Berthing
Anchorages many of which have visitors' moorings which are charged for in season

Facilities
Boat vendors, restaurant and small shop in season. No water

Charts
BA 2820 (50), 3640 (30)
SHOM 7146 (50), 6648 (20)
Imray C37 (77)

Radio
Glénans sailing school VHF Ch 16

Beautiful archipelago with a famous sailing school, the Centre Nautique des Glenans (CNG)

The Îles de Glénan is a beautiful archipelago of small islands about 12M south-southeast of Bénodet. It has crystal clear water, white sandy beaches and in good weather is as close to the Caribbean as you can get in South Brittany.

PILOTAGE

Charts

A large-scale chart is strongly recommended. The plans in this book will suffice for the main channels but should not be used for exploration.

Îles de Glénan approaches

By day

The main islands are easily distinguished by the conspicuous lighthouse on Île de Penfret and by the stone fort on the southeast side of Île Cigogne which has a tall, partially black-topped concrete tower. The west edge is marked by Bluiniers tower, the south and east by buoys. When approaching La Pie IDM beacon tower from the north the most conspicuous mark is the disused lighthouse on Le Huic 47°43'·9N 4°00'·69W.

Other useful daymarks are a conspicuous disused factory chimney on Île du Loc'h; some houses on the southeast side of Île de Drénec and the buildings on Île de St-Nicolas.

The easiest entrances are from the north and northeast but take care to avoid Les Porceaux rocks in the north approaches.

By GPS

From Penmarc'h use:
⊕109-Spineg, ⊕129-La Pie

This route passes close to the north edge of the Îles de Glénan. Most of the rocks never cover but some outliers on the northwest corner are dangerous.

From Loctudy or Bénodet pass west of Île aux Moutons using:
⊕115-Roustolou, ⊕129-La Pie

Alternatively, from Bénodet pass E of Île aux Moutons using;
⊕128-Pourceaux, ⊕129-La Pie

From the Baie de la Forêt:
⊕129-La Pie or ⊕132-N Penfret

can be approached directly.

From the south or southeast:
⊕138-Brilimec or ⊕136-Ruolh

can be approached directly. However, neither the Brilimec nor the Ruolh channels are advisable for a first visit.

Îles de Glénan entrances

In the descriptions of the entrances, the letters refer to the plan. Note that all routes go to La Chambre so appropriate changes must be made for the other anchorages.

By day

The letters A to E refer to *plan opposite*.

Îles de Glénan old lighthouse on le Huic

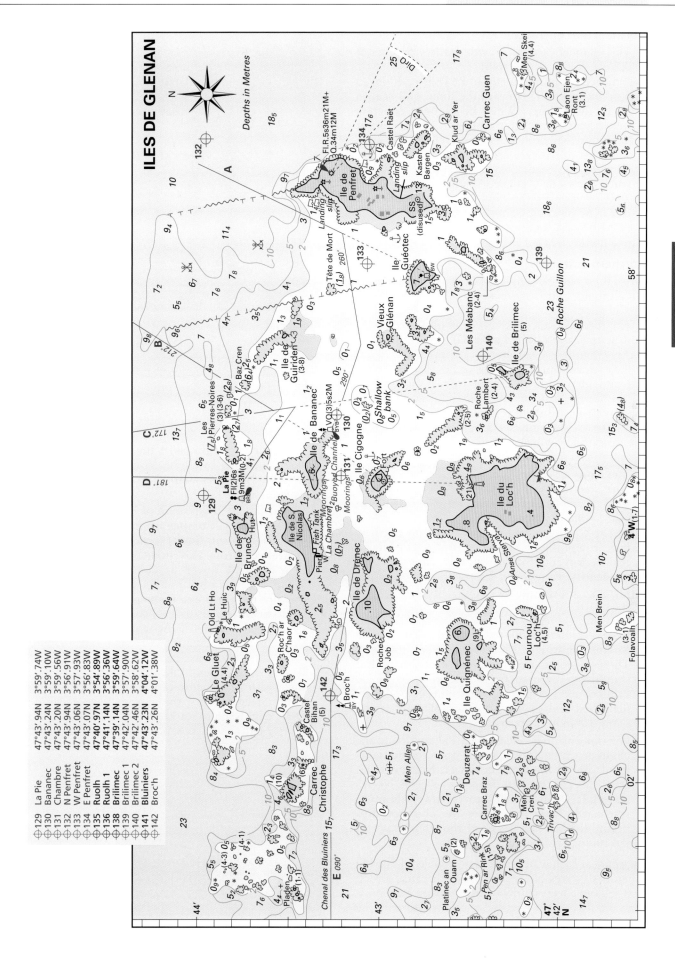

ÎLES DE GLÉNAN

Depths in Metres

⊕129	La Pie	47°43'.94N	3°59'.74W
⊕130	Bananec	47°43'.24N	3°59'.10W
⊕131	Chambre	47°43'.20N	3°59'.56W
⊕132	N Penfret	47°43'.94N	3°56'.91W
⊕133	W Penfret	47°43'.06N	3°57'.93W
⊕134	E Penfret	47°43'.07N	3°56'.83W
⊕**135**	**Ruolh**	**47°40'.97N**	**3°54'.89W**
⊕**136**	**Ruolh 1**	**47°41'.14N**	**3°56'.36W**
⊕**138**	**Brilimec**	**47°39'.14N**	**3°59'.64W**
⊕139	Brilimec 1	47°42'.04N	3°57'.90W
⊕**140**	**Brilimec 2**	**47°42'.46N**	**3°58'.62W**
⊕141	Bluiniers	47°43'.23N	4°04'.12W
⊕**142**	**Broc'h**	**47°43'.26N**	**4°01'.38W**

Northeastern entrance

A This channel carries 1m with shallow patches of 0.7m very close to the route.

Leave the northern end of Le Penfret 300m to port and steer 205° toward the stone wall beacon on Île de Guéotec. When Île Cigogne concrete tower bears 260° alter course to 260°. Penfret lighthouse will be dead astern. If the ECM beacon southeast of Bananec can be located, alter course for it when it bears 290°. This avoids the shallow patch east of Île Cigogne. Alternatively alter onto 283°, steering for the wind generator on the west end of St-Nicolas. Using either course, leave the ECM beacon southeast of Bananec to starboard to enter the buoyed channel of La Chambre.

Northern entrances

These three entrances should be regarded as carrying 1m although a little more water can be found with careful pilotage.

The three entrances are taken in order from east to west; the easiest being La Pie (D). The marks for B and C are four above-water rocks: Baz Cren (3.5m) in the east, two adjacent rocks of Les Pierres Noires (5.6 and 5m) and finally, in the west, a single Pierre Noire (4.6m) with others to its southwest which seldom cover. All these rocks stand on rocky bases and must be distinguished from Île de Guiriden to the southeast, which has a considerable sandy expanse that covers near high water.

B The entrance leaves Baz Cren 50m to 100m to port steering on Fort Cigogne tower, bearing 212°. Once Baz Cren is passed it is possible to bear to port as convenient.

The CNG use the chimney on Île du Loc'h in transit with the ECM beacon southeast of Île de Bananec on 200° for this entrance. Although easy to identify, this transit leaves an outlier of Les Pierres Noires (dries 2.8m) only 60m to starboard.

C This entrance leaves the two adjacent heads of Les Pierres Noires 20m to 60m to port. Île de Brilimec, bearing 172°, leads fairly into the pool. This is a popular entrance for local boats, but should not be used for a first visit, as Île de Brilimec and Les Pierres Noires must be positively identified and there is a rocky plateau drying 2.7m, 100m to starboard.

D For this entrance, identify La Pie and bring the chimney on Île du Loc'h just open to the right-hand side of the Cigogne tower, bearing 181°. Steer this course until inside Les Pierres Noires leaving La Pie IDM light beacon tower abeam to starboard. Near low water the chimney dips behind the fort but it is good enough to leave La Pie 100m to starboard.

Except near high water there is no problem knowing when Les Pierres Noires are passed because a rock that seldom covers marks their southwest extremity. Once La Pie beacon is passed and in transit with the north side of Île de Brunec, steer into the pool

The lighthouse on the north end of the Île de Penfret
M&G Barron

towards the ECM beacon at the east end of Île de Bananec.

Western entrance

E The Chenal des Bluiniers dries 0.5m, but it is safer to regard it as drying 0.8m. If this gives insufficient margin, skirt the north edge of the rocks and enter by La Pie. Visibility of three miles is needed for this channel except towards high water.

Start about 200m south of Les Bluiniers WCM tower beacon. Coming from the northwest be sure to give this tower beacon at least 200m clearance. From this point, steer east for Le Broc'h NCM tower beacon, keeping at least 100m south of a line joining all the dangers that show to the north and keeping Penfret lighthouse open to the north of Le Broc'h tower beacon, bearing about 090°. Approaching Le Broc'h tower beacon, leave it 100m to starboard and bring the semaphore, near the southern point of Île de Penfret, open to the left of Fort Cigogne by the width of the fort (not the tower), bearing 100°. Steer so until the eastern part of Île de Drénec is abeam to starboard; this island is in two clearly defined parts separated by a sandy strip

The stone wall beacon on Île de Guéotec is the mark for the northeast approach *M&G Barron*

which covers at HW. Now steer 035° on the summer cottages to the east of the shellfish tank to enter La Chambre. Near HW the detailed directions above can be disregarded; having passed Le Broc'h tower beacon it is only necessary to sail 100m north of Île de Drénec and then make straight for La Chambre or the pool as required.

For those already familiar with the islands the transits shown on BA chart 3640 may be used, but it is necessary to identify the semaphore mast on Penfret at a distance of 5M as well as the farm buildings on Drénec.

By GPS

Warning

If using GPS as an aid to navigation within the archipelago, the use of an incorrect GPS datum could be very dangerous. See page 6 for a note on GPS pilotage and datum correction.

The easiest route into La Chambre is from the north using:

⊕129-La Pie, ⊕130-Bananec, ⊕131-Chambre

Once La Pie IDM beacon has been identified, the waypoints are hardly necessary.

The NE route is almost as easy using:

⊕132-N Penfret, ⊕133-W Penfret, ⊕131-Chambre

The dangers are Tête de Mort, the two shallow patches south of Île de Guiriden and the shallow patch between Île Cigogne and Vieux Glénan.

The Brilimec Channel from the south uses:

⊕138-Brilimec, ⊕138-Brilimec 1, ⊕140-Brilimec 2, ⊕131-Chambre

This is an easy route using GPS and is worth knowing because, by replacing ⊕131-Chambre with ⊕132-N Penfret it provides a short-cut straight through the Îles de Glénan from south to north or vice versa.

The southeast entry uses:

⊕135-Ruolh, ⊕136-Ruolh 1, ⊕140-Brilimec 2, ⊕131-Chambre

There are dangers very close to this route so it would be best to start by using it as an exit in conjunction with the transits and in any case to ensure there is adequate rise of tide to cover minor deviations from the track.

The west entry requires visual pilotage and can only be used with sufficient rise of tide. However ⊕141-Bluiniers, ⊕142-Broc'h may assist with the approach.

ANCHORAGES

⚓ East of Île de Penfret

Sheltered from the west but exposed to the *brise de terre*, this anchorage is in the sandy bay south of the hill on which the lighthouse stands. Approach with the middle of the bay bearing 270°. There is a potentially dangerous rock 150m north of Castel Raët, which is the islet in the south of the bay.

There is a large metal mooring buoy on the north side of the bay. However, it is preferable to anchor closer to the beach on sand, taking care to avoid the patches of weed.

South of Castel Raët is another bay with a slip and some CNG moorings. This bay is unsuitable for anchoring.

⊕134-E Penfret 47°43'·07N 3°56'·83W

⚓ Southwest of Île de Penfret

Sheltered from the west by Guéotec and from the east by Penfret, there is a good anchorage in 2.5m outside the CNG moorings between Penfret and Guéotec. The tide runs fairly hard.

The easy approach is from the north. An approach from the south is possible but requires intricate pilotage and a large-scale chart.

⊕133-W Penfret 47°43'·06N 3°57'·93W

Îles de Glénan north beach at St-Nicolas

Île de Penfret looking north. Anchored boats can be seen on the east side of the island near the lighthouse. There is an alternative anchorage to the southwest of the island

Île de Glénan St-Nicolas anchorage at Île Cogogne

⚓ East of Île Cigogne

Anchor in 1m to 1.4m, north of the rocky ledge running southeast from Île Cigogne.

⊕131-Chambre 47°43'·20N 3°59'·56W

⚓ La Chambre

This anchorage south of Île de St-Nicolas is the most popular one for visitors although there are now many moorings. The depths are up to 3m but avoid anchoring in the vedette channel, which is marked by small port and starboard buoys.

A rocky ledge extends 100m along the south shore of St-Nicolas and Bananec. The shoal also extends east of Bananec and an ECM beacon marks its limit. Between the islands there is a sandy ridge with shallow sandy bays (drying 1m) to the north and south. These make excellent anchorages for yachts that can take the ground.

Enter La Chambre from a position 100m south of the ECM beacon southeast of Île de Bananec. If La Chambre is full of yachts, follow the marked channel until a suitable anchorage is found. If the shellfish tank is not obscured, keep it on 285° until Bananec is passed and then bear a little to port if wishing to proceed further into La Chambre. At low water depths of less than 1m may be encountered in La Chambre. The water is clear and it is necessary to look for a sandy patch on which to anchor, as there is much weed.

⊕131-Chambre 47°43'·20N 3°59'·56W

The anchorage east of Île de Penfret can be a convenient night stop when sailing along the South Brittany coast. It is protected from the west but exposed to the *brise de terre* which can blow from the northeast during the night and early morning. The small boats in the picture are the Centre Nautique training boats *M&G Barron*

Île du Loc'h in the foreground looking north. The small island with the tower is Île Cigogne. Beyond that, the long islands are Île de St-Nicolas which is connected to the smaller Île de Bananec by a sandy isthmus that covers at HW

⚓ North of Île de Bananec

Sheltered, except from north and east at high water, the bay northwest of Bananec and east of St-Nicolas is a popular fair-weather anchorage. The bay shoals from 2m and has a clean sandy bottom so choose a spot outside the moorings according to draught.

⊕129-La Pie 47°43'·94N 3°59'·74W

⚓ North of Île du Loc'h

Sheltered from the north by Île Cigogne and from the south by Île du Loc'h, there is a neap anchorage about 400m north of the Île du Loc'h chimney.

ASHORE IN ÎLES DE GLENAN

Facilities

After mid June enterprising vendors tour the anchorages each morning with bread, seafood and, occasionally, fresh vegetables. And, again in season, there is a famous restaurant and a bar on Île St-Nicolas together with a small shop that occasionally stocks very limited provisions.

Fresh water is in short supply and visitors should not expect to obtain any.

There are islands that can be explored but the best activities are on the extraordinary clear water. The shallow areas between the islands are sometimes just a few inches deep depending on the tide. Viewed from a rowing dinghy, the underwater gardens just below the surface are quite unique.

Centre Nautique des Glénans

The Îles de Glénan is home to the Centre Nautique des Glénans (CNG). It was founded in 1947 by Hélène and Philipe Viannay, former members of the French Resistance, and is one of the first and one of the largest sailing schools in Europe. The school's main base is on Île Cigogne but their fleets of training boats are in evidence throughout the islands. They are very hospitable to visitors, but obviously that hospitality should not be abused.

Sailing dinghies from the Centre Nautique on the southwest shore of Île de Penfret
M&G Barron

23 Port-la-Forêt

Location
47°54'N 3°58'W

Shelter
Excellent in marina

Hazards
Rocks on SW corner and E side of Baie de la Forêt

Depth restrictions
0.6m bar at entrance of channel

Tidal restrictions
Depth restricts entry at LW±0130

Night entry Partially lit

HW time
Brest HW–0015 neaps, –0030 springs

Mean height of tide (m)

	HWS	HWN	LWN	LWS
Concarneau	5.0	3.9	1.9	0.8

Tidal stream
Weak in the bay, strong in entrance

Berthing
Large modern marina

Fuel
Root of visitors' pontoon

Facilities
All repair facilities and some marina shops. 1M walk to town

Charts
BA 2820 (50), 3641 (20)
SHOM 7146 (50), 6650 (15)
Imray C38 (large scale)

Radio
Marina VHF Ch 9

Telephone
Marina ① 02 98 56 98 45

Port-la-Forêt

Huge marina in sheltered bay

Port-La-Forêt is a large modern marina complex. The facilities are good and the staff helpful so it is a good place to leave a yacht.

Shopping is limited but there is a pleasant walk over the causeway and footbridge to the town at La Forêt-Fouesnant.

PILOTAGE

Port-La-Forêt approach and entrance

By day

In the approach, there are marked dangers off Beg-Meil. There are also extensive unmarked dangers west of Concarneau. Many of these rocks never dry but they can be avoided by keeping the slender Le Scoré SCM beacon open east of the end of Cap Coz breakwater or, more simply, by keeping well off the east side of the bay.

The entrance to Port-La-Forêt lies to the east of the wooded promontory of Cap Coz. The channel to the marina is dredged to 1.2m below chart datum and is well marked.

By night

The white sector of Cap Coz light marks the deepest water. The green sector guards a 2.6m shallow patch in the mouth of the bay.

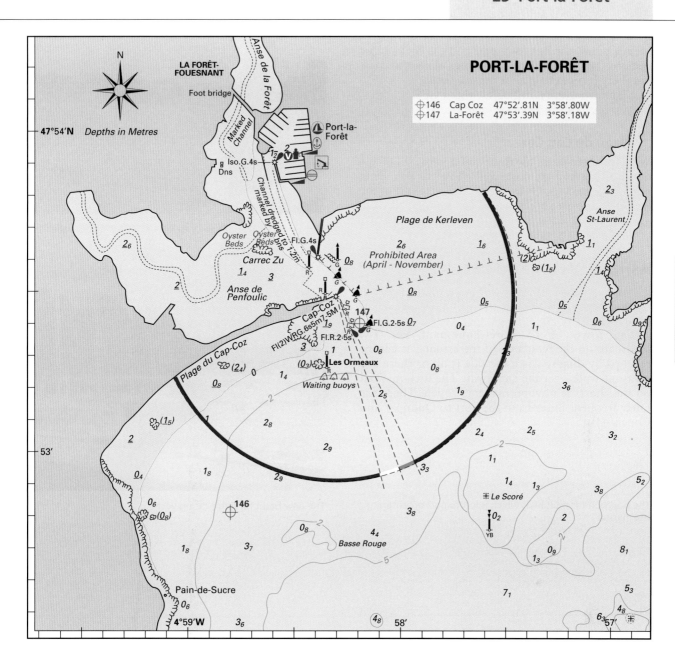

By GPS

From Loctudy or Bénodet use:

⊕126-Mousterlin, ⊕143-SE Beg-Meil, ⊕147-La-Forêt

In good weather with enough rise of tide it is possible to use:

⊕125-La Voleuse, ⊕127-Men Vras, ⊕144-Laouen Pod, ⊕147-La-Forêt

This route passes very close to several unmarked dangers and must be used with care.

From Concarneau use:

⊕149-Concarneau, ⊕148-Vas Hir, ⊕147-La-Forêt

From Glénan use:

⊕129-La Pie, ⊕143-SE Beg-Meil, ⊕147-La-Forêt

or

⊕132-N Penfret, ⊕143-SE Beg-Meil, ⊕147-La-Forêt

BERTHS AND ANCHORAGES

Port-La-Forêt marina

On the west side of the marina entrance is a long pontoon projecting southward on the east side of which are berths for multihulls. On entering the marina, the visitors' pontoon is immediately ahead. Secure here and visit the helpful harbour office to be allocated a berth. The marina has recently been enlarged northwards and the area dredged to accommodate large racing yachts with drafts up to 5m.

⚓ Beg Meil

Sheltered from the west, Beg-Meil is a pretty holiday resort in the southwest corner of Baie de la Forêt. Approach from the east to avoid the dangers off the point. Also avoid the Louen Jardin shallow patch (depth 0.8m) off Beg-Meil pier and the rocks close inshore. There are a lot of moorings along the coast but there is room to anchor outside them.

Night departure is difficult without GPS.

⊕145-Beg-Meil 47°51'·87N 3°58'·53W

⚓ Plage de Cap Coz

Well sheltered from northwest and west, the Plage du Cap-Coz is in the northwest corner of Baie de la Forêt. The best spot is usually at the west end of the beach. There are several rocky patches but all close inshore. Night departure is difficult without GPS.

⊕146-Cap Coz 47°52'·81N 3°58'·80W

ASHORE IN PORT-LA-FORÊT

Port-la-Forêt has all the facilities of a large modern marina and yacht sales centre. There are pleasant beaches nearby.

The town of La Forêt-Fouesnant lies 1M upstream on the west side of the estuary. It can be reached by dinghy when the tide is up or there is a pleasant walk over the causeway. The lock marked on the charts is now permanently open. There are fairly frequent buses from the port to Quimper and Concarneau.

Port-La-Forêt. The village of La Foret-Fouesnant from the foot bridge

The new basin for large racing yachts

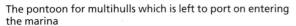

The pontoon for multihulls which is left to port on entering the marina

24 Concarneau

Location
47°52'N 3°55'W

Shelter
Good in marina

Hazards
Rocks on E side of Concarneau bay
Intricate entrance
Rocks by fuel berth wall

Depth restrictions
1m to 5m in marina

Night entry Well lit

HW time
Brest HW–0015 neaps, –0030 springs

Mean height of tide (m)

	HWS	HWN	LWN	LWS
Concarneau	5.0	3.9	1.9	0.8

Tidal stream
Weak in bay but stronger in entrance

Berthing
Visitors' pontoon and inside floating breakwater

Fuel
S corner of marina

Facilities
All facilities

Charts
BA 2820 (50), 3641 (20)
SHOM 7146 (50), 6650 (15)
Imray C38 (large scale)

Radio
Marina VHF Ch 9

Telephone
Marina ① 02 98 97 57 96

Ancient fort and fishing port

The remarkable old town of Concarneau is on an island connected to the mainland by a drawbridge. Secure within massive defensive walls is a labyrinth of beautifully preserved little streets that are packed with tourist shops and restaurants and an excellent museum.

Concarneau from the southeast

PILOTAGE

Concarneau approach and entrance

By day

From any direction, the buildings on the hill at the back of the town are unmistakable. Steer for a position about half a mile west of the promontory of Pointe de Cabellou.

The official leading line is Beuzec belfry, on the ridge a mile inland, in transit with La Croix lighthouse, on the seafront, bearing 028.5°. This works at night but is not clear by day. Le Cochon

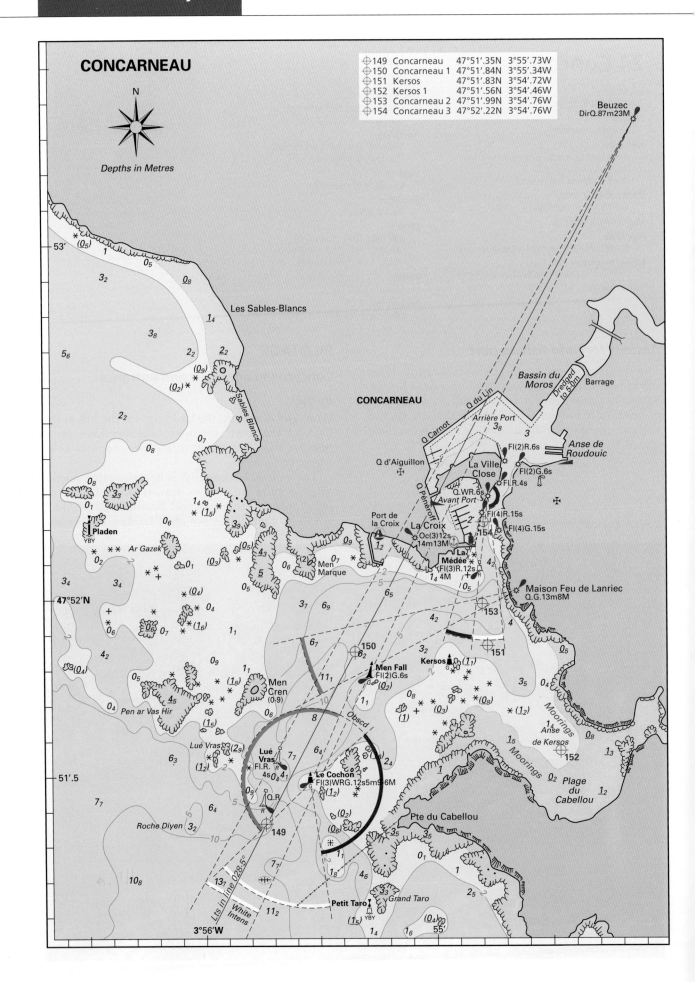

CONCARNEAU

N

Depths in Metres

⊕149	Concarneau	47°51'.35N	3°55'.73W
⊕150	Concarneau 1	47°51'.84N	3°55'.34W
⊕151	Kersos	47°51'.83N	3°54'.72W
⊕152	Kersos 1	47°51'.56N	3°54'.46W
⊕153	Concarneau 2	47°51'.99N	3°54'.76W
⊕154	Concarneau 3	47°52'.22N	3°54'.76W

Beuzec
DirQ.87m23M

Les Sables-Blancs

Sables Blancs

CONCARNEAU

Bassin du Moros

Dredged to 5.0m

Barrage

Arrière Port

Anse de Roudouic

Fl(2)R.6s

Fl(2)G.6s

Q du Lin

Q Carnot

Q d'Aiguillon

La Ville Close

Q.WR.6s

Fl.R.4s

Avant Port

Q Péneroff

Port de la Croix

La Croix
Oc(3)12s
14m13M

Fl(4)R.15s

154

Fl(4)G.15s

La Médée
Fl(3)R.12s
4M

Maison Feu de Lanriec
Q.G.13m8M

Pladen
YBY

Ar Gazek

153

Men Marque

47°52'N

150

Men Fall
Fl(2)G.6s

Kersos
G

151

Men Cren
(0.9)

Moorings

Anse de Kersos

152

Pen ar Vas Hir

Obscd

Lué Vras
Lué Vras
Fl.R.
4s

Le Cochon
Fl(3)WRG.12s5m9-6M

Moorings

Plage du Cabellou

Q.R
R

149

Pte du Cabellou

Roche Diyen

Lts in line 028.5°

White Intens

Petit Taro
YBY

Grand Taro

51'.5

53'

3°56'W

SHM beacon tower is more easily identified and it is sufficient to pass midway between it and the two PHM buoys on a course of about 030°.

Continue on this course for 600m towards Men Fall SHM lightbuoy. Round the buoy and steer 065° for Lanriec light. This is the end gable of a white house, among many, and is hard to spot. Binoculars may reveal a black window in the upper half and the name in green under the window. Fortunately, the channel is wide. Simply leave Kersos SHM beacon tower 200m to starboard and La Médée PHM beacon tower to port to reach the marina entrance.

By night

Approach in the white sector of Le Cochon and bring Beuzec and La Croix lights in transit on 029°. Hold this course past Le Cochon and Basse du Chenal buoy towards Men Fall buoy. As Men Fall is passed, Lanriec Q.G light will open. Steer about 070° in the green sector until the Passage de Lanriec light on the Ville Close opens red. Continue to head for Lanriec until the red light turns white. Then alter to about 000° to keep in the white sector, leaving La Médée to port and No. 1 beacon to starboard.

The floodlights, illuminating La Ville Close, give plenty of background light to the marina area. The channel beyond the marina, past the Ville Close, is marked by further red and green lights.

By GPS

The entrance to Concarneau requires careful visual pilotage. The following waypoints may assist:

⊕149-Concarneau, ⊕150-Concarneau 1,
⊕153-Concarneau 2, ⊕154-Concarneau 3

The following suggested approaches terminate at F149-Concarneau

From Penmarc'h use:

⊕115-Roustelou, ⊕124-Astrolabe, ⊕126-Mousterlin,
⊕143-SE Beg-Meil, ⊕149-Concarneau

This route passes close to several shallow patches between ⊕115-Roustelou and ⊕124-Astrolabe

From Loctudy and Bénodet use:

⊕126-Mousterlin, ⊕143-SE Beg-Meil, ⊕149-Concarneau

In good weather with enough rise of tide it is possible to use:

⊕125-La Voleuse, ⊕127-Men Vras, ⊕143-SE Beg Meil,
⊕149-Concarneau

This shortcut passes very close to several dangerous rocks, particularly off Beg Meil, so use it with care.

From Port-La-Forêt use:

⊕147-La-Forêt, ⊕148-Vas Hir, ⊕149-Concarneau

From east and southeast use:

⊕159-SW Trévignon, ⊕158-W Trévignon,
⊕157-An Houarnou, ⊕149-Concarneau

From south of Belle-Île use:

⊕160-E Glénan, ⊕158-W Trévignon,
⊕157-An Houarnou, ⊕149-Concarneau

From Glénan use:

⊕129-La Pie, ⊕149-Concarneau or
⊕132-N Penfret, ⊕149-Concarneau

Concarneau entrance to la Ville Close

La Croix front leading light

Lanriec lighthouse

BERTHS AND ANCHORAGES

Concarneau visitors' pontoons

Larger yachts can berth on the inner side of the floating wave breaker and others on the marked visitors' pontoon, directly inside the marina entrance. The wave breaker is claimed to be less disturbed by the wash of passing fishing boats coming from the fishing harbour. Only ferries can use the outside of the wave breaker.

Beware of the shallow rocky patch by the fuel berth. It is a hazard near low water.

Concarneau visitors' berth on the wavebreaker

⚓ Anse de Kersos

Sheltered from the north through east to southwest, but exposed to the west and northwest, the Anse de Kersos is a large bay in the approach to Concarneau. Go in clear of the moorings as far as draught permits.

⊕152-Kersos 47°51'·56N 3°54'·56W

⚓ Baie de Pouldohan

Sheltered from the east, the Baie of Pouldohan is about 1.5M south of Concarneau. It is surrounded by rocks and best visited in quiet weather at neaps. A large-scale chart is essential.

Port de la Croix small fishing harbour to the west

Start from a position about 1M south of Pointe de Cabellou and enter on 060° between Roche Tudy SHM beacon tower and Karek Steir PHM beacon. This route passes over a 2.3m shallow patch.

⊕156-Pouldohan 47°50'·81N 3°54'·08W

ASHORE IN CONCARNEAU

There are all the facilities of a sizeable town and busy fishing and leisure port. All repairs can be undertaken. Shops, including a large supermarket, banks, hotels and restaurants are close. Internet café on the quay.

There is a delightful beach just over a mile northwest of the port. The Ville Close and the Fishing Museum are interesting tourist attractions.

A bus service connects Concarneau to the railway at Quimper and Rosporden.

III. Groix and the Rias

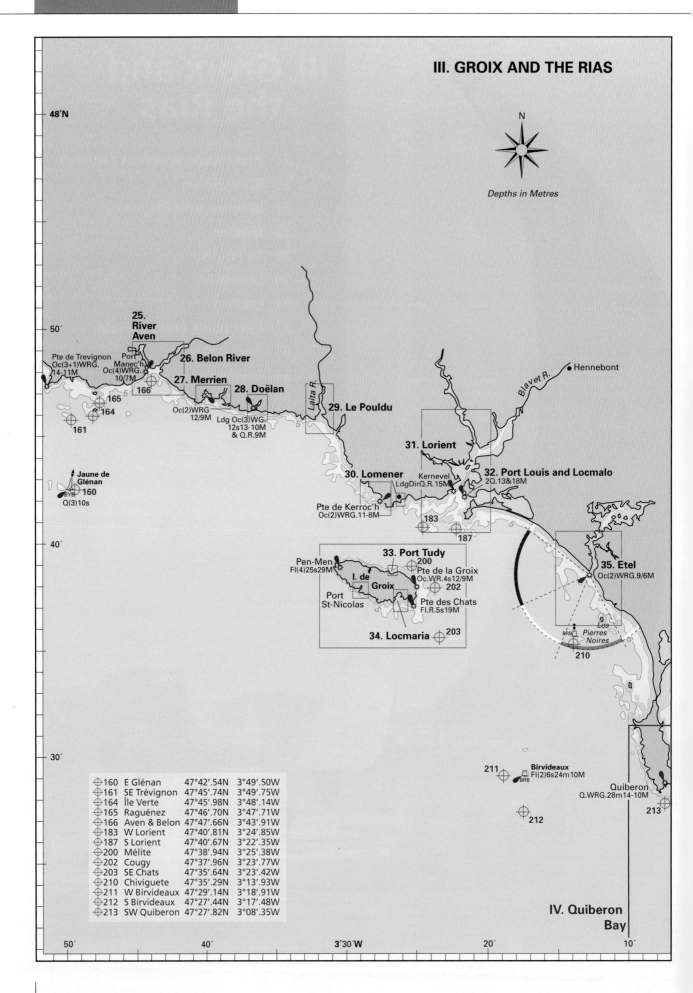

III. GROIX AND THE RIAS

N

Depths in Metres

48°N

50′

Pte de Trevignon
Oc(3+1)WRG.
14-11M

**25.
River
Aven**

Port
Manec'h
Oc(4)WRG.
10/7M

26. Belon River

27. Merrien

166

Oc(2)WRG
12/9M

165

164

161

Laita R.

28. Doëlan

Ldg Oc(3)WG.
12s13-10M
& Q.R.9M

29. Le Pouldu

Blavet R.

● Hennebont

31. Lorient

Jaune de
Glénan

BYB

160

Q(3)10s

30. Lomener

Kernevel
LdgDirQ.R.15M

32. Port Louis and Locmalo
2Q.13&18M

Pte de Kerroc'h
Oc(2)WRG.11-8M

183

187

40′

35. Etel
Oc(2)WRG.9/6M

Pen-Men
Fl(4)25s29M

33. Port Tudy
200

Pte de la Groix
Oc.WR.4s12/9M

202

**I. de
Groix**

Port
St-Nicolas

Pte des Chats
Fl.R.5s19M

LGS

BRB

Pierres
Noires

210

34. Locmaria

203

30′

211

Birvideaux
Fl(2)6s24m10M

BRB

Quiberon
Q.WRG.28m14-10M

213

212

⊕160	E Glénan	47°42′.54N	3°49′.50W
⊕161	SE Trévignon	47°45′.74N	3°49′.75W
⊕164	Île Verte	47°45′.98N	3°48′.14W
⊕165	Raguénez	47°46′.70N	3°47′.71W
⊕166	Aven & Belon	47°47′.66N	3°43′.91W
⊕183	W Lorient	47°40′.81N	3°24′.85W
⊕187	S Lorient	47°40′.67N	3°22′.35W
⊕200	Mélite	47°38′.94N	3°25′.38W
⊕202	Cougy	47°37′.96N	3°23′.77W
⊕203	SE Chats	47°35′.64N	3°23′.42W
⊕210	Chiviguete	47°35′.29N	3°13′.93W
⊕211	W Birvideaux	47°29′.14N	3°18′.91W
⊕212	S Birvideaux	47°27′.44N	3°17′.48W
⊕213	SW Quiberon	47°27′.82N	3°08′.35W

**IV. Quiberon
Bay**

50′   40′   3°30′W   20′   10′

25 River Aven and Port Manec'h

Location
48°47'N 3°44'W

Shelter
Reasonable from SW to NE

Hazards
Unmarked rocks in W approach

Depth restrictions
Visitors' buoys at Port Manec'h 1m.
Bar dredged to 0.6m
River dries 1.5m

Night entry Well lit to Port Manec'h

HW time
Brest HW–0015 neaps, –0030 springs

Mean height of tide (m)

	HWS	HWN	LWN	LWS
Concarneau	5.0	3.9	1.9	0.8

Tidal stream
Weak in bay, strong in the river
3 knots in Rosbraz narrows

Berthing
Visitors' moorings and anchorages, drying quays at Rosbraz and Pont Aven

Facilities
Water, a few shops, bars and restaurants

Charts
BA 2821 (50)
SHOM 7031 (50), 7138 (10)
Imray C38 (large scale)

Telephone
Yacht Club ① 02 98 06 84 30

Lovely river scenery to Pont Aven

The Aven is a popular and very pretty river. The holiday resort of Port Manec'h is at its mouth on the west bank. It is a further 7M inland to the picturesque artists' town of Pont Aven.

PILOTAGE

Approach to the River Aven

By day

The entrance is easy to locate using the lighthouse at Port Manec'h. There is also a large white masonry beacon with a black vertical stripe on the east side of the entrance to the Belon river

The approach can be made from any direction but take care to avoid the unmarked Les Cochons de Rospico (dries 0.5m) to the west; and Le Cochon (dries 0.8m) 0.4M northwest of Les Verrès IDM tower beacon to the east.

The 0.5M passage between Les Verrès and the land, has a least depth of 2.6m. The passage between Île Raguenez and Île Verte is deep but there is a 1m shallow patch south of the channel west of Île Verte.

By night

Use either of the white sectors of Port Manec'h light. The red sector covers the dangers of Les Verrès.

The entrance to the River Aven and River Belon looking northeast. The insets are (left) the Port Manec'h lighthouse and (right) the Amer at Pointe de Kerhermen *M&G Barron*

III. GROIX AND THE RIAS

By GPS

From northwest (*see page 64*) use:
⊕159-SW Trévignon, ⊕161-SE Trévignon, ⊕164-Île Verte, ⊕166-Aven and Belon, ⊕167-Port Manec'h

In good weather it is possible to use the short cut:
⊕159-SW Trévignon, ⊕165-Raguenez, ⊕166-Aven and Belon

This route requires care because it passes close to the unmarked Cochons de Rospico.

From Glénan use:
⊕164-Île Verte, ⊕166-Aven and Belon, ⊕167-Port Manec'h

From south use:
⊕166-Aven and Belon, ⊕167-Port Manec'h

but take great care to avoid Le Cochon (dries 0.8m) 0.4M northwest of Les Verrès IDM beacon tower.

The River Aven to Pont Aven

The mouth of the river is shallow and the position of the bar changes periodically. Within 0.5M of the mouth it dries apart from a few pools.

Enter on a rising tide leaving the Le Roc'h PHM beacon well to port and proceed up the centre of the river. Half a mile up there is an inlet called Anse de

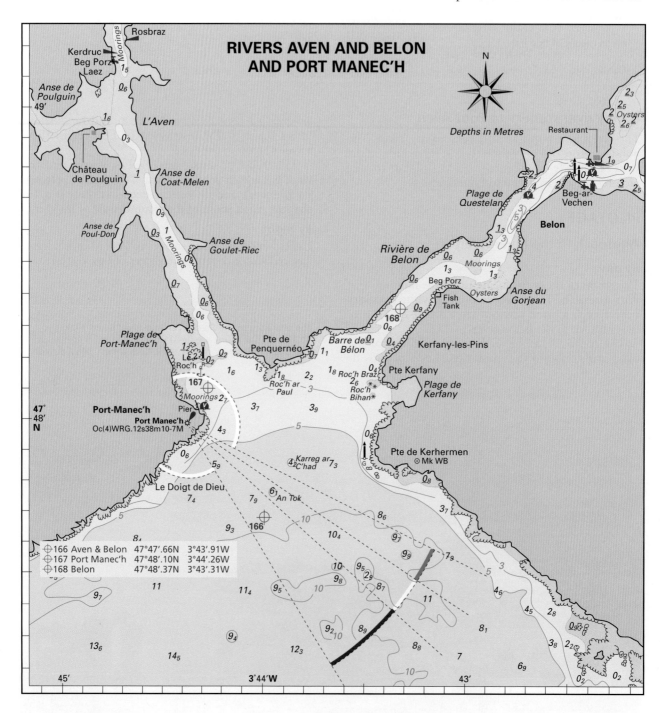

Port Manec'h looking west.
Port Manec'h is a small holiday village. There are a few white visitors' moorings and room to anchor outside the moorings. From here you can access the beautiful GR34 coastal footpath

Goulet-Riec on the east side. Here the river deepens and 2m or more may be found.

Further on the river shoals to dry 0.6m in places and there is a large drying creek branching off to the west with a château on the point. Then the river narrows between the quays and slips of Kerdruc on the west bank and Rosbraz on the east.

Above Rosbraz the river widens and shoals, but is navigable on the tide or by dinghy a further 2.5M to Pont Aven. The channel is marked by buoys and easy to follow.

Aven River

BERTHS AND ANCHORAGES

Port Manec'h

The short Port Manec'h breakwater runs north from the point. Behind it is a small quay and slipway. To the east are three white visitors' mooring buoys in 1.0m but exposed from southwest to southeast through south. Upstream are some fore and aft moorings in 2m depth. They are occasionally available for boats of less than 10m. During the season, all of these moorings are likely to be taken by early afternoon but there may be room to anchor outside them.

Rosbraz

It is possible to dry out alongside the quays on mud at Kerdruc or on shingle and mud at Rosbraz or to borrow a mooring. No visitors' moorings.

The ebb runs at over 3kns and there is so little space between the moorings that it is difficult for a yacht of over 10m to turn.

Pont Aven

There are drying quays but these tend to be crowded.

ASHORE

Port Manec'h

There is water on the quay and modest shops and restaurants.

Pont Aven

All the facilities of a tourist town. Gauguin lived and worked here and it is still a magnet for artists and connoisseurs. Pont Aven Museum and Art Gallery is particularly worth visiting.

26 River Belon

Location
47°48′N 3°44′W

Shelter Good in river

Hazards
Unmarked rocks in W approach
Bar dangerous in strong SW wind

Depth restrictions
Bar dries 0.1m
Visitors' moorings have 3m or more

Night entry Not recommended

HW time
Brest HW−0015 neaps, −0030 springs

Mean height of tide (m)

	HWS	HWN	LWN	LWS
Concarneau	5.0	3.9	1.9	0.8

Tidal stream
Weak in bay, moderate in the river

Berthing
Visitors' moorings

Facilities
Excellent seafood

Charts
BA 2821 (50)
SHOM 7031 (50), 7138 (10)
Imray C38 (large scale)

Telephone
Harbourmaster ☏ 06 25 53 06 65

Oyster lovers' paradise

Belon, home of the Belon oyster, is a must for seafood enthusiasts. It is a pretty, sheltered river with some visitors' buoys. However, in bad southerly weather the bar is impassable.

PILOTAGE

(See plan on page 98)

Approach to the River Belon

By day

The outer entrance is easily identified by a large white day mark with a black vertical stripe on the east side of the entrance at Pointe de Kerhermen.

The approach can be made from any direction. Be sure to avoid Les Cochons de Rospico (dries 0.5m) to the west; and Le Cochon (dries 0.8m) 0.4M northwest of Les Verrès IDM tower beacon to the east. Both are unmarked.

The passage between Les Verrès and the land has a least depth of 2.6m. The passage between Île Raguenez and Île Verte is deep but there is a 1m shallow patch south of the channel west of Île Verte.

By night

Not recommended.

The River Belon looking east.
The village consists of the attractive row of houses on the south bank. There are no shops, only a small fish market. The famous restaurant and fish shop, Chez Jacky, is the white building on the opposite bank.

By GPS

From northwest use:

⊕159-SW Trévignon, ⊕161-SE Trévignon, ⊕164-Île Verte, ⊕166-Aven & Belon, ⊕168-Belon

In good weather it is possible to use the short cut:

⊕159-SW Trévignon, ⊕161-SE Trévignon, ⊕165-Raguenez, ⊕166-Aven and Belon

This route requires care because it passes close to the unmarked Cochons de Rospico.

From Glénan, use:

⊕164-Île Verte, ⊕166-Aven and Belon, ⊕168-Belon

From south use:

⊕166-Aven and Belon, ⊕168-Belon

but take great care to avoid Le Cochon (dries 0.8m) 0.4M northwest of Les Verrès IDM.

River Belon

It is best to enter the river above half tide. Start from a position midway between the headland at Port Manec'h and Pointe de Kerhermen and enter the river from the southwest. When Pointe Kerfany is abeam to starboard, steer down the middle of the dredged channel on 035°.

Just after Beg Porz, a bar extends from the north bank. The deepest water is on the south side, close to the stakes marking the oyster beds. Half a mile further the river turns to starboard and on the north side of the curve there are three large white metal head and stern visitors' buoys, suitable for rafting.

Beyond the visitors' moorings is a quay and there are six more fore and aft visitors' moorings for smaller vessels just beyond Chez Jacky's large white restaurant on the north bank. All the moorings are in strong tidal currents but the smaller ones are

particularly difficult to pick up when the tide is ebbing strongly as the current is diagonally across the moorings. The Belon River winds further inland through steep, wooded valleys. It may be possible to explore in a dinghy or else on foot. The GR34 coastal footpath leads for miles around the banks of both the Aven and the Belon rivers. The TOP25 map of Quimperlé No. 0620 is recommended for those with time to explore further.

ASHORE IN BELON

Belon village is on the south bank. There is water, fuel and a public toilet block on the quay and a few bars but no shops. Fish can sometimes be bought from the fishermen at high water. The Plage de Kerfany is a pleasant walk and, in season, has a shop for the campsite.

Chez Jacky on the north bank is a famous seafood restaurant that also has a shop selling shellfish.

Belon River Chez Jacky restaurant on north bank

Looking upriver, the three white head and stern visitors' buoys are vacant on the left

III. GROIX AND THE RIAS

27 Merrien and Brigneau

Location
47°47'N 3°39'W

Shelter
Good in the Merrien river, but visitors' buoys are exposed.

Hazards
Marked rocks in entrances

Depth restrictions
Approach to Merrien 1m, Brigneau 2.1m
At Merrien the river dries 0.6m except in channel
At Brigneau the river dries completely

Night entry Possible but not recommended

HW time
Brest HW neaps, –0030 springs

Mean height of tide (m)

	HWS	HWN	LWN	LWS
Port Tudy	5.1	4.0	2.0	0.9

Tidal stream
Weak in bay, stronger in harbours

Berthing
Anchorages and visitors' buoys at Merrien

Facilities
Pleasant walking

Charts
BA 2821 (50)
SHOM 7031 (50), 7138 (10)
Imray C38 (large scale)

Telephone
Belon Harbourmaster ☎ 06 25 53 06 65

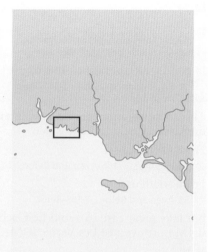

Attractive drying creek

Merrien is delightful, particularly for boats that can take the ground. There are two fine weather visitors' buoys in the bay outside. Inside it dries apart from a dredged channel.

PILOTAGE

Merrien approach and entrance

By day

From the west, Merrien is easily identified 0.75M beyond the ruined factory at Brigeau. From the east, the entrance will open after passing a headland topped by some white houses with grey roofs, 1.75M west of Doëlan.

There are marked dangers on both sides of the entrance. The official transit is the white lighthouse at the head of the pool with a large grey-roofed house with a gable on 005°. Unfortunately the lighthouse is almost obscured by the trees and it is adequate to line up the grey roof on 005°.

By night

Entry to the pool is possible, though not recommended without GPS, using the narrow red sector of the light on 005°.

Merrien looking north.
The white light tower is visible just below the building at the top of the hill on the north bank *M&G Barron*

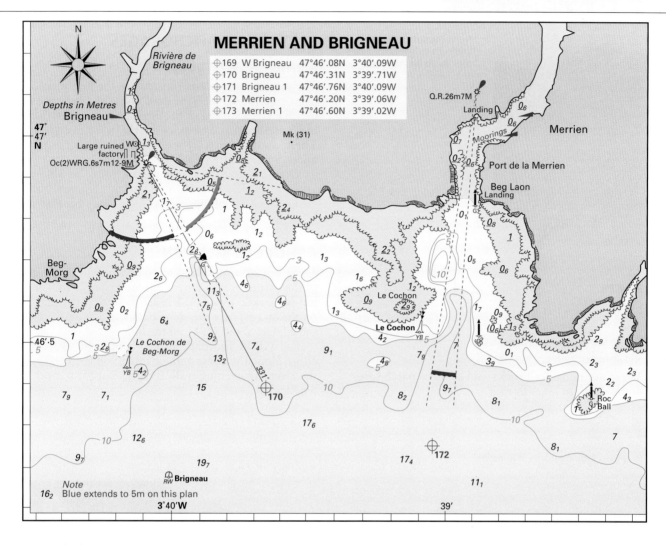

MERRIEN AND BRIGNEAU

⊕	169	W Brigneau	47°46'.08N	3°40'.09W
⊕	170	Brigneau	47°46'.31N	3°39'.71W
⊕	171	Brigneau 1	47°46'.76N	3°40'.09W
⊕	172	Merrien	47°46'.20N	3°39'.06W
⊕	173	Merrien 1	47°46'.60N	3°39'.02W

Merrien looking south *R Rundle*

III. GROIX AND THE RIAS

From the sea (below), the light tower is concealed by the trees *M&G Barron*

BERTHS AND ANCHORAGES

Merrien visitors' buoys

The two visitors' buoys outside are the best place in calm conditions. Merrien Pool inside the entrance is inviting but keep out of the fairway and at least 50m offshore because the sides of the pool are rocky. There are fore and aft moorings for visitors up to about 9m length in depths of about 1m.

Vessels able to take the ground may be able to anchor in the river outside the channel but anchoring is prohibited off Merrien quay because of a submarine cable.

ASHORE IN MERRIEN

There is a stone jetty and steps on the starboard side of the entrance. The jetty is submerged at high water but is marked by a SHM beacon. Water is available on the quay. There are some bars and a restaurant in the village, about 0.5M up the hill.

The GR34 footpath offers wonderful walking either along the coast path or inland on the banks of the river. An evening walk to Brigneau for a meal is worthwhile.

By GPS

From the west use:
⊕169-W Brigneau, ⊕172-Merrien, ⊕173-Merrien 1

From south and southeast use:
⊕172-Merrien, ⊕173-Merrien 1

There are unmarked rocks and shallow patches for 400m south of ⊕173-Merrien 1.

Brigneau looking north *R Rundle*

Merrien *R Rundle*

The ruined factory at Brigneau.
In good weather Brigneau is an interesting place to visit
but it is completely exposed to the southeast and untenable
in swell *M&G Barron*

Brigneau looking south *R Rundle*

BRIGNEAU

Brigneau is completely exposed to the southeast so wind or swell from the south makes it untenable. It is 0.75M west of Merrien and in good weather is an interesting place to visit. It was once a major sardine port but now has a small amount of fishing and a sailing school.

Brigneau approach

By day

330° on the ruined factory chimney.

By night

In the west sector of Brigneau Light 329/339° Oc(2)WRG 6s.

By GPS

From the west use:

⊕169-W Brigneau, ⊕170-Brigneau, ⊕171-Brigneau 1

From south and southeast use:

⊕170-Brigneau, ⊕171-Brigneau 1

The port dries but it is possible to anchor outside the harbour or borrow a mooring. Small boats may be able to use the fore and aft moorings just inside the harbour. Ashore fuel is available and there are two good restaurants and a chandler.

III. GROIX AND THE RIAS

28 Doëlan

Location
47°46'N 3°36'W

Shelter Exposed to S

Hazards
Marked rocks in entrance.

Depth restrictions
Channel dredged 2.0m

Night entry Lit

HW time
Brest HW neaps, –0030 springs

Mean height of tide (m)

	HWS	HWN	LWN	LWS
Port Tudy	5.1	4.0	2.0	0.9

Tidal stream
Little stream in bay or harbour

Berthing
Visitors' moorings and drying quay

Facilities
Bars, restaurants, fish market but no shops

Charts
BA 2821 (50)
SHOM 7031 (50), 7138 (10)
Imray C38 (large scale)

Radio VHF Ch 16, 69

Telephone
Harbourmaster ☏ 02 98 39 60 67

Small friendly fishing port

The port of Doëlan is larger than the other ports on this stretch of coast but is still very small. There is a small but active fishing fleet and some boats that take the ground at the back of the harbour. It is a pretty place and popular with artists.

PILOTAGE

Doëlan approach and entrance

By day

Identify a pink house on the east headland and a conspicuous factory with a tall, slender chimney.

Two lighthouses provide the entry transit on a bearing of 014°. This transit passes a PHM beacon marking Basse le Croix and the SHM buoy that replaced the destroyed Le Four tower.

By night

Approach and enter with the leading lights in line on 014°. Coming from the direction of Lorient, a vessel can avoid the rocks southeast of Le Pouldu (Les Grand et Petit Cochons) by keeping out of the green sector of the front light, which covers them.

By GPS

⊕174-Doëlan, ⊕175-Doëlan 1

Doëlan looking north.
A large white metal mooring buoy is visible just inside the breakwater. Not shown in the picture is another similar mooring buoy just outside the breakwater

BERTHS

Doëlan visitors' buoys

Visitors raft to a large white metal buoy with a rail round its edge. There is one of these just outside and another inside the breakwater on the west side of the entrance. Care is needed when mooring to the buoy inside the breakwater as the rock line extends close to the buoy from the west and south.

The fishermen are friendly, and it may be possible to borrow one of their moorings. A boat that can take the ground may be able to borrow a mooring up-harbour.

Doëlan quays

It is possible to dry out at one of the quays. Near the entrance to the harbour there is a landing slip and quay on the west side, a pair of slips forming a V on the east side. Other quays lie further up. Local advice should be obtained before drying out. The inner quay on the west is not suitable as the bottom slopes outwards. The first two quays on the east dry about 1.5m and should be suitable.

ASHORE IN DOËLAN

Water and electricity are available on the quays and there is a fish market on the outer port-side quay, Quay Neuf.

There are bars and restaurants on both sides of the river and a good chandlery but apart from that, the nearest shops are at Clohars Carnoet, 3km inland.

The GR34 footpath is easy to access and can be followed along the rocky coast or inland beside the banks of the river.

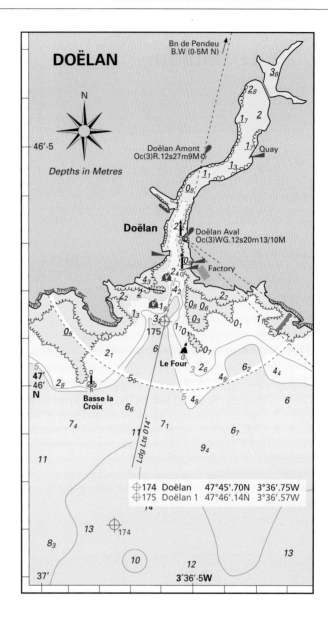

The approach to Doëlan with the leading lighthouses almost in transit. The slender chimney associated with the factory is further up the hill *M&G Barron*

29 Le Pouldu

Location
47°46'N 3°32'W

Shelter
Good in river. Exposed to S in outer anchorage

Hazards
Dangerous bar at entrance. Possibility of being trapped inside

Depth Restrictions
Bar dries 2.2m. 2.0m in marina and parts of river

Night entry Not lit

HW time
Brest HW at neaps, -0030 at springs

Mean height of tide (m)

	HWS	HWN	LWN	LWS
Port Tudy	5.1	4.0	2.0	0.9

Tidal stream
Weak in bay, up to 6 kns in river

Berthing
Very small marina. Visitors' buoys and anchorages

Facilities
Bars, restaurants and supermarket. Other shops 1M away

Charts
BA 2821 (50)
SHOM 7031 (50), 7138 (10)
Imray C38 (large scale)

Telephone
HM ① 02 97 05 99 / 06 07 18 11 54

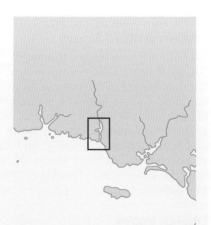

Shifting sands and sluicing tide

Le Pouldu is challenging. The entry is difficult and can only be attempted an hour before HW in calm offshore weather with no swell. The sandbanks shift, the tide is very strong at springs and there is not much water over the bar at neaps but with a tidal co-efficient of 85 or more there is said to be plenty of water over the bar for a boat drawing 1.5m. Once inside, there is little room for visitors, but the river is attractive and the harbourmaster is very helpful and welcoming.

PILOTAGE

Approach and entrance to Le Pouldu

Warning

The stream in the river runs very hard and except near slack water a yacht going aground will be slewed round uncontrollably and possibly dangerously.

Le Pouldu looking northeast.
The River Laita flows 9M from the town of Quimperlé and in the 19th-century ships of 150-tonnes used to go up at high tide. Notice the tide race at the mouth of the river

By day

The harbour entrance can be identified by the former pilot's house, white with a round tower, situated on the W headland. The final approach is made with the pilot's house bearing 010°.

Entry should only be attempted in calm conditions about an hour before HW. This means there will be no indication of where the channel lies.

It is not possible to give precise directions since the channel moves. The guide-line on the plan is as drawn by the HM in 2009. The main channel usually follows the west bank. It is marked by the PHM beacon tower at the entrance and by a PHM beacon pole. The channel then curves to starboard where a second port-hand beacon pole marks the end of a small rocky spit. Except for the stream from the river, this channel dries at LW.

To take the main channel, leave the second beacon pole 40m to port and keep this distance off to avoid a rocky shelf. The river opens out, with a wide shallow bay to starboard, and the protecting breakwater of the marina will be seen ahead on the east bank.

The river is navigable by dinghies at HW up to Quimperlé, but a bridge with 10m clearance two miles from the entrance prevents the passage of masted vessels.

By night

Night entry should not be attempted.

By GPS

The entrance requires careful visual pilotage. The following may be helpful in the approach.

⊕176-Pouldu, ⊕177-Pouldu 1

BERTHS AND ANCHORAGE

Le Pouldu visitors' buoys

There are two white dumbell visitors' buoys, where there is sufficient water at neaps, off the marina and another further up in the trot moorings where there is more depth. Another option is to continue upriver to find 2m or more for anchoring but the deeper water is very full of moorings. The holding appears to be good in spite of the stream and some weed.

There is a drying sandbank in the middle of the river and there are many small-craft drying moorings on the east side and in the bay downstream.

The Guidel marina on the east side is small but there are three visitors' berths, max length 9.5m and max draft 1.5m.

⚓ Outside Le Pouldu

In settled offshore weather an anchorage can be found outside the bar. The best spot seems to be with the marina bearing 000° as far in as draught permits. The bottom is hard sand.

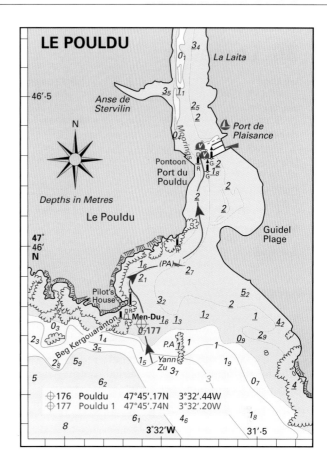

| ⊕176 | Pouldu | 47°45'.17N | 3°32'.44W |
| ⊕177 | Pouldu 1 | 47°45'.74N | 3°32'.20W |

ASHORE IN LE POULDU

The pontoon on the west bank is for fishermen but there is space to leave a dinghy. There are two hotels close by and the shops of Le Pouldu are 1M along the road.

The harbour office is on the east bank at Guidel by the marina. Further south there are restaurants catering for a camping site and there is a large supermarket a short walk round the bay towards the entrance.

The former pilot's house with a round tower above Men-Du beacon tower *M&G Barron*

30 Loméner

Location
47°42'N 3°26'W

Shelter
Good from NW to NE

Hazards
Marked and unmarked rocks

Depth restrictions
3.0m at breakwater

Night entry Lit

HW time
Brest HW neaps, –0030 springs

Mean height of tide (m)

	HWS	HWN	LWN	LWS
Port Tudy	5.1	4.0	2.0	0.9

Tidal stream
Weak in approach and anchorage

Berthing
Anchorages

Facilities
As of a beach resort

Charts
BA 2821 (50)
SHOM 7031 (50), 7139 (20)
Imray C38 (78)

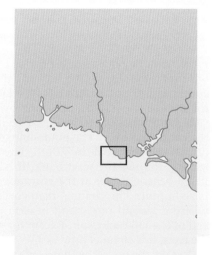

Pleasant seaside resort

The port of Loméner and the adjacent Anse de Stole, form a small harbour on the mainland opposite Île de Groix.

It is open to the south but sheltered from the north and the *brise de terre*. In settled weather, it can be a better option than Port Tudy.

Loméner has good beaches and all facilities of a small seaside resort.

PILOTAGE

Approach and entrance to Loméner

By day

The harbour is easy to identify by a prominent block of flats behind the breakwater.

Enter by keeping the white tower with a red top on 357°. Close-in the dangers on the west side are well marked but there are unmarked shallow patches to the west of the leading line further out at Les Trois Pierres (0.9m) and Basse des Chats (0.1m). The dangers on the east are also not well marked and in particular Grasu SCM tower beacon should be given a good berth because rocks extend west of it.

By night

Enter using the white sector of Anse de Stole light 355°/359°. Beware of the many unlit fishing floats and moorings.

By GPS

⊕181-Loméner, ⊕182-Loméner 1

BERTHS AND ANCHORAGES

⚓ Anse de Stole

Anchor in the Anse de Stole where space and depth permit or borrow a mooring but it is open to the south. The beaches behind the breakwater and in the Anse de Stole are excellent for drying out. There is a landing slip on the spur inside the harbour. Avoid the breakwater wall, as there are vicious rocks at its foot.

⚓ Kerroc'h

Sheltered from all directions except west when swell can enter near HW, this small harbour is about 4M west of Lorient. Approach from due south steering to pass about 150m west of the WCM beacon marking Les Deux Têtes. This is necessary to avoid the unmarked Les Soeurs rocks on the west side of the entrance. Once past the WCM, turn to starboard to enter the harbour. Anchor where depth permits or borrow a mooring.

⊕179-Kerroc'h 1 47°42'·18N 3°28'·09W

Le Pérello looking east.
This stretch of rocky coast has several small, sandy bays which make useful anchorages. The first bay in the picture is Le Pérello. Further east, beyond the long breakwater is Loméner and the large curved bay is Anse de Stole. In the distance is the entrance to Lorient harbour

⚓ Le Pérello

Exposed to wind or swell from the south and southeast, Le Pérello is about 1M east of Kerroc'h. Approach from the south-southeast. The drying rocks on either side of the entrance can be avoided by aligning the elbow of the small slipway on the northeast side of the bay with the seaward-facing gable end of the house behind it on 353°. The house is the one closest to the beach.

There are some moorings but there is also room to anchor.

⊕180-Pérello 47°41'·69N 3°26'·40W

ASHORE IN LOMENER

There is water at the root of the quay and shops, bars and restaurants. There is also a large supermarket close to the quay. Shellfish can often be bought direct from local fishermen.

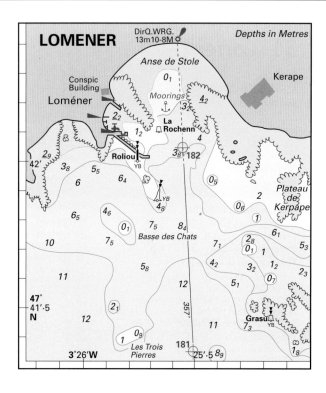

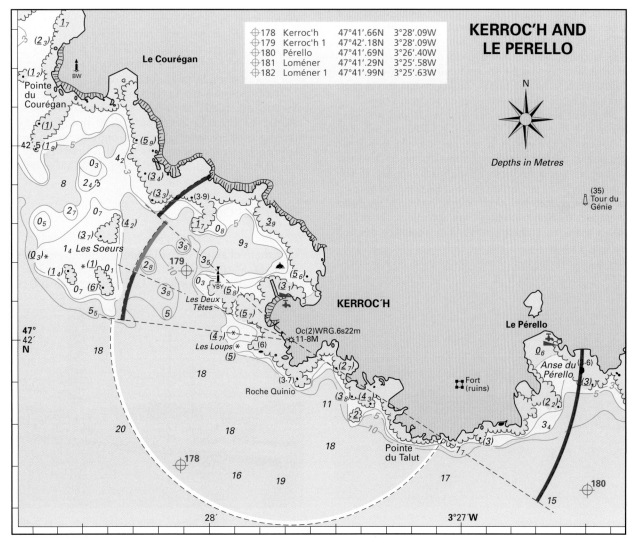

⊕178	Kerroc'h	47°41'.66N	3°28'.09W
⊕179	Kerroc'h 1	47°42'.18N	3°28'.09W
⊕180	Pérello	47°41'.69N	3°26'.40W
⊕181	Loméner	47°41'.29N	3°25'.58W
⊕182	Loméner 1	47°41'.99N	3°25'.63W

III. GROIX AND THE RIAS

31 Lorient

Location
47°42'N 3°22'W

Shelter
Excellent in marinas

Hazards
Marked rocks in entrance

Depth restrictions None

Night entry Well lit

HW time
Brest HW +0005 neaps, -0020 springs

Mean height of tide (m)

	HWS	HWN	LWN	LWS
Lorient	5.1	4.0	2.0	0.8
Hennebont	5.0	3.9	1.8	0.7

Tidal stream in entrance:
Flood – Brest HW–0500 to –0200
(3.5kts)
Slack – Brest HW–0200 to +0200
Ebb – Brest HW+0200 to +0500 (4.0kns)
Slack – Brest HW+0500 to –0500

Berthing
Several marinas

Fuel
Kernéval S basin

Facilities
All facilities

Charts
BA 2821 (50), 304 (10)
SHOM 7031 (50), 7140 (20)
Imray C38 (large scale)

Radio All marinas VHF Ch 9

Telephone:
Lorient Marina ① 02 97 21 10 14
Kernéval ① 02 97 65 48 25
Locmiquélic ① 02 97 33 59 51
Base de Sous-Marin ① 02 97 87 00 46

Major port with good facilities

Lorient was once an important commercial port, founded originally in the 17th century as a base for France's India Company, hence the original name L'Orient. A naval dockyard followed in the north of the harbour (now closed) and during the Second World War the huge concrete submarine pens were built for German U-Boats. Today it has the largest fishing fleet in Brittany and seven yacht marinas.

Parts of the harbour are industrial and not very attractive but against that, it is possible to moor in the heart of the city, in a marina near the beach, or anchor in perfect peace in a beautiful river. Also the sailing is good because Île de Groix protects the approaches. Thus Lorient is an ideal place to hole up in bad weather but well worth visiting in good weather. Communications are excellent so it is a good place to change crews. The recently opened sailing exhibition 'Cité de la Voile Eric Tabarly' situated close to the submarine pens is also worth a visit.

PILOTAGE

Warnings

Yachts must keep to the edges of channels wherever possible and must keep out of the way of large vessels. In particular they must keep well to the appropriate side of the narrows at the citadel whether or not a large ship is present.

Traffic signals for large ships, on the simplified system, are made from the signal station on the citadel of Port Louis. Boats may not enter the narrows when one of these signals is shown. Appropriate announcements are also made on VHF and boats must maintain watch on Ch 16 when underway in the harbour.

Passe de l'Ouest

By day

This channel starts 0.75M south of the conspicuous Grasu SCM tower beacon. The outer leading line is the red and white tower on Les Soeurs rocks and the

Lorient submarine pens

Lorient. Three of Eric Tabarly's Pen Duicks at Cité de la Voile

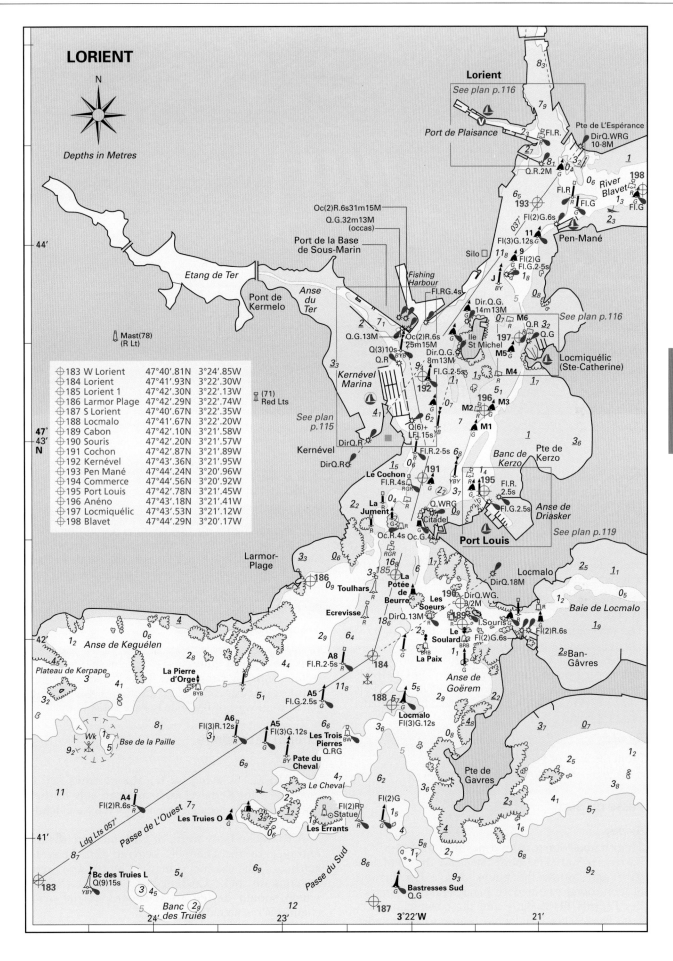

LORIENT

N

Depths in Metres

⊕ 183	W Lorient	47°40'.81N	3°24'.85W
⊕ 184	Lorient	47°41'.93N	3°22'.30W
⊕ 185	Lorient 1	47°42'.30N	3°22'.13W
⊕ 186	Larmor Plage	47°42'.29N	3°22'.74W
⊕ 187	S Lorient	47°40'.67N	3°22'.35W
⊕ 188	Locmalo	47°41'.67N	3°22'.20W
⊕ 189	Cabon	47°42'.10N	3°21'.58W
⊕ 190	Souris	47°42'.20N	3°21'.57W
⊕ 191	Cochon	47°42'.87N	3°21'.89W
⊕ 192	Kernével	47°43'.36N	3°21'.95W
⊕ 193	Pen Mané	47°44'.24N	3°20'.96W
⊕ 194	Commerce	47°44'.56N	3°20'.92W
⊕ 195	Port Louis	47°42'.78N	3°21'.45W
⊕ 196	Anéno	47°43'.18N	3°21'.41W
⊕ 197	Locmiquélic	47°43'.53N	3°21'.12W
⊕ 198	Blavet	47°44'.29N	3°20'.17W

See plan p.116

Lorient

Port de Plaisance

Pte de L'Espérance

River Blavet

Pen-Mané

Oc(2)R.6s31m15M
Q.G.32m13M
(occas)

Port de la Base
de Sous-Marin

Fishing Harbour

Silo

Anse du Ter

Etang de Ter

Pont de Kermelo

Mast(78)
(R Lt)

(71)
Red Lts

See plan p.116

Locmiquélic
(Ste-Catherine)

Dir.Q.G.
14m13M

Q.G.13M

Oc(2)R.6s
25m15M

Q(3)10s

Q.R

Dir.Q.G.
8m13M

Kernével Marina

See plan p.115

DirQ.R

Kernével

DirQ.R

Ile St Michel

Banc de Kerzo

Pte de Kerzo

Anse de Driasker

See plan p.119

Le Cochon

La Jument

Citadel

Q.WRG

Port Louis

Larmor-Plage

Toulhars

La Potée de Beurre

Les Soeurs

Ecrevisse

Locmalo

Baie de Locmalo

Ban-Gâvres

Le Soulard

La Paix

Anse de Goërem

Anse de Keguélen

Plateau de Kerpape

La Pierre d'Orge

A8
Fl.R.2·5s

184

A5
Fl.G.2·5s

188

Locmalo
Fl(3)G.12s

Pte de Gavres

A6
Fl(3)R.12s

A5
Fl(3)G.12s

Les Trois Pierres
Q.RG

Pate du Cheval

Le Cheval

Les Errants

Fl(2)R
Statue

Fl(2)G

A4
Fl(2)R.6s

Les Truies O

Ldg Lts 057°

Passe de L'Ouest

Passe du Sud

183

Bc des Truies L
Q(9)15s

Banc des Truies

Bastresses Sud
Q.G

187

3°22'W

III. GROIX AND THE RIAS

Kernével Marina from south with Port de la Base de Sous-Marin in the background

red and white banded day mark above the citadel walls (right of a conspicuous church spire) on 057°. The channel is well buoyed.

Soon after passing Les Trois Pierres beacon tower (BW horizontal bands), the narrows will open. The transit is two white towers with green tops on the west side of Île Saint-Michel on 016°. However, the huge white grain silo in the commercial harbour also provides a useful landmark.

By night

The intensified sector of the leading lights on 057° covers the channel and all the lateral buoys are lit. Use Les Trois Pierres to identify the position of the turn to port on to 016° with the two Dir.QG lights on the west side of Île Saint-Michel in line. This takes one through the narrows marked by the citadel and La Jument.

By GPS

From the west or Port Tudy use:
⊕183-W Lorient, ⊕184-Lorient, ⊕191-Cochon

Passe du Sud

By day

This channel starts from a position 0.25M SW of Bastresses Sud SHM buoy. Steer for the citadel on 010° and follow the buoys. Leave Les Errants beacon tower (white with black square topmark), Les Errants PHM buoy and the conspicuous Les Trois Pierres (black and white beacon tower) to port.

The main channel, the Passe de l'Ouest, is then joined and is well marked to the citadel.

By night

The leading lights for this channel are no longer lit so that at night those without local knowledge should use the Passe de l'Ouest as Basse de la Paix SHM buoy is unlit as are several tower beacons just off the track.

By GPS

From east or southeast use:
⊕187-S Lorient, ⊕185-Lorient 1, ⊕191-Cochon

This route passes quite close to a 2.2m shallow patch 400m south-southeast of Les Trois Pierres black and white tower beacon and to another 1.4m shallow patch southwest of Basse de la Paix SHM buoy.

Chenal Secondaire

By day

This channel is a bypass for the narrows and is convenient for Kernével marina. It can only be used above half tide because it passes over Le Cochon (dries 1m).

A RGR can buoy south of La Jument marks the entrance to the channel. Leaving this buoy to starboard, the channel is marked by red and green beacons up to Le Cochon beacon tower (RGR), which should be left to starboard as the main channel is re-entered.

By night

The Chenal Secondaire is unlit and should not be used at night.

Proceeding up the harbour

By day

Once through the narrows, the harbour opens out and navigation is straightforward. Within the harbour, the dangers are marked, and the chart is the best guide.

If bound for the Lorient Harbour (Port de Commerce) or the River Blavet, either the channel to the east or to the west of Île Saint-Michel may be used. Note that there is an unmarked shallow patch, with 0.5m over it, on the eastern edge of the east channel.

By night

The usual route up harbour is to the west of Île Saint-Michel although there is often enough background light to see the unlit buoys in the eastern channel. The shallow area south-southwest of this island (Banc du Turc) is a hazard below half tide, so use the 350° DirOc(2)R.6s leading lights on top of the submarine pens until the middle of the Kernével Marina is abeam to port when the white sector of Pte de L'Espérance light (DirQ.WRG) then leads all the way up the harbour on 037°. The QR light on the end of the jetty at the RoRo terminal can be used to identify the entrance to the marina.

The entrance to the Blavet channel is marked by lit port and starboard lateral buoys and the starboard-hand buoys in the lower reaches of the river are also lit. Using these, it is possible to find a temporary anchorage out of the channel.

By GPS

Visual pilotage is required in the harbour. The following waypoints may provide assistance.

For Kernével, Pen Mané, or the Port de Commerce use:

⊕191-Cochon, ⊕192-Kernével, ⊕193-Pen Mané, ⊕194-Commerce

For the Blavet replace ⊕194-Commerce with ⊕198-Blavet

For Locmiquélic use:

⊕191-Cochon, ⊕196-Anéno, ⊕197-Locmiquélic

BERTHS AND ANCHORAGES

Kernével Marina

Kernével is on the west of the harbour 0.5M beyond the narrows. It is protected by a line of floating wavebreakers secured to piles. These have recently been moved eastwards and the marina enlarged. The north entrance is used when looking for a berth. The south entrance leads to the fuel pontoon, a slipway for hauling out and scrubbing berths. The visitors' pontoon is at the southern end of the north basin. Beware that since the marina has been enlarged out into the tideway the current in the marina can cause dificulties when berthing.

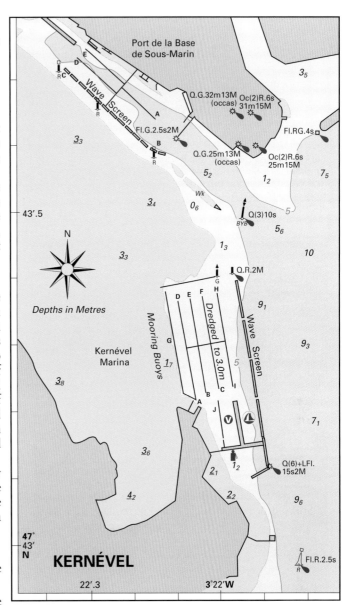

Apart from a chandler there are limited facilities nearby but bicycles are available free of charge from the helpful marina staff. Wi-Fi available. Two large supermarkets are situated about a mile northwest round the bay and there is a frequent bus service to Lorient, where workshops and engineers can be found.

Lorient Harbour (Port de Commerce)

The marina is a fully pontooned yacht harbour in pleasant surroundings. At busy times yachts will be met by marina staff in a launch and directed to a pontoon; otherwise tie up on the south side where convenient and arrange a berth with the helpful staff in the capitainerie. Only those planning to stay more than a few days can berth in the wet basin which is entered via a lifting bridge and a lock gate. Entry to and exit from the wet basin is only possible for one hour either side of HW at springs, less at neaps.

The pontoons between the entrance to the avant-port and the Île de Groix ferry terminal are reserved for local boats.

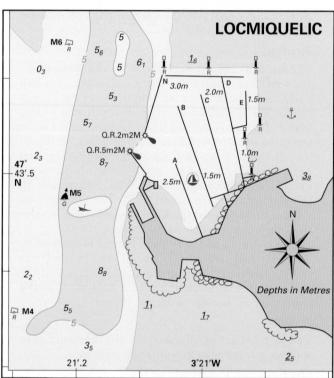

Lorient Marina (formerly the Port de Commerce) looking northwest.
The Wet Basin at the top of the harbour is only open for one hour either side of HW at springs and less at neaps. Visitors usually stay in the Avant Port near the capitainerie

It is a lively place and has all facilities including a 45 tonne travel-lift. Fuel is at Kernével. Covered market seven minutes walk away in Avenue Anatole France. The rail and bus services from Lorient are good and Lorient Airport has flights to Paris.

Locmiquélic (Ste-Catherine)

This marina has all the normal facilities and space for visitors can usually be found. It is entered from the channel east of Île Saint-Michel. There is a wreck with only 0.4m over it, marked by M5 SHM buoy, just south of the marina entrance and a boat should pass west of this buoy when the tide is low.

The marina has recently been enclosed with floating breakwaters and the facilities upgraded with a new shower/toilet block and laundry. At night the entrance is lit but, as the channel is unlit, it is easiest for the stranger to approach from north of Île Saint-Michel. There are no dedicated visitors' berths but

Lorient. Locmiquelic Marina ferry *R Rundle*

visitors are welcome. Call the Capitainerie on VHF 09 or ☎ 02 97 33 59 51 for a berth (office hours). Fuel is at Kernével but there is a pump-out facility. Wi-Fi available.

Locmiquélic Marina (formerly St-Catherine's) with Pen-Mané at middle right and the entrance to Lorient Marina at the top left of picture

There are shops and the usual facilities of a small town about 500m from the marina. Free bicycles available. Frequent waterbus to Lorient where it links with a bus into the town centre.

Pen-Mané marina

This modern marina at the mouth of the Blavet is attractive and peaceful and is under the same management as Locmiquélic. Repair and servicing for both marinas takes place at Pen-Mané where there is a yachtyard. It is a long way from the shops but there is a waterbus to Lorient.

There are no visitors' berths but a place can usually be found by speaking to the management at Locmiquélic on VHF 09 or ✆ 02 97 33 59 51 (office hours).

Base de Sous-Marin

This is a brand new marina at the submarine pens close to the 'Cité de la Voile Eric Tabarly' exhibition. The marina is dedicated to professional yachtsmen and women in the Eric Tabarly and Ellen MacArthur mould. Several of the late Eric Tabarly's Pen Duick yachts are berthed here. The casual cruiser will be politely told to find somewhere else unless he has a yacht over 20m long and/or a very deep draft up to 6m and cannot be accommodated elsewhere. Large multihulls will also be found a berth.

There are excellent facilities and they are willing to help sort out complex electronic and constructional problems. ✆ 02 97 87 00 46, *Mobile* 06 28 56 3149 or VHF Ch 09 for advice.

The marina also specialises in hosting national and international rallies and in being a 'stop' for passage races.

⚓ The River Blavet and Hennebont

The upper reaches of this little-visited river are most attractive, with an abundance of bird-life. At half tide it is possible to find plenty of water all the way to Hennebont. The two shallowest patches lie just after Pointe de Beger Vil and in the reach before the power cables after the second road bridge where only 1.5m could be found at LW neaps.

Three bridges cross the river between the entrance and Hennebont. The first two have 22m clearance and the last 21m. Power cables cross the river above the second bridge. Their height is unknown but they appear to be higher than the bridges.

The channel is marked by buoys or beacons to the second road bridge. Above the first bridge at Bonhomme the river narrows and winds a further four miles to Hennebont.

A concrete obstruction, which dries, is reported to lie under the second road bridge, approximately one third of the way out from the left supporting column (heading upriver). When passing under the bridge keep to the centre, or to starboard if proceeding upriver.

There are many possible anchorages on the way to Hennebont, where there is a small, short-stay pontoon (12 hours max) just before the bridge. The bottom is very soft mud so an overnight stay may be possible. There is also one head and stern visitors' mooring for yachts less than 10m at the far end of the trot.

Hennebont is a pleasant walled market town with a market in the square on Thursday mornings. There are shops, including a large supermarket, banks and restaurants. Fuel can be obtained from a garage close to the bridge and there is a water tap close to the pontoon. It has good rail connections.

32 Port Louis and Locmalo

Location
47°42'N 3°22'W

Shelter
Excellent in marina

Hazards
Intricate entry to Locmalo

Depth restrictions
1.1m in approach to Port Louis
0.2m in approach to Locmalo

Night entry
Partially lit but not recommended

HW time
Brest HW +0005 neaps, −0020 springs

Mean height of tide (m)

	HWS	HWN	LWN	LWS
Port Louis	5.1	4.0	2.0	0.8

Tidal streams
Approach as Lorient
4kns in entrance to Locmalo

Berthing
Marina at Port Louis;
anchorage at Locmalo

Facilities
All facilities; interesting historic town

Charts:
BA 2821 (50), 304 (10)
SHOM 7031 (50), 7140 (20)
Imray C38 (large scale)

Radio VHF Ch 9

Telephone
Port Louis Marina
☏ 02 97 82 59 55

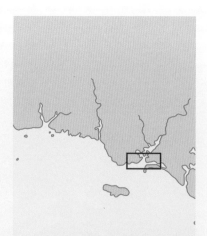

The other side of Lorient

Port Louis is no distance from Lorient by water but a world away in charm and character. It is a small tuna port and seaside resort with a magnificent 16th century citadel which contains several interesting museums with a nautical theme including an excellent lifeboat museum and one about the Compagnie des Indes.

There is a marina on the north side of the town. To the south, completely protected by the Gâvres peninsula, is the delightful bay of Locmalo.

PILOTAGE

(see plan on page 113).

Port Louis entrance

By day

Leave the main channel north of the citadel near Le Cochon RGR tower beacon and steer about 100° leaving two SHM buoys to starboard. Just beyond the second SHM buoy is a SHM beacon marking the end of a slip and the beginning of the channel to the marina. Keep close to the starboard side of the channel because the bay shoals quickly.

By night

Not recommended.

By GPS

Use the instructions for the Passe de l'Ouest or Passe du Sud to ⊕191-Cochon and continue towards ⊕195-Port Louis.

Locmalo NW entrance

Warning

A large-scale chart is essential.

By day

Pass north of La Potée de Beurre SHM beacon tower with the north side of Île aux Souris in transit with the end of the ferry slip on the south side of the entrance to the Baie de Locmalo, bearing 112°.

A Tall ship in the Narrows approaching Port Louis Citadel

Port Louis from the south with some of the new pontoons in position

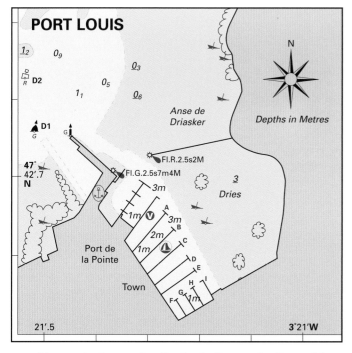

Alternatively use La Potée de Beurre in line with Larmor church spire on a back bearing of 278°. On approaching Île aux Souris, with a green light tripod on its western side, alter course to leave the islet to starboard and steer on the north side of the channel. Leave a green buoy to starboard and pass between the red and green beacon towers. The channel then curves northeast towards the jetty at Locmalo.

By night

Not recommended.

By GPS

This entrance requires careful visual pilotage.
⊕185-Lorient 1, ⊕190-Souris
may provide some assistance.

Locmalo southwest entrance

Warning

A large-scale chart is essential.

By day

Start at the Locmalo SHM buoy 0.75M southwest of Île aux Souris and head for Île aux Souris, on a heading of 045°. Once past Le Soulard IDM tower beacon alter course to about 000° to pass between Le Cabon reef and Île aux Souris. Beware that neither the beacon on Le Cabon, nor the light beacon on Île aux Souris mark the extremities of the dangers. Le Pesquerez SHM pole beacon astern should be kept just open west of Le Soulard. After Île aux Souris has been passed the channel described above is joined.

By night

Partially lit but not recommended.

By GPS

This entrance requires careful visual pilotage.
⊕188-Locmalo, ⊕189-Cabon, ⊕190-Souris
may provide some assistance.

BERTHS AND ANCHORAGES

Port Louis

Port Louis welcomes visitors but in 2009 the harbour was closed for dredging and expansion of berthing space. The harbour is to be re-opened in 2010. The visitors' pontoon will be the second one in from the entrance. A new capitainerie and shower block is to follow.

There are also some moorings in the shoaling bay to the east of the citadel, which may be available on application to the yacht club.

The nearest fuel and repair facilities are at Kernével.

Locmalo

There are many moorings off Pen-er-Run and it may be possible to borrow one. The pool east of the Grand and Petit Belorc'h beacons is clear of moorings and offers good anchorage in up to 4m.

Facilities at Locmalo

There are shops, banks and restaurants at Port Louis. The best dinghy landing is at Locmalo jetty.

Ban-Gâvres

There is a marina at Ban-Gâvres, opposite Locmalo. It has six berths for visitors (max length 10m) on a pontoon in 2m but with difficult manoeuvring. ☎02 97 65 48 25. There are also moorings available.

⚓ Larmor-Plage

Protected from west and north there is a rather open anchorage opposite Port Louis in the approaches to Lorient. Leave the main channel near Toulhars PHM buoy and head towards the two red beacons near Larmor breakwater. It is possible to anchor near the north red beacon. At neaps anchor beyond the beacons towards the Plage de Toulhars. Keep clear of the two cardinal beacons that mark a wreck. A large-scale chart is essential.
⊕186-Larmor Plage 47°42'·29N 3°22'·74W

⚓ Anse de Goërem

Sheltered from the east there is a useful bay at the west end of the Gâvres peninsula. Anchor south of La Pesquerez beacon. It is rather exposed for a night anchorage but it possible to leave at night using the lit Locmalo SHM buoy south-southwest of La Paix.
⊕188-Locmalo 47°41'·67N 3°22'·20W

ASHORE IN PORT LOUIS

There are plenty of shops, bars and restaurants. Port Louis itself is a pleasant and interesting 18th century walled town. Frequent waterbus to Lorient. The citadel contains museums and there are good views of Lorient and Groix from the ramparts.

III. GROIX AND THE RIAS

33 Port Tudy

Location
47°38'N 3°28'W

Shelter
Good except from N or NE

Hazards
Unmarked rocks near leading line
Ferries manoeuvring in harbour

Depth restrictions
2.0m on visitors' moorings

Lock to inner harbour HW ±0200

Night entry Lit

HW time
Brest HW neaps, -0025 springs

Mean height of tide (m)

	HWS	HWN	LWN	LWS
Port Tudy	5.1	4.0	2.0	0.9

Tidal stream in approaches
E – Brest HW–0400 to HW (0.4kns)
Slack – Brest HW to +0200
W – Brest HW +0200 to +0600 (0.4kns)
Slack – Brest HW -0600 to -0400

Berthing
Visitors' buoys and marina

Fuel
SE corner of inner harbour (cans)

Facilities As of a small port

Charts
BA 2821 (50)
SHOM 7031 (50), 7139 (20/5)
Imray C38 (large scale)

Radio VHF Ch 9

Telephone
Harbourmaster ① 02 97 86 54 62

Attractive busy harbour

Port Tudy is an attractive 19th-century tuna port that is now almost entirely devoted to tourism. The outer harbour is rather exposed to the north and northeast, which makes it uncomfortable if the *brise de terre* blows in the early hours of the morning.

It is the only real port in Île de Groix (*see plan on page 125*) and gets very crowded, particularly at weekends. The large number of tourists and the noisy ferries make Port Tudy lively but rarely peaceful.

Port Tudy looking south.
All three harbours may be used by visitors if there is space. Boats can moor fore and aft between buoys in the outer harbour. There are pontoon berths in the inner harbour or boats raft to the pontoons in the wet dock

PILOTAGE

Port Tudy approach and entrance

By day

The harbour is easily identified and the approach from the west and north is straightforward; there are some mooring buoys and a fishfarm off Port Lay, but no other dangers.

From the east and southeast there are some unmarked dangers. The safe transit uses the harbour pierhead lights in line on 217°. This leaves a rock (depth 0.8m) 200m to port. A red beacon marks some other dangers closer inshore.

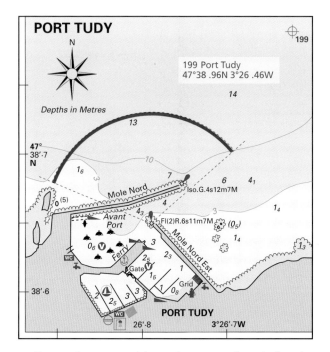

PORT TUDY

N

Depths in Metres

199 Port Tudy
47°38 .96N 3°26 .46W

14

13

47°
38'·7
N

10

1₆

7

6

4₁

Mole Nord

Iso.G.4s12m7M

4

3

1₄

0 (5)

Avant
Port

4₃

Fl(2)R.6s11m7M

(0₅)

1₄

0₆ ⓥ

Ferry

3

Mole Nord Est

2₃

1

1₃

WC

Gate ⓥ

2₅

1₅

1

0₈

Grid

2

2₅

3

PORT TUDY

WC

26'·8

3°26'·7W

Enter the port midway between the pierheads, then steer parallel to the north mole to avoid the rocks at the end of the east mole. If a ferry is manoeuvring, stand off as it needs all the room there is.

By night

The buoys in the approach are unlit. The east pierhead light is obscured over the dangers to the east of the harbour. It is therefore safe to keep this light showing and just open to the left of the north pierhead light. If they are exactly in transit the rear light is obscured.

By GPS

From Lorient or the northwest use:
⊕199-Port Tudy

From Etel use:
⊕200-Mélite, ⊕199-Port Tudy

From the SE use:
⊕202-Cougy, ⊕200-Mélite, ⊕199-Port Tudy

BERTHS AND ANCHORAGES

Port Tudy outer harbour

In season yachts entering the harbour will be met by a harbour launch and directed to a berth. In the outer harbour yachts moor fore and aft between the large white mooring buoys, ensuring that there is room for the ferry to manoeuvre. Long warps are necessary and springs are advisable to ensure that spreaders will not foul if the swell gets up. The landing slip is reserved for ferries.

Port Tudy inner harbour

The inner harbour shoals inward but there is plenty of water for most yachts. There are pontoon berths and alongside berths where rafting may be necessary. The inner harbour berths are much more expensive than those in the outer harbour.

Port Tudy wet dock

Entry to the wet dock is possible for two hours either side of HW. If waiting for the gates to open it is better to moor to a pontoon rather than the inner landing slip as there is a stone shelf which protrudes below the top end of the slip near the gates.

Visitors will be directed to a berth in 2–3m. The wet basin is the most crowded part of the harbour; yachts are rafted to the pontoons and it is really only useful for a prolonged stay.

⚓ Port Tudy anchorage

The harbour has no room to anchor and the bottom is foul. In settled weather it is possible to anchor outside the harbour provided that the ferries are not obstructed. However, their wash makes the anchorage rather uncomfortable.

⚓ Port-Melin and Beg-er-Vir

Open to the north but protected from the south Port-Melin is a small cove 1M west of Port Tudy and Beg-er-Vir is the larger bay west of Port-Melin. Approach from the north at LW taking care to avoid the rock ledges. Anchor in 2m on sand. A large scale chart is essential.

Port-Lay

Open to the north, this very pretty harbour is believed to be one of the tiniest in Brittany. It is 0.5M west of port Tudy and anchoring is forbidden but the local sailing school has some mooring buoys which can sometimes be borrowed.

⚓ Pointe de la Croix

Protected from the southwest but otherwise rather exposed there are a number of possible anchorages off the beach near Pointe de la Croix.
⊕201-Pte de la Croix 47°38'·14N 3°24'·87W

ASHORE IN PORT TUDY

Fuel is available in cans from the depot at the southeast corner of the inner harbour. There is a marine engineer, a hauling-out slip, some chandlery and a launderette on the quay. There are cafés around the harbour and bread may be obtained nearby. All other shops, including a supermarket, are available up the hill in the town.

Bicycles may be hired to explore this picturesque island and there are frequent ferries to Lorient.

Port Tudy. Fore-and-aft visitors' moorings in outer harbour

III. GROIX AND THE RIAS

34 Locmaria

Location
47°37′N 3°26′W

Shelter
Locmaria – open to S

Hazards
Many unmarked rocks

Depth restrictions
1.0m in Loc Maria anchorage

Night entry Not recommended

HW time
Brest HW neaps, −0030 springs

Mean height of tide (m)

	HWS	HWN	LWN	LWS
Port Tudy	5.1	4.0	2.0	0.9

Tidal stream Pte des Chats
NE – Brest HW−0600 to −0200 (0.5kns)
Slack – Brest HW−0200 to +0100
SW – Brest HW+0100 to +0500 (0.5kns)
Slack – Brest HW+0500 to −0600

Berthing
Moorings and Anchorages

Facilities
A few shops and bars, good beach, nice 1.5 M walk to Port Tudy

Charts
BA 2821 (50)
SHOM 7031 (50), 7139 (20)
Imray C38 (large scale)

Charming unspoilt harbour

This charming unspoilt little harbour is situated on the south of Île de Groix, 0.75M west of Pointe des Chats (*see plan on page 125*). It is well worth a visit under the right conditions.

The approach is open to the Atlantic, and the anchorage is dangerously exposed to swell or wind with any south in it. However, it is well sheltered from the west through north to east. The harbour dries but outside there is space to moor or anchor in depths of 1m or more.

Locmaria harbour looking east.
The harbour itself is full of moorings but there are 20 visitors' buoys outside

PILOTAGE

Locmaria approach and entrance

By day

Coming from the north, east or southeast it will be necessary to make a detour round Les Chats (*see plan on page 125*).

From an initial position S of Les Chats, Locmaria will be seen on the east side of the bay, together with Er Brazelleg SHM beacon tower and a white masonry beacon on the land. There is another village on the west side. Between the villages, on the northwest side of the bay, is a small group of cottages with a small white masonry beacon in front of them. These form the leading line. (See photo).

Approach Er Brazelleg on 005° until the cottages and beacon have been identified. The transit for the

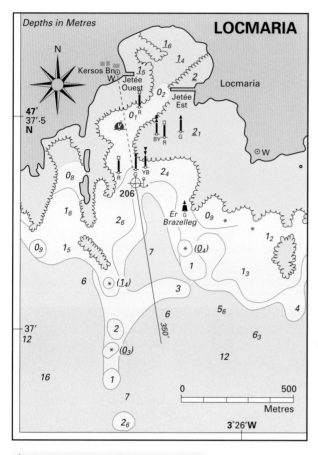

Locmaria visitors' moorings

entrance is the Kersos small white masonry beacon on the edge of the cliff in line with the centre window of a white cottage on 350°. There are several cottages in the area but the correct one is the right-hand, lowest one of a group of three. Unfortunately the centre window was obscured by a fig tree in 2009 but the middle of the roof of the cottage can still be used once the right one has been identified by a bearing of 350° on the small white beacon in front of it. The group of cottages is distinctive because the left-hand one shows its gable end.

Follow the transit between the first port and starboard beacons. The line to the second port beacon passes close to the rocks so keep on the transit until the pier head bears about 055°. Then bear to starboard for the pier head, keeping rather closer to the inner port-hand beacon.

Locmaria. The cottage, whose middle window used to be the rear marker, with the white beacon in front of it

The drying harbour from the visitors' moorings

III. GROIX AND THE RIAS

By night

There are no lights and a night entry should not be attempted.

By GPS

From Port Tudy use:

⊕199-Port Tudy, ⊕200-Mélite, ⊕202-Cougy, ⊕203-SE Chats, ⊕204-Les Chats, ⊕205-Locmaria, ⊕206-Locmaria 1

In good weather with enough rise of tide, ⊕203-SE Chats (*see plan on page 125*) can be omitted but the resulting route must be used with care because it passes close to the unmarked dangers of Les Chats.

From Lorient, join the above route at:

⊕202-Cougy; from Etel join at⊕203-SE Chats (plan 33C)

BERTHS AND ANCHORAGES

⚓ Locmaria

The harbour is choked with small-boat moorings and there is no room to anchor and remain afloat. There are 20 visitors' mooring buoys laid just outside the harbour in about 1m but they are quite usable at neaps. There is also a good anchorage just outside the reef, south of the SCM beacon, in about 2m. It is not possible to lie alongside the jetty because it may be used for landing.

Locmaria is an attractive white painted village that feels like somewhere much further south. There are shops, a bar and a crêperie and good beaches. It is a pleasant walk of 1.5M to Port Tudy and there are many other walks in the area.

⚓ Port Saint-Nicolas

Protected from northwest to east and from the *brise de terre* but wide open to the southwest, this magical crack in the cliffs is about 1M east of Pen Men. It can be identified by a masonry day mark 900m to the west of the cove.

Approach from the southwest and, leaving Pointe Saint-Nicolas to starboard, steer for the centre of the cove. The bottom is sand with a lot of rock and weed so it is best to buoy the anchor. Since there is not much swinging room, it may be necessary to use two anchors.

Port St-Nicolas

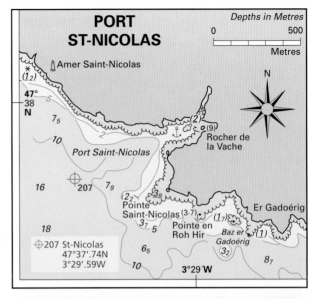

Port St-Nicolas looking northeast.
This magical and challenging crack in the cliffs has very little swinging room

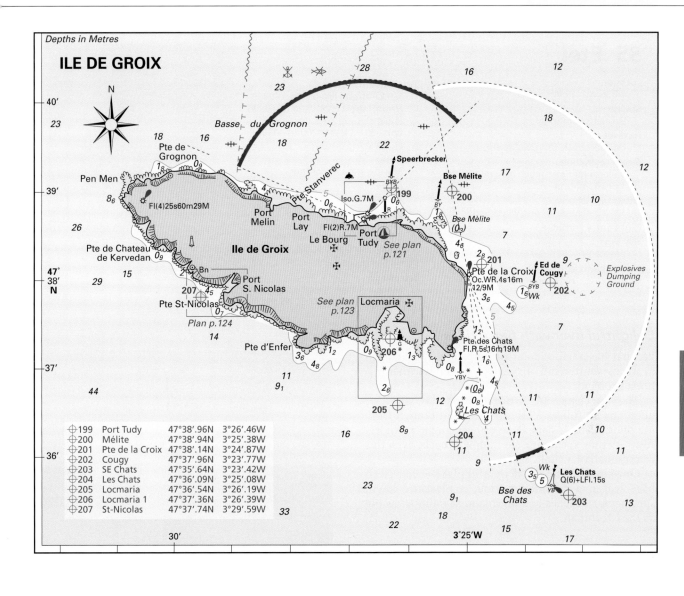

Depths in Metres

ILE DE GROIX

⊕199	Port Tudy	47°38'.96N	3°26'.46W
⊕200	Mélite	47°38'.94N	3°25'.38W
⊕201	Pte de la Croix	47°38'.14N	3°24'.87W
⊕202	Cougy	47°37'.96N	3°23'.77W
⊕203	SE Chats	47°35'.64N	3°23'.42W
⊕204	Les Chats	47°36'.09N	3°25'.08W
⊕205	Locmaria	47°36'.54N	3°26'.19W
⊕206	Locmaria 1	47°37'.36N	3°26'.39W
⊕207	St-Nicolas	47°37'.74N	3°29'.59W

35 Etel

Location
47°39'N 3°13'W

Shelter
Excelent in marina

Hazards
Dangerous shifting bar at entrance

Depth restrictions
0.6m, sometimes much less, on bar
1.5m in marina

Other restrictions
Must call pilot for entry instructions

Night entry Forbidden

HW time
Brest HW +0020 neaps, -0010 springs

Mean height of tide (m)

	HWS	HWN	LWN	LWS
Etel	4.9	4.1	2.2	1.5

Tidal stream in river
Slack – Brest HW–0500 to –0400
Flood – Brest HW–0400 to +0200
(1.5kns)
Ebb – Brest HW+0200 to –0500
(1.3kns)

Berthing
Marina and anchorages

Facilities
All facilities

Charts
BA 2821 (50), 304 (10)
SHOM 7031 (50), 7138 (10)
Imray C38 (large scale)

Radio Semaphore d'Etel VHF Ch 13

Telephone
Marina ① 02 9755 46 62
Semaphore ① 02 97 55 35 59

Delightful river with fierce tides

Etel bar has a bad reputation and should be avoided in strong south wind or swell. In settled weather it is not a problem.

The bar can shift from day to day so it is necessary to follow VHF directions in French from the pilot, Mme Josiane Pene or her daughter, André-Ann. As they speak in clear simple French, even this is not much of a challenge.

Once inside, Etel is a delightful place. It has clean blue water, a friendly marina, a pleasant town, spectacular beaches and an inland sea almost as big as the Morbihan.

PILOTAGE

Etel Bar and the semaphore

During the approach it is essential to make contact with the semaphore station and until then to keep at least 0.5M off. The following visual signals are displayed:

- Arrow horizontal: no entry for any vessels
- Black ball: no entry for undecked vessels under 8m length
- Red flag: Not enough water or pilot not on duty.

Once VHF contact has been established, Madame Josiane Pene or her daughter, will give instructions in clear, simple French. If no VHF notify ETA by phone beforehand.

The semaphore is hardly ever used but if necessary it is easy to understand. Mme Pene simply points the arrow right or left depending on the direction she wants the boat to turn or leaves it vertical to signal to maintain present course. (Beware that the vertical position is also the stowed position.)

The harbourmaster recommends crossing the bar between Port Tudy HW–0200 and –0100 (roughly Brest HW–0230 to –0130). Note that the flood stream will still be running strongly.

The semaphore station at Etel with the semaphore arrow in the vertical position. If it is horizontal it means that there is no entry for vessels. If the red flag is flying then either there is not enough water or the pilot is not on duty

ETEL APPROACH AND ENTRANCE

By day

The position of the deepest water across the bar varies considerably and can change overnight. However, it is usually best to approach with the distinctive 76m red and white radio mast at the back of the town on 020°.

The stream is weak outside the bar, but may reach six knots as the port-hand beacon is passed. Shortly after entering the river continue along the west side, leaving an unlit red beacon to port, a green buoy and beacon to starboard and a final red buoy to port. From there, keep in the centre of the channel where the water is deep.

By night

Visitors must not attempt to enter at night.

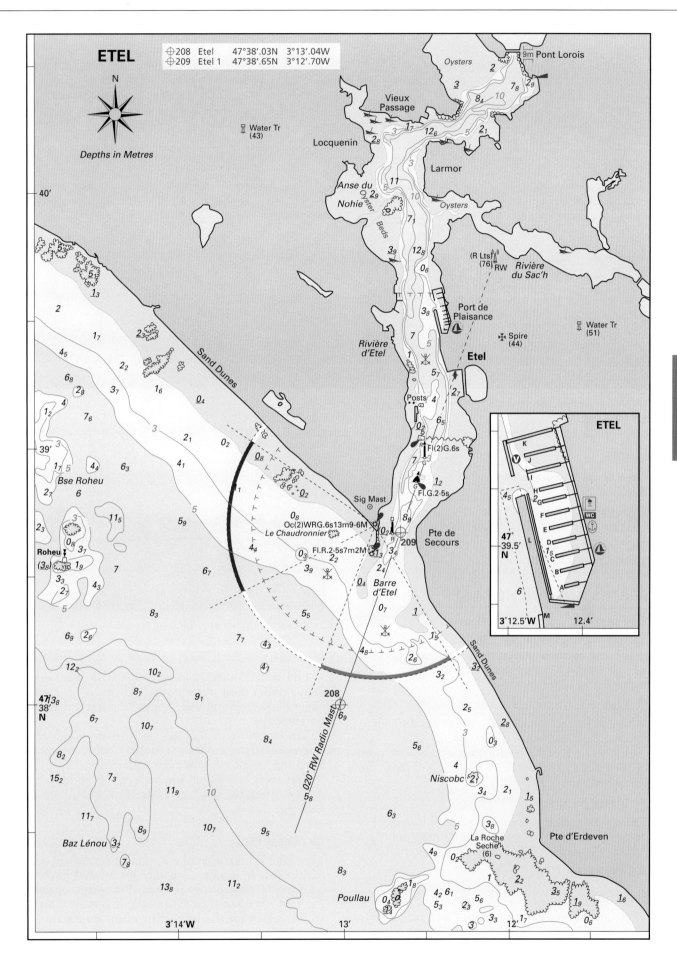

ETEL

| ⊕208 | Etel | 47°38'.03N | 3°13'.04W |
| ⊕209 | Etel 1 | 47°38'.65N | 3°12'.70W |

N

Depths in Metres

Water Tr (43)

Oysters

Vieux Passage

Pont Lorois
9m

Locquenin

Larmor

Anse du Nohie

Oyster Beds

Oysters

Rivière du Sac'h
(R Lts) (76) RW

Port de Plaisance

Water Tr (51)

Spire (44)

Etel

Rivière d'Etel

Sand Dunes

Posts

Fl(2)G.6s

Fl.G.2·5s

Sig Mast

Oc(2)WRG.6s13m9-6M
Le Chaudronnier

Fl.R.2·5s7m2M

209

Pte de Secours

Bse Roheu

Roheu (3₈) VBS

Barre d'Etel

208

020° RW Radio Mast

Niscobc

La Roche Seche (6)

Pte d'Erdeven

Baz Lénou

Poullau

3°14'W

13'

12'

ETEL (inset)

K J V L M

47° 39.5' N

3°12.5'W

12.4'

III. GROIX AND THE RIAS

The visitors' berths are on the inside of the wavebreaker in the front on the left

By GPS

From the west or south use

⊕208-Etel

From the south use

⊕210-Chivguete, ⊕208-Etel

The continuation into the river will depend on instructions from the pilot.

BERTHS AND ANCHORAGES

Etel marina

The marina has a depth of 2.5m. Larger boats secure to the new northern wave-breaker. Smaller boats use a finger berth. Beware that the current is much less strong once inside the marina.

⚓ Etel

Moorings occupy the best places and it is difficult to find an anchorage out of the stream.

Just above Etel the holding is good on both sides of the river, but springs run at 6kns and there are oyster beds in the shallows.

⚓ Vieux passage

There is an anchorage just above Vieux Passage, but do not go far into the bay as the bottom is foul.

ASHORE IN ETEL

Facilities

There are limited repair facilities and fuel is only available in cans.

Etel Marina entrance seen between the two yachts

Etel is a thriving holiday resort with plenty of shops, bars and restaurants. There is a good supermarket, several fish shops and a street market on Tuesdays.

The beaches on either side of the river mouth are interesting. They have a particularly rich sand dune flora and are also very popular with male nudists.

The tuna festival is on the second Sunday in August when the town gives itself over to fun and feasting.

La Mer d'Etel

The Mer d'Etel is a like a small version of the Morbihan. It is not navigable by masted yachts because the road bridge only has 9m clearance and the tide runs very fast. However, it is well worth seeing it from the tourist boat that runs several times a day in season.

IV. Quiberon Bay

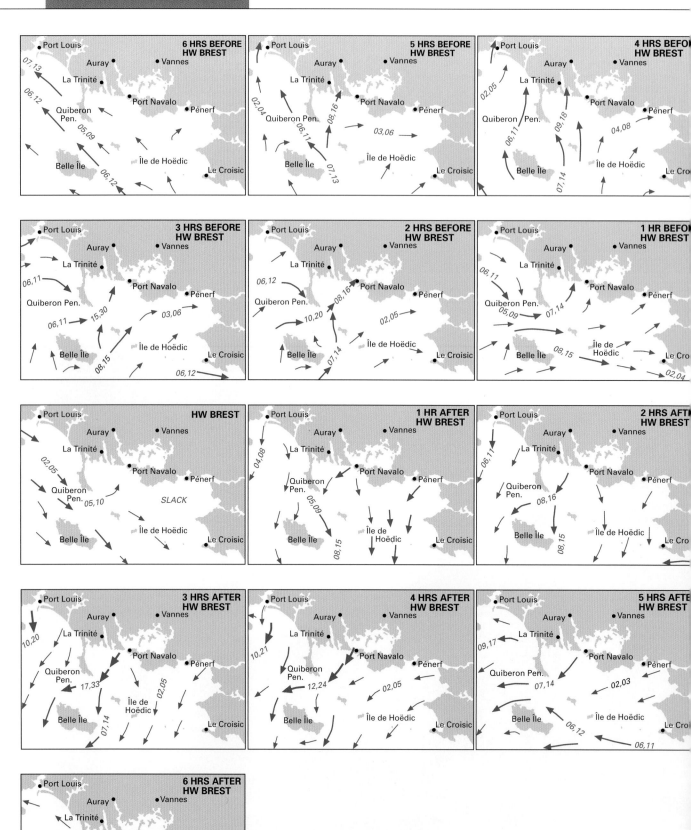

QUIBERON BAY TIDAL STREAMS

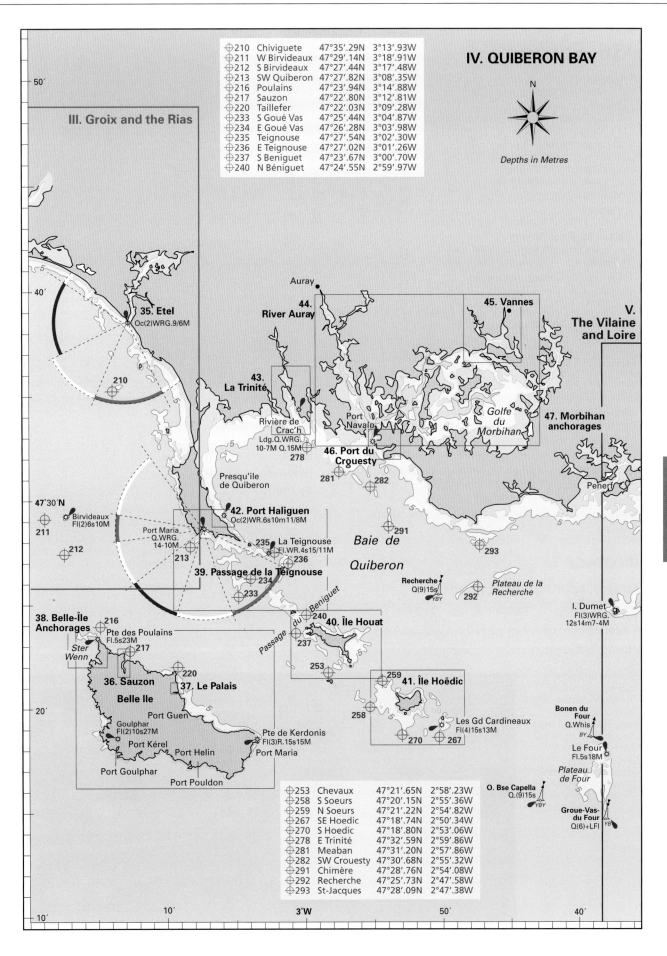

⊕	210	Chiviguete	47°35'.29N	3°13'.93W
⊕	211	W Birvideaux	47°29'.14N	3°18'.91W
⊕	212	S Birvideaux	47°27'.44N	3°17'.48W
⊕	213	SW Quiberon	47°27'.82N	3°08'.35W
⊕	216	Poulains	47°23'.94N	3°14'.88W
⊕	217	Sauzon	47°22'.80N	3°12'.81W
⊕	220	Taillefer	47°22'.03N	3°09'.28W
⊕	233	S Goué Vas	47°25'.44N	3°04'.87W
⊕	234	E Goué Vas	47°26'.28N	3°03'.98W
⊕	235	Teignouse	47°27'.54N	3°02'.30W
⊕	236	E Teignouse	47°27'.02N	3°01'.26W
⊕	237	S Beniguet	47°23'.67N	3°00'.70W
⊕	240	N Béniguet	47°24'.55N	2°59'.97W

IV. QUIBERON BAY

N

Depths in Metres

III. Groix and the Rias

50'

40'

47°30'N

20'

10'

Auray

44. River Auray

45. Vannes

V. The Vilaine and Loire

43. La Trinité

Rivière de Crac'h
Ldg.Q.WRG.
10-7M Q.15M
278

Port Navalo

Golfe du Morbihan

47. Morbihan anchorages

46. Port du Crouesty

281

282

Penerf

Presqu'île de Quiberon

35. Etel
Oc(2)WRG.9/6M

210

Birvideaux
Fl(2)6s10M

211

212

Port Maria.
Q.WRG.
14-10M

213

42. Port Haliguen
Oc(2)WR.6s10m11/8M

235

La Teignouse
Fl.WR.4s15/11M

236

234

233

Baie de

Quiberon

291

293

39. Passage de la Teignouse

Recherche
Q(9)15s
YBY

Plateau de la Recherche

292

I. Dumet
Fl(3)WRG.
12s14m7-4M

38. Belle-Île Anchorages

216

Pte des Poulains
Fl.5s23M

217

Ster Wenn

220

36. Sauzon

Belle Ile

37. Le Palais

Port Guen

Goulphar
Fl(2)10s27M

Port Kérel

Pte de Kerdonis
Fl(3)R.15s15M

Port Maria

Port Helin

Port Goulphar

Port Pouldon

240

237

40. Île Houat

253

259

41. Île Hoëdic

258

Les Gd Cardineaux
Fl(4)15s13M

270

267

Bonen du Four
Q.Whis
BY

Le Four
Fl.5s18M

Plateau de Four

O. Bse Capella
Q.(9)15s
YBY

Groue-Vas-du Four
Q(6)+LFl
YB

⊕	253	Chevaux	47°21'.65N	2°58'.23W
⊕	258	S Soeurs	47°20'.15N	2°55'.36W
⊕	259	N Soeurs	47°21'.22N	2°54'.82W
⊕	267	SE Hoedic	47°18'.74N	2°50'.34W
⊕	270	S Hoedic	47°18'.80N	2°53'.06W
⊕	278	E Trinité	47°32'.59N	2°59'.86W
⊕	281	Meaban	47°31'.20N	2°57'.86W
⊕	282	SW Crouesty	47°30'.68N	2°55'.32W
⊕	291	Chimère	47°28'.76N	2°54'.08W
⊕	292	Recherche	47°25'.73N	2°47'.58W
⊕	293	St-Jacques	47°28'.09N	2°47'.38W

10'

10'

3°W

50'

40'

36 Sauzon

Location
47°22'N 3°13'W

Shelter
Reasonable from S to W but exposed to N and *vent solaire*

Depth restrictions
2.5m on visitors' moorings
1.0m in outer harbour
Inner harbour dries 1.8m

Night entry Lit

HW time
Brest HW −0005 neaps, −0025 springs

Mean height of tide (m)

	HWS	HWN	LWN	LWS
Le Palais	5.1	4.0	1.9	0.7

Tidal stream Sauzon approaches
SE – Brest HW−0530 to −0130 (0.8kns)
Slack – Brest HW−0130 to +0030
NW – Brest HW+0030 to +0530 (0.9kns)
Slack – Brest HW+0530 to −0530

Berthing
Visitors' buoys and drying harbour
Anchoring outside possible

Facilities
Cafés, restaurants, a few shops and bike hire

Charts
BA 2822 (50)
SHOM 7032 (50), 7142 (25)
Imray C38 (78)

Radio VHF Ch 9

The jewel of Belle-Île

Sauzon is an attractive little harbour on the north coast of Belle-Île. It is well placed for exploring the magnificent northwest coast and not far from Le Palais by bicycle.

The inner harbour dries but it is well set up for visitors and offers a secure haven for vessels that can take the ground. The outer harbour has a number of visitors' buoys. These are well sheltered from the south and west but exposed to the north and east and the *brise de terre*. There are also about 20 visitors' buoys outside the harbour.

PILOTAGE

Sauzon approach and entrance

By day

The harbour is easy to identify. The Gareau SHM beacon tower off the Pointe du Cardinal north of the entrance is distinctive. Low white lighthouses, with red and green tops, mark the ends of the two outer breakwaters. In addition, the taller main lighthouse, also with a green top, can be seen behind the breakwater lights.

The official transit aligns the two green-topped lighthouses on 205°. However, this need not be followed closely.

By night

The approach uses the day transit of the pier head and main green light in line on 205°. Note that these lights are obscured by the Pointe du Cardinal when approaching from the northwest so keep well north until they are positively identified.

There is very little light from the shore so a powerful spotlight will be necessary to find and pick up a buoy.

Sauzon Harbour looking southwest. The inner visitors' buoys are the two rows of bow and stern moorings on the west side near the ferry berth. The drying harbour, through the gap in the breakwater, has space available for boats that can take the ground

The entrance to Sauzon harbour *M&G Barron*

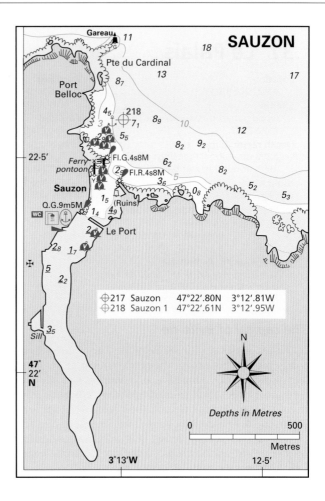

⊕217 Sauzon   47°22'.80N   3°12'.81W
⊕218 Sauzon 1   47°22'.61N   3°12'.95W

By GPS

From Penmarc'h use:

⊕137-S Glénan, ⊕216-Poulins, ⊕217-Sauzon, ⊕218-Sauzon 1

From Lorient or Groix use:

⊕211-W Birvideaux, ⊕217-Sauzon, ⊕218-Sauzon 1

Otherwise, from northwest through east, ⊕217-Sauzon can be approached directly.

From the southwest and Le Palais use:

⊕220-Taillefer, ⊕217-Sauzon, ⊕218-Sauzon 1

BERTHS AND ANCHORAGES

Outer visitors' buoys

There are visitors' buoys outside the outer north mole. These are suitable for boats up to 45ft and, with the harbourmaster's permission, it may be possible to use the larger buoys used by vedettes after they have departed for the night. Anchoring on the east side of the entrance is permitted when the mooring buoys are full.

Inner visitors' buoys

Between the outer and inner moles on the east side there are some white buoys that are reserved for fishermen. On the west side are two rows of bow and stern moorings for boats up to 12m. When the harbour is crowded, up to eight yachts may be rafted between each pair of buoys.

Inner harbour

The inner harbour dries to a firm sandy bottom. Boats able to take the ground may moor, secured bow and stern in the lines of red buoys inside the entrance, or anchor further up the harbour. It may also be possible to lie against a wall after consulting the harbourmaster.

The creek is over 500m long and if there is a crowd near the entrance there is plenty of room higher up for those prepared to dry out for longer each tide.

ASHORE IN SAUZON

There is a tap at the root of the inner west jetty. Showers and toilets are on the west wall of the inner harbour, near the harbourmaster's office. There are hotels, restaurants, bars but food shops are hard to find. Bicycles and scooters can be hired from a van in the carpark but walkers may prefer to explore the spectacular coast path.

Sauzon inner harbour *M&G Barron*

Sauzon outer visitors' moorings *W Krusekopf*

37 Le Palais

Location
47°21′N 3°09′W

Shelter
Good in harbour, anchorage sheltered
from SW

Depth restrictions
3.0m on visitors' moorings
1.7m or more in wet basin

Night entry Lit

HW time
Brest HW−0005 neaps, −0025 springs

Mean height of tide (m)

	HWS	HWN	LWN	LWS
Le Palais	5.1	4.0	1.9	0.7

Tidal stream Pte de Taillefer
SE – Brest HW−0530 to +0030 (1.1kns)
Slack – Brest HW+0030 to +0130
NW – Brest HW+0130 to −0530 (1.2kns)

Berthing
Visitors' buoys and wet basin
Anchorage outside harbour

Facilities
As of a busy tourist port

Charts
BA 2822 (50)
SHOM 7032 (50), 7142 (25)
Imray C38 (large scale)

Radio VHF Ch 9

The capital of Belle-Île

Le Palais is the capital of Belle-Île and a good base for exploring this magnificent island. It is also the site of the citadel, a massive, star-shaped fort built by Vauban in the 18th century. It was thought to be invulnerable but the British took it in 1761. It was restored to France two years later in exchange for Novia Scotia. Several Nova Scotian families settled on the island and introduced the potato some years before it became popular on the mainland.

Le Palais is the main ferry port for Belle-Île and unfortunately it gets very crowded in summer. To add to the fun, the frequent ferries need to maintain quite a high speed while they manoeuvre. They don't have much room, so it is vital for other craft to keep out of their way.

Le Palais looking east.
The harbour is in three parts: the outer harbour which contains the busy ferry terminal and a few moorings, the inner harbour which dries, and the wet basin and La Saline marina that extend past the citadel like a canal

PILOTAGE

Le Palais approach and entrance

By day
The citadel is easy to identify and there are no dangers in the approach. Steer for the lighthouse with the green top on the end of the north jetty and keep a sharp lookout for the ferries. They enter and leave at speed and take up most of the channel. In the entrance, keep in the middle of the channel because there are dangers off both pier heads.

By night
Steer for the lighthouse, flashing Q.G. and keep a sharp lookout for the unlit buoys near the entrance.

By GPS
From Penmarc'h use:

⊕137-S Glénan, ⊕216-Poulains, ⊕220-Taillefer,
⊕221-Le Palais

From Lorient use:

⊕220-Taillefer, ⊕221-Le Palais

From Etel use:

⊕210-Chiviguete, ⊕220-Taillefer, ⊕221-Le Palais

From the Teignouse, Beniguet or Sœurs passage,
⊕221-Le Palais can be approached directly.

From the southeast use:

⊕270-S Hoedic, ⊕221-Le Palais

BERTHS AND ANCHORAGES

Outer harbour

The outer harbour is well sheltered from the south and west. However, strong northeast winds cause seas to break over the breakwater and strong winds from any north or east direction can cause some swell to enter the harbour.

Yachts raft between bow and stern mooring buoys or between buoys and chains suspended from the breakwater wall. Either way, a dinghy is needed to get ashore. The moorings are subject to ferry wash

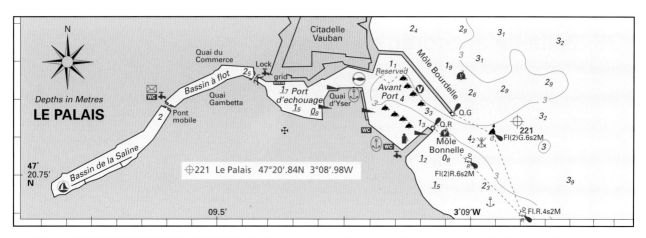

The Citadel from the Bassin à Flot

Visitors' moorings in the outer harbour

so it is necessary to check that spreaders are clear of adjacent yachts. If it is possible to arrange to arrive close to HW, when the gate is open, it is certainly much more comfortable in the wet basin but it is more expensive.

Inner harbour

It is possible to dry out in the inner harbour. Either moor bow to the north wall on either side of the grid, or alongside the quay if a space can be found. The bottom is foul in places so consult the harbourmaster. Note that the white stripes on the harbour walls reserve spaces for fishing boats and that anchoring is forbidden in the harbour.

The wet basin and La Saline marina

The gate to the wet dock opens local HW +0030 at neaps and +0130 at springs between the hours of 0600 and 2130. The opening times vary according to the tidal co-efficient so consult the harbourmaster for exact times. The lifting bridge, which gives access to the marina, is operated by the harbourmaster when required during the time the gate is open. In the wet dock, yachts raft up to a pontoon in 2.5m or there are finger berths in the marina.

⚓ Anchorage outside

Outside the harbour, anchor to the southeast of the south jetty in 3m, keeping well clear of the fairway. In offshore winds, this is safe and has good holding. Large mooring buoys have been placed east of the north pier for the use of local *vedettes* but, with the harbourmaster's permission, they can be used by visiting yachts after the *vedettes* have gone in the evening. There are also some smaller visitors' buoys to the south of the harbour entrance.

Anchoring is prohibited between the citadel at Le Palais and the approaches to Sauzon because of cables.

ASHORE IN LE PALAIS

Water, showers and toilets are available by the harbourmaster's office and also in the wet basin. Fuel, by long hose, can be purchased with a card at the root of the south breakwater. There are haul-out facilities, marine and electrical engineers, and chandlery.

Le Palais is a bustling tourist resort with a wide range of restaurants, bars and shops. It is possible to hire bicycles and cars to explore the island.

The Vauban citadel is a museum and also has fine views from the belvedere that runs round the central fortifications.

Le Palais entrance.
The Citadel on the right

IV. QUIBERON BAY

38 Belle-Île anchorages

Location
   47°23'N 3°15'W

Shelter
   All southern anchorages exposed to S and W

Night entry Not recommended

HW time
   Brest HW -0005 neaps, –0025 springs

Mean height of tide (m)

	HWS	HWN	LWN	LWS
Le Palais	5.1	4.0	1.9	0.7

Tidal streams
   Complex, strong at E and W ends of Belle Isle

Berthing Anchorages

Facilities Limited.

Charts
   BA 2822 (50)
   SHOM 7032 (50), 7142 (25)
   Imray C38 (78)

Beautiful Island

(See plan on page 139)

Belle-Île is 10M long and up to 5M wide, which makes it the largest island off the Brittany coast. There are many attractive anchorages that can be used as day anchorages or overnight in good weather. The north coast anchorages are well protected from the southwest but mostly open to the north and the *brise de terre*. The south coast is rugged, deeply indented and has a profusion of rocks. There are a number of anchorages that can be used in settled weather but it is no place to be in bad weather or if there is any swell from the south or west.

The Port du Vieux Château looking southeast.
The port is divided into two parts: the main inlet Stêr-Vraz, and a smaller inlet, Stêr-Wenn

Stêr-Wenn *W Krusekopf*

The inlet and anchorage of Stêr-Wenn looking south. Stêr-Vraz, the main inlet, can also be used as a day anchorage in very calm weather

Ster-Wenn
(Port du Vieux Château)

The most beautiful harbour in France

Stêr-Wenn is a beautiful fjord on the northwest coast of Belle-Île, about a mile south of Pointe des Poulains. The anchorage itself is perfectly sheltered except in strong onshore winds but the entrance (or exit) becomes a death trap in bad weather or heavy swell. It has been likened to a lobster pot: easy to get in but hard to get out. However, the French rate it as the most beautiful harbour in France so it is usually crowded. Needless to say, at the first hint of bad weather or swell, it is essential to get out.

The directions and plan should be used with caution because the largest-scale published chart is too small a scale to show much detail. The names Pointe Dangéreuse and Pointe Verticale are unofficial but they are appropriate.

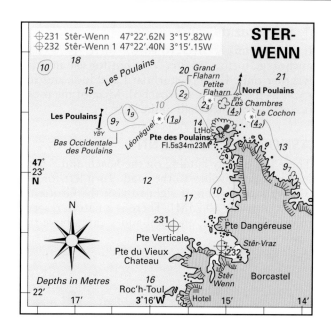

Stêr-Wenn on a busy summer day *M&G Barron*

PILOTAGE

Stêr-Wenn approach and entrance

By day

Coming from the north the dangers off the Pointe des Poulains must be avoided. The completely safe route goes outside Basse Occidentale des Poulains buoy. The Port du Vieux Château is divided into two parts: the main inlet, Stêr-Vraz, and a smaller inlet, Stêr-Wenn. The latter opens from the south side of the former. Stêr-Vraz is 400m wide and 900m long; Stêr-Wenn is only 50m wide and 500m long.

The entrance to Stêr-Vraz is quite hard to locate because there are several inlets that look similar from seaward but closer to it is quite distinctive. The north side is encumbered with rocks as much as 300m offshore and should not be approached too closely. However, the south side, shown on the plan as Pointe Verticale, is steep to and forms a cliff that makes identification easy. Also, there is a conspicuous hotel on the skyline about 0.75M south of Pointe Verticale.

Do not cut the corner on the north side of Stêr-Vraz but start from a position at least 0.5M offshore and approach on about 120°. Both the tidal stream and the swell will weaken as Stêr-Vraz is entered.

Coming from the south, the cliffs along the southern shore of Stêr-Vraz are steep to. However, unless another yacht is entering or leaving, Stêr-Vraz will not be seen until it opens up, quite dramatically, to starboard. When it is fully open, alter course sharply to starboard and enter.

By GPS

Stêr-Wenn requires very careful visual pilotage. The following waypoint may be helpful.

⊕232-Ster-Wenn 47°22′.40N 3°15′.15W

ANCHORAGES

⚓ Stêr-Wenn

Stêr-Wenn is deep near the entrance and shoals gradually up to a sandy beach after a small fork. A cable is slung across the inlet at the fork to provide moorings for small fishing boats. On both sides iron rings are set into the rock above the high-water line. Drop anchor in the middle of the inlet (1.5m or more) and take a stern line ashore to one of the rings. The holding is good, but make sure that the anchor is well dug in before going ashore. Do not allow other yachts to raft to you with slack cables and shore lines if you are to survive a *brise de terre* during the night. Also, in the event of a *brise de terre*, check that the anchor is not dragging.

The water is smooth in all winds except northwest. But surge does enter when there is a heavy onshore wind, and the anchorage becomes dangerous.

Stêr-Vraz day anchorage *M&G Barron*

⚓ Stêr-Vraz day anchorage

If Stêr-Wenn is overcrowded, there is a day anchorage further up Stêr-Vraz but for use in calm weather only. Keep to starboard and look out for rocks as the beach is approached. Most of the rocks occupy the northern half of the inlet.

ASHORE IN STÊR-WENN

There is a dinghy landing on the beach and a path leading up the valley to the road. Turn left for the 3M walk to Sauzon or right to visit the Grotte de l'Apothicairerie (0.75M). There is a nature reserve information centre, an hotel and a café above the cave.

Port Jean anchorage on the north coast *M&G Barron*

Ancient Fort Larron at Port Salio *M&G Barron*

Goulphar lighthouse, Belle-Île *M&G Barron*

North coast anchorages

PILOTAGE

These anchorages all require a large-scale chart.

⚓ Port Jean

Sheltered from the south but completely exposed to the northeast, Port Jean is about a mile east of Sauzon and a useful alternative if Sauzon is very crowded. Approach from the north-northeast and anchor off the beach. It is relatively easy to leave at night.

⊕219-Port Jean 47°21'·94N 3°11'·29W

⚓ Port Guen and Port Salio

Protected from the south and west but exposed to the northeast, this bay is 1M east of Le Palais. There are no dangers in the approach but it is necessary to tuck in well to minimise the swell and ferry wash.

⊕222-Salio 47°19'·84N 3°08'·19W

Anchorage at Port Yorc'h *M&G Barron*

⚓ Port Yorc'h

Protected from the west through south to southeast but exposed to the northeast, this bay is 1.5M east of Le Palais. There are a number of local moorings but it is possible to anchor outside them to the west or off the beach.

⊕223-Yorc'h 47°19'·65N 3°07'·23W

South coast anchorages

PILOTAGE

These anchorages all require a large-scale chart.

⚓ Port Goulphar

Sheltered from the north but completely open to the south, Port Goulphar is a mini-fjord close to Goulphar lighthouse. There are a lot of rocks in the entrance and it is necessary to start from a position close to ⊕228-Goulphar. Approach the bay with Goulphar lighthouse on 015°, which will put it a bit to the right of the hotel on the cliff top. Hold this course through the outer rocks and bear to starboard into the bay. Anchor outside the local moorings. A French cruising guide classifies Port Goulphar as a mouillage gastronomique because of the excellent restaurant in the hotel.

⊕230-Goulphar 2 47°18'·11N 3°13'·72W

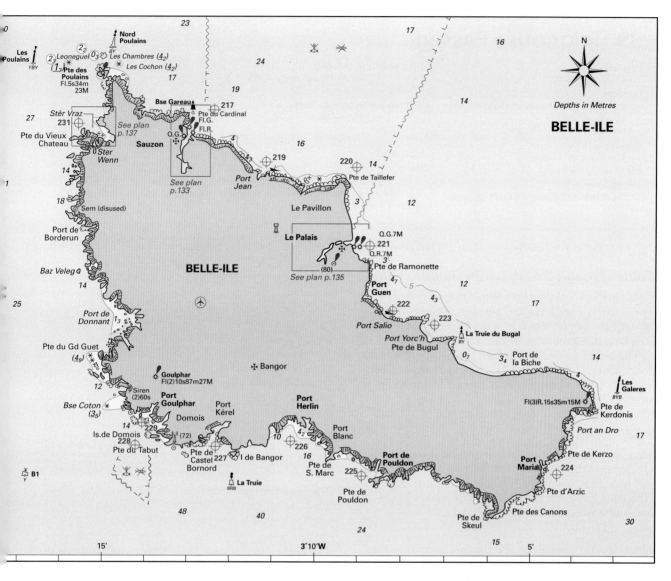

IV. QUIBERON BAY

⚓ Port Kérel

Sheltered from the north but completely open to the south, Port Kérel is a very attractive little bay about 1M east of Port Goulphar. Approach from due south starting from a position west of La Truie IDM. Locals anchor in the fjords but the easiest spot is off the beach in the northeast part of the bay.

⊕227-Kerel 47°17'·79N 3°12'·22W

⚓ Port Herlin

Sheltered from northwest to northeast but completely open to the south, Port Herlin is a fairly wide bay about 1.5M east of Port Kérel. Approach from due south to avoid the rocks on either side of the bay. Anchor almost 0.25M from the shore because of the rocky foreshore.

⊕226-Herlin 47°17'·94N 3°12'·22W

⚓ Port de Pouldon

Sheltered from north through east, Port de Pouldon is 2M west of Pointe du Skeul. Approach from the west-southwest and anchor close to the north side of the headland. There are drying rocks just off the north side of the bay.

⊕225-Pouldon 47°17'·29N 3°08'·58W

⊕217	Sauzon	47°22'.80N	3°12'.81W
⊕218	Sauzon 1	47°22'.61N	3°12'.95W
⊕219	Port Jean	47°21'.94N	3°11'.29W
⊕220	Taillefer	47°22'.03N	3°09'.28W
⊕221	Le Palais	47°20'.84N	3°08'.98W
⊕222	Salio	47°19'.84N	3°08'.19W
⊕223	Yorc'h	47°19'.65N	3°07'.23W
⊕224	Port Maria Bl	47°17'.56N	3°04'.38W
⊕225	Pouldon	47°17'.29N	3°08'.58W
⊕226	Herlin	47°17'.94N	3°10'.39W
⊕227	Kerel	47°17'.79N	3°12'.22W
⊕228	Goulphar	47°17'.51N	3°14'.10W
⊕229	Goulphar 1	47°17'.99N	3°13'.92W
⊕230	Goulphar 2	47°18'.11N	3°13'.72W
⊕231	Stêr-Wenn	47°22'.62N	3°15'.82W
⊕232	Stêr-Wenn 1	47°22'.40N	3°15'.15W

⚓ Port Maria

Protected from west to north, Port Maria is an attractive little creek between Point de Kerdonis and Pointe du Skeul. The tide can be strong along the ends of Belle-Île so approach with caution from the southeast. Port Maria is quite narrow and it is best to keep in the middle steering 315°. It is possible to leave at night but not to enter.

⊕224-Port Maria Bl 47°17'·56N 3°04'·38W

39 Teignouse Passage

Location
47°26'N 3°06'W

Hazards
Strong tide over uneven seabed
Rough water
Many well marked rocks

Depth restrictions
The channel is deep

Night entry Well lit

HW time
Brest HW+0015 neaps, –0030 springs

Mean height of tide (m)

	HWS	HWN	LWN	LWS
Le Palais	5.3	4.1	2.1	0.9

Tidal stream Teignouse passage
NE – Brest HW–0600 to +0030
(1.8kns)
SW – Brest HW+0030 to +0600
(2.1kns)

Charts
BA 2823 (50), 2357 (20)
SHOM 7033 (50), 7141 (20)
Imray C38 (78)

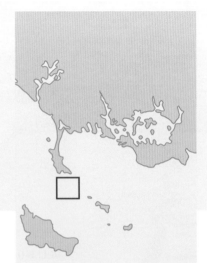

Route through the reefs into Quiberon Bay

There are several passages into Quiberon Bay. The Teignouse is a well-marked big ship passage that can be used by day or night. It is 0.25M wide and there is deep water either side of the marked channel.

The other passages through the Quiberon reefs are described below under Houat and Hoëdic. There are also many shortcuts that can be found using a large-scale chart.

PORT MARIA

This harbour at the southern end of Presqu'île de Quiberon is the ferry port for Belle-Île and yachts are not welcome so it will not be described further here. However there is a possible anchorage sheltered in northwest to east winds off the beach.

Warning

The tides run strongly in the channel and the seabed is very uneven. As a result, surprisingly steep seas build up even with only a moderate wind against the tide. If possible take it at slack water and treat it with great respect if there is any swell running.

Teignouse passage from southwest

By day

Bring the white lighthouse on La Teignouse to bear 036°. This line leads south of Goué Vaz Sud SCM buoy, which must not be confused with Goué Vaz Nord NCM buoy, situated 0.5M to the northwest. Steer 036°, leaving Goué Vaz Sud SCM to port, Basse du Milieu SHM buoy to starboard and Goué Vas Est PHM buoy to port.

When this last buoy is abeam alter course to 068°. The official line is St-Gildas, 10M away, on 068°, but it is only necessary to leave Basse Nouvelle PHM buoy to port and northeast Teignouse SHM buoy to starboard.

By night

Enter the white sector (033°-039°) of La Teignouse light before Port Maria main light turns from white to green. Steer in this sector between the buoys. When between Basse du Milieu SHM and Goué Vaz

The Teignouse lighthouse

Est PHM alter course to 068° to pass between the Basse Nouvelle PHM buoy and northeast Teignouse SHM buoy.

By GPS

The big ship route is:

⊕233-S Goué Vas, ⊕234-E Goué Vas, ⊕236-E Teignouse

With good weather and sufficient rise of tide, ⊕236-E Teignouse can be replaced with ⊕235-Teignouse. This shortcut passes close to a 1m shallow patch and the rocks near the Teignouse light.

Teignouse passage from east or north

By day and by GPS

Reverse the above courses.

By night

Use the white sector of Port Haliguen light to keep off the dangers between Haliguen and La Teignouse light. Then enter the Teignouse Passage between the Basse Nouvelle PHM buoy and NE Teignouse SHM buoy. Steer 248° to pass between Basse du Milieu SHM buoy and Goué Vaz PHM buoy. Steer out on 216° using the white sector of La Teignouse light. When Port Maria main light turns from green to white all dangers are passed.

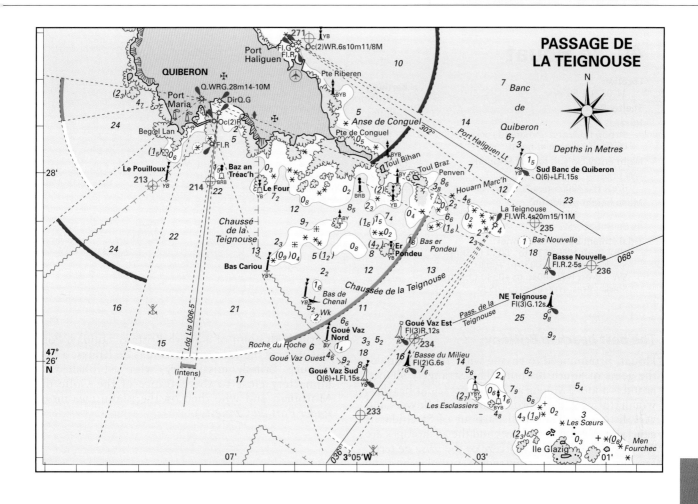

Port Maria and the Teignouse Passage looking southeast.
The passage opens the way to the Morbihan and the Vilaine estuary.
It is bordered on either side by many reefs and the tides run strongly

IV. QUIBERON BAY

40 Île Houat

Location
47°02'N 2°58'W

Shelter Poor

Hazards
Strong tides and unmarked rocks
Difficult to leave at night

Night entry Only lit to Port St-Gildas

HW time
Brest HW+0005 neaps, −0025 springs

Mean height of tide (m)

	HWS	HWN	LWN	LWS
Île de Houat	5.2	4.1	2.0	0.8

Tidal stream Beniguet channel
NE – Brest HW−0530 to −0030 (1.5kns)
Slack – Brest HW −0030 to +0030
SW – Brest HW +0030 to +0530 (1.3kns)
Slack – Brest HW+0530 to −0530

Berthing
Anchorages

Facilities
Very limited but good
beaches, walking and wild
flowers

Charts
BA 2823 (50), 2835 (20)
SHOM 7032 (50), 7143 (25)
Imray C38 (78)

The best beach in Brittany

Houat, pronounced to rhyme with '*that*', is one of the gems of South Brittany. This strangely shaped island is about 2M long and has spectacular beaches, wonderful walking, a profusion of wild flowers and very little else. The small harbour of St-Gildas is generally full of fishing boats and the anchorages are exposed either to the sea breeze or the *brise de terre*. Despite this, Houat is extremely popular and the anchorage off the best beach, Tréac'h-er-Gourhed, can be uncomfortably crowded. However, don't be put off. A visit to Houat in good weather is likely to be the high point of a South Brittany holiday. Port St-Gildas is named after St-Gildas de Rhuys, a 6th century British missionary who established a monastery close to the entrance of the Golfe du Morbihan and who died on the island (*see more under Port du Crouesty*).

Houat looking southeast.
The harbour and anchorage of Port St-Gildas is shown in the bottom of the picture. The wide curving bay of Tréac'h er Gourhed is at the top left

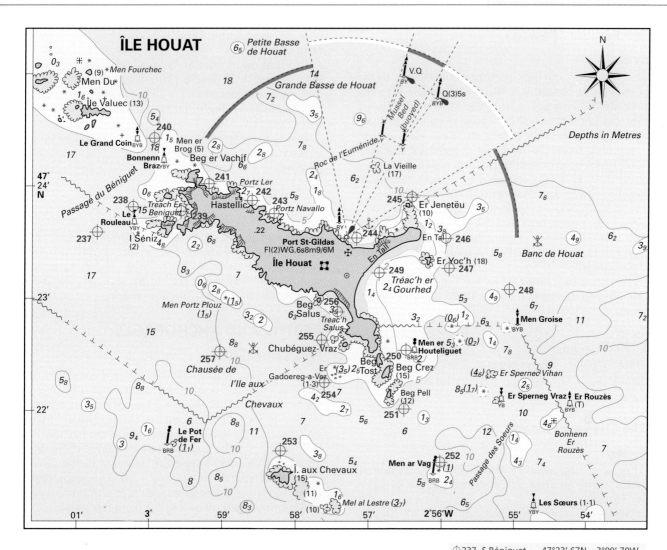

ÎLE HOUAT

PILOTAGE

Port St-Gildas approach

By day

The easiest approach is from the north and east. If possible come down with the ebb stream but, if planning to enter the harbour, do not arrive too near low water because manoeuvring room is much reduced.

From the north steer towards the east end of the island. Nearly one mile north is a conspicuous rock, La Vieille (14m high), and north-northeast of it is a mussel bed marked by buoys. Once La Vieille is identified it is easy to locate the harbour, which bears 200°, 0.75M from it. Pass either side of the mussel bed. La Vieille is clean to the north and east but to the south the shoals extend about 200m.

From the east, the outer northeast rock, Er Jenetëu (16m high), is distinctive. It can be passed at a distance of 100m but there are rocks in the direct line to the harbour so keep well out before turning for St-Gildas.

By night

Green sectors of the breakwater light cover La Vieille and the dangers to the east and west of the

⊕237	S Béniguet	47°23'.67N	3°00'.70W
⊕238	Rouleau	47°23'.79N	3°00'.36W
⊕239	Béniguet	47°23'.79N	2°59'.62W
⊕240	N Béniguet	47°24'.55N	2°59'.97W
⊕241	Portz Ler	47°24'.02N	2°59'.26W
⊕242	Hastellic	47°23'.89N	2°58'.74W
⊕243	Portz Navallo	47°23'.76N	2°58'.42W
⊕244	St-Gildas	47°23'.61N	2°57'.26W
⊕245	Er Jeneteu	47°23'.94N	2°56'.51W
⊕246	En Tal	47°23'.61N	2°56'.08W
⊕247	Er Yoc'h	47°23'.27N	2°56'.08W
⊕248	E Houat	47°23'.19N	2°55'.17W
⊕249	Gourhed	47°23'.17N	2°56'.99W
⊕250	Houteliguet	47°22'.54N	2°56'.48W
⊕251	Beg Pell	47°22'.03N	2°56'.63W
⊕252	SE Houat	47°21'.52N	2°56'.08W
⊕253	Chevaux	47°21'.65N	2°58'.23W
⊕254	Gadoérec	47°22'.24N	2°57'.68W
⊕255	Chubéguez	47°22'.64N	2°57'.68W
⊕256	Salus	47°22'.81N	2°57'.50W
⊕257	SW Houat	47°22'.52N	2°59'.08W

harbour. Approach in either white sector and anchor off the harbour. The mussel bed is in the green sector of the breakwater light, and the buoys on its north side are lit.

By GPS

From northwest to northeast:

⊕244-St-Gildas can be approached directly. Take care to avoid the well-marked mussel beds northnortheast of St-Gildas

From the east use:

⊕245-Er Jeneteu, ⊕244-St-Gildas

IV. QUIBERON BAY

The Béniguet Passage

By day

This is an easy daylight passage, immediately to the northwest of Houat. It is the shortest route between Belle-Île and Port St-Gildas or the Vilaine. The strong tide and uneven seabed can cause steep seas in wind against tide conditions so take it close to slack water.

Coming from the southwest, leave Le Rouleau WCM beacon tower 600m to starboard and make good 030° to pass between Le Grand Coin ECM beacon tower and Bonnenn Braz WCM beacon tower. Keep closer to Le Grand Coin tower and well clear of Bonnenn Braz and the shoals (depth 1.5m) that extend 600m north-northeast. Le Grand Coin tower in transit with Le Palais citadel on 240° clears these shoals.

Use the 240° transit when leaving Quiberon Bay and alter to 210° when about 400m from Le Grand Coin.

By GPS

From the south use:

⊕237-S Béniguet, ⊕240-N Béniguet

Avoid the 1.5m shallow patch east of Le Grand Coin.

The Chevaux Passage

By day

This is a fine-weather route from Le Palais to Hoëdic, and an attractive alternative to Le Beniguet for Houat.

Steer for a position 0.25M north of Île aux Chevaux, watching out for Pot de Fer IDM and the rocks on the north side of Île aux Chevaux.

Bound for Houat, steer to leave Beg Pell (12m high) 200m to port. Don't go too much further out because there is a rock (depth 0.6m) about 0.5M to the southeast of Beg Pell. Then leave the Men er Houteliguet tower 100m to starboard. A detour to visit the spectacular Tréac'h er Gourhed beach may be in order.

Proceeding to Port St-Gildas, cross the bay and leave the rock Er Yoc'h (18m high) 100m to port and the beach on point En Tal well to port. Round Er Jenetëu (10m high), leaving it 100m to port and enter Port St-Gildas.

Instructions for getting to Hoëdic via the Chevaux Passage are given under Hoëdic.

By GPS

From the south use:

⊕253-Chevaux, ⊕231-Beg Pell, ⊕250-Houteliguet, ⊕247-Er Yoc'h, ⊕246-En Tal

Continue to ⊕245-Er Jeneteu for St-Gildas and the north coast of Houat. This route should not be attempted in poor visibility or at night. In good visibility the waypoints are hardly necessary because they are all close to conspicuous marks.

BERTHS AND ANCHORAGES

Port Saint-Gildas

Port St-Gildas is so small that a yacht over 10m is unlikely to find a berth. The breakwater is reserved for fishing boats but there is a row of head and stern moorings for yachts parallel to the breakwater. Do not obstruct the access for the ferry. If the harbour is full, anchor in the bay to the east where there are also some visitors' buoys but these are rather close and not suitable for boats over 12m. This anchorage and the visitors' buoys are open to the northwest and the *brise de terre* and suffer from ferry wash.

⚓ Tréac'h er Béniguet

Sheltered from the east but exposed to south and west, this attractive bay is on the west end of Houat. Approach from a position north of Le Rouleau

Port St-Gildas

Port St-Gildas commercial quay

Tréac'h er Beniguet

WCM beacon tower. Steer east into the middle of the bay and anchor off the beach. It is difficult to leave at night without GPS.
⊕239-Béniguet 47°23'·79N 2°59'·62W

⚓ Portz Ler

Sheltered from the south but open to north and east, this bay is at the west end of the north coast. The approach from the north is straightforward. There are two distinct bays and it is important to anchor in one of them and not on the rocks between them. It is easy to leave at night.
⊕241-Portz Ler 47°24'·02N 2°59'·26W

Tréac'h Salus

⚓ Hastellic

This bay, sheltered from south and west but open to the north and east, is between Beg Run er Vilin and Er Hastellic. The approach is straightforward from the northeast and it is easy to leave at night.
⊕242-Hastellic 47°23'·89N 2°58'·74W

⚓ Portz Navallo

Sheltered from south and west but open to the north and east, this bay is just east of Er Hastellic. The approach is simple from the northeast and it is easy to leave at night.
⊕243-Portz Navallo 47°23'·76N 2°58'·42W)

⚓ Tréac'h er Gourhed

Sheltered for the west but horribly exposed to the *brise de terre*, this bay on the east end of Houat offers one of the finest beaches in South Brittany. It can be approached from the north or east by keeping clear of Er Jenetëu, En Tal and Er Yoc'h or from the southwest using the Chevaux passage. Anchor wherever there is a space. It is important to plan for a night departure because the anchorage is famous for its *brise de terre* pyjama parties, with yachts rolling from beam to beam and dragging all over the place. The waypoint ⊕248-E Houat may provide an escape route but note that it is not safe to move round to Tréac'h Salus after dark.
⊕249-Gourhed 47°23'·17N 2°56'·19W

⚓ Tréac'h Salus

Protected from the north and east and the *brise de terre* but exposed to the south and west, this magnificent beach is the other side of the headland from Tréac'h er Gourhed. It can be approached directly from the southwest but from the north or Tréac'h er Gourhed it is necessary to round the many dangers off southeast Houat. Anchor as close to the beach as draught permits. Shelter is often a little better at the west end but there is a wreck with a doubtful position marked on the chart.

Tréac'h Salus is exposed to the sea breeze and is often less crowded than Tréac'h er Gourhed. It is better protected from the *brise de terre* so is often a better place to spend the night. It is possible to escape to the southwest at night, using waypoint ⊕257-SW Houat.
⊕256-Salus 47°22'·81N 2°57'·50W

ASHORE IN HOUAT

There is water from the public tap in the centre of the pretty village of Saint-Gildas or at the toilets on the pier. The shops can supply simple needs, but they are limited. There are some bars, a medical centre, and a post office. The island is noted for its succession of wild flowers: roses in May, carnations in June, yellow immortelles in July and sand lilies in August. There are wonderful beaches on the north side of En Tal, at Tréac'h er Gourhed in the east, Tréac'h Salus in the southeast and Tréac'h er Beniguet in the west.

41 Île Hoëdic

Location
47°02'N 2°52'W

Shelter
Generally poor

Hazards
Strong tides and unmarked rocks
Difficult to leave at night

Night entry
Only lit to L'Argol

HW time
Brest HW+0010 neaps, –0035 springs

Mean height of tide (m):

	HWS	HWN	LWN	LWS
Hoëdic	5.1	4.0	1.9	0.7

Tidal stream Sœurs channel
NE – Brest HW–0530 to –0030 (1.4kns)
Slack – Brest HW–0030 to +0030
SW – Brest HW+0030 to +0530 (1.3kns)
Slack – Brest HW+0530 to –0530

Berthing
Visitors' buoys and anchorages

Facilities
Very limited

Charts
BA 2823 (50), 2835 (20)
SHOM 7032 (50), 7143 (25)
Imray C38 (78)

Picture postcard island

Hoëdic is 1M long and 0.5M wide and lies 4M southeast of Houat. Argol, the main harbour, is on the north side. It is very small and yachts may prefer to lie outside. Port de la Croix in the south dries but in fine weather it is an attractive anchorage.

PILOTAGE

Argol approach from north and east

By day

From the north make directly for the island passing either side of La Chèvre IDM. From Houat, be sure to leave Men Groise ECM beacon and Er Rouzès ECM buoy to starboard. From the east give Beg Lagad a clearance of at least 400m.

By night

Approach in one of the white sectors of the harbour light. Green sectors cover La Chèvre and the dangers east and west of the approach.

By GPS

From the Morbihan or Lorient approach:
⊕261-Argol

From the northeast use:
⊕262-N Hoëdic, ⊕261-Argol

From the east use:
⊕263-NE Hoëdic, ⊕262-N Hoëdic, ⊕261-Argol

From Houat use:
⊕248-E Houat, ⊕261-Argol

Argol via the Soeurs Passage

By day

Start from a position about 0.25M west of Er Palaire WCM beacon tower. Steer about 020° to leave Les Soeurs WCM beacon tower 100m to starboard. Avoid Men er Guer and Bonen Bras shoals by keeping Er Spernec Bras SCM beacon tower open to the left of Men Groise ECM beacon.

Bound for Hoëdic, do not let Les Soeurs WCM beacon tower bear more than 255° until Pointe du Vieux Château, bearing 175°, hides the west side of Hoëdic. This is necessary to avoid the shoals north and west of Point du Vieux-Château.

Bound north, leave Er Rouzèz ECM buoy at least 200m to port.

By GPS

From the south use:
⊕258-S Soeurs, ⊕259-N Soeurs, ⊕260-NW Hoëdic

Continuing to Argol, add:
⊕261-Argol

Argol via the Chevaux Passage

By day

Start from a position about 0.25M north of Île aux Châteaux. Steer due east to leave Men er Vag IDM buoy well to starboard. Continue on the same course, keeping well north of Les Soeurs WCM beacon tower until the Pointe du Vieux Château, bearing 175°, hides the west side of Hoëdic. It is then safe to steer for Argol.

By GPS

From the southwest use:
⊕253-Chevaux, ⊕252-SE Houat, ⊕260-NW Hoëdic, ⊕261-Argol

Take care to avoid the unmarked rocks and shallow patch between Les Soeurs WCM beacon tower and the northwest headland of Hoëdic.

Port de la Croix approaches

A large-scale chart is required.

By day

From the north pass outside the Plateau des Cardinaux and then steer southwest until the Madavoar SCM tower beacon is in line with the right-hand edge of the fort on 320°. Approach Port

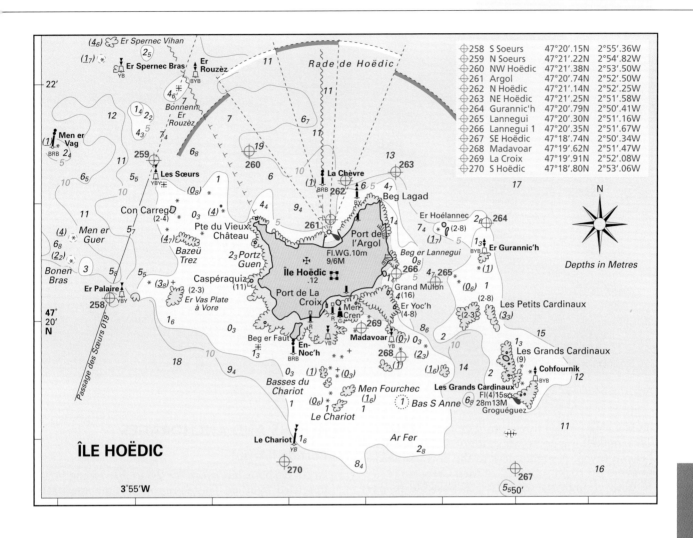

⊕258	S Soeurs	47°20'.15N	2°55'.36W
⊕259	N Soeurs	47°21'.22N	2°54'.82W
⊕260	NW Hoëdic	47°21'.38N	2°53'.50W
⊕261	Argol	47°20'.74N	2°52'.50W
⊕262	N Hoëdic	47°21'.14N	2°52'.25W
⊕263	NE Hoëdic	47°21'.25N	2°51'.58W
⊕264	Gurannic'h	47°20'.79N	2°50'.41W
⊕265	Lannegui	47°20'.30N	2°51'.16W
⊕266	Lannegui 1	47°20'.35N	2°51'.67W
⊕267	SE Hoëdic	47°18'.74N	2°50'.34W
⊕268	Madavoar	47°19'.62N	2°51'.47W
⊕269	La Croix	47°19'.91N	2°52'.08W
⊕270	S Hoëdic	47°18'.80N	2°53'.06W

ÎLE HOËDIC

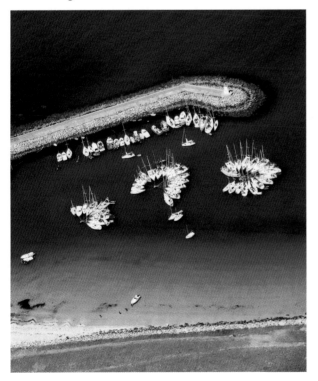

More than 40 visiting boats rafted to the visitors' buoys in Port de L'Argol

Looking northwest to the anchorage at Pointe du Vieux Château

Argol harbour looking south

de la Croix on this transit until close to Madavoar. Then make for a point just south of Men Cren SHM beacon tower. A slight curve to the north is needed to avoid the rocks southeast of Men Cren.

With enough rise of tide it is possible to pass inside the Plateau des Cardinaux. This hazard is a chain of unmarked drying rocks east of Madavoar. Those closest to the Madavoar beacon dry 0.8m but those further out dry 2.3m. If there is enough water to pass safely over the inner rocks, the outer ones can be avoided by staying within 400m of the beacon.

By GPS

From the southeast use:

⊕267-SE Hoëdic, ⊕268-Madavoar, ⊕269-La Croix

From the north, with enough rise of tide, use:

⊕263-NE Hoëdic, ⊕265-Lannegui, ⊕268-Madavoar, ⊕269-La Croix

This shortcut passes close between unmarked drying rocks east of Madavoar tower.

Yachts aground on the western-most visitors' buoy in Argol harbour

BERTHS AND ANCHORAGES

Port de l'Argol

Argol harbour has room for 20 to 30 visiting boats in settled weather. There are rocks in the approach; to avoid them keep the bearing to the east pier head less than 180°.

In the harbour, there are three visitors' buoys where yachts can raft. The boats on the innermost one dry out at LW. There may also be room for one or two yachts bow to the principal breakwater and stern to a buoy at its eastern end. Alternatively, anchor just inside the entrance to port.

It is usually preferable to anchor outside the harbour but be sure to keep the bearing to the east pier head less than 180° to keep clear of the ferries. There is another anchorage further to the west, off the beach near the old lifeboat slip.

⚓ Port de la Croix

The harbour dries 2.8m and is often crowded so it is usually necessary to anchor outside. The shelter is good from the northwest to northeast but the anchorage is very exposed to any wind or swell from the south.

Anchor south of Men Cren tower or further in at neaps. Do not go in too close to the shore because there are some short posts set in concrete.

⚓ Beg er Lannegui

Sheltered from northwest to west, there is a secluded anchorage on the east side of Hoëdic just south of Beg er Lannegui. Approach from about 0.5M offshore and anchor on sand, avoiding any patches of weed. It is only possible to stay overnight in perfect conditions.

⊕266-Lannegui 1 47°20'·35N 2°51'·67W

Porz Guen on the west side of Hoëdic

Port de l'Argol

Other anchorages

Other anchorages around the island can be found. The water is so clear that in calm weather many of the submerged hazards can be seen and avoided but beware of submarine cables in the north-facing bays west of Argol.

ASHORE ON HOËDIC

Hoëdic has even fewer facilities than Houat but there is a small hotel, a food shop and some bars and crêperies. There is also a primitive shower and toilet block with a fresh-water tap near the harbour. A museum in the fort gives interesting insights into life on the island in the past.

IV. QUIBERON BAY

42 Port Haliguen

Location
47°29'N 3°06'W

Shelter Excellent

Night entry: Lit

HW time
Brest HW+0010 neaps, –0020springs

Mean height of tide (m)

	HWS	HWN	LWN	LWS
Haliguen	5.2	4.1	2.0	0.7

Tidal stream Haliguen approaches
NW – Brest HW–0530 to –0230 (0.5kns)
Slack – Brest HW–0230 to +0030
SE – Brest HW+0030 to +0530 (0.6kns)
Slack – Brest HW+0530 to –0530

Berthing
Marina

Facilities
Good marina facilities but
shopping is 1M away

Charts
BA 2823 (50), 2357 (20)
SHOM 7032 (50), 7141 (20)
Imray C39 (large scale)

Radio VHF Ch 9

Telephone
Marina ☎ 02 97 50 20 56
Yacht club ☎ 02 97 29 53 61

Large modern marina on the Quiberon Peninsula

Port Haliguen is the marina for Quiberon. It is pleasant with excellent facilities. There is a good beach nearby but Quiberon town and the magnificent Côte Sauvage are on the other side of the peninsula.

Haliguen marina looking north.
Visitors tie up to the long pontoon in the northeast corner of the west basin just to starboard of the entrance. The fuel pontoon is in the east basin on the south side of the quay wall

PILOTAGE

Port Haliguen approach and entrance

By day

The approach from the south is easy. Pass midway between La Teignouse lighthouse and the Sud Banc de Quiberon SCM buoy on a course of 305°, leaving Port Haliguen SCM buoy to starboard.

Enter between the breakwaters and turn to starboard. The visitors' pontoon runs along the inside of the breakwater.

By night

Approach in one of the white sectors of Port Haliguen Marina light or in the white 246°-252° sector of Port Maria light. Keep a lookout for unlit buoys and avoid the protective spur off the east breakwater head on entering.

By GPS

From the Teignouse Passage use:

⊕235-Teignouse, ⊕271-Haliguen

or

⊕236-E Teignouse, ⊕271-Haliguen

From Trinité use:

⊕276-Trinité, ⊕271-Haliguen

From the Morbihan use:

⊕285-Kerpenhir, ⊕282-SW Crouesty, ⊕271-Haliguen

or with care and enough tide for a useful shortcut:

⊕285 -Kerpenhir, ⊕281-Meaban, ⊕271-Haliguen

BERTHS AND ANCHORAGES

Port Haliguen marina

Anchoring is not permitted in the harbour. Visitors moor in the west basin where there is a long visitors' pontoon just to starboard of the entrance. Floating pontoons for very large yachts may be available in the west basin. If the visitors' berths are full, go to the reception pontoon. It is beside the fuel pontoon, on the inside quay wall of the East basin.

⚓ Port d'Orange

Sheltered from the west but open to the east and the *brise de terre*, Port d'Orange is a small drying harbour 2.25M north of Port Haliguen. Approaching from the south, keep well offshore to avoid the dangers along the east coast of Quiberon. Approach from the southwest and anchor off the pier.

⊕272-Orange 47°31'·32N 3°07'·37W

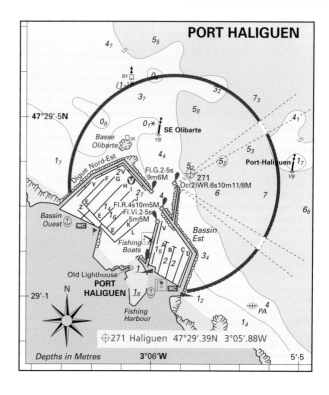

ASHORE IN PORT HALIGUEN

Port Haliguen has all the facilities of a major marina. There is a fuel pontoon, slip, crane, travel-lift, engineers, and a yacht club. Bread and limited shopping is available in the port. A 15-minute walk along the road to Quiberon finds a large supermarket with fish and oysters on sale outside. Quiberon town is about 1M away. It has all the facilities of a sizeable market town including a good market on Saturday. Market day at Port Haliguen is Wednesday. There are connections by bus, train and plane to all parts.

Quiberon town and Port Maria looking southwest.
Port Maria is only open to fishermen and ferries and is not covered in this edition. The town has good shops and a beach. It is possible to walk to the headland and explore the magnificent Côte Sauvage on the west of Quiberon peninsula

IV. QUIBERON BAY

43   La Trinité

Location
47°35'N 3°01'W

Shelter
Excellent except at HW

Hazards
Marked and unmarked rocks on E side of approach

Other restrictions
Power vessels >20m and oyster boats have right of way

Night entry Lit but intricate

HW time
Brest HW+0025 neaps, –0020 springs

Mean height of tide (m)

	HWS	HWN	LWN	LWS
Haliguen	5.4	4.3	2.1	0.8

Tidal stream
Fairly weak and complex in the bay; up to 3kns in the river

Berthing
Marina

Facilities
All facilities of a major yachting centre and busy town

Charts
BA 2823 (50), 2357 (20)
SHOM 7032 (50), 7141 (20)
Imray C39 (large scale)

Radio VHF Ch 9

Telephone
Marina ① 02 97 55 71 49

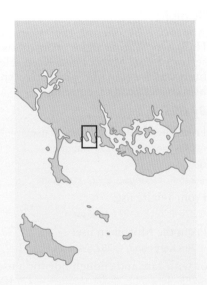

Major yachting centre

La Trinité is a flourishing oyster river and one of the most important sailing centres in the Bay of Biscay. It is a pleasant place and a perfect base for cruising or racing.

The town has excellent sailing facilities, plenty of bars, restaurants and shops and good connections to the rest of the world.

PILOTAGE

La Trinité approach and entrance

There is an official speed limit of 5kns. Power vessels over 20m, barges and oyster-culture vessels under tow have priority.

By day

La Trinité can be identified by a wooded hill to the west and a lighthouse on the skyline to the east.

Approach from the south, steer for the lighthouse until Le Petit Trého PHM buoy is identified. This buoy marks the outer dangers on the west side of the entrance.

From the south or southeast leave the conspicuous island of Méaban and Buissons de Méaban SCM buoy to starboard. The official transit is the two lighthouses in line on 347°. However, the many dangers east of the line are well marked so the transit need not be followed exactly.

La Trinité

La Trinité multihull berths

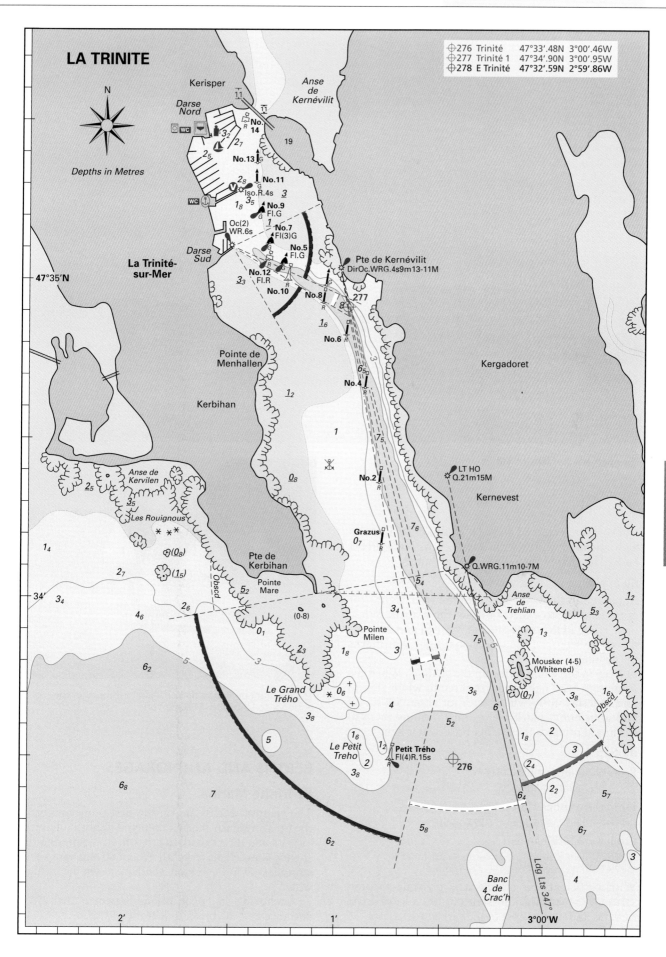

LA TRINITÉ

N

Kerisper

Darse
Nord

Depths in Metres

Anse
de
Kernévilit

⊕276	Trinité	47°33'.48N	3°00'.46W
⊕277	Trinité 1	47°34'.90N	3°00'.95W
⊕278	E Trinité	47°32'.59N	2°59'.86W

No.14

No.13 G

No.11
Iso.R.4s

No.9
Fl.G

Oc(2)
WR.6s

No.7
Fl(3)G

La Trinité-
sur-Mer

Darse
Sud

47°35'N

No.5
Fl.G

No.12
Fl.R

No.10

No.8

Pte de Kernévilit
DirOc.WRG.4s9m13-11M

277

No.6

Pointe de
Menhallen

Kergadoret

Kerbihan

No.4

LT HO
Q.21m15M

Kernevest

Anse de
Kervilen

Les Rouignous

No.2

Grazus

Q.WRG.11m10-7M

Pte de
Kerbihan

Obscd

Pointe
Mare

Pointe
Milen

Anse de
Trehlian

34'

Mousker (4.5)
(Whitened)

Obscd

Le Grand
Trého

Pointe
Milen

Le Petit
Trého

Petit Trého
Fl(4)R.15s

276

Banc
de
Crac'h

Ldg Lts 347°

2'   1'   **3°00'W**

IV. QUIBERON BAY

The approach to the marina at La Trinité

The river is entered between Mousker rock (4.5m high), painted white on top and Le Petit Trého PHM buoy. The channel is well marked by buoys.

By night

Approach in the white sector of the front light, it is not necessary to exactly follow the transit. When Petit Trého PHM comes abeam, steer to port to enter the white sector of the directional light that marks the channel.

Keep in the white sector up the channel. When the south pier-head light turns from red to white alter to port and stay in the white sector for about 500m. Lit and unlit buoys mark the channel. Follow them to starboard towards the marina breakwater light.

By GPS

From the south or west use:

⊕276-Trinité, ⊕277-Trinité 1

From the southeast use:

⊕278-E Trinité, ⊕276-Trinité, ⊕277-Trinité 1

From the Morbihan use:

⊕285-Kerpenhir, ⊕282-SW Crouesty, ⊕281-Meaban, ⊕278-E Trinité, ⊕276-Trinité, ⊕277-Trinité 1

With sufficient rise of tide it is possible to omit ⊕282-SW Crouesty but this shortcut has a least depth of 0.5m and passes close to unmarked rocks.

The low light on Pointe de Kerbihan to the east of the entrance to La Trinité *M&G Barron*

BERTHS AND ANCHORAGES

La Trinité Marina

The visitors' berths are on the first pontoon above the breakwater. A marina launch will normally meet visitors and direct them to a berth. In the marina the shelter is excellent from all except strong south and southeast winds, which send in a sea near high water.

Anchoring is prohibited between the river entrance and the bridge (clearance 11m).

La Trinité looking south

⚓ Pointe Saint-Colomban

Moderately sheltered from the north and northeast, there is a pleasant neap anchorage near Saint-Colomban in the northwest corner of Quiberon Bay. The approach is straightforward. Anchor close west of the Pointe St-Colomban.

⊕273-Colomban 47°33'·79N 3°05'·93W

⚓ Carnac

Sheltered from the north but exposed to the southwest and southeast, the dinghy sailing centre and holiday town of Carnac has two distinct bays. A rocky spur, marked by a SCM beacon, separates them. Approach from the south and watch the depth carefully because the bays shoal quickly. Anchor where depth permits.

⊕275-E Carnac 47°33'·92N 3°03'·32W

⚓ Saint-Philbert River

Sheltered from all directions except south, this unspoilt river just east of Trinité offers a quiet neap anchorage. Start from a position about 0.25M east of Er Gazeg SCM beacon and steer north to leave Le Grand Pellignon PHM beacon to port. Beyond that point there are only a few withies and some moorings to indicate the deepest water. The best spot is on the west side about 0.5M north of Le Grand Pellignon.

⊕280-Philbert 1 47°33'·76N 2°58'·90W

ASHORE IN LA TRINITÉ

Facilities

La Trinité has all the facilities that would be expected of a major yachting centre and small holiday town. Walking distances round the marina are considerable but in season there is a free water-taxi; call on VHF Ch 09, *Service de Rade*. Wi-Fi is available but the Capitainerie also offers free use of a computer for weather information and emails.

The Carnac Alignments

The Quiberon district is famous for a large number of carved menhirs, long mounds, stone circles, passage graves and alignments. This ritual landscape, created between 4000 and 2700 BC, was built by an energetic society that must have been living well above subsistence level. But nobody knows why they were such active builders. The monuments may have been religious, or astronomical or they may simply have been a means of expression.

A visit to the most extensive Alignments at Le Ménec, near Carnac, is highly recommended. The alignments are 1km long with stones in 12 rows laid out between two enclosures.

There is a bus service to Carnac, from which the Alignments can be reached on foot. It is also possible to hire bicycles in La Trinité.

IV. QUIBERON BAY

44 River Auray

Location
47°35′N 2°57′W
Shelter
Reasonable
Depth restrictions
Deep to Le Rocher, 1.0m beyond
Height restriction
14m under bridge at Auray
HW time Port Navalo
Brest HW+0030 neaps, -0005 springs
HW time Auray:
Brest HW+0035 neaps, HW springs
Mean height of tide (m)

	HWS	HWN	LWN	LWS
Auray	4.9	4.0	1.8	0.8

Tidal stream Auray River
Flood – Brest HW–0500 to +0030 (3½ kns)
Ebb – Brest HW +0030 to –0500 (3½ kns)

Berthing
Visitors' moorings and anchorages
Facilities
Boatyard at Port du Parun, shops, cafés and restaurants at several locations
Charts
BA 2371 (20)
SHOM 7034 (25)
Imray C39 (78)
Telephone
Auray HM ① 02 97 56 29 08
Le Bono HM ① 02 97 57 88 98
Port du Parun ① 02 97 57 88 98

Attractive oyster river

Auray is a historic town in the northwest corner of the Morbihan. It is approached by an oyster river that is somewhat less crowded than the rest of the Morbihan.

PILOTAGE

(See plan on page 168)

Approach to the Morbihan

Tidal strategy

The tides in the Morbihan entrance are very strong and the final approaches can be rough in wind against tide conditions. Ideally, pass through the narrows a bit before local HW. The tide to Auray will still be flooding or slack for a couple more hours.

At Auray, the tide stands for quite a long time and then drops very quickly at about half tide. This causes strong currents in the narrows by Le Grand Huernic.

By day

From the south, the outer approaches to the Morbihan present no difficulties. Méaban island to the west and the hill of Petit Mont, southwest of Crouesty to the east are both distinctive. Approach leaving Méaban SCM buoy and Bagen Hir ECM beacon tower to port.

The entrance transit is Petit Vezid white pyramid in line with Baden Church on 001°. In reasonable visibility, these marks are easy to identify, although Petit Vezid can be confused with a white sail. The channel is deep so the transit need not be followed precisely. Watch out for the tide because the flood

River Auray looking north from the narrows at Le Grand Huernic

Gregan SCM (right) marks the turning point for the River Auray. Petit Vezid (left,) a white pyramid that can easily be confused with a white sail, is the front mark of the transit with Baden Church. (Viewed from the southwest) *M&G Barron*

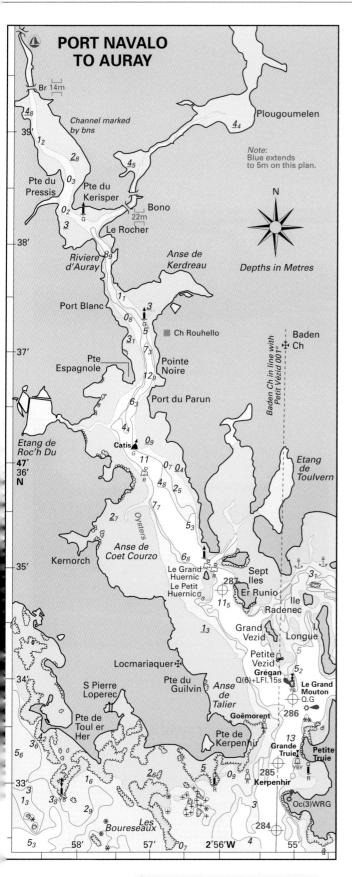

Map labels (Port Navalo to Auray chart):

PORT NAVALO TO AURAY

Br 14m
Channel marked by bns
Plougoumelen
Note: Blue extends to 5m on this plan.
Pte du Pressis
Pte du Kerisper
Bono
22m
Le Rocher
Riviere d'Auray
Anse de Kerdreau
Depths in Metres
Port Blanc
Ch Rouhello
Baden Ch
Pte Espagnole
Pointe Noire
Baden Ch in line with Petit Vézid 001°
Port du Parun
Etang de Roc'h Du
Catis
Etang de Toulvern
Kernorch
Anse de Coet Courzo
Oysters
Le Grand Huernic
Le Petit Huernic
Sept Iles
Er Runio
Ile Radenec
Grand Vezid
Longue
Locmariaquer
Petite Vezid
Grégan Q(6)+LFl.15s
Le Grand Mouton Q.G
S Pierre Loperec
Pte du Guilvin
Anse de Talier
Goëmorent
286
Pte de Toul er Her
Pte de Kerpenhir
13
Grande Truie
Petite Truie
YBY
285 Kerpenhir
Oc(3)WRG
Les Boureseaux
284
2°56'W

⊕285 Kerpenhir 47°33 .21N 2°55 .27W
⊕286 Grégan 47°33 .74N 2°55 .04W
⊕287 Huernic 47°34 .87N 2°56 .02W

past Port Navalo sweeps first west towards Kerpenhir and then east towards Grégan.

Just inside the entrance, a shallow patch (0.9m depth) extends east of Goëmorent beacon. This is very close to the Petit Vezid transit so, at low water, it is better to use Grégan SCM beacon tower in line with Baden Church on 359° for the final approach. Don't go east of this transit because the tide sets very strongly onto the Grand and Petit Moutons.

By night

The river is unlit beyond Grégan tower and night passage is not recommended.

By GPS

Warning

Beware that because of the sluicing tides close visual pilotage is essential. However the following waypoints may be helpful.

From the south use:

⊕282-SW Crouesty, ⊕285-Kerpenhir, ⊕286-Grégan

From the southeast with sufficient rise of tide use:

⊕281-Méaban, ⊕285-Kerpenhir, ⊕286-Grégan

This shortcut has a least depth of 0.5m and passes within 0.25M of unmarked rocks.

THE RIVER AURAY TO AURAY

Pilotage in the river

The strong tides and confusingly large number of islands can make pilotage quite difficult. It is a good idea to mark all courses and their compass bearings on a large-scale chart and to tick off the marks as they are passed.

Auray visitors' moorings with landing pontoon below the bridge *R. Rundle*

The footbridge at Bono

Auray bridge

The height of the bridge just below Auray is 14m above MHWS but with care and nerves of steel it is possible to get under it with more than 14m of air draught.

The distance from the riverbed to the bridge is 19.3m and there are height gauges on either side of the bridge. Thus by careful calculation, and use of the height gauges, it may be possible to find a combination of depth and height that works. For example at half tide there should be about 3m of water and about 16m of height.

By day

When 0.25M S of Grégan, steer about 330° for Le Grand Huernic island. Pass it to the north and continue on the same course past Kerlavarec PHM buoy and Catis SHM buoy. From Catis SHM, steer due north for Point Espagnole and, except at high water, do not cut the corner to the PHM beacon beyond the point.

After Pointe Espagnole, it is easy to follow the river through the attractive narrows at Le Rocher to Bono.

Beyond Bono the river is shallow and it is only possible to continue to Auray with enough rise of tide. The shallowest patch (depth 0.2m) is just beyond Bono near César PHM buoy, which marks the ruins of an ancient Roman bridge.

Beacons mark the remainder of the river to Auray.

By GPS

The River Auray requires careful visual pilotage. The following waypoints may be helpful in the first stretch.

⊕286-Grégan, ⊕287-Huernic

Auray River. Looking downstream from the footbridge at Bono

BERTHS AND ANCHORAGES

Port de Bono

Bono is an attractive inlet on the east side of the river just above Le Rocher. There is no room to anchor, but there are some visitors' buoys in the Auray River opposite the inlet and some in the narrows south of Le Rocher. In addition there are head and stern moorings, in the creek, just beyond the first bridge (height 20m). The tide runs hard so be careful when arriving or departing.

Bono is a pleasant village with a few shops, bars and restaurants. Also the hamlet and chapel of St-Avoye, beyond the second bridge, can be visited by dinghy.

St-Goustan visitors' moorings *R Rundle*

St-Goustan (Auray)

There are moorings in the middle of the river opposite the quays and for high-masted yachts there are visitors' bow and stern moorings below the bridge. Both have enough water at most tides but a mooring near Le Bono and a visit by dinghy is a good alternative.

As the old bridge in the town is approached, the water shoals rapidly. At springs, the ebb pours violently through this bridge and eddies make the upper end of the mid-stream moorings uncomfortable. The quay should only be used as a temporary berth at high water.

ASHORE IN AURAY

Benjamin Franklin landed at St-Goustan from America to negotiate a treaty with France during the American War of Independence. At the port, there are a few shops and restaurants and a fish market in the square. The old town of Auray is up the steep hill. The harbour office has showers and a dinghy pontoon. Auray has all the facilities of a substantial town, including a marine engineer. Market day is Monday.

The train service is good, though the station is some way from St-Goustan. There are buses to all parts, including La Baule for the airport and Carnac for the megaliths.

The quay and visitors' moorings *R Rundle*

The old bridge at St-Goustan was first built in 1295 but was not able to withstand the tidal stream. It was rebuilt several times and the existing successful bridge was built in the 14th century. Originally, Auray was a whaling port but by the 16th and 17th centuries it dealt in grain and wine and was one of the largest ports in Brittany *M&G Barron*

IV. QUIBERON BAY

ATLANTIC FRANCE   *159*

45 Vannes

Location
47°38'N 2°46'W

Shelter
Excellent in Vannes marina

Depth restrictions
Least depth 0.7m

Vannes lock
Opens Vannes HW ±0230

HW time Port Navalo
Brest HW+0030 neaps, −0005 springs

HW time Vannes
Brest HW+0200 neaps, +0150 springs

Mean height of tide (m)

	HWS	HWN	LWN	LWS
Port Navalo	4.9	3.9	1.8	0.7
Vannes	3.3	2.7	1.0	0.5

Tidal stream Grand Mouton
Flood – Brest HW−0430 to +0130 (8kns)
Ebb – Brest HW +0130 to −0430 (9kns)
Times may be 30 minutes later at neaps

Berthing
Marina

Facilities
Limited repairs but plenty of cafés, restaurants and shops

Charts
BA 2371 (20)
SHOM 7034 (25)
Imray C39 (78)

Radio Vannes HM VHF Ch 9

Telephone
Vannes HM ☎ 02 97 54 16 08

The heart of the Morbihan

Vannes has been the capital of the Morbihan since pre-Roman times. It has an old town with narrow streets and plenty of attractive old buildings but it is also a vibrant modern city with smart shops and excellent transport.

The marina is in a locked basin alongside the old town. It gets rather crowded but as it is completely sheltered the tight packing does not really matter. In 2009 the whole area round the marina was being developed and when it is finished it will be most attractive with wide promenades and open-air cafés. There is a brand new marina building with excellent showers, laundry and restaurant.

PILOTAGE

(See plan on page 168).

Morbihan approach

See 44 River Auray

The Vannes channel to Vannes

Tidal strategy

High water at Vannes is two hours after high water Port Navalo. Go through the Morbihan entrance at least half an hour before HW Port Navalo to carry the flood all the way to Vannes.

The entry gate and swing bridge at Vannes

The gate is open between Vannes HW ±0200 between the hours of 0830–2130 local time but times vary according to the tidal co-efficient. Beware that if HW is before 0800 or after 2200 the bridge will not open during that period. Telephone the marina or contact on VHF Ch 09 for confirmation of opening and closing times.

The swing bridge is 0.25M to seaward of the gate and opens on demand in the first and last 30 minutes and on every hour that the entry gate is open. When the entry gate first opens there is a depth of at least

Vannes swing bridge and canal

2.3m over the sill. Between 15 June and 15 September, it also opens on every half hour when the gate is open.

The traffic signals at the bridge are:

- fixed red lights – no passage
- occulting red lights – prepare to move
- fixed green lights – passage permitted
- occulting green lights – proceed only if already underway and the passage is clear.

Pink house on the corner of the channel to Vannes

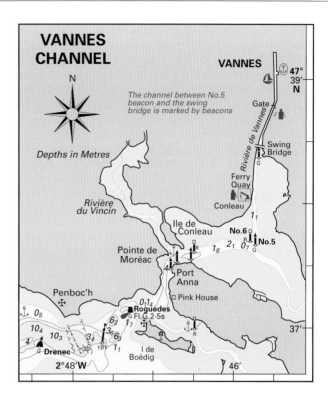

There are waiting pontoons on both sides of the bridge.

In recent years, there has been serious silting in the vicinity of the bridge and dredging has been needed. The possibility of being neaped could exist. Make a note of the minimum depth on entry.

Pilotage in the Morbihan

Strong tides and a large number of islands can make pilotage confusing. It is a good idea to mark courses and compass bearings on a large-scale chart and tick off the marks as they are passed.

By day

In the entrance, the Grand and Petit Moutons are dangerous because the tide sets directly onto them at up to 8kns. To avoid them, hold the transit until close to Grégan. Then turn sharply to starboard.

The channel passes south of Îles Longue, Gavrinis and Berder before entering a larger area of water west of Île aux Moines. Hold more or less the same course until north of Île Crëizig.

After passing Île Crëizig, turn north to pass through the narrows between Point de Toulingdag on Île aux Moines and the mainland. Keep towards the east side of the channel to avoid the Banc de Kergonan. Beacons mark the narrows but take care because the stream runs very strongly.

Once through the narrows, pass between the north tip of Île aux Moines and Pointe d'Arradon. Follow the mainland shore north of Îles Logoden and Roguédas beacon. The channel then turns north past a very distinctive pink house. It is important not

The channel to Vannes

to cut the corner because there are rocks and a shallow patch between Roguédas and the pink house.

Follow the channel past Port Anna to beacon No.6, which is the start of the canalised section to Vannes. The channel silts and carries only 0.5m at LAT in the section leading to the swing bridge.

The swing bridge is a short distance past the vedette quay. It is operated from the capitainerie at Vannes, using closed-circuit TV cameras. If the bridge is not open, secure to the waiting pontoon on the starboard side until the bridge opens.

In season, a marina launch may meet visiting boats and direct them to a berth. Otherwise, moor alongside in front of the marina office on the east side. Rafting may be necessary. A depth of 2.10m is maintained in the marina.

By GPS

Because of the sluicing tides the Golfe du Morbihan requires very careful visual pilotage at all times but ⊕286-Grégan, ⊕288-Creizig may be helpful in the first stretch.

ASHORE IN VANNES

Vannes has limited sailing facilities but excels in most other respects. The marina is adjacent to the medieval old town with its lovely buildings, narrow streets and masses of little shops, bars and restaurants. On Wednesdays, Saturdays and Sundays there is a colourful street market where entertainers often perform. History buffs will enjoy the fine cathedral and museum and will no doubt walk along the ramparts. The modern shopping area is just beyond the old town.

Vannes is a main rail centre and communications by rail and bus (including a direct bus to Roscoff) are excellent. Buses from Conleau and Vannes marina pass the railway station. There is an airfield north of the city and a regular ferry service from the swing bridge to Conleau, Île aux Moines, Port Navalo, Auray and other points in the Morbihan.

Vannes marina

Vannes visitors' berths and new marina office

The opening section of the swing bridge is on the west side ahead of the motor cruiser

46 Port du Crouesty

Location
47°32'N 2°55'W

Shelter
Excellent

Hazards
Entrance dangerous in strong SW wind

Depth restrictions
Channel dredged 1.8m

Night entry Lit

HW time
Brest HW+0010 neaps, -0025 springs

Mean height of tide (m)

	HWS	HWN	LWN	LWS
Port Navalo	4.9	3.9	1.8	0.7

Tidal stream – Crouesty approaches
Slack – Brest HW–0430 to –0330
NW – Brest HW–0330 to +0130 (0.9kns)
SE – Brest HW+0130 to –0430 (1.4kns)

Berthing
Huge marina

Facilities
All facilities

Charts
BA 2823 (50), 2357 (20)
SHOM 7032 (50), 7141 (20)
Imray C39 (large scale)

Radio VHF Ch 9

Telephone
Marina ℡ 02 97 53 73 33

Huge marina on the edge of the Morbihan

Port du Crouesty is a huge, six basin marina about 2M from the entrance to the Morbihan. It has all facilities, plenty of visitors' berths, a good range of marina shops, restaurants and an excellent supermarket. It is an ideal place to stock up before a visit to the Morbihan. There is a good beach but few other tourist attractions.

PILOTAGE

Crouesty approach and entrance

By day

From the south, Crouesty can be identified by the hill of Petit Mont and Crouesty lighthouse to the east of Méaban island. Leave Méaban SCM buoy to port.

Use the Morbihan entrance transit of Petit Vezid white pyramid in line with Baden Church on 001° until, just past Petit Mont, the Crouesty channel buoys are seen to starboard. The leading marks are the lighthouse in line with a red panel with a vertical white stripe on 058°.

Port du Crouesty

IV. QUIBERON BAY

Port du Crouesty entrance with the leading marks in line

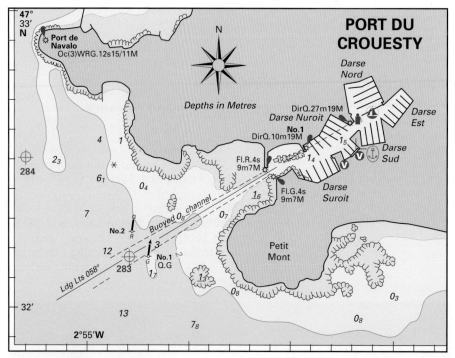

By night

Approach in the white sector of Port Navalo light on about 010°. When Crouesty leading lights come in transit on 058°, turn to starboard and follow the transit into the marina.

By GPS

From south or west use:
⊕282-SW Crouesty,
⊕283-Crouesty

From the Vilaine use:
⊕293-St-Jacques, ⊕291-Chimère, ⊕282-SW Crouesty,
⊕283-Crouesty

⊕283 Crouesty   47°32'.19N 2°54'.77W
⊕284 NE Crouesty 47°32'.51N 2°55'.28W

Port du Crouesty marina, visitors' basin looking southwest

BERTHS AND ANCHORAGES

Port du Crouesty

In season, boats are normally met by a launch and directed to a vacant berth. Otherwise use the visitors' berths in the second basin on the starboard side.

⚓ Port Navalo

The bay is full of moorings and it may be possible to borrow one. Otherwise there is a tolerable anchorage in 1.5m off the end of the pier, among the moorings. This spot is exposed to the west and disturbed by the wash from ferries.

⚓ La Plage de Fogeo

Sheltered from north and east but wide open to wind or swell from the south, this sandy bay is the other side of Petit Mont from Crouesty. Approach from the south to avoid the rocks just east of Petit Mont. Anchor where depth permits. It is easy to move to Crouesty at night but be sure to clear the rocks east and south of Petit Mont.

⊕289-Fogeo 47°32'·04N 2°53'·26W

St-Gildas chapel to the south of the Crouesty entrance
M&G Barron

⚓ Anse de Cornault

Sheltered from north and east but open to wind and swell from the southwest, this bay is 2M southeast of Petit Mont. Approach from the southwest and anchor where depth permits. It is easy to leave at night but get well offshore before turning for Crouesty as there are several dangers close to the shore. The easiest escape route is to aim for ⊕282-SW Crouesty.

⊕290-Cornault 47°30'·86N 2°51'·37W

ASHORE IN CROUESTY

Facilities

The marina has all boating facilities including chandlers, engineers, crane, scrubbing berth, fuel berth, 45-tonne travel-lift and all repairs. Around the marina are bars, restaurants and a number of shops including a launderette. There is an excellent supermarket and fish market just northwest of the marina. The supermarket is quite a long way round the marina from the visitors' berths so that for a big shop it is worth taking the dinghy across to the north basin where there is a designated victualing pontoon. (There is no access to the supermarket from the fuel berth).

History

St-Gildas de Rhuys, a 6th-century British missionary, established a monastery near the entrance to the Morbihan. When St-Gildas died in 570 he was visiting Houat. His body, as he had wished, was placed in a boat and pushed out to sea. Two months later it came ashore at what is now the entrance to Crouesty Marina. A chapel was built at the spot, and it can be seen on the south side of the marina entrance.

The Morbihan entrance looking north

47 Morbihan anchorages

Location
47°35′N 2°36′W

Shelter
Reasonable

HW time Arradon and Le Logeo
Brest HW+0200 neaps, +0145 springs

Mean height of tide (m)

	HWS	HWN	LWN	LWS
Arradon	3.2	2.7	1.0	0.5
Le Logeo	3.2	2.7	1.0	0.5

Tidal stream Arradon
Slack – Brest HW–0430 to –0330
Flood – Brest HW–0330 to +0030
(0.5kns)
Slack – Brest HW+0030 to +0230
Ebb – Brest HW+0230 to –0430 (0.7kns)

Berthing
Buoys and anchorages

Facilities
Limited cafés, restaurants and shopping

Charts
BA 2371 (20)
SHOM 7034 (25)
Imray C39 (78)

Telephone
Larmor Baden HM ① 02 97 57 20 86
Port Blanc HM ① 02 97 26 30 57
Île Aux Moines HM ① 02 97 26 30 57

Sixty islands in an inland sea

The Morbihan (*see plan on pages 168–169*) contains about 50 square miles of sheltered water and 60 islands (counting above-water rocks). All but Île aux Moines and Île d'Arz are privately owned and most are uninhabited.

Navigation is not difficult as the islands are easy to identify. There is deep water in the main channels and beacons and buoys mark most of the dangers.

Tidal streams are a major factor. They are fast enough for their direction to be seen on the surface and, except in the entrance, tend to follow the channels. There are plenty of counter-currents so it is often possible to make good progress against a foul tide. Nevertheless, the best time for cruising is neaps.

Moorings now fill most of the traditional anchorages so it is often necessary to borrow a buoy rather than anchor. When anchoring, it is important to tuck well in out of the stream and to avoid obstructing the many *vedettes*.

Only the popular places have been described here. Many other anchorages can be found using a large-scale chart.

Lamor Baden from the south

RIVER AURAY ANCHORAGES

(See plan on pages 168–9)

⚓ Locmariaquer

This village is on the west side of the river near the entrance. There is a channel to it, with about 1m, marked by port-hand beacons, but it is narrow and used by the ferries. The quay dries 1.5m. Boats can take the ground between the village quay and the *vedette* jetty. Deep-keeled yachts may be able to dry out against the outer side of the jetty. It is possible to anchor off the entrance but it is a long way from the shore.

⚓ Larmor Baden

This village is usually approached from the Vannes channel but it can be approached from the Auray River between Grand Vezid and Er Runio. Leave Île Radenec to starboard and keep in the north half of the channel because there is a rock and shallow patch northeast of Radenec. Anchor near Pointe de Berchis or borrow a mooring closer to the pier.

⚓ Le Rocher

This is an attractive and popular spot. There is no room to anchor but there are some visitors' buoys or it may be possible to borrow a private one.

CENTRAL MORBIHAN ANCHORAGES

(see plan on pages 168–9).

⚓ Île Longue

There is a northeast-facing bay on the southeast end of this island which is protected from the tide. The bottom shelves rapidly, but there is room to anchor outside the moorings. The island is private and landing not allowed.

⚓ Île de la Jument

There is a little bay on the east side. Go in as far as depth allows. Access from the north is easy; access from the south is possible with a large-scale chart.

⚓ Île Berder

There is a little east-facing bay on the northeast side of Île Berder. Alternatively, anchor further north towards the Anse de Kerdelan. Moorings occupy the best spots.

⚓ Locmiquel

Île aux Moines has a small marina on the northwest side at Locmiquel. The marina has no designated berths for visitors but there are two pontoons moored off in deeper water with alongside berths for visitors. Beware the drying Réchauds rocks, marked by two beacons, close to the approach to the pontoons and there is also a 0.6m shallow patch, marked by a SCM buoy, in the middle of the moorings area. It is therefore best to approach the pontoons round south of Les Réchauds from the Vannes channel. A free water taxi operates in season. Ashore there are a few shops, bars and restaurants.

Marina and moorings at Locmiquel

The visitors' pontoon Locmiquel, Île aux Moines

Beg Men Du, Île aux Moines

The beach at Beg Men Du, Île aux Moines

IV. QUIBERON BAY

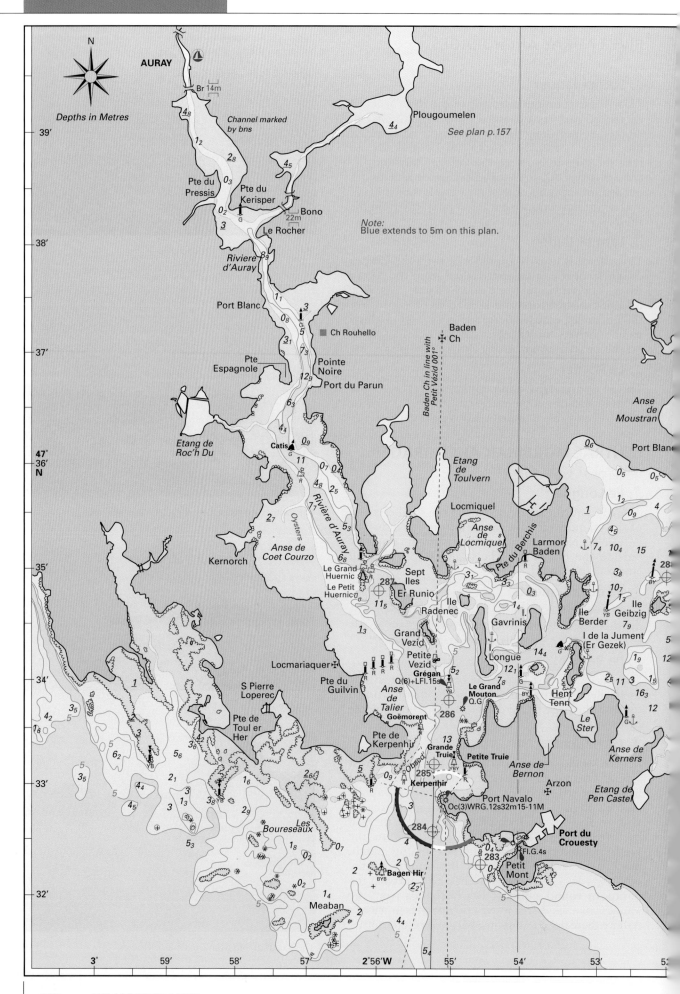

N

AURAY

Depths in Metres

Br 14m

4₈

Channel marked by bns

1₂

2₈

Plougoumelen

4₄

See plan p.157

0₃

Pte du Pressis

Pte du Kerisper

0₂

G

22m Bono

3

Le Rocher

Note:
Blue extends to 5m on this plan.

8₉

Riviere d'Auray

Port Blanc

1₁

0₈

3

G

5

Ch Rouhello

Baden Ch

3₁

7₃

Pte Espagnole

Pointe Noire

12₉

Port du Parun

6₃

4₄

Etang de Roc'h Du

Catis

G

0₉

0₄

Baden Ch in line with Petit Vézid 001°

Etang de Toulvern

Anse de Moustran

0₆

Port Blanc

Locmiquel

0₅ 0₅

11

0₇

4₈ 2₅

7₇

Rivière d'Auray

Oysters

2₇

5₃

Anse de Coet Courzo

Kernorch

6₈

Le Grand Huernic

Le Petit Huernic

Sept Iles

Er Runio

Anse de Locmiquel

Pte du Berchis

3₁

0₃

1

1₂

0₉ 4

4₅ 7₄ 10₄ 15

3₈

Larmor Baden

10₇

1₃

Ile Geibzig

7₉

Ile Berder

287

11₅

Ile Radenec

Gavrinis

1₄

I. Longue

14₄

I de la Jument (Er Gezek)

G

1₉

12

2₅ 11 3 1₅

16₃

1₃

Locmariaquer

Grand Vezid

Petite Vezid

Grégan
Q(6)+LFl.15s

5₂

7₈

Le Grand Mouton
Q.G

12₁

G

Hent Tenn

12

Le Ster

S Pierre Loperec

Pte du Guilvin

Anse de Talier

Goëmorent

286

BY

G

Anse de Kerners

1

Pte de Toul er Her

3₅

2₂

3₆

4₂

5₆

5

3₈

Pte de Kerpenhir

13

Grande Truie

Petite Truie

Anse de Bernon

Arzon

Etang de Pen Castel

4₂

1₆

YB

6₂

5

1

0₉

285

Kerpenhir

R

3

BY

Port Navalo
Oc(3)WRG.12s32m15-11M

2₁

2₆

5

4₄

4₅

3

1₃

3₈

2₉

Les Boureseaux

1₈

0₇

0₉

284

4

5

283

0₄

Fl.G.4s

Port du Crouesty

Petit Mont

2

Bagen Hir
BYB

0₂

2₂

Meaban

1₄

2

4₄

5₄

3' 59' 58' 57' 2°56'W 55' 54' 53' 52'

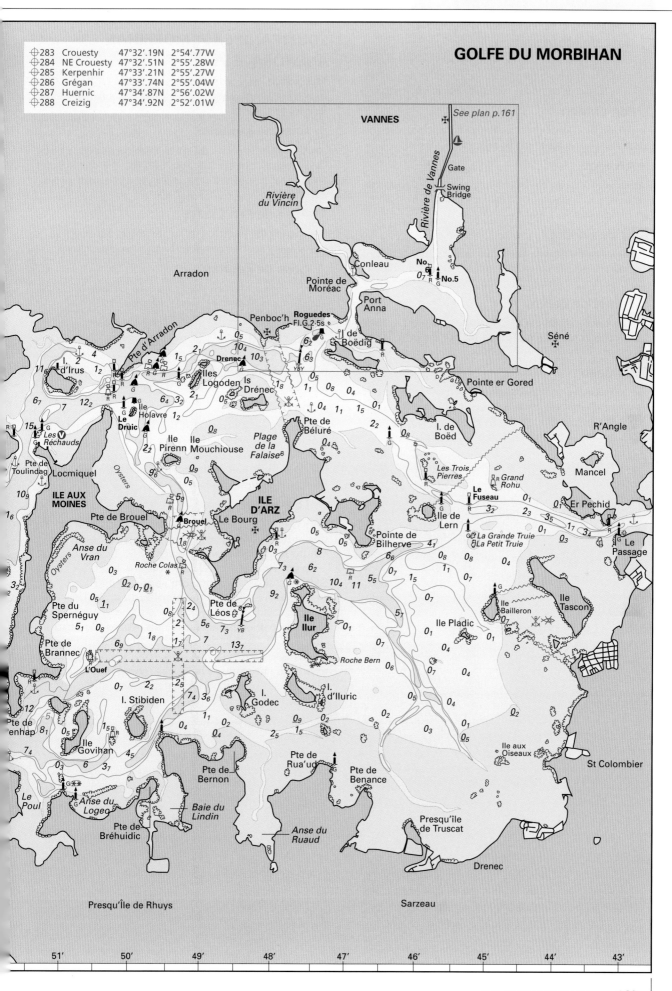

⊕283	Crouesty	47°32'.19N	2°54'.77W
⊕284	NE Crouesty	47°32'.51N	2°55'.28W
⊕285	Kerpenhir	47°33'.21N	2°55'.27W
⊕286	Grégan	47°33'.74N	2°55'.04W
⊕287	Huernic	47°34'.87N	2°56'.02W
⊕288	Creizig	47°34'.92N	2°52'.01W

GOLFE DU MORBIHAN

See plan p.161

VANNES

Rivière du Vincin

Gate

Swing Bridge

Rivière de Vannes

Conleau

Arradon

Pointe de Moréac

Port Anna

No.6

No.5

Séné

Penboc'h

Roguedes Fl.G.2·5s

I. de Boëdig

Drenec

Illes Logoden

Is Drénec

Pte d'Arradon

Pointe er Gored

I. d'Irus

Ile Holavre

Le Druic

Ile Pirenn

Ile Mouchiouse

Plage de la Falaise

Pte de Béluré

I. de Boëd

R'Angle

Les Réchauds

Pte de Toulindag

Locmiquel

Les Trois Pierres

Grand Rohu

Mancel

Er Pechid

ILE AUX MOINES

Pte de Brouel

Brouel

Le Bourg

ILE D'ARZ

Pointe de Bilherve

Le Fuseau

Ile de Lern

La Grande Truie

La Petit Truie

Le Passage

Anse du Vran

Oysters

Roche Colas

Pte de Léos

Ile Ilur

Ile Pladic

Ile Bailleron

Ile Tascon

Pte du Spernéguy

Pte de Brannec

L'Ouef

Roche Bern

I. Stibiden

I. Godec

I. d'Iluric

Ile aux Oiseaux

St Colombier

Pte de Bernon

Pte de Rua'ud

Pte de Benance

Ile Govihan

Le Poul

Anse du Logeo

Baie du Lindin

Presqu'île de Truscat

Pte de Bréhuidic

Anse du Ruaud

Drenec

Presqu'Île de Rhuys

Sarzeau

| 51' | 50' | 49' | 48' | 47' | 46' | 45' | 44' | 43' |

IV. QUIBERON BAY

⚓ Anse de Moustran

This is the bay just north of Port Blanc, opposite Locmiquel. The best spots are occupied by moorings and it is difficult to find a comfortable anchorage.

⚓ Pen er Men

North of Île d'Irus there is room to anchor off the mainland shore, clear of the moorings.

⚓ Arradon

Rather exposed to the southwest at high water, this popular yachting centre has moorings for visitors but little room to anchor.

⚓ Île de Boëdig

There is a pleasant, secluded anchorage off the northeast end of the island in the Chenal de Badel. The island is private and landing is not allowed.

⚓ Pointe de Beluré

On the north tip of Île d'Arz, there is an anchorage east of the green beacon which marks the end of the ferry slip.

⚓ Conleau

The inlet to the southwest of the peninsula is full of moorings. The best anchorage is in the bight on the port side just before the far end of the narrows. There is a good restaurant.

SOUTH AND EAST MORBIHAN ANCHORAGES

The south and east parts of the Morbihan are slightly less crowded and more peaceful than the Vannes channel.

⚓ Anse de Kerners

Southwest of Île aux Moines there is a large drying bay. Anchor outside the local boats. Water, showers and provisions are available at the campsite in season.

⚓ Anse de Pen Castel

Opposite the south tip of Île aux Moines, it is possible to anchor outside the moorings.

⚓ Anse de Penhap

This is a nice spot in the southeast corner of the Île aux Moines. There is plenty of space to anchor but tuck in well to get out of the stream.

⚓ Île Pirenn

There is a quiet anchorage southwest of Île Pirenn but watch out for the oyster beds. It is possible to land at Pointe de Brouel on Île aux Moines.

⚓ Île d'Arz

There is an anchorage in the bay on the east side. Anchor outside the moorings and do not go in too far because it shoals quickly. Land at the slipway, marked by a red beacon to visit Le Bourg where there are modest shops.

⚓ Le Passage

This is in the extreme east of the Morbihan. It can be difficult to identify and the secret is to first identify Grand Rohu red beacon tower.

In the final approach, do not pass too close to the red beacon on the northern shore. It marks the end of a slipway and not the southern extremity of the dangers.

Anchor midstream in the narrows to the north of the island if space can be found among the moorings. Alternatively, in settled weather, anchor east of the narrows. The tide is strong and there may be some silting so check the depth carefully.

V. The Vilaine and the Loire

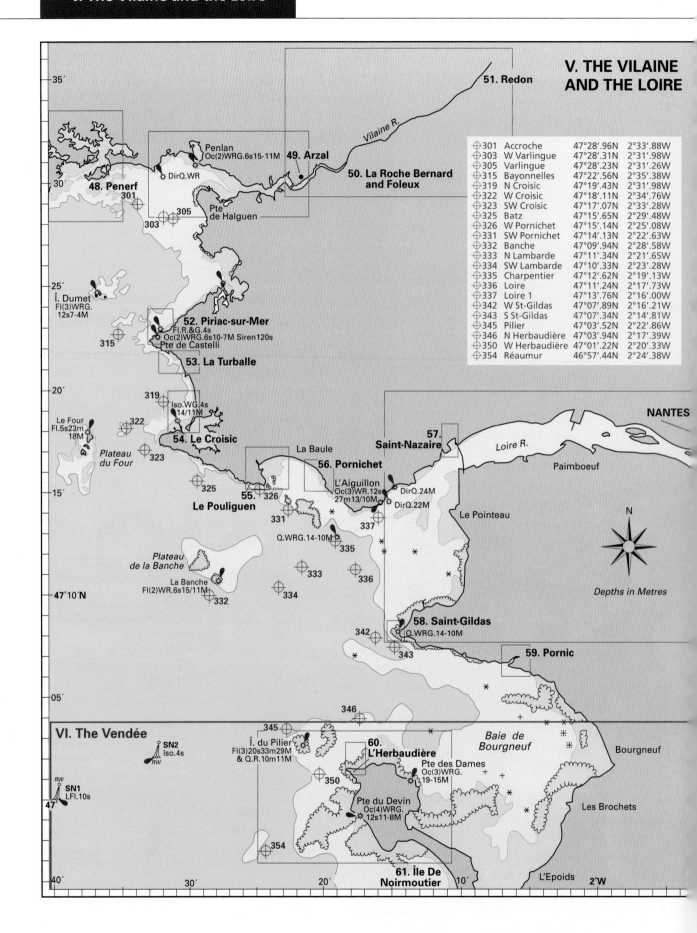

V. THE VILAINE AND THE LOIRE

51. Redon

Vilaine R.

49. Arzal

Penlan
Oc(2)WRG.6s15-11M

☼ DirQ.WR

50. La Roche Bernard and Foleux

Pte de Halguen

48. Penerf
301
305
303

⊕301	Accroche	47°28'.96N	2°33'.88W
⊕303	W Varlingue	47°28'.31N	2°31'.98W
⊕305	Varlingue	47°28'.23N	2°31'.26W
⊕315	Bayonnelles	47°22'.56N	2°35'.38W
⊕319	N Croisic	47°19'.43N	2°31'.98W
⊕322	W Croisic	47°18'.11N	2°34'.76W
⊕323	SW Croisic	47°17'.07N	2°33'.28W
⊕325	Batz	47°15'.65N	2°29'.48W
⊕326	W Pornichet	47°15'.14N	2°25'.08W
⊕331	SW Pornichet	47°14'.13N	2°22'.63W
⊕332	Banche	47°09'.94N	2°28'.58W
⊕333	N Lambarde	47°11'.34N	2°21'.65W
⊕334	SW Lambarde	47°10'.33N	2°23'.28W
⊕335	Charpentier	47°12'.62N	2°19'.13W
⊕336	Loire	47°11'.24N	2°17'.73W
⊕337	Loire 1	47°13'.76N	2°16'.00W
⊕342	W St-Gildas	47°07'.89N	2°16'.21W
⊕343	S St-Gildas	47°07'.34N	2°14'.81W
⊕345	Pilier	47°03'.52N	2°22'.86W
⊕346	N Herbaudière	47°03'.94N	2°17'.39W
⊕350	W Herbaudière	47°01'.22N	2°20'.33W
⊕354	Réaumur	46°57'.44N	2°24'.38W

Î. Dumet
Fl(3)WRG.
12s7-4M

52. Piriac-sur-Mer
Fl.R.&G.4s
Oc(2)WRG.6s10-7M Siren120s
Pte de Castelli
315

53. La Turballe

319
Iso.WG.4s
14/11M

NANTES

Loire R.

Paimboeuf

54. Le Croisic
322

Le Four
Fl.5s23m
18M

Plateau
du Four

323
325

La Baule

56. Pornichet

57. Saint-Nazaire

L'Aiguillon
Oc(3)WR.12s
27m13/10M

DirQ.24M
DirQ.22M

Le Pointeau

55. Le Pouliguen
326

331
337

Plateau
de la Banche

Q.WRG.14-10M
335

333
336

La Banche
Fl(2)WR.6s15/11M
332
334

N

Depths in Metres

58. Saint-Gildas
342
Q.WRG.14-10M

343

59. Pornic

Baie de
Bourgneuf

Bourgneuf

346

VI. The Vendée

345

SN2
Iso.4s
RW

Î. du Pilier
Fl(3)20s33m29M
& Q.R.10m11M

60. L'Herbaudière

350

Pte des Dames
Oc(3)WRG.
19-15M

Les Brochets

RW
SN1
LFl.10s
47°

Pte du Devin
Oc(4)WRG.
12s11-8M

354

61. Île De Noirmoutier

L'Epoids

2°W

48 Pénerf

Location
  47°30'N 2°39'W
Shelter
  Good except in strong W wind
Hazards
  Intricate approach
Depth restrictions
  0.5m in Central passage
  4.5m in E passage
  Deep inside
Night entry Lit but not recommended
HW time
  Brest HW+0015 neaps, -0025 springs
Mean height of tide (m)

	HWS	HWN	LWN	LWS
Pénerf	5.4	4.3	2.0	0.7

Tidal stream in passages
  3kns when rocks are uncovered, 2kns when
  rocks are covered

Berthing
  Visitors' buoys and anchorage
Facilities
  Bar, restaurant and a few
  shops
Charts
  BA 2823 (50)
  SHOM 7033 (50), 7135 (15)
  Imray C39 (78)
Radio VHF Ch 09
Telephone
  ① 02 97 41 20 67,
  Mobile 06 30 95 82 79

Quiet unspoilt river

The Pénerf is an unspoilt oyster river about 6M west of the Vilaine. There are many rocky ledges at the entrance that provide good protection but also make the entrance a bit tricky. A first visit should be in good weather close to high water.

The villages of Pénerf and Cadenic are both small, quiet and attractive. They offer excellent oysters but not a great deal else.

PILOTAGE

Pénerf west passage

Local fishing boats use this entrance in strong west winds. It can only be used safely with local knowledge.

Pénerf Central passage

This passage is the easiest of the three. It can only be used above half tide when Pénerf presents a daunting expanse of water with only Le Pignon for guidance.

By day

Start from a position close to ⊕297-Pénerf but watch out for extensive fishing nets. The distinctive white Tour des Anglais will be roughly in line with Pénerf church on 030° and Le Pignon red beacon tower will be due north.

The entry transit is Le Pignon in line with the steeple of Le Tour du Parc on 001°. If trees obscure the steeple, use Le Pignon in line with the prominent white house on 359°. The house has a single gable and is just right of the water tower (*see below*). Borenis SHM buoy and La Traverse SHM beacon mark the dangers to starboard. Do not confuse the two PHM beacons of the east passage with those of the Central one.

On close approach, turn to starboard leaving Le Pignon 40m to port. Then steer to leave Bayonnelle and Petit Bayonelle beacons to starboard and follow one more starboard beacon into the river. At the last beacon, turn onto about 060° and head for the moorings off Pénerf village. On the way there is a red beacon. Do not go too close as it is in very shallow water.

By night

Le Pignon is lit but otherwise the river is unlit and night entry is not recommended.

By GPS

Careful visual pilotage is required. The following waypoints may help in the approach
⊕297-Pénerf, ⊕298-Pénerf 1

Pénerf E passage

This passage is deep but very narrow and there are rocky shoals close east of it. Also, the front mark is not easy to see from a distance and trees may hide the back mark. It should not be used in poor visibility.

Le Pignon and the steeple showing just above the trees to the right of the white house with the gable *M&G Barron*

V. THE VILAINE AND THE LOIRE

The River Pénerf looking northeast.
The Port of Pénerf is on the east side of the river near the jetty. The anchorage at Cadenic is ½M further on the north side. The River Pénerf is mostly devoted to oyster farming

By day

Start from a position near Borénis SHM buoy. The transit is the first PHM beacon of the east passage (southeast of Le Pignon) in line with Le Tour du Parc steeple on 354°. Both marks may be hard to see. Above half-tide it is safe to go in cautiously towards Le Pignon. However, do not attempt the passage unless the first PHM beacon can be positively identified, particularly if the tide is running strongly.

Leave the PHM beacon fairly close to port. Then steer to leave Le Pignon to port and join the central passage described above.

By GPS

Careful visual pilotage is required. The following waypoints may help in the approach
⊕299-E Pénerf, ⊕300-E Pénerf 1

BERTHS AND ANCHORAGES

Pénerf

There are three marked visitors' buoys off Pénerf quay and there are two more some 200m upstream. All are in a minimum depth of 4m. It may be possible to anchor outside the moorings but beware of oyster beds. This anchorage is quite choppy when wind and tide are opposed.

Cadenic

Cadenic is on the north bank less than 0.5M beyond Pénerf. Leave the IDM beacon, just north of Pénerf, to port and aim for the PHM beacon and SHM buoy just off Cadenic. There are some fishing boat moorings off the pier and a quiet neap anchorage upstream of the moorings. There is not much room at springs and the holding in deeper water is reported to be poor.

⚓ Pointe de St-Jacques

Sheltered from northwest to northeast, there is a small harbour off the south tip of the Presqu'île de Rhuys. Approach from St-Jacques SCM and anchor off the pier. A night departure is possible using the pierhead light.
⊕294-St-Jaques 47°28'·97N 2°47'·08W

⚓ Anse de Suscinio

Well protected from the north and northwest but completely open to the south, this wide shallow bay is 3M west of Pénerf entrance. Approach from due south and anchor where depth permits. A night departure without GPS would be unsafe. The ruins of the Château de Suscinio are visible from the anchorage and can be visited.
⊕296-Suscinio 47°29'·94N 2°43'·38W

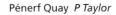

Pénerf Quay P Taylor

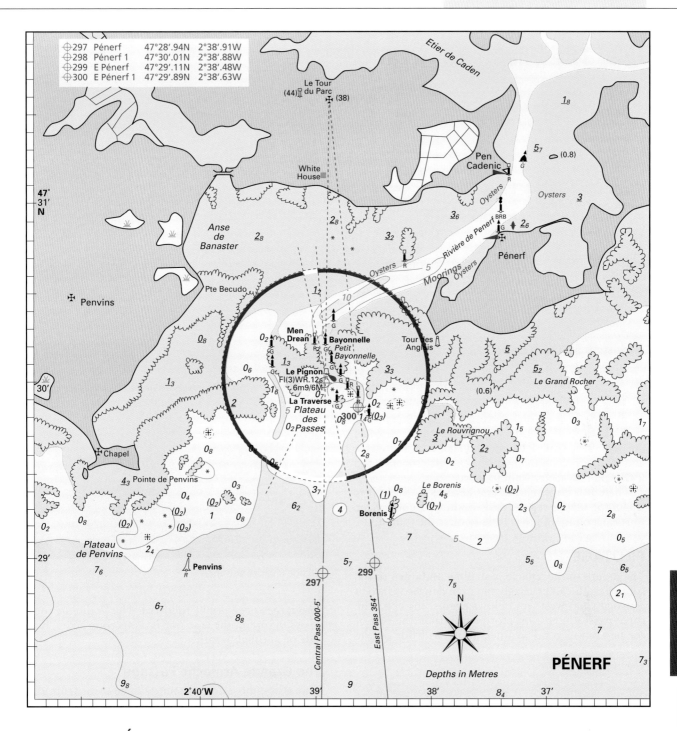

⊕297	Pénerf	47°28'.94N	2°38'.91W
⊕298	Pénerf 1	47°30'.01N	2°38'.88W
⊕299	E Pénerf	47°29'.11N	2°38'.48W
⊕300	E Pénerf 1	47°29'.89N	2°38'.63W

ASHORE IN PÉNERF AND CADENIC

Pénerf has shops, bars and two restaurants. Toilets at the lifeboat station but no showers. Oysters are sold on the quay. There is also a nice chapel with a couple of traditional model fishing boats as votive offerings.

Cadenic has almost no facilities but, like Pénerf, it is often possible to buy seafood from the fishermen.

The Bureau du Port at Pénerf *P Taylor*

49 The Vilaine to Arzal

Location
47°30'N 2°28'W

Shelter
Excellent

Depth restrictions
0.5m over the bar

Night entry
Partially lit

Arzal lock Opens on most hours

HW time
Brest HW+0035 neaps, –0020 springs

Mean height of tide (m)

	HWS	HWN	LWN	LWS
Tréhiguier	5.5	4.4	2.1	0.7

Tidal stream in the river
Flood 2kns, ebb 3kns in river but much influenced by inland rain

Berthing
Two marinas

Fuel
W side of Arzal marina

Facilities
Good marina facilities

Charts
BA 2823 (50)
SHOM 7033 (50)
Imray C39 (78)

Radio
Lock VHF Ch 18
Marina VHF Ch 9

Telephone
Lock ☎ 02 97 41 28 39
Marina ☎ 02 97 45 02 97
Call *Marina* or ☎ 02 97 45 01 15 for lock opening times

Gateway to the Vilaine

(See page 179)

The Vilaine has a large lock at Arzal through a barrage built to protect the area from flooding and to provide a reservoir of fresh water. It keeps the water level permanently at 3.0m or more. This has created a beautiful, long boating lake with flat water and almost no commercial traffic. Once through the lock, you may never want to leave.

There is a large marina just beyond the lock. It is useful for fuel or repairs and would be a good place to leave a boat but it has little to offer the tourist.

PILOTAGE

The mouth of the Vilaine is shallow and open to the southwest. It can be rough and even dangerous when a strong southwest wind blows against the ebb. The three passes have a bit more depth than the rest of the bay but in good weather, above half tide on the

Vilaine River at entrance

flood, they need not be followed. The Varlingue rock (dries 0.3m) on the east side is dangerous below half tide or in rough weather.

The Grande Accroche Passage

This is the most convenient passage to or from the Morbihan but the seas break heavily in strong west and southwest winds.

By day

Start from a position 0.5M SE of Les Mâts SCM buoy. The transit is Penlan lighthouse in line with the Abbaye de Prières on 052°. Both marks are fairly easy to see but in practice it is good enough to steer for Penlan lighthouse, keeping a reasonable distance from Kervoyal tower beacon.

Once Kervoyal tower is due west, steer due east to enter the river between the buoys. A useful transit is Kervoyal tower beacon in line with Tour des Anglais tower beacon (at Pénerf) on 267°.

By night

The Grande Accroche is lit by the white sector of Penlan and the narrow white sector of Kervoyal.

Vilaine River entrance

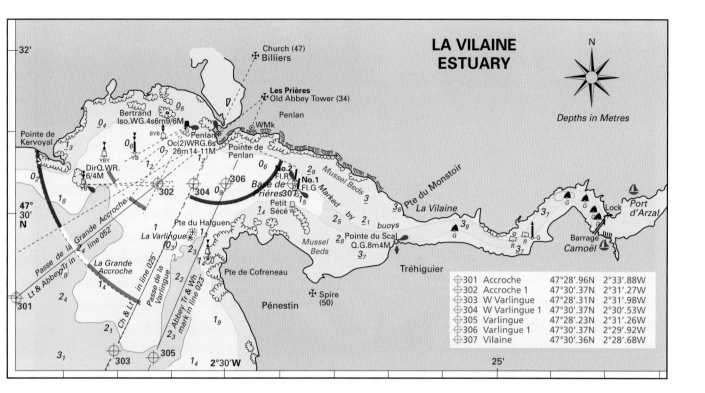

LA VILAINE ESTUARY

Depths in Metres

⊕301	Accroche	47°28'.96N	2°33'.88W
⊕302	Accroche 1	47°30'.37N	2°31'.27W
⊕303	W Varlingue	47°28'.31N	2°31'.98W
⊕304	W Varlingue 1	47°30'.37N	2°30'.53W
⊕305	Varlingue	47°28'.23N	2°31'.26W
⊕306	Varlingue 1	47°30'.37N	2°29'.92W
⊕307	Vilaine	47°30'.36N	2°28'.68W

However, the river is not lit beyond Tréhiguier so night entry is not recommended.

By GPS

⊕301-Accroche, ⊕302-Accroche 1, ⊕307-Vilaine

The west Varlingue passage

By day

Start towards the east side of the bay with Penlan lighthouse bearing about 025°. The transit is Biliers church in line with Penlan lighthouse on 025°. At low water, it is important to hold it accurately because it passes close to La Varlingue rock (dries 0.3m).

Once Kervoyal tower beacon is due west, steer due east to enter the river between the buoys.

By GPS

⊕303-W Varlingue, ⊕304-W Varlingue 1, ⊕307-Vilaine

This route passes close west of La Varlingue (dries 0.3m).

The Varlingue passage

This is the most convenient passage from the south. It is also the deepest and the most protected in bad west and southwest weather.

By day

The official transit is the Abbaye de Prières in line with a small white daymark on 023°. The front mark will be invisible to a stranger. Fortunately a WCM tower beacon on the shore indicates the approximate position of La Varlingue (dries 0.3m).

Once Kervoyal tower is due west, or Petit Sécé white tower beacon bears 105° steer due east to enter the river between the buoys.

The Vilaine entrance to the Arzal lock

By day

The channel is well buoyed to Tréhiguer. There will be as little as 0.8m or even less in places so take the curves wide and if possible go in or out at high water.

Beyond Tréhiguier there are fewer marks, but the channel is still easy to follow with red and green buoys and the occasional beacon. The approach to the lock is marked with starboard-hand buoys.

By GPS

⊕305-Varlingue, ⊕306-Varlingue 1, ⊕307-Vilaine

This route passes close east of La Varlingue (dries 0.3m).

The Arzal lock

The lock is on the north side of the river, adjacent to the conspicuous control tower. The lower gates are normally left open so yachts arriving from seaward can wait in the lock. There are some mooring buoys

River Arzal lock and barrage with bridge raised *S. Parkes*

The barrage from southeast with Arzal Marina on the northeast side and Camoël on the southwest

below the dam and room to anchor. The danger area around the dam spillway is marked off by yellow buoys.

The lock is worked in daylight hours between 0700 and 2200, during the season. The opening times depend on the tide and are displayed at the local marinas and in an invaluable booklet available at the lock. The lock may be closed for more than one hour at lunch time or close to low water. Otherwise, it opens on the hour.

The lock is big and crowded and, except close to high water, quite turbulent. Moor to the vertical chains and make sure the fenders do not pop out. Also wait until the turbulence has subsided before casting off. Fortunately, the lock-keeper manages the potential chaos with great charm and skill. If possible it is best to avoid times of heavy use such as early on Saturdays, Sunday evenings and early or late on fête days.

BERTHS AND ANCHORAGES

⚓ Tréhiguier

Sheltered from south and east but exposed to west and northwest, there is a convenient anchorage near the entrance on the seaward side of the lock. Anchor outside the moorings in soft mud. Land at the slip.

The Vilaine below Arzal

There are many places in the river where anchoring is possible on the edge of the channel. Sound the area carefully before anchoring because in places the depths shoal rapidly when the channel is left. Two anchors may be necessary.

Arzal Lock looking southeast towards Camoël Marina
S. Parkes

Arzal and Camoël marinas

There is a large marina on the north bank above the dam at Arzal and a smaller, quieter one at Camoël on the south side.

Facilities at Arzal

Arzal has all the facilities of a major marina complex including fuel, all repairs, 15-tonne crane, masting, haul out, laying up outside or under cover. There are bars and restaurants, but no shops within 2M. The dam has a fish pass which is worth seeing.

Camoël marina on the south side is more peaceful, but has no facilities other than showers and toilets.

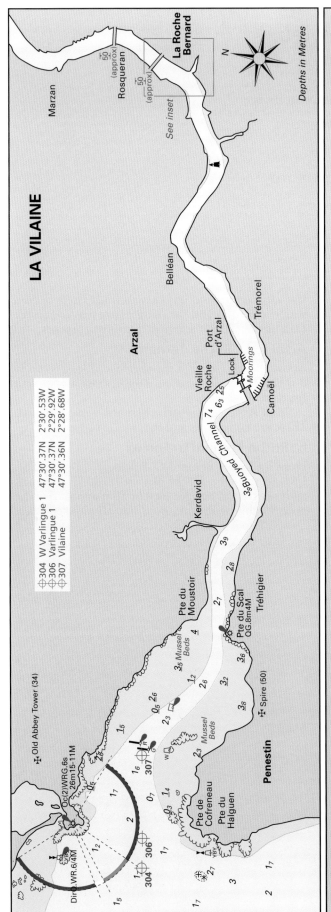

LA VILAINE

Depths in Metres

⊕304	W Varlingue 1	47°30'.37N	2°30'.53W
⊕306	Varlingue 1	47°30'.37N	2°29'.92W
⊕307	Vilaine	47°30'.36N	2°28'.68W

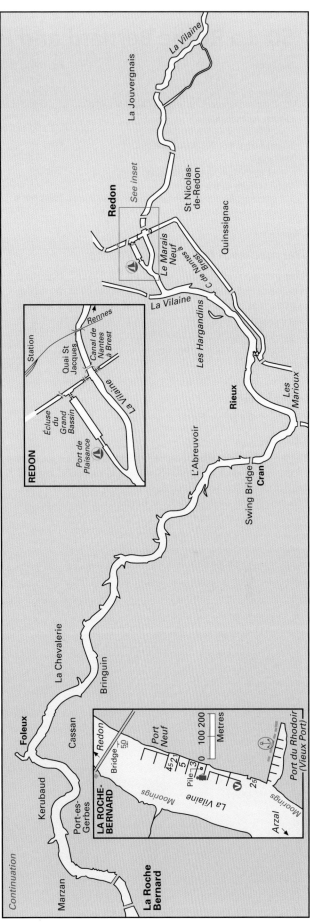

V. THE VILAINE AND THE LOIRE

50 La Roche Bernard and Foleux

Location
47°31'N 2°19'W

Shelter
Excellent except in very strong SW wind

Depth restrictions
3.0m or more beyond Arzal

Night entry Not recommended

HW time
Above Arzal there is no tide

Tidal stream in the river
There is usually a slight stream to seaward.
This can be strong after very heavy rain

Berthing
Marina and visitors' buoys

Facilities
Good marina facilities plus
attractive town with shops, cafés
and restaurants

Fuel
At Port Neuf

Charts
IGN Top25 1022OT (25)

Telephone
Harbourmaster ☎ 02 99 90 62 17

The medieval heart of the Vilaine

The attractive holiday town of La Roche Bernard was once an important river port and boat building centre. Today its quaint medieval streets and houses have been beautifully restored to make it the main tourist destination on the Vilaine.

There are two marinas and plenty of visitors' buoys.

PILOTAGE

(See plan on page 179).

Charts

Beyond the dam, the river is not charted. The section from Arzal to La Roche Bernard is covered by the land map IGN Top25 1022OT (*La Roche Bernard*). However, beyond La Roche Bernard, land maps are less satisfactory and less easy to find. There is deep water to Redon and the dangers are marked so the plan on page 179 is adequate for most purposes.

Arzal to La Roche Bernard

Above the dam most of the river has at least 3.0m so it is only necessary to use common sense and not cut the corners.

From Arzal to La Roche Bernard is about 3.75M. There are no hazards and the river is very attractive.

La Roche Bernard to Foleux

From La Roche Bernard to Foleux is about 4.75M. Just north of La Roche Bernard, the river passes under two road bridges (height 50m approx.) and a power cable with unknown but ample clearance.

Vilaine River. La Roche Bernard from west

The Vilaine River, Foleux

La Roche Bernard Old
Marina in Port du Rhodoir

Just before Foleux another power cable crosses the river, again with unknown but ample clearance.

After La Roche Bernard, the river becomes less steep sided but it still winds between wooded hills and is most attractive.

BERTHS AND ANCHORAGES

Port du Rhodoir marina

Port du Rhodoir marina, the Old Port, is in a small inlet on the south side of La Roche Bernard. Local boats mainly use it but the first pontoon is a reception pontoon. The harbourmaster's office is on the quay.

Port Neuf

Port Neuf is the main marina in the river at La Roche Bernard. The visitors' pontoon is the westernmost one (pontoon A). If it is full call the marina office.

Visitors' moorings

There are many moorings in the river and it is usually possible to borrow one.

Foleux

Foleux has a marina, boatyard and visitors' pontoon. Ashore there are toilets, showers and a restaurant but not much else.

ANCHORAGES IN THE VILAINE

It is possible to anchor almost anywhere in the river except where anchoring is explicitly forbidden. Note that a similar charge to that in the marina will be made for anchoring in the vicinity of La Roche Bernard or Foleux.

ASHORE IN LA ROCHE BERNARD

The marina can carry out most repairs but there is no chandlery and no fuel berth. Bread can be delivered to yachts each morning.

Ashore, there are cafés, shops and restaurants to suit every taste. The medieval town is well worth exploring. A map showing a recommended walk through the old streets and alleys is available from the tourist office. The maritime museum has models and reconstructions to show what life was like by the Vilaine. Market day is Thursday.

La Roche Bernard Bureau du Port

V. THE VILAINE AND THE LOIRE

51 Redon

Location
  47°38′N 2°05′W
Shelter
  Excellent in Redon marina
Depth restrictions
  3.0m or more in river beyond Arzal
  2.2m in Redon basin
Cran bridge opening (local time)
  0900, 1000, 1100, 1430, 1630, 1830
  and 1930
  1 April to 31 October
Night entry Not recommended
HW time
  Above Arzal there is no tide
Stream in the river
  There is usually a slight stream to seaward.
  This can be strong after very heavy rain

Berthing
  Marina at Foleux and Redon,
  several riverside pontoons and
  anchorages
Facilities
  Marina at Foleux, substantial
  market town at Redon
Fuel
  Diesel at Redon
Radio
  Vilaine navigation VHF Ch 10
  Redon Marina VHF Ch 9
Telephone
  Foleux ② 02 99 91 80 87
  Redon ② 02 99 71 61 73,
  Mobile 06 65 13 69 65

Gateway to the canals

Redon is a pleasant market town and major canal port with direct access to the Nantes to Brest canal via a lock at the northeast end of the marina basin. It is 26M from the sea and has a completely different atmosphere from most yacht ports. The town is interlaced with canals and locks, and there are many fine buildings that provide evidence of Redon's important role in Breton history.

PILOTAGE

(See plan on page 179).

Foleux to Redon

The swing bridge at Cran (closed clearance 5.8m)

Between April and October the swing bridge at Cran opens at 0900, 1000, 1100, 1430, 1630, 1830 and 1930 (local time). There is a waiting pontoon on the upstream side and a waiting buoy on the downstream side. The bridge does not open for long and it is important to watch the signals and be ready. Two reds means no passage; one red means get ready; and two greens means go.

By day

From Foleux to Cran is about 7M. The river winds between fields and wooded hills and is most attractive. A nature reserve with a pontoon will be passed in this section. There are no hazards except a power cable just below Cran with 27m headroom. The speed limit in the river is 5.5knots.

From Cran bridge to Rieux is just under 3M and shortly afterwards the vista widens out for the last 3M to Redon and the river becomes much more like an inland waterway with junctions and signposts.

The marina is in the old sea lock of the Nantes-Brest canal and it is necessary to follow the signposts to the Port du Redon. The lock gate is permanently open since the barrage at Arzal now maintains the water level.

The visitors' pontoon and café at Foleux *M&G Barron*

Traditional fishing on the Vilaine *M&G Barron*

One of the two pontoons at Rieux *M&G Barron*

The marina at Redon looking west

Redon. View of approach canal from the entrance to the marina basin

BERTHS AND ANCHORAGES

Redon

The marina is through the lock on the port side. Maximum depth is 2.20m but could be less. Canal boats use the starboard side. There are no specific visitors' berths and usually the harbourmaster allocates berths. If he is not on duty, find an empty berth (the ones nearer to the entrance are deepest) and report to the office.

Rieux

There are two visitors' pontoons in attractive surroundings and fairly deep water 3M upstream from Cran close to the village of Rieux.

ASHORE IN REDON

Redon is a market town and a major port for canal boats so most yachting requirements can be satisfied. The diesel berth is on the porthand side just inside the entrance to the marina basin.

The town has an excellent covered market (open in the morning on Mondays, Fridays and Saturdays), good shops and restaurants, and an interesting canal museum. There are some fine 15th to 18th century town houses and a surprisingly large abbey church. For a town that has been sacked repeatedly in its history it has all the appearances of a wealthy past.

There are markets every day except Friday and Sunday, a hypermarket a mile away on the road to Nantes and the railway station is within easy walking distance of the marina and has direct trains to Nantes and St-Malo and along the coast to Vannes and Quimper.

Redon yacht basin looking east

52 Piriac-sur-Mer

Location
47°23'N 2°33'W

Shelter
Good in the marina

Depth restrictions
Sill dries 1.0m and opens when there is
2.4m of tide.
The marina has 2.4m

Night entry Lit

HW time
Brest HW+0015 neaps, −0030 springs

Mean height of tide (m)

	HWS	HWN	LWN	LWS
St-Nazaire	5.4	4.3	2.0	0.7

Tidal stream in approach
NE – Brest HW−0600 to −0100 (0.7kns)
SW – Brest HW−0100 to −0600 (0.7kns)

Berthing
Marina

Fuel
On quay

Facilities
Limited repairs; adequate shops,
cafés and restaurants; good
market

Charts
BA 2823 (50)
SHOM 7033 (50), 7136 (15)
Imray C39 (78)

Radio VHF Ch 9

Telephone
Harbourmaster ☏ 02 40 23 52 32

Delightful holiday resort

Piriac is a delightful place. It is a small 17th century town that has been beautifully renovated as a holiday resort. The town is full of flowers that make the cafés and restaurants seem particularly inviting. For the more adventurous, it is a good base for visiting the swampy area of Grand Brière for bird-watching or the medieval town of Guérande although both can be reached just as easily from La Baule or St-Nazaire.

The marina is fairly new and usually has room for visiting yachts up to 12m. It is located in a drying harbour with a sill and a flap gate. The gate opens above half tide and retains the depth in the marina at 2.4m. The depth over the sill is signified by a digital read-out at the sill and is visible from seaward and from within the marina.

PILOTAGE

Approach and entrance to Piriac

Piriac flap gate

The sill dries 1.0m and the gate automatically drops open when the height of tide reaches 2.4m, which gives 1.4m over the sill. The digital depth gauge shows the actual depth over the sill.

There is no large-scale chart of the approaches but the channel seems to be deeper than the sill. However, yachts regularly go aground in the approach and just outside the marina entrance so there may be some shallower patches.

By day

From the north, a distinctive belfry on the seafront identifies Piriac. The approach is rocky so start from a position 100m northeast of Grand Norven NCM beacon. Steer about 165° and pass between the green and red beacons to enter the harbour. The line from the PHM beacon to the harbour is reported to have the deepest water.

From the south or west, avoid the rocks off Pointe du Castelli by keeping outside Les Bayonnelles WCM buoy and well outside Rohtrès NCM beacon tower and then approaching Piriac from the north as above.

The entrance to the marina is to port, immediately inside the breakwaters. It is only about 50 feet wide and is marked by two red and two green beacons. Red lights indicate that the gate is closed; green lights indicate that it is open.

By night

Approach in the white sector of the Inner Mole WRG light and remain in this sector until past the breakwater lights.

By GPS

From the north use:
⊕312-Piriac, ⊕313-Piriac 1

From the west use:
⊕314-Rohtrès, ⊕312-Piriac, ⊕313-Piriac 1

From the southwest use:
⊕315-Bayonnelles, ⊕314-Rohtrès, ⊕312-Piriac, ⊕313-Piriac

Piriac-sur-Mer from the east

BERTHS AND ANCHORAGES

Piriac marina

Visitors are normally met by a launch and allocated a berth. If there is no launch, berth on the visitors' pontoon (pontoon E), which is immediately ahead on entering.

⚓ Grand Norven

In settled weather, there is a temporary anchorage, to wait for the tide, east of the Grand Norven beacon in about 2.5m.

⚓ Mine d'Or

Protected from the east, this wide bay is just south of the mouth of the Vilaine. Approach from north of west to avoid the dangers near Île de Belair. Anchor 0.5M northeast of Île de Belair where depth permits. A night escape to Piriac or the Vilaine is possible using Penlan light.

⊕308-Mine d'Or 47°28'·16N 2°29'·87W

⚓ Mesquer

Sheltered from the east, Mesquer is a little harbour and large drying bay 4M northeast of Piriac. Approach from a position between Basse Normande NCM buoy and Laronesse IDM beacon and steer about 110° towards Mesquer. Enter the harbour between the red and green beacons. At neaps it is possible to anchor east of the jetty. Boats that can take the ground can go further in for better shelter but beware of shellfish beds.

⊕310-Mesquer 47°25'·44N 2°28'·20W

⚓ Île Dumet

Slightly sheltered from the southwest, Île Dumet is a bird sanctuary 3M west-northwest of Piriac. There are shallow patches northeast and northwest of the island so approach with the lighthouse on about 215°. Anchor northeast of the lighthouse.

In the 18th century Île Dumet was used by Admiral Hawke as a market garden to provide vegetables for his sailors when they were blockading the French Fleet in the harbours of Quiberon Bay. He was one of the first naval commanders to appreciate the importance of fresh vegetables in preventing disease in men confined on ships for long periods.

⊕311-Dumet 47°24'·77N 2°36'·94W

ASHORE IN PIRIAC

Piriac has a fuel pontoon and a chandlery but otherwise it has limited harbour facilities. The town is charming. It has a reasonable range of shops and a market on Monday, Wednesday and Saturday. There are many cafés and restaurants.

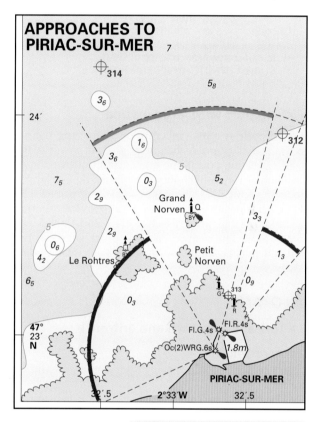

⊕312 Piriac   47°23'.89N 2°32'.26W
⊕313 Piriac 1   47°23'.17N 2°32'.66W
⊕314 Rohtrès   47°24'.22N 2°33'.60W

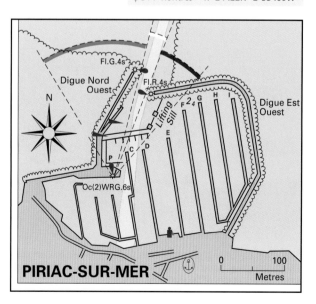

Piriac-sur-Mer

V. THE VILAINE AND THE LOIRE

53 La Turballe

Location
47°21′N 2°31′W

Shelter
Good except from SSW

Depth restrictions
2.2m in approach
2.0m in marina

Night entry Lit

HW time
Brest HW+0015 neaps, −0040 springs

Mean height of tide (m):

	HWS	HWN	LWN	LWS
Le Croisic	5.4	4.3	2.0	0.7

Tidal stream in approach
N – Brest HW−0600 to −0100 (0.5kns)
S – Brest HW−0100 to +0400 (0.5kns)
Slack – Brest HW+0400 to −0600

Berthing Marina

Fuel SW harbour wall

Facilities
As of a major fishing port

Charts
BA 2823 (50)
SHOM 7033 (50), 7145 (25)
Imray C39 (large scale)

Radio:
Marina VHF Ch 9
Must call before entry

Telephone
Harbourmaster ☎ 02 40 23 41 65

Fishing port with large marina

La Turballe is a nice mixture of a working fishing port and a popular beach resort. It is now the leading fishing port in the Loire-Atlantique region.

There are two harbours. The Basin de Garlahy is locked and totally dedicated to fishing boats. The Port de Plaisance is dredged to provide all tide access; fishing boats use one half and yachts the other half. The visitors' area is quite small so the harbourmaster sometimes has to turn visiting boats away.

PILOTAGE

La Turballe approach and entrance

Entry restrictions

Entry is not recommended in strong west wind or swell.

The marina gets very crowded in season and it is necessary to call on VHF Ch 9 before entering. When the marina is full, the harbourmaster may broadcast announcements on VHF Ch 9.

By day

The long white-walled fish market, the water tower at the back of town and the long beach to the south make La Turballe easy to identify from any direction. However, it must only be approached from the southwest to avoid the rocky shoals to the north.

Aim for the north end of the beach. When about 0.25M south of the harbour, the south facing entrance will open. Make a sharp turn to port to make the final entry on about 007°. Keep towards the west breakwater because rocks extend from the east side. Once past the inner breakwater head, turn sharply to starboard to enter the Port de Plaisance.

By night

Approach in the white sector of the west jetty head light. Enter with the leading lights in line on 007°. After passing the west breakwater head, make a sharp turn to starboard round the green light that marks the entrance to the Port de Plaisance.

By GPS

⊕316-Turballe, ⊕317-Turballe 1, ⊕318-Turballe 2

A sharp turn to port is required at ⊕317-Turballe 1.

The main harbour is split into two. Fishing vessels are on the north side nearest to the fish market and pleasure boats are on the south side *M&G Barron*

The visitors' pontoons form a U-shape beyond the finger pontoons. There is a small aluminium kiosk on the end of the first pontoon. An extra pontoon, without shore access, is sited in the middle of the 'U' *M&G Barron*

BERTHS AND ANCHORAGES

La Turballe marina

The visitors' pontoons are clearly indicated and are in the southwest part of the marina, just past a little aluminium kiosk. Space for berthing and manoeuvring a 12m boat is quite limited and in fact the area designated for visiting boats can become one big raft in season.

⚓ South of La Turballe harbour

In offshore winds there is pleasant anchorage off the long sandy beach to the south of the harbour.

ASHORE IN LA TURBALLE

There is a fuel berth on the south breakwater, a 25-tonne crane, a 250-tonne travel-lift and a slipway. All repairs can be undertaken on yachts up to 16m. The town is a lively holiday resort with plenty of restaurants, shops and cafés close to the marina.

A magnificent 2M beach is just south of the marina and there is easy access to the salt marshes to see the wildlife.

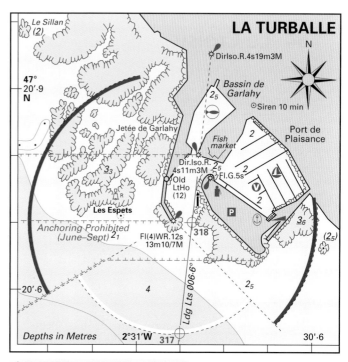

LA TURBALLE

⊕316 Turballe   47°20′.54N 2°31′.63W
⊕317 Turballe 1 47°20′.60N 2°30′.91W
⊕318 Turballe 2 47°20′.70N 2°30′.88W

La Turballe looking northeast.
It is easy to identify La Turballe from the sea as the white wall of the fish market is particularly distinctive. Visitors entering the marina turn to starboard into the main marina. The harbourmaster's office is in the corner of the car park

V. THE VILAINE AND THE LOIRE

54 Le Croisic

Location
47°18'N 2°31'W

Shelter
Good in drying harbour
Exposed to NW in anchorage

Depth restrictions
Channel dredged to 2.3m on leading line
Yacht harbour dries 1.7m

Night entry Lit

HW time
Brest HW+0015 neaps, –0040 springs

Mean height of tide (m)

	HWS	HWN	LWN	LWS
Le Croisic	5.4	4.3	2.0	0.7

Tidal stream in entrance
5kns at half-flood and half-ebb

Berthing
Drying harbour, 2m in Le Pool
anchorage

Facilities
As of fishing port and holiday
resort.

Charts
BA 2823 (50)
SHOM 7395 (50), 7145 (25)
Imray C39 (large scale)

Radio
Marina VHF Ch 9

Telephone
Marina ① 02 40 23 10 95

Historic salt port

Le Croisic is a fascinating town. It has been important as a salt port since before the middle ages. The salt was very good for fish curing and Le Croisic had a large sardine fishing fleet. Then in the 19th century it became one of the first swimming resorts.

Today it is a thriving tourist resort and an excellent base from which to visit the salt marshes, the beautiful walled town of Guérande, the salt museum at Batz-sur-Mer or the nearby beaches.

The harbour is made up of a curious series of islands with drying basins between them. Fishing

Le Croisic looking southeast.
The largest basin in the foreground is the Grande Chambre, then there are several small, strangely-shaped basins and finally the Port de Plaisance. All the harbours dry

boats and sailing boats that can take the ground use these. Boats wishing to remain afloat must anchor or use a mooring outside the harbour in Le Pool.

PILOTAGE

Le Croisic approach and entrance

Warning

The streams are strong and the flood sets onto the submerged training wall so enter on the last hours of the flood if possible. On the ebb, with strong winds between west-southwest and north, the entrance is dangerous.

By day

Start from a position about 0.5M north of Basse Hergo SHM beacon tower. This can be approached directly from the northwest. However, coming from the west, particularly at low water, it is necessary to keep at least 1M off shore to avoid the reef between Basse Castouillet WCM buoy and Basse Hergo SHM beacon tower.

Le Croisic can be identified by a distinctive belfry in town and a conspicuous hospital at Pen Bron on the east side of the channel. Steer for the belfry on 156°. The outer leading marks are rather slender light structures with black stripes on yellow boards almost in line with the belfry. They are lit continuously. Bring them in line on 156° and follow them into the channel. This will leave Basse Hergo SHM and the Jetée du Trehic to starboard.

Follow the transit to the bend in the breakwater. Then steer 174° to follow the second leading marks, which are yellow rectangles each with a vertical black stripe. These marks are located in a bay at the root of the breakwater and are not lit during the day.

At Les Rouzins PHM buoy turn onto 135° and the third transit which is a pair of red and white chequered rectangles on the fish market roof and on the quay in front of the fish market. These are also not lit during the day. This channel is buoyed because it moves.

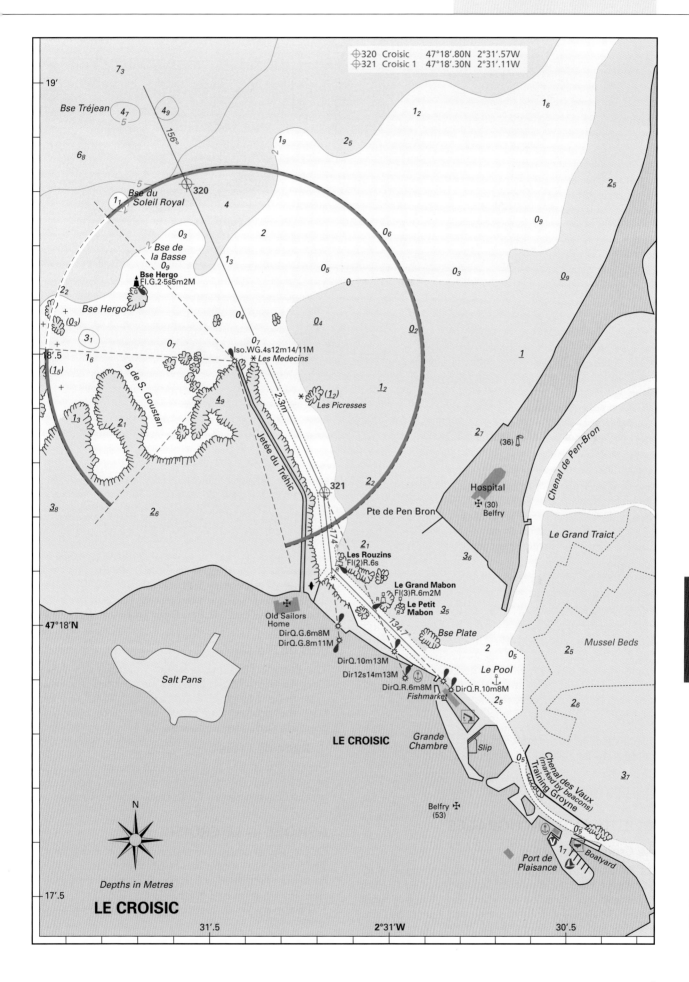

	Croisic	47°18′.80N	2°31′.57W
⊕320	Croisic	47°18′.80N	2°31′.57W
⊕321	Croisic 1	47°18′.30N	2°31′.11W

19′

Bse Tréjean

320

Bse du
Soleil Royal

Bse de
la Basse

Bse Hergo
Fl.G.2·5s5m2M

Bse Hergo

B de S. Goustan

18′.5

Iso.WG.4s12m14/11M
✳ Les Medecins

Les Picresses

Jetée du Tréhic

321

Pte de Pen Bron

Hospital

⊕ (30)
Belfry

Le Grand Traict

Chenal de Pen-Bron

Les Rouzins
Fl(2)R.6s

Le Grand Mabon
Fl(3)R.6m2M

Le Petit
Mabon

Bse Plate

Mussel Beds

Old Sailors
Home
DirQ.G.6m8M
DirQ.G.8m11M

DirQ.10m13M
Dir12s14m13M

DirQ.R.6m8M   DirQ.R.10m8M
Fishmarket

Le Pool

47°18′N

Salt Pans

LE CROISIC

Grande
Chambre

Slip

Chenal des Vaux
(marked by beacons)
Training Groyne

N

Belfry ⊕
(53)

Port de
Plaisance

Boatyard

Depths in Metres

17′.5

LE CROISIC

31′.5   2°31′W   30′.5

Hold the transit until close to the fishing quay to avoid Basse Plate, drying 2.5m and when the fishmarket is abeam turn to port to enter Le Pool for a mooring or, for the yacht basin, continue along the channel leaving the PHM stakes marking the training wall about 25m to port. The entrance to the yacht basin is the fifth one on the starboard side

By night
The white sector of Jetée du Tréhic light clears all the distant dangers, including Le Four and Île Dumet. However, it leads onto the rocks nearer to the harbour entrance so make the final approach using the east green sector with the Dir.QW leading Lights in line. The three transits are easier to identify by night than by day and it is only necessary to keep on them. The street lighting on the quays is good and there is no difficulty once they are reached.

By GPS
From the north or northwest use:
⊕319-N Croisic, ⊕320-Croisic, ⊕321-Croisic 1

From the west, with sufficient rise of tide, use:
⊕322-W Croisic, ⊕320-Croisic, ⊕321-Croisic 1

BERTHS AND ANCHORAGES

Le Croisic Pool
Le Pool is a fair size but moorings occupy much of it. However visitors are permitted to moor to vacant ones and are charged for their use. Mussel beds cover the drying banks of Le Grand Traict, but the narrow and steep-sided Chenal de Pen Bron runs up the east side of the peninsula. It contains more

Le Croisic entrance looking north.
The first transit is followed as far as the bend in the Jetée du Tréhic and the second transits are located at the root of the jetty. The third transits are on the roof of the fish market which is the building on the quay with the long grey roof. The moored boats are in The Pool and the Chenal de Pen-Bron

moorings. Anchoring is forbidden in the Pen Bron channel. If anchoring in Le Pool, use a trip-line, as the bottom is foul with old chain. The ebb runs very hard in the Chenal de Pen Bron and quite hard in Le Pool.

Port de Plaisance
The Port de Plaisance is in the Chambre des Vases. Deep-keel yachts can dry out against the wall outside on a hard, level bottom and boats that can take the ground can enter and secure bow-to a pontoon with a stern mooring.

⚓ Rade de Croisic
Sheltered from the east but horribly exposed to wind or swell from the west, there are many anchorages off the beach between La Turballe and Le Croisic.

ASHORE IN LE CROISIC
Le Croisic is an active fishing and yachting port. There is a 180-tonne travel-lift and boatyard with haul-out facilities, a marine engineer and good chandlery but no fuel berth.

The town is an attractive, busy holiday resort with a full range of shops, cafés and restaurants. There are good markets on Monday (July and August), Thursday and Saturday.

Le Croisic looking south.
The town has been built on a slender peninsula extending to the west of La Baule. The town on the far coast,
6M south of Le Croisic, is Batz-sur-Mer, the City of Salt. Between the two towns there are many salt pans

V. THE VILAINE AND THE LOIRE

55 Le Pouliguen

Location
47°16'N 2°25'W

Shelter
Good except in strong S and SE

Depth restrictions
Entrance dries 1.2m
About 1.3m on visitors' pontoon

Night entry Not recommended

HW time
Brest HW+0015 neaps, –0030 springs

Mean height of tide (m)

	HWS	HWN	LWN	LWS
Le Pouliguen	5.4	4.3	2.0	0.7

Tidal stream in river
4kns at half-flood and half-ebb

Berthing
Marina with visitors' pontoon

Facilities
All marina facilities plus busy
and attractive holiday resort

Fuel By visitors' pontoon

Charts
BA 2986 (50)
SHOM 7033 (50), 7145 (25)
Imray C39 (large scale)

Radio
Marina VHF Ch 9

Telephone
Marina ① 02 40 11 97 97

The genteel marina at La Baule

Le Pouliguen marina is at the west end of the magnificent 5M beach at La Baule. It is ideally situated for the fashionable resorts of La Baule and Le Pouliguen. There is space for 30 visitors of less than 11.5m length in depths of 1.3m on the visitors' pontoon.

Le Pouliguen looking southeast.
The marina occupies most of the east side of the river as far as the bridge. The harbourmaster's office is close to the entrance on the east side

PILOTAGE

Le Pouliguen approach and entrance

Warning

The approach dries, the sands shift and it is not very well marked, so enter close to high water. Avoid Le Pouliguen altogether if there is strong wind or swell from the southeast, particularly on the ebb when the seas break in the shallow water.

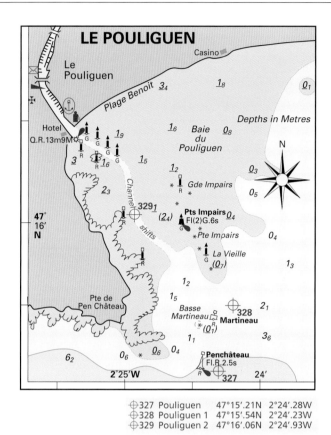

LE POULIGUEN

Casino

Le Pouliguen

Plage Benoît

Depths in Metres

Baie
du
Pouliguen

Hotel
Q.R.13m9M

N

**47°
16'
N**

Channel shifts

Gde Impairs

Pts Impairs
Fl(2)G.6s

Pte Impairs

La Vieille
(Q.7)

Pte de
Pen Château

Basse
Martineau
(*) (Q.1)

328
Martineau

Penchâteau
Fl.R.2.5s

2°25'W

327

24'

⊕327 Pouliguen   47°15'.21N 2°24'.28W
⊕328 Pouliguen 1 47°15'.54N 2°24'.23W
⊕329 Pouliguen 2 47°16'.06N 2°24'.93W

By day

The best approach is from the west between Penchâteau PHM buoy and Les Guérandaises SHM buoy. Leave Penchâteau PHM to port and steer 020° to leave Martineau PHM buoy to port. Come round onto about 320° and steer for a point just east of the second of the two PHM beacons. This will leave La Vieille SHM beacon and Les Petits Impairs SHM tower beacon well to starboard.

When the second red beacon is abeam turn to starboard on about 340° and steer for the channel marked by the four starboard and two port beacons.

Le Pouliguen visitors' berths are to starboard on entry

Follow these into the river, if necessary also using the transit of the church spire between the pier heads.

The channel is quite narrow with high sands on either side so caution is needed. Also some of the beacons are quite slender and not very conspicuous.

By night

There are a few lights but night entry is not recommended. The entry into Pornichet 5M to the east is well lit.

By GPS

From the west or south, use:

⊕326-W Pornichet, ⊕327-Pouliguen, ⊕328-Pouliguen 1, ⊕329-Pouliguen 2

From Pornichet use:

⊕327-Pouliguen, ⊕328-Pouliguen 1, ⊕329-Pouliguen 2

BERTHS AND ANCHORAGES

Le Pouliguen marina

The visitors' pontoon is to starboard near the entrance where there are also a new harbour office and showers in the old YC building. The fuel berth is also there. The marina continues upriver and occupies most of the east side of the river as far as the bridge.

⚓ Pointe de Penchâteau

If waiting for the tide, there is a temporary anchorage in about 1m some 400m north of Martineau buoy.

ASHORE IN LE POULIGUEN

There are all the facilities of a sophisticated yachting centre with a yard, chandlers and engineers close at hand. The yacht club on the east side above the bridge is hospitable to visitors.

Le Pouliguen is a smart holiday resort with a full range of shops, restaurants and cafés.

V. THE VILAINE AND THE LOIRE

56 Pornichet

Location
47°16'N 2°21'W

Shelter
Excellent

Depth restrictions
2.5m in marina

Night entry Lit

HW time
Brest HW+0015 neaps, –0045 springs

Mean height of tide (m)

	HWS	HWN	LWN	LWS
Pornichet	5.5	4.4	2.1	0.8

Tidal stream in approach
Streams are weak and irregular

Berthing
Large modern marina

Facilities
All marina facilities, town is
0.5M away

Charts
BA 2986 (50)
SHOM 7033 (50), 7145 (25)
Imray C39 (large scale)

Radio
Marina VHF Ch 9

Telephone
Marina ① 02 40 61 03 20
Tourist Office ① 02 40 61 33 33

The parking lot at La Baule

Pornichet is a huge modern and rather dull marina at the east end of the 5M beach at La Baule. It is a long way from the casino and the fashionable part of La Baule but the marina has easier access and much more room than Le Pouliguen.

PILOTAGE

Pornichet approach and entrance

By day

From the west, pass between Penchâteau PHM buoy and Guérandaises SHM buoy. Then steer about 085° for the forest of masts at the east end of La Baule. This route passes close north of a SHM buoy.

The marina entrance faces north and the red and green beacons marking the entrance can only be seen on close approach. Pass between the beacons to enter the marina.

From the south and east, the easy route is the west entrance described above. However, with a large-scale chart, there are some more interesting possibilities. A good approach from the southwest is to enter the reef between the PHM and SHM buoys marking Les Evens and Les Troves and approach the marina on 040°. From the east it is possible to enter the reef between the Grand and the Petit Charpentier but this requires a detailed chart because there are several unmarked rocks.

By night

Approach from the west using the white sector of Pornichet pierhead light. Watch out for the unlit SHM buoy 0.5M east of Penchâteau PHM. The beacons in the entrance are lit.

By GPS

From the west use:
⊕326-W Pornichet, ⊕330-Pornichet

From the south or southwest by day use:
⊕331-SW Pornichet, ⊕330-Pornichet

From the southeast, with a large-scale chart and careful pilotage, it is possible to use:
⊕335-Charpentier, ⊕330-Pornichet

However, this is not a safe straight-line route.

BERTHS AND ANCHORAGES

Pornichet marina

There are 10 pontoons (A–J) on the south side of the harbour and four (K–N) on the north. The heads of all these are allocated to visitors. Also, visitors under 10m can use the whole of pontoon J and the outer side of pontoon I. All the main berths have a depth of 2.8m.

⚓ Saint-Marc

Adventurous film buffs may wish to use a large-scale chart to work through the Charpentier reef and visit the pretty holiday resort of Saint-Marc where Jacques Tati made *Monsieur Hulot's Holiday*. The anchorage is completely exposed to the south and only suitable as a day anchorage in good weather.

ASHORE IN PORNICHET

Facilities

Pornichet is a well-equipped modern marina. The fuel pontoon is immediately to port on entry and all repairs can be carried out. Wi-Fi available in capitainerie. There is a chandlery, restaurants, cafés and a wine merchant in the marina, but no food shops or bakery.

The marina is about 0.5M from town, which offers all the delights of a fair-sized beach resort. There is a good market on Wednesday and Saturday.

History

In the late 19th century holiday resorts developed along many of the beautiful French beaches. As soon as the railway arrived at the seaside, developers took the opportunity to build resorts for the new fashion of sea swimming.

The green-topped light marking the entrance to Pornichet

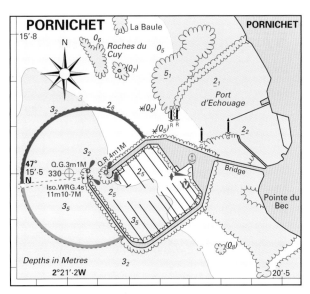

⊕330 Pornichet 47°15'.50N 2°21'.19W

This is just how La Baule began. What is particularly interesting is that it became the playground for some of the wealthier families who had more money to invest in holiday homes. During a 60-year development period architects competed with each other to design something different. A walk along the promenade and back through the side streets is fascinating. Every architectural style has been used, from half-timbered cottages to exotic Art Deco designs.

Pornichet marina fuelling pontoon to port of the entrance

Pornichet from southeast

V. THE VILAINE AND THE LOIRE

57 Saint-Nazaire and Nantes

Location
47°16'N 2°12'W

Shelter
Excellent in St-Nazaire basin

Depth restrictions none

Night entry Lit

HW time
St-Nazaire Brest HW+0030 neaps, −0040 springs
Nantes Brest HW+0135 neaps +0055 springs

Mean height of tide (m)

	HWS	HWN	LWN	LWS
St-Nazaire	5.8	4.6	2.2	0.8
Nantes	6.3	5.1	1.8	0.9

Tidal stream in Loire approaches
Flood – Brest HW−0600 to HW
Ebb – Brest HW to −0600
Very strong at St-Nazaire at half-flood and half-ebb

Berthing
Alongside in southernmost commercial dock

Facilities
As of a commercial dock

Charts
BA 2986 (50), 2989 (15), 2985
SHOM 7033 (50), 6797 (25), 7396 (15)
Imray C39 (large scale)

Radio
Loire port control and E Lock VHF Ch 14

Telephone
St-Nazaire Plaisance Harbourmaster at E Lock
☏ 02 40 00 45 24
Anne de Bretagne Pontoon, Nantes Gestion Equipement (NGE) ☏ 02 40 37 04 62
Capitainerie VHF Ch 12

Busy commercial river

A third of France's maritime trade comes into the Loire but for cruising boats there are only two berthing options. Saint-Nazaire offers visitors a berth in an old commercial dock by the submarine pens and Nantes now has a visitors' pontoon close to the centre of town.

The southern big ship lock into the commercial dock at St-Nazaire was the scene of a courageous action by the Royal Navy and Royal Marines during the Second World War when the destroyer HMS *Campbeltown* was rammed into the lock gates and detonated to prevent the use of the submarine pens. A stele about it faces the sea on Bd de Verdun.

Bassin de St-Nazaire showing the east lock entrance and submarine pens opposite

PILOTAGE

The Loire to Saint-Nazaire

By day

The approach is straightforward. The big ship channel is well marked by buoys, but it is not necessary to adhere to it until past Pte de l'Aiguillon as there is plenty of water either side. There are some isolated dangers outside the channel but they are mostly marked. After Pte de l'Aiguillon it is best to keep close to the main channel, although there is generally space to pass outside the buoys if necessary to avoid commercial traffic.

Approach along Chenal de Bonne-Anse leaving the two long breakwaters, which mark the big-ship entrance to the docks, to port. Leave the main channel at this point to pass between the SE Vieux Môle PHM buoy and Basse Sud Nazaire SCM buoy. Turn to port on about 340° until the East lock, which lies east/west, will open up to port.

The lock (24 hours) opens for exit on the even hours and for entry about 10 minutes later except the times are 10 minutes earlier at 0800 and are at 2300 instead of midnight.

By night

The Passe des Charpentiers leading lights close to Pointe de l'Aiguillon are very conspicuous and lit buoys mark the channel.

By GPS

From the west use:

⊕335-Charpentier, ⊕337-Loire 1, ⊕339-St-Nazaire

From the south use:

⊕336-Loire, ⊕337-Loire 1, ⊕339-St-Nazaire

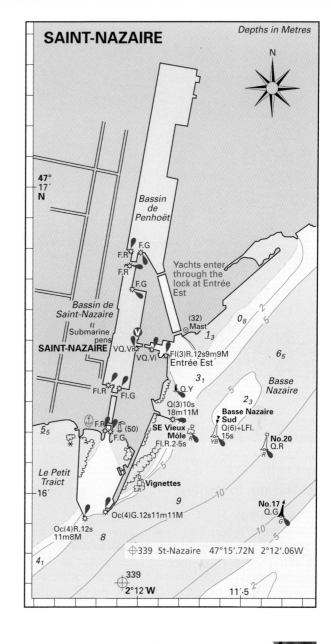

A ship entering the Bassin de St-Nazaire by the south lock viewed from the submarine pens pontoon

V. THE VILAINE AND THE LOIRE

Nantes. The Madeleine branch of the Loire

St-Nazaire to Nantes

Tidal strategy

Leave Saint-Nazaire an hour before low water and expect to carry a fair tide all the way to Nantes. But heading down river, leave Nantes about an hour before high water and expect to encounter some foul tide as LW St-Nazaire is less than five hours after HW Nantes.

By day

The channel from St-Nazaire to Nantes is well marked. The river is wide and deep, until Paimbœuf, and a significant sea can build up. Further upstream there can still be a considerable chop in strong winds.

The passage is interesting but not particularly attractive.

By night

Lit but not recommended.

BERTHS AND ANCHORAGES

Bassin de St-Nazaire

Once through the lock, pass through the swing bridge into the Bassin de St-Nazaire, where yachts berth against the east wall to the north of the lock. The long pontoon on the west side, by the submarine pens, is used for organised events but it is not secure as the submarine pens can be frequented by petty criminals at night.

In 2009 yachts were berthed free-of-charge for the first three days and classic traditional craft were totally free.

There are few facilities but repairs could probably be arranged. No showers or toilets but water and electricity are available on the pontoon. The town has all facilities and there is a supermarket close to the submarine pens. The submarine museum in the pens (complete with submarine) as well as make-believe tours of shipyards, cruise liners and the world is a small boys' paradise.

St-Nazaire visitors' pontoon by the old submarine pens

Ponton Anne de Bretagne at Nantes

This new pontoon has replaced Ponton Des Chantiers, Ponton D'Aiguillon and Trentemoult Marina as the visitors' berths and is situated on the north side of the Madeleine branch of the Loire immediately below the Anne de Bretagne fixed bridge. It has water/electricity on the pontoon and showers/toilets are scheduled for 2010. There is a minimum depth of 3–4m and it is immediately adjacent to the city. It is necessary to telephone NGE for the digicode for the security gate (*see summary box above*). Trentemoult marina is silted up and no longer accepts visitors.

⚓ Trébézy

Sheltered from west to north, this wide, attractive bay is just north of the Phare de l'Aiguillon. Approach from the southeast and anchor where depth permits outside the moorings. There are several more anchorages in the bays between Trébézy and Saint-Nazaire.

⊕338-Trébézy 47°14'·88N 2°15'·33W

Looking east

Ponton des Chantiers on the south side   *R. Rundle*

Pontoon Anne de Bretagne   *R. Rundle*

V. THE VILAINE AND THE LOIRE

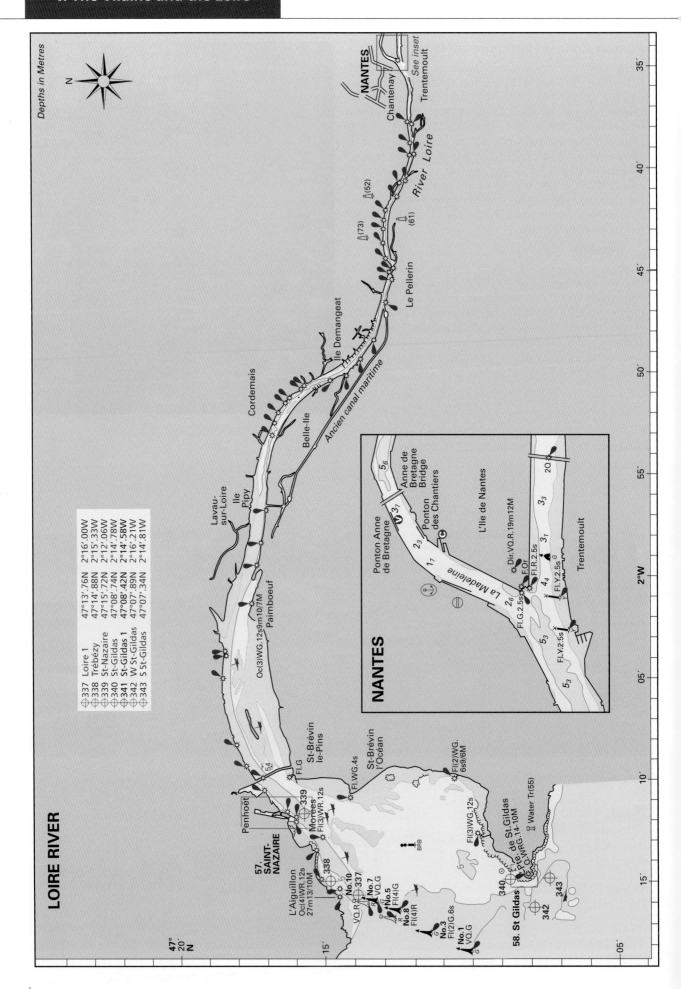

LOIRE RIVER

Depths in Metres

N

337	Loire 1	47°13'.76N	2°16'.00W
338	Trébézy	47°14'.88N	2°15'.33W
339	St-Nazaire	47°15'.72N	2°12'.06W
340	St-Gildas	47°08'.74N	2°14'.78W
341	St-Gildas 1	47°08'.42N	2°14'.58W
342	W St-Gildas	47°07'.89N	2°16'.21W
343	S St-Gildas	47°07'.34N	2°14'.81W

NANTES

Chantenay

Trentemoult

River Loire

See inset

(52)

(73)

(61)

Le Pellerin

Ile Demangeat

Cordemais

Belle-Ile

Ancien canal maritime

Ile Pipy

Lavau-sur-Loire

Oc(3)WG.12s9m10/7M

Paimboeuf

54

St-Brévin le-Pins

Penhoët

339

Mordées Fl(3)WR.12s

Fl.G

Fl.WG.4s

St-Brévin l'Océan

Fl(2)WG. 6s9/6M

57. SAINT-NAZAIRE

L'Aiguillon Oc(4)WR.12s 27m13/10M

No.10

338

337

No.7 VQ.G

VQ.R

No.5 Fl(4)G

No.8 Fl(4)R

No.3 Fl(2)G.6s

No.1 VQ.G

Fl(3)WG.12s

Pte. de St-Gildas Q.WRG.14-10M

340

Water Tr(55)

58. St Gildas

343

342

BRB

NANTES

Ponton Anne de Bretagne

Anne de Bretagne Bridge

Ponton des Chantiers

La Madeleine

L'Ile de Nantes

Trentemoult

Dir.VQ.R.19m12M

F.Or

Fl.R.2.5s

Fl.Y.2.5s

Fl.G.2.5s

Fl.Y.2.5s

5_6

3_7

2_3

1_7

2_6

4_4

3_1

3_3

$2Q$

5_3

5_3

5_3

47° 20' N

47° 20' N

58 Saint-Gildas

Location
47°08′N 2°15′

Shelter
Good from S, reasonable from W but exposed to N

Depth restrictions
1.5m on moorings

Night entry Lit

HW time
Brest HW−0045 neaps, +0025 springs

Mean height of tide (m)

	HWS	HWN	LWN	LWS
St-Gildas	5.6	4.4	2.1	0.8

Tidal stream approach
E – Brest HW−0600 to HW (1.0kn)
W – Brest HW to −0600 (1.3kns)

Berthing
Dry out on anchor or pick up a mooring.

Facilities
Limited facilities

Charts
BA 2986 (50)
SHOM 7395 (50)
Imray C40 (109)

Radio
Harbourmaster VHF Ch 9

Telephone
Harbourmaster ① 02 40 21 60 07

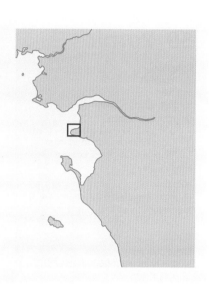

Small port and anchorage

Saint-Gildas is a small harbour (also known as the Anse de Boucau) on the north side of Pointe de Saint-Gildas.

PILOTAGE

St-Gildas approach and entrance

By day

From the north or northwest identify St-Gildas lighthouse and the large white tide gauge near the end of the jetty. Steer for the lighthouse, just left of the tide gauge, on 177°. L'Ilot PHM beacon, just north of the harbour, marks a dangerous rock (dries 1.7m). A SHM beacon marks the end of the jetty and in summer there is also a lit SHM buoy.

From the south, avoid the Banc de Kerouars, give Pointe de St-Gildas a wide berth and then follow the north entrance.

By night

The white sector of Pointe de St-Gildas light leads into the harbour and the breakwater end is lit.

By GPS

From the west or northwest use:
⊕340-St-Gildas, ⊕341-St-Gildas 1

St-Gildas from southwest

From south or southwest use:
⊕342-W St-Gildas, ⊕340-St-Gildas, ⊕341-St-Gildas 1

but in rough weather or at LW it would be safer to leave La Couronnée SHM lightbuoy to starboard.

BERTHS AND ANCHORAGES

⚓ Anse du Boucau

This is a crowded, holiday-resort mooring with numerous numbered buoys for small fishing boats. Anchor outside the moorings or dry out on the sandy beach at the head of the harbour.

The bay is sheltered from the south but exposed to the west at HW springs and completely open to the north and northeast.

ASHORE IN SAINT-GILDAS

There is a tap at the dinghy pontoon and the usual facilities of a small holiday village.

⊕340	St-Gildas	47°08′.74N	2°14′.78W
⊕341	St-Gildas 1	47°08′.42N	2°14′.58W

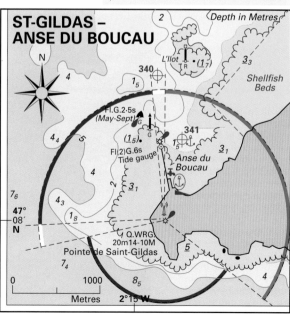

ST-GILDAS – ANSE DU BOUCAU

V. THE VILAINE AND THE LOIRE

59 Pornic

Location
  47°06′N 2°07′W
Shelter
  Very good in marina
Depth restrictions
  Old harbour dries from entrance
  1.0m in approach to marina
  Marina dredged 2.0m but silts
Night entry Lit
HW time
  Brest HW–0050 neaps, +0030 springs
Mean height of tide (m)

	HWS	HWN	LWN	LWS
Pornic	5.8	4.6	2.2	0.8

Tidal stream approach
  E – Brest HW–0600 to HW (1.0kn)
  W – Brest HW to –0600 (1.0kns)

Berthing Large marina
Facilities
  All marina facilities, 0.75M to
  smart holiday resort
Charts
  BA 2986 (50), 2981 (50/15),
  SHOM 7395 (50), 7394 (50/15)
  Imray C40 (large scale)
Radio
  Harbourmaster VHF Ch 9
  Wi-Fi at the Capitainerie.
Telephone
  Harbourmaster ☎ 02 40 82 05 40
  Tourist office ☎ 02 40 82 04 40

Attractive town with large marina

Pornic is an attractive seaside resort within easy reach of Nantes. It has a delightfully southern feel, with elegant holiday villas set in large gardens. There are numerous pine trees as well as grape vines growing near the marina.

The modern, well-managed marina has excellent road, rail and air communications. It is a pleasant 0.75M walk to town past the old drying harbour and Bluebeard's castle. There is a good beach next to the marina.

PILOTAGE

Pornic approach and entrance

By day

From the north, round Pointe de Saint-Gildas at least 0.5M off. The long marina wall is distinctive.

From the southwest avoid the well-marked dangers northwest of Noirmoutier and the dangers off Île du Pilier that extend 1M to seaward of the lighthouse.

From the south or west, the Banc de Kerouars is a hazard. The unmarked shallow patches are dangerous in rough weather or below half tide.

The marina entrance is at the southeast corner and is not visible in the approach. Steer for the fairway buoy and be ready to turn sharply to port between the red and green beacons. Once inside keep clear of the south wall, which is lined with submerged rocks. The east breakwater head is also foul. Pornic entrance silts so assume a depth of 1.0m. The approach can be dangerous in strong winds from the southwest to southeast at LW.

By night

Approach in the white sector of Pornic light, which clears the Banc de Kerouars and Notre Dame rock. Enter the marina between the entrance lights.

By GPS

From north or west use:

⊕342-W St-Gildas, ⊕343-S St-Gildas, ⊕344-Pornic

Pornic marina looking north.
Pornic, like La Baule, was developed in the 19th century after the railway arrived. The green of the pine trees makes it particularly attractive and is the origin of the name, the Jade Coast. A walk from the marina beside the estuary passes the fine 11th-century château and the old harbour. In town there is a maze of winding streets that fill with stalls on market day

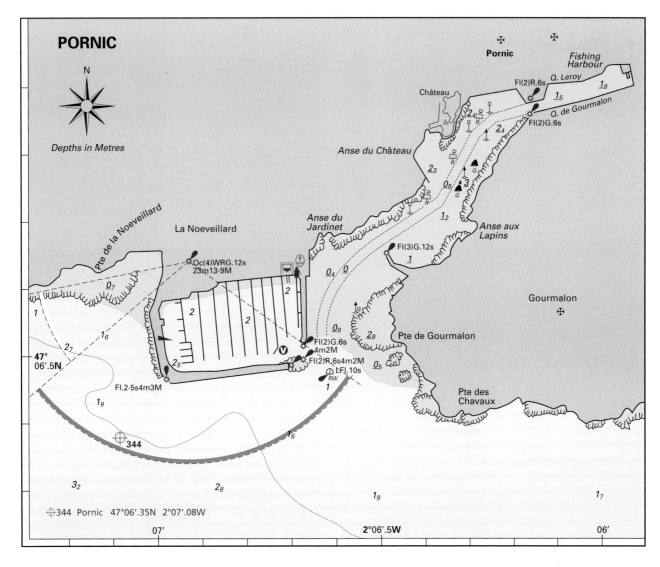

PORNIC

N

Depths in Metres

Pte de la Noeveillard

La Noeveillard

Oc(4)WRG.12s
23m13-9M

Anse du Jardinet

Anse du Château

Château

Pornic

Fishing Harbour

Q. Leroy

Fl(2)R.6s

Q. de Gourmalon

Fl(2)G.6s

Fl(3)G.12s

Anse aux Lapins

Gourmalon

Pte de Gourmalon

Fl(2)G.6s
4m2M

Fl(2)R.6s4m2M

L.Fl.10s

Fl.2·5s4m3M

Pte des Chavaux

47°
06′.5N

344

⊕344 Pornic 47°06′.35N 2°07′.08W

07′   2°06′.5W   06′

From Herbaudière use:

⊕347-Herbaudière, ⊕346-N Herbaudière, ⊕344-Pornic

At high water, it is possible to omit ⊕346-N Herbaudière but this route passes close to a 1.1m shallow patch and two rocks that dry 0.7m.

BERTHS AND ANCHORAGES

Pornic marina

The reception berth in the marina is directly ahead on entering and clearly marked.

Drying harbour

Visitors are discouraged from using the old drying harbour. The channel (dries 1.8m) is marked by buoys and beacons. Night entry is not recommended.

ASHORE IN PORNIC

Pornic has all the facilities of a major marina and the marina staff are particularly helpful. The fuel dock is at the base of the narrow first aisle and rather awkward for a 12m yacht.

On the north side of the marina there are cafés, restaurants and chandlers and some of the bars supply bread and croissants in the early morning. It is a very pleasant 10-minute walk along the riverbank to the town, where there are shops and restaurants and a market four times a week.

Pornic is within easy reach of Nantes Airport for crew changes.

Pornic. The old harbour

V. THE VILAINE AND THE LOIRE

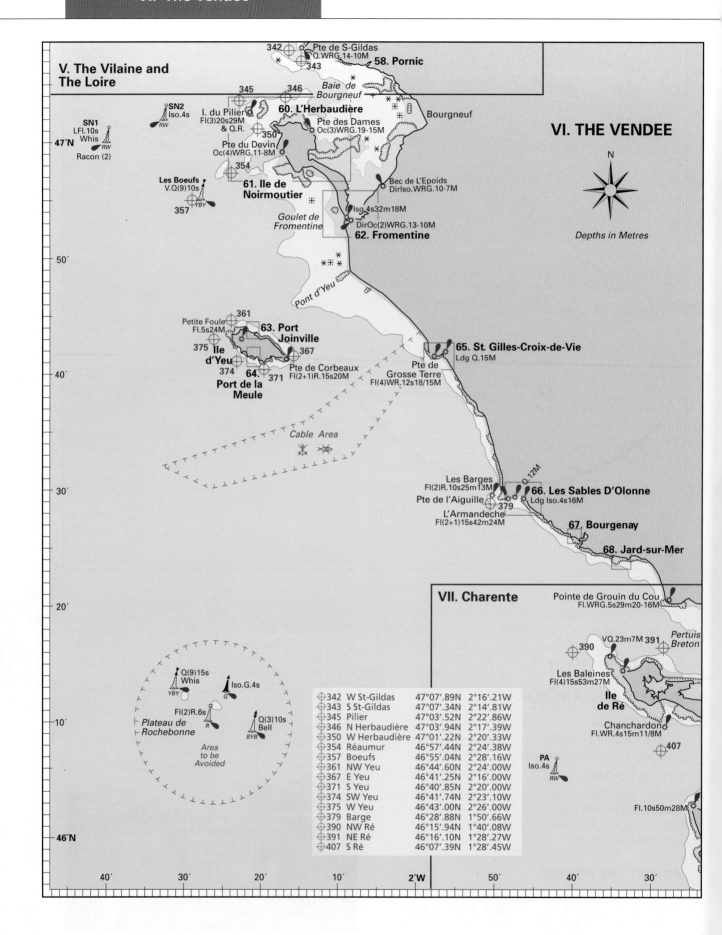

V. The Vilaine and
The Loire

342 ⊕ Pte de S-Gildas
Q.WRG.14-10M
343

58. Pornic

345 ⊕ 346 ⊕ *Baie de*
Bourgneuf

SN2
Iso.4s

SN1
LFI.10s
Whis
RW
47°N
Racon (2)

I. du Pilier 350
Fl(3)20s29M
& Q.R.

60. L'Herbaudière

Bourgneuf

VI. THE VENDEE

Pte des Dames
Oc(3)WRG.19-15M

Pte du Devin
Oc(4)WRG.11-8M

354

Les Boeufs
V.Q(9)10s

61. Ile de
Noirmoutier

357 YBY

Bec de L'Epoids
Dirlso.WRG.10-7M

Iso.4s32m18M

DirOc(2)WRG.13-10M
62. Fromentine

Goulet de
Fromentine

Depths in Metres

50'

Pont d'Yeu

Petite Foule 361
Fl.5s24M

63. Port
Joinville

375 Ile 367
d'Yeu

374 64. 371
Port de la
Meule

Pte de Corbeaux
Fl(2+1)R.15s20M

65. St. Gilles-Croix-de-Vie
Ldg Q.15M

Pte de
Grosse Terre
Fl(4)WR.12s18/15M

40'

Cable Area

Les Barges
Fl(2)R.10s25m13M

Q.12M

66. Les Sables D'Olonne
Ldg Iso.4s16M

Pte de l'Aiguille
379

L'Armandeche
Fl(2+1)15s42m24M

30'

67. Bourgenay

68. Jard-sur-Mer

VII. Charente

Pointe de Grouin du Cou
Fl.WRG.5s29m20-16M

20'

VQ.23m7M 391 *Pertuis*
Breton

390

Les Baleines
Fl(4)15s53m27M

Ile
de Ré

Q(9)15s
Whis
YBY

Iso.G.4s
G

Fl(2)R.6s
R

Q(3)10s
Bell
BYB

Plateau de
Rochebonne

Area
to be
Avoided

Chanchardon
Fl.WR.4s15m11/8M

PA
Iso.4s
RW

407

10'

Fl.10s50m28M

⊕ 342	W St-Gildas	47°07'.89N	2°16'.21W
⊕ 343	S St-Gildas	47°07'.34N	2°14'.81W
⊕ 345	Pilier	47°03'.52N	2°22'.86W
⊕ 346	N Herbaudière	47°03'.94N	2°17'.39W
⊕ 350	W Herbaudière	47°01'.22N	2°20'.33W
⊕ 354	Réaumur	46°57'.44N	2°24'.38W
⊕ 357	Boeufs	46°55'.04N	2°28'.16W
⊕ 361	NW Yeu	46°44'.60N	2°24'.00W
⊕ 367	E Yeu	46°41'.25N	2°16'.00W
⊕ 371	S Yeu	46°40'.85N	2°20'.00W
⊕ 374	SW Yeu	46°41'.74N	2°23'.10W
⊕ 375	W Yeu	46°43'.00N	2°26'.00W
⊕ 379	Barge	46°28'.88N	1°50'.66W
⊕ 390	NW Ré	46°15'.94N	1°40'.08W
⊕ 391	NE Ré	46°16'.10N	1°28'.27W
⊕ 407	S Ré	46°07'.39N	1°28'.45W

46°N

40'   30'   20'   10'   **2°W**   50'   40'   30'

VI. The Vendée

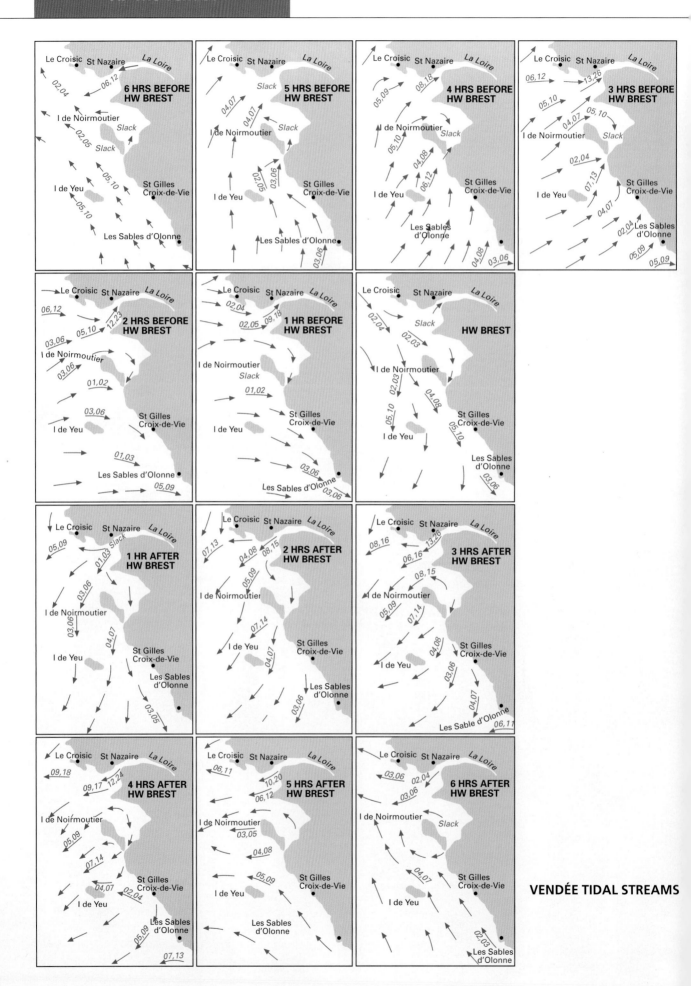

VENDÉE TIDAL STREAMS

60 L'Herbaudière

Location
47°02'N 2°18'W
Shelter
Good except from N and NE
Depth restrictions
Entrance dredged 1.2m
Marina 1.5m to 2.9m
Night entry Lit
HW time
Brest HW−0045 neaps, +0025 springs
Mean height of tide (m)

	HWS	HWN	LWN	LWS
L'Herbaudière	5.5	4.4	2.1	0.8

Tidal stream in approach
ESE – Brest HW−0600 to HW (1.9 kn)
WNW – Brest HW to −0600 (1.6 kns)

Berthing
Raft on visitors' pontoon
Facilities
All facilities.
Charts
BA 2986 (50), 2981 (50/15)
SHOM 7395 (50), 7394 (50/15)
Imray C40 (large scale)
Radio
Harbourmaster VHF Ch 9
Telephone
Harbourmaster ① 02 51 39 05 05

VI. THE VENDÉE

The main port on Noirmoutier

Île de Noirmoutier is well worth visiting. It is about 10M long by about 3M wide, mostly flat and sandy, with much of the north part given over to salt ponds. Bicycles are a perfect way to get about and can be hired in L'Herbaudière.

L'Herbaudière is the only all tide port on Île de Noirmoutier. It is shared between fishing boats and yachtsmen and has a pleasant genuine atmosphere.

PILOTAGE

(See also plan on page 210).

L'Herbaudière approach and entrance

By day

From the north, L'Herbaudière can be identified by a 40m radio mast to the west and the stone breakwater.

L'Herbaudière from the west

Start from a position about 0.5M west of Basse du Martroger NCM tower beacon but do not approach the beacon from due north because there are several shallow patches. From this position, steer for the harbour on 188° keeping the breakwaters just open. The last 0.25M is marked by buoys and beacons and, if visibility is poor, the leading lights are switched on. Beware the rock awash at LAT on the east side approximately opposite the halfway distance between No.1 and No.3 SHM buoys and quite close to the leading line.

The harbour entrance faces east so it is necessary to round the west breakwater and turn fairly sharply to starboard.

From the southwest, use the Chenal de la Grise. Start south of Passe de la Grise SCM buoy. Then steer 058° towards Basse de Martroger NCM tower beacon. About 0.25M before Matroger, when the harbour bears 188°, turn onto this course and enter the harbour as described above. Note that the tide runs very strongly in the Passe de la Grise.

L'Herbaudière entrance

By night

From north, approach in either of the two north white sectors of Basse du Martroger light. Then use the white sector of L'Herbaudière breakwater light on 188°. Identify the leading lights on 188° and follow this transit into the harbour, leaving the red and green lit buoys to port and starboard. As by day beware the rock awash at LAT on the east side of the near approach.

From the south, through the Chenal de la Grise, use the white sector of Basse du Martroger light, bearing between 055° and 060°. When the breakwater head light turns white, steer 188° and proceed as above.

By GPS

From the northwest and northeast use:

⊕346-N Herbaudière, ⊕347-Herbaudière,
⊕349-Herbaudière 2

This route passes close west of several shallow patches in the outer approaches.

From the west and southwest via Chenal de la Grise use:

⊕350-W Herbaudière, ⊕348-Herbaudière 1,
⊕349-Herbaudière 2

This passage is quite narrow and the tide runs very strongly but the dangers are well marked.

BERTHS

L'Herbaudière marina

Visitors' berth on the ends of the two pontoons M and N to port on entering or on the west side of the next one. These berths are a little exposed and may be uncomfortable if the wind is from the north or northeast but they have recently been re-arranged to give more protection. The harbourmaster's dory usually meets visitors and guides them to a berth in season.

ASHORE IN L'HERBAUDIERE

L'Herbaudière has all the facilities of a yacht and fishing port. There is a fuel berth, a 30-tonne travel-lift, chandlers and all repairs. The town is small but

L'Herbaudière visitors' berths on right

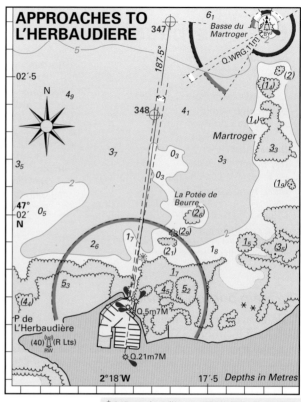

⊕347 Herbaudière   47°02'.69N 2°17'.62W
⊕348 Herbaudière 1 47°02'.36N 2°17'.69W

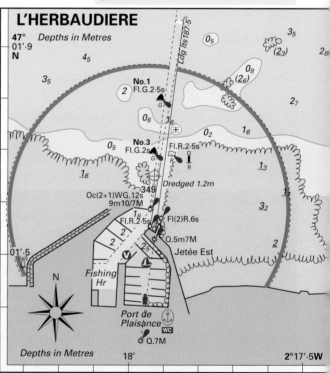

⊕349 Herbaudière 2 47°01'.67N 2°17'.83W

has a good range of shops, cafés and restaurants. Fresh fish can be bought near the fish market. Bicycles can be hired and provide an excellent way to see the island. The local beaches, the saltpans and the main town of Noirmoutier-en-Île are all worth visiting. If time and tide permit, the causeway to the mainland is also interesting, if only to see the scale and diligence of the pêche à pied.

61 Noirmoutier anchorages

Location
47°01'N 2°13'W

Depth restrictions
Noirmoutier dries 2.5m
Bois de la Chaise about 1.0m
Port Morin harbour 0.9m

Night entry
Lit to Bois de la Chaise and Port Morin

HW time
Brest HW–0045 neaps, +0025 springs

Mean height of tide (m)

	HWS	HWN	LWN	LWS
L'Herbaudière	5.5	4.4	2.1	0.8

Facilities
Noirmoutier has good shops, Bois de la Chaise has a few shops, Port Morin only has a good beach and a seasonal shop

Charts
BA 2981 (50/15)
SHOM 7394 (50/15)

Telephone
Noirmoutier HM ① 02 51 39 08 39

Bois de la Chaise

Attractive anchorage

Sheltered from west and south and to some extent from north and east, this attractive anchorage is on the northeast corner of the island, near Pointe des Dames.

PILOTAGE

Bois de la Chaise approach and entrance

By day

From the northwest, keep outside Banc de la Blanche NCM buoy and Basse des Pères ECM buoy. Then steer 150° for La Chaise SWM buoy. The headland is steep and tree covered and only the lighthouse top is visible.

From L'Herbaudière, stay inside Banc de la Blanche using a back-bearing of the red and white radio tower in line with Martroger tower on 215°.

By night

Approach in the white sector of Pointe de Dames light.

By GPS

From Pornic use:
⊕352-Chaise

but watch out for the rocks that extend southeast of Notre-Dame WCM beacon tower.

From L'Herbaudière use:
⊕346-N Herbaudière, ⊕351-Pères, ⊕352-Chaise

BERTHS AND ANCHORAGES

This is a popular holiday beach and sailing school base with a large number of small craft moorings for the summer visitors. There is room to anchor and there are several white mooring buoys for visitors.

There are a few shops and restaurants in Bois de la Chaise but Noirmoutier-en-Île is only 1M away. There is a big campsite with a shop just to the south.

Noirmoutier-en-Île

Busy drying port

Noirmoutier-en-Île is a nice place but best visited by bicycle. It dries 2.5m leaving steeply sloping, unstable mud. Rafting is normally necessary and rafted boats may tip and cross masts, or fall outwards into the scoured channel.

PILOTAGE

Noirmoutier approach and entrance

By day

From the Bois de la Chaise anchorage, keep about 400m offshore, inside the mussel bed. There is a line of green beacons along the shore. Continue into the entrance and up the marked channel to town. The best water at the entrance is on the south side near the training wall.

By GPS

The entrance requires careful visual pilotage:
⊕352-Chaise, ⊕353-Noirmoutier

may help in the approach.

Moored in the soft mud at Noirmoutier-en-Île *M&G Barron*

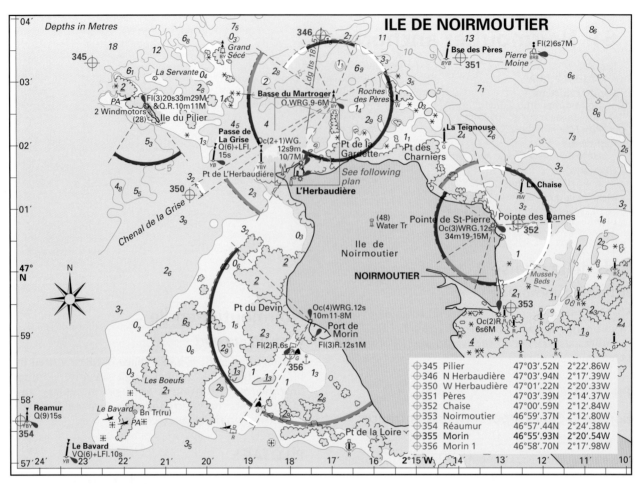

ILE DE NOIRMOUTIER

⊕345	Pilier	47°03'.52N	2°22'.86W
⊕346	N Herbaudière	47°03'.94N	2°17'.39W
⊕350	W Herbaudière	47°01'.22N	2°20'.33W
⊕351	Pères	47°03'.39N	2°14'.37W
⊕352	Chaise	47°00'.59N	2°12'.84W
⊕353	Noirmoutier	46°59'.37N	2°12'.80W
⊕354	Réaumur	46°57'.44N	2°24'.38W
⊕355	Morin	46°55'.93N	2°20'.54W
⊕356	Morin 1	46°58'.70N	2°17'.98W

BERTHS AND ANCHORAGES

Moor to the first quay on the starboard side, just before the crane. Further up, the quays are shallower. The mud is very soft so, with luck, a fin keel may sink in, leaving the boat upright.

ASHORE IN NOIRMOUTIER-EN-ÎLE

Noirmoutier has all facilities. It is a pleasant market town and well worth visiting. Markets are held on Tuesday, Friday and Sunday, in season.

Noirmoutier. Port de Morin looking southeast   *R Rundle*

Port de Morin

Shallow harbour and anchorage

This harbour is on the west of the island. The original west breakwater has been supplemented with a new east breakwater to enclose the harbour in which there are now several pontoons but it is really a place for locals and holidaymakers to keep their shallow-draft boats during the season. Good shelter in all winds except southeast and south. There is a pool outside the harbour where deep draught yachts can anchor in good weather.

PILOTAGE

Port de Morin approach and entrance

By day

Starting from ⊕355-Morin, steer 032° towards the lighthouse at the root of the north breakwater close to a large white reservoir. First there is a PHM lightbuoy and then a SHM buoy about 1M apart. The route crosses a shallow patch (dries 1.3m), with deeper water to starboard.

The entrance channel is marked by a red and a green buoy. Pass between them then steer for the end of the breakwater.

By GPS

⊕355-Morin, ⊕356-Morin 1

Port de Morin from the southwest

BERTHS AND ANCHORAGE

The Capitainerie may be contacted on VHF Ch 09.

Berth on the south side of the first pontoon inside the entrance. There is 0.9m depth at LW springs. Maximum length allowed is 12m. Water and electricity on the pontoon.

Anchor in the pool to the southeast of the inner red and green buoys or pick up one of the two red visitors' moorings.

ASHORE IN PORT DE MORIN

There are very few facilities apart from a magnificent beach, a 5-tonne mobile crane and a seasonal shop.

Noirmoutier. Port du Morin looking southeast *R Rundle*

62 Fromentine

Location
46°54'N 2°10'W

Shelter
Fairly exposed

Hazards
Shifting bar with very strong tides

Depth restrictions
Bar dries 1.5m

Night entry Lit but not recommended

HW time
Brest HW–0045 neaps, +0020 springs

Mean height of tide (m)

	HWS	HWN	LWN	LWS
Fromentine	5.2	4.1	1.8	1.9

Tidal stream in entrance
Flood – Brest HW–0600 to –0130 (5kn)
Ebb – Brest HW–0100 to +0530 (8kns)
Tidal Stream at Le Goéland SHM beacon
S – Brest HW–0500 to -0030 (2kns)
N – Brest HW+0030 to +0600 (1.5kns)

Berthing
Anchorage

Facilities
All facilities of small holiday resort

Charts
BA 2981 (50)
SHOM 7394 (50)
Imray C40 (large scale)

Telephone
Harbourmaster ✆ 02 51 39 05 05

Small resort with challenging access

The Goulet de Fromentine is the passage between the south end of Île de Noirmoutier and the mainland. The streams are very strong, the sand bar shifts and the anchorage is uncomfortable. Although Fromentine is a pleasant holiday resort, a visit is probably not worth the effort.

PILOTAGE

Tidal strategy

The tide ebbs for eight hours and floods for four and the streams, particularly on the ebb, are very strong. Only attempt to enter in the last hours of the flood and do not attempt to enter if there is strong southwest wind or swell.

Fromentine approach and entrance

By day

The Goulet can be identified by a conspicuous water tower on Noirmoutier and Notre-Dame-de-Monts lighthouse. Start well offshore at L'Aigle SCM buoy and steer 050° for Fromentine fairway buoy. Be prepared for some south stream. From the landfall buoy, follow the channel buoys to the red and white tower beacons that mark the entrance. Passing between the beacons, the channel deepens and a

Fromentine from the west

SHM buoy indicates the course to the navigation arch of the bridge (clearance 24m). After the bridge, a PHM buoy marks the channel to Fromentine pier. North of this buoy are two wrecks, exposed at LW.

By GPS

The sand shifts and the buoys are moved to reflect this. The following waypoints only provide a general indication of the channel in from the west:

⊕358-Fromentine, ⊕359-Fromentine 1, ⊕360-Fromentine 2

BERTHS AND ANCHORAGES

⚓ Fromentine and Pointe de la Fosse

Depending on draught, anchor off the jetty on the Noirmoutier side at Pte de la Fosse, with less tidal stream, or just west of the Fromentine ferry jetty and just east of the cable area. The streams in the fairway are very strong, about 5kns, but they moderate towards the shore. Anchor as far in as draught and tide allow.

Owing to the strength of the tide it is said to be unwise to leave a yacht unattended while at anchor, and this would certainly be true at the top of springs. If going in to the Pte de la Fosse side, beware of the wrecks just north of the channel; they lie between the first and second red buoys after the bridge, so turn in either before the first red buoy or after the second. It is not practical to row across the stream to Fromentine in the dinghy.

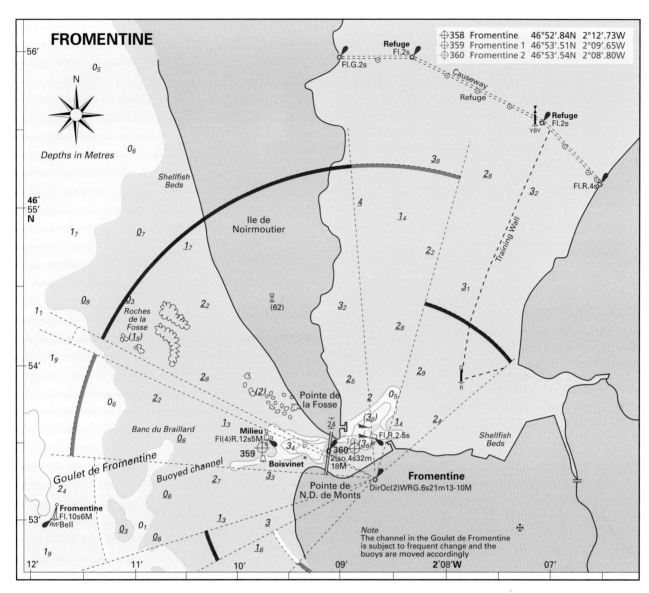

Within the chart:

FROMENTINE

56'

N

0_5

Depths in Metres

0_6

46° 55' N

1_7 0_7 1_7

0_9 0_3 Roches de la Fosse (1_5)

54'

1_1

1_9

0_6 2_2 2_8

Banc du Braillard 0_6

Goulet de Fromentine 2_4

1_3 Milieu Fl(4)R.12s5M

Buoyed channel 2_7 0_6

359 Boisvinet 3_4 3_3

Pointe de N.D. de Monts

53' Fromentine Fl.10s6M RW Bell

1_9

0_3 0_1 0_6

1_3 3 1_6

Shellfish Beds

Ile de Noirmoutier

1

(62)

3_2

2_2 2_5 (2) Pointe de la Fosse

2_4 360 10 Fl.R.2.5s 2Iso.4s32m 18M

Fromentine DirOc(2)WRG.6s21m13-10M

3_8 2_8

4 1_4 2_2 Training Wall 3_2

3_1 2_8 2_9

2 0_5 (3_8) 1_4 3_6

R

Shellfish Beds

Note
The channel in the Goulet de Fromentine is subject to frequent change and the buoys are moved accordingly

Refuge Fl.2s Fl.G.2s Causeway Refuge Refuge Fl.2s YBY Fl.R.4s

⊕358 Fromentine 46°52'.84N 2°12'.73W
⊕359 Fromentine 1 46°53'.51N 2°09'.65W
⊕360 Fromentine 2 46°53'.54N 2°08'.80W

12' 11' 10' 09' 2°08'W 07'

ASHORE IN FROMENTINE

Water can be obtained from the ferry jetty. Fromentine is a small holiday resort with typical facilities, including a ferry to Île d'Yeu. Berthing at the ferry pier is not permitted.

THE GOIS CAUSEWAY

Warning

The adventurous may wish to use the Goulet de Fromentine as a shortcut to Pornic or L'Herbaudière by crossing the causeway 2M north of Fromentine. The combination of very shallow water and very strong tides make this passage unsafe for deep draught yachts.

However for shallow draught boats which can dry out in an upright position if they run aground and in calm conditions the passage is possible.

The passage is 7M long from Fromentine pier to Le Goéland SHM beacon and the Gois Causeway dries 3m. There is said to be more than 1.5m over the causeway 2hrs before HW at springs and less

The causeway joins Île de Noirmoutier to the mainland. It dries 3m and is used as a road during low water *M&G Barron*

than 1.0m at HW neaps. The causeway is about 30m wide with a 10m wide cobbled road on top. South of the causeway it dries 3.2m in places. There are three refuges on the causeway for pedestrians who get caught by the tide. The usual crossing point is between the middle and easternmost refuges but the best place is sometimes marked (starboard-hand marks on the west side, porthand marks on the east). An up-to-date large scale chart is essential to identify the deepest water and the position of shellfish beds.

63 Port-Joinville

Location
46°44'N 2°21'W
Shelter
Good in marina
Hazards
Entrance dangerous in strong N and E winds
Depth restrictions
Entrance 1.2m, marina 1.5m to 2.5m
Night entry Lit
HW time
Brest HW–0040 neaps, +0015 springs
Mean height of tide (m)

	HWS	HWN	LWN	LWS
Joinville	5.0	4.0	1.9	0.4

Berthing
Marina
Fuel
At entrance to marina
Facilities
All facilities. Wi-Fi available
Charts
BA 3640 (10)
SHOM 7410 (20/10)
Imray C40 (large scale)
Radio
Harbourmaster VHF Ch 9
Telephone
Harbourmaster ① 02 51 58 38 11

Attractive tuna port

Île d'Yeu is a delightful island and well worth a visit. Port-Joinville is the only safe harbour and is an excellent base from which to explore. The marina is modern and welcoming. The town is an active fishing and ferry port with lots of shops, cafés and restaurants; the fishmonger alone makes the visit worthwhile.

PILOTAGE

Port-Joinville approach and entrance

By day

Port-Joinville is easy to locate from seaward and steering 224° for the conspicuous water tower behind the town leads straight into the harbour.

Enter the harbour leaving the northwest breakwater head 50m to starboard. After passing the old lighthouse bear to port and round the inner end of the breakwater to enter the marina. Do not stray to starboard in the outer harbour because the southwest corner is very shallow and beware that the ferry may be manoevring inside.

By night

Approach in either of the white sectors of the northwest breakwater light and enter the harbour with the leading lights in line on 219°. Remember to avoid the drying patch in the southwest corner of the outer harbour.

By GPS

From the northwest use:
⊕364-Joinville, ⊕365-Joinville1

From the north use:
⊕357-Boeufs to clear the dangers W of Île de Noirmoutier

From St-Gilles use:
⊕366-E Joinville, ⊕365-Joinville 1

From Sables-d'Olonne or further south use:
⊕367-E Yeu, ⊕366-E Joinville, ⊕365-Joinville1

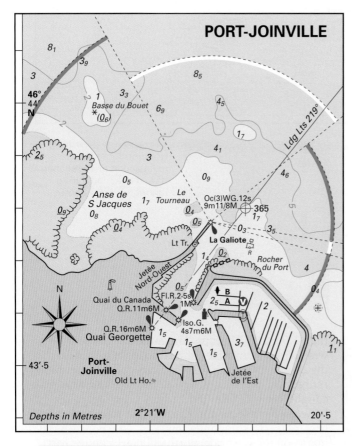

Port-Joinville old lighthouse is half way along the northwest breakwater
M&G Barron

⊕364	Joinville	46°44'.22N	2°20'.23W
⊕365	Joinville 1	46°43'.77N	2°20'.76W
⊕366	E Joinville	46°43'.34N	2°18'.00W

BERTHS AND ANCHORAGES

Port-Joinville Marina

Visiting boats berth in the marina according to size. Pontoons A, B and the west sides of C, D and E are available. To reach the reception pontoon follow the inside of the breakwater and turn to starboard at the end of B pontoon in front of the harbourmaster's office. At busy times, visiting yachts are met by a launch and directed to a vacant berth.

⚓ Anse de Ker Châlon

Sheltered from south and west but exposed to the north, there is a convenient bay 0.5M east of Joinville harbour. There are rocky outcrops on either side and some rocks close inshore so it is best to anchor quite well out.

ASHORE IN JOINVILLE

Joinville has all marine facilities including a big chandler and a fuel berth. In the town there is a full range of shops, cafés and restaurants, two good supermarkets and an outstanding fishmonger selling the tuna for which the island is famous.

Marshal Pétain, head of the collaborationist Vichy government from 1940 to 1944, was imprisoned here from 1945 to 1951.

Bicycle hire is easy and very popular with the hundreds of visitors. Those who enjoy walking may prefer to visit the magnificent south coast on foot because the footpath and bicycle path are mostly separate and the bicycle path is a bit of a racetrack. Cars can also be hired and the island is just about large enough to make this worthwhile. Maps are available from the harbourmaster's office.

There is a regular ferry service to Fromentine and, in summer, to St-Gilles and, less frequently, Les Sables-d'Olonne.

A typical Île d'Yeu cottage *M&G Barron*

The waterfront at Port-Joinville *M&G Barron*

VI. THE VENDÉE

Port-Joinville looking southeast. The marina has plenty of space for visitors on pontoons located just inside the entrance and close to the Bureau du Port. Smaller, local boats are moored at the far end of the marina. The remainder of this large harbour is devoted to deep-sea fishing boats and ferries coming from the mainland

64 Port de la Meule

Location
46°42'N 2°21'W

Shelter
Moderate from the N, dangerously
exposed to S

Hazard
Unsafe in S wind or swell

Depth restrictions
Harbour dries

Night entry Lit but not recommended

HW time
Brest HW–0040 neaps, +0015 springs

Mean height of tide (m)

	HWS	HWN	LWN	LWS
Joinville	50	4.0	1.9	0.7

Berthing
Anchorage outside tiny harbour

Facilities
Restaurants

Charts
SHOM 7410 (20)

Tiny fishing harbour

Port de la Meule is a tiny, picturesque fishing
harbour on the south side of Île d'Yeu. The harbour
is packed with small fishing boats and mostly dries
so it is necessary to anchor outside.

If you do not have the time or the settled offshore
weather to visit by boat, then Port de la Meule is a
worthwhile walk or bike ride. A round trip to
include the Vieux Château (*see page 217*) and the
coast path works very well.

Port de la Meule and the rocky west coast of Ile
d'Yeu looking east.
The path along the cliffs is for walkers while the
large path inland is for cyclists

PILOTAGE

Port de la Meule approach and entrance

By day

Port de la Meule is between Pointe du Châtelet, with
its distinctive white stone cross, and Pointe de la
Tranche with a conspicuous white semaphore tower
and a red and white radio mast. The entrance can
only be identified from almost due south when the
lighthouse and white chapel become visible.

The bay is clear of off-lying rocks so it is safe to
steer for the lighthouse on 022°. On close approach,
keep clear of the headland on the west side, which
has rocks projecting to the southeast. These can
usually be seen but it is best to keep towards the

Map labels:
PORT DE LA MEULE
372 Meule 46°41'.19N 2°20'.91W
373 Meule 1 46°41'.49N 2°20'.78W
etc.

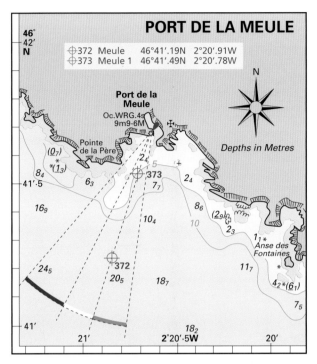

The tiny fishing harbour of Port de la Meule *M&G Barron*

starboard side of the channel. Once inside, the reef is normally marked by PHM lobster pots.

If proceeding to the quay, keep towards the port side to avoid some rocks close to the east side of the entrance and be prepared to turn sharply to port into the harbour.

The harbour is sheltered in winds from west through north to east but in south winds, the swell surges right into the harbour.

By night
The entrance is lit but night entry is not recommended.

By GPS
From Joinville via the east:

⊕366-E Joinville, ⊕367-E Yeu, ⊕368-SE Yeu, ⊕371-S Yeu, ⊕373-Meule 1

This route does not enter Port de Meule by the normal transit and the harbour will only open when the final waypoint is reached.

From Joinville via the west use:

⊕364-Joinville, ⊕361-NW Yeu, ⊕375-W Yeu, ⊕374-SW Yeu, ⊕372-Meule, ⊕373-Meule 1

BERTHS AND ANCHORAGES

Port de la Meule
The harbour dries but in settled offshore winds it is possible to anchor in the entrance, though some swell enters even in northeast winds. The bottom is rocky and there is little swinging room, so two anchors are necessary. There is not really room in the harbour for a boat to dry out but it might be possible with advice from the local fishermen.

⚓ Anse des Vieilles
Sheltered from the north, this attractive sandy bay is just over 1M east of Port de la Meule. It should be approached from the southeast to avoid the Ours des Vieilles reef that extends nearly 0.5M southeast of Pointe des Vieilles. Anchor in about 3m in the centre of the bay.

⊕370-Vieilles 1 46°41'.53N 2°18'.70W

⚓ Anse des Broches
Sheltered from southwest through south to east, this fair-weather anchorage is on the northwest coast of Île d'Yeu.

Approach with the Petite Foule lighthouse bearing 145°. There are drying and above-water rocks on both sides of the bay but this approach passes well clear of them. When Les Chiens Perrins WCM beacon tower bears about 225° turn to port onto 125° and go in as far as depth and draught allow. Anchor on sand, with Petite Foule bearing about 155° and Les Chiens Perrins WCM about 250°. The GPS route from ⊕362-Broches to ⊕363-Broches 1 is more direct.

⊕363-Broches 1 46°43'.85N 2°23'.50W

ASHORE IN PORT DE LA MEULE
There are three restaurants, but almost no other facilities. The cliff walks to east and west are magnificent and there is an interesting ruined castle about 1M to the west.

The Vieux Château, built in the 11th century, is thought to have been a pirates' lair at some time in its history *M&G Barron*

65 Saint-Gilles-Croix-de-Vie

Location
46°41'N 1°56'W

Shelter
Good in marina

Hazards
Entrance dangerous in strong SW wind or swell

Depth restrictions
Entrance 1.5m but silts to 0.8m
Marina and reception pontoon 1.5m

Night entry Lit

HW time
Brest HW–0030 neaps, +0015 springs

Mean height of tide (m)

	HWS	HWN	LWN	LWS
Saint-Gilles	5.1	4.1	2.0	0.7

Tidal streams
Weak in the bay but 6kns on ebb in harbour, much affected by rain

Berthing
Marina and visitors' buoys

Fuel
Next to the visitors' berth

Facilities
All facilities

Charts
BA 3640 (10),
SHOM 7402 (50/10)
Imray C40 (large scale)

Radio
Harbourmaster VHF Ch 9

Telephone
Harbourmaster ① 02 51 55 30 83

Fishing port and beach resort

Saint-Gilles and Croix-de-Vie are two towns on opposite sides of the Vie River. Saint-Gilles, on the south, is a beach resort whereas Croix-de-Vie is an important fishing port and sizeable town. The river separating them has a fishing harbour and a large marina. The combination of resort and bustling river gives the place a very pleasant atmosphere.

PILOTAGE

Saint-Gilles approach and entrance

Warning

The entrance is shallow and exposed to winds from the southwest; the ebb runs at up to 6kns. Entry is therefore dangerous in strong wind against tide conditions. Even in moderate conditions it is better to enter and leave on the last of the flood.

By day

The entrance can be located by the low rocky headland of Grosse Terre, to the north, and the high lighthouse of Croix-de-Vie. On closer approach, Pill'Hours island can be seen in front of the harbour entrance and the red-topped leading lighthouses.

With the leading lighthouses in line on 043° the approach should preferably be made shortly before high water because the strong currents at mid-tide, particularly the ebb, make manoevring difficult. This leaves Pilours SCM to port and leads between the breakwater heads into the buoyed channel. The stream runs very hard and the buoys should be given a good berth as they are moored on the high ground beside the channel.

After a 90° turn to starboard, the channel passes the fishing-boat basins to reach the marina. The reception berth lies at the far end, beyond the fuel berth and round the bend to port. There is not much room to manoeuvre near the pontoon. Beware of the

Croix-de-Vie and Ste-Gilles looking northeast.
Croix-de-Vie on the bend in the river is the largest fishing town in the Vendée. Ste-Gilles, on the opposite bank, is a holiday resort. The marina is up river past the fishing harbour on the Croix-de-Vie side.
The ebb runs very strongly in the river and the exposed entrance can be rough

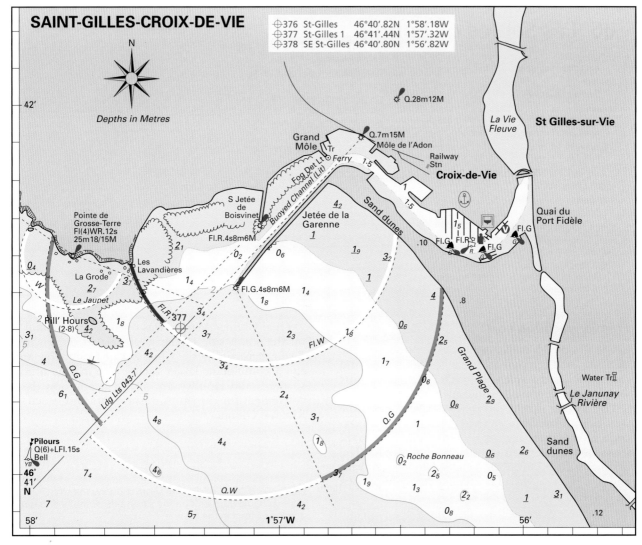

SAINT-GILLES-CROIX-DE-VIE

⊕376	St-Gilles	46°40'.82N	1°58'.18W
⊕377	St-Gilles 1	46°41'.44N	1°57'.32W
⊕378	SE St-Gilles	46°40'.80N	1°56'.82W

VI. THE VENDÉE

shallow water marked by green buoys and the strong stream.

Departure should be made before high water, as the strong ebb quickly raises a sea at the entrance.

By night

The entrance is well lit. Get the leading lights in line before passing Pilours SCM buoy. Once the southeast breakwater head is reached, follow the lit channel buoys. Unless conditions are ideal, borrow a vacant berth in the main part of the marina rather than attempt to berth on the visitors' pontoon in the dark.

By GPS

From the northwest or west use:

⊕376-St-Gilles, ⊕377-St-Gilles 1

From the south use:

⊕377-St-Gilles 1

From east of south use:

⊕378-SE St-Gilles, ⊕377-St-Gilles 1

to avoid getting too close to Roche Bonneau (depth 0.2m).

The red-topped lighthouse is one of a pair marking the leading line on 043°. The green-topped lighthouse is on the north jetty in the harbour entrance at the start of the buoyed channel *M&G Barron*

BERTHS AND ANCHORAGES

St-Gilles Marina

The visitors' pontoon is often crowded and a berthing master may direct yachts, particularly those over 10m, to a vacant berth in the main part of the marina so it is worth calling on VHF Ch 09 on the way in.

ASHORE IN ST-GILLES

The marina has all facilities including a fuel berth near the visitors' pontoon. St-Gilles and Croix-de-Vie have a full range of cafés, restaurants and shops with a good supermarket over the bridge in St-Gilles. There are connections by rail to Nantes.

66 Les Sables d'Olonne

Location
46°30'N 1°48'W

Shelter
Good in marina

Hazards
Entrance rough in strong SW wind or swell, particularly on the ebb

Depth restrictions
Entrance 1.1m
Visitors' berths 2.0m in both marinas,

Night entry Well lit

HW time
Brest HW–0030 neaps, +0015 springs

Mean height of tide (m)

	HWS	HWN	LWN	LWS
Sables	5.2	4.1	2.0	0.7

Tidal streams
Weak in the bay but 2.5kns on ebb in harbour

Berthing Marinas

Facilities All facilities and Wi-Fi.

Charts
BA 3640 (10), 3638 (10)
SHOM 7411 (10)
Imray C40 (large scale)

Radio
Both Marinas VHF CH 9, 16
Port Control VHF CH 12

Telephone
Port Olona Marina ☎ 02 51 32 51 16
Quai Garnier Marina ☎ 02 51 96 43 34
Mobile 06 73 76 94 65

Premier yachting port

Les Sables d'Olonne is a sophisticated resort on the east side of the river. It has a casino, shops and restaurants and a splendid beach. The fishing port with its market and cafés is just behind the beach.

Port Olona, the large modern marina, is on the west side above the town of La Chaume. Ferries run continuously between the two towns and the walk from the marina to La Chaume is about 0.5M. The marina is the home of the Vendée Globe yacht race and has every facility. La Chaume has cafés, shops on the river front and a market.

Quai Garnier Marina was opened in 2008 and is on the south side of the west part of the Fishing Basin. It is run by the Chamber of Commerce and can accommodate larger yachts. The marina office, showers and laundry are all on a pontoon. It is convenient for the shops, restaurants and beach of Sables d'Olonne.

Les Sables d'Olonne from the south showing the two marinas. Quai Garnier is on the south side of the near basin and Port Olona in the far one

PILOTAGE

Sables d'Olonne approach and entrance

Warning

Entry under sail is prohibited.

The approach can be very rough and even dangerous in strong southeast, south or southwest winds, especially if there is any swell. Avoid entering or leaving in these conditions. In bad weather, the southeast approach is reported to be safer.

By day

Les Sables d'Olonne can be identified by two large blocks of flats and the tall L'Armadèche lighthouse. The harbour entrance has a conspicuous red-topped white lighthouse at the end of the west breakwater, while the green-topped lighthouse on the east breakwater is less easy to spot.

From the southeast, use the transit of the green-topped breakwater light with the crenellated, white-topped, La Chaume lighthouse on 320°. This leaves all the shoals to port and the water is deep until within 400m of the harbour entrance. This approach should always be used in bad weather.

From the north or northwest, start close to La Petite Barge SCM buoy and make good 100° to leave Nouch Sud SCM buoy to port. Turn onto 033° and identify the harbour entrance. The leading line on the left of the beach front is between the belfry and two blocks of flats. The front light is above a red board on the beach. They are permanently lit.

Near LW, after passing the end of the west breakwater, alter to port to bring the red panels on the starboard side in transit on 328°. Above half tide the dangers are covered and the transit need not be followed precisely.

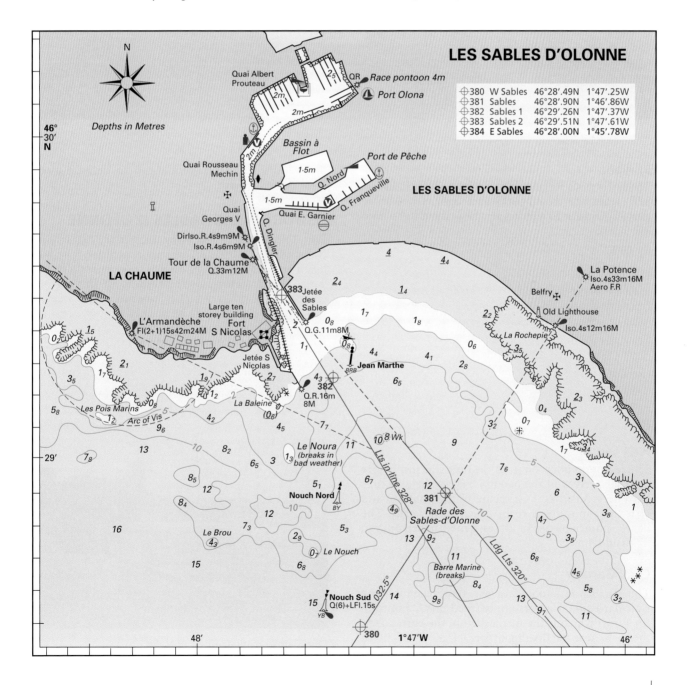

Quai Garnier Marina   *P Taylor*

By night

The harbour is well lit. Follow the leading lights on 320° until the west breakwater light is abeam to port. Then turn to port to get the leading lights into line on 328°.

By GPS

From the northwest use:

⊕379-Barge, ⊕380-W Sables, ⊕381-Sables

From the southwest use:

⊕380-W Sables, ⊕381-Sables

From the south use:

⊕384-E Sables, ⊕381-Sables

Continue using:

⊕382-Sables 1, ⊕383-Sables 2

BERTHS

Port Olona

The reception pontoon is on the port side just before the fuel berth and the marina basin. The ebb runs hard here. Visitors must secure to the pontoon and visit the capitainerie to be allocated a berth. The nearer pontoons are in 2m and the further ones in 2.5m and 4m.

Quai Garnier

The marina is situated in the first basin on the starboard side. Visitors are berthed on 'A' pontoon (in 1.7m) which is the furthest from the entrance to the basin near the floating office. Larger yachts berth on the outside. Visitors should call on VHF Ch 09 to be allocated a berth.

ASHORE IN LES SABLES D'OLONNE

Port Olona has all facilities including a 28-tonne travel-lift, two slips and all repair facilities. The fuel berth is near the reception pontoon and there are some shops, cafés and restaurants in the marina complex. The shops of La Chaume are nearby and the delights of Les Sables can be reached by ferry from La Chaume or from the marina in high season. There is a large car park and excellent communications by train, bus and air.

Quai Garnier has good basic facilities but fuel must be obtained from Port Olona.

Quai Garnier marina office   *P Taylor*

67 Bourgenay

Location
46°26′N 1°41′W

Shelter
Good in marina

Hazards
Entrance dangerous in moderate SW wind or swell

Depth restrictions
Entrance 1.0m
Visitors' berths 1.5m to 2.0m

Night entry Lit

HW time
Brest HW–0030 neaps, +0015 springs

Mean height of tide (m)

	HWS	HWN	LWN	LWS
Sables	5.2	4.1	2.0	0.7

Tidal streams in approaches
SE – Brest HW-0530 to +0030 (0.9kns)
Slack – Brest HW +0030 to +0130
NW – Brest HW+0130 to –0530 (1.3kns)

Berthing Marina

Fuel S breakwater

Facilities All marina facilities

Charts
BA 2998 (50)
SHOM 7403 (50)
Imray C40 (large scale)

Radio
Harbourmaster VHF Ch 9, 16

Telephone
Harbourmaster ☎ 02 51 22 20 36

Modern marina and holiday complex

Bourgenay is a large, artificial yacht harbour and marina village about 6M southeast of Les Sables d'Olonne. The nearest town is 2M inland. There is a beach to the south, oyster farms on the Payré River and pinewoods and marshes to explore.

Bourgenay is conveniently placed on passage to and from Île de Ré or La Rochelle and is a popular port of call for rallies.

Bourgenay leading lights in line

PILOTAGE

Bourgenay approach and entrance

Warning

Entry should not be attempted in strong west or southwest winds. Even in moderate winds there will be confused water in the entrance. However, once inside, there is good shelter.

By day

Bourgenay is identified by the sandy beach at the mouth of the Payre River to the south and the white roofs of the two marina buildings.

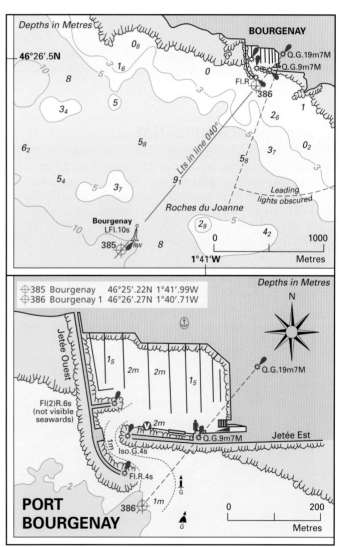

Locate the landfall buoy 1M southwest of the marina. The leading marks on 040° are green panels with the rear one on a tall white column. This column can be seen easily and it is sufficient to keep this on 040° at the low point between the two white roofs until the front mark is seen on the breakwater.

On close approach leave a green buoy and a green beacon to starboard; then make a 90° turn to port followed by a 90° turn to starboard to enter the marina. Fluorescent red and white chevrons indicate this latter turn.

By night

Follow the leading lights until the entrance is reached. The breakwater heads are lit but the green buoy and beacon are not.

By GPS

⊕385-Bourgenay, ⊕386-Bourgenay 1

BERTHS

Bourgenay Marina

The visitors' pontoon is on the south side of the marina along the south breakwater. Visiting yachts should secure to it unless met by a marina launch and shown to a berth. There are 45 berths for visitors; maximum length 20m.

ASHORE IN BOURGENAY

There is a fuel berth in the southeast corner of the marina, a grid, a slip, a 20-tonne travel-lift, a chandlery and engineers. There are cafés, a few small shops and bicycle hire in the marina complex. Up the hill is a supermarket and a post office but all other shops are about two miles away in Talmont-St-Hilaire.

Bourgenay entrance warning about the exit being difficult in swell

The visitors' pontoon looking southwest

Bourgenay marina looking north.
The inset is the landfall buoy 1M southwest of the marina

68 Jard-sur-Mer

Location
46°24'N 1°35'W

Shelter
Good in marina

Hazards
Entrance dangerous in strong SW wind or swell

Depth restrictions
Entrance dries, access HW±0200

Night entry Not recommended

HW time
Brest HW−0030 neaps, +0015 springs

Mean height of tide (m)

	HWS	HWN	LWN	LWS
Sables	5.2	4.1	2.0	0.7

Tidal streams in approaches
SE – Brest HW−0530 to +0030 (1.0kns)
Slack – Brest HW+0030 to +0130
NW – Brest HW+0130 to −0530 (1.4kns)

Berthing Drying harbour

Facilities Limited

Charts
BA 2998 (50)
SHOM 7403 (50)
Imray C40 (large scale)

Radio
Harbourmaster VHF Ch 9

Telephone
Harbourmaster ② 02 51 33 90 61

Small drying harbour

Jard-sur-Mer is a small drying harbour that lies about 10M north of the tip of Île de Ré. It is a pleasant spot for those with shallow draft or who can take the ground. The village of Jard-sur-Mer has reasonable facilities and there are good beaches nearby.

In offshore weather at neaps a deeper draught yacht could find a pleasant day anchorage off the harbour.

PILOTAGE

Jard-sur-Mer approach and entrance

By day

Jard is easy to identify as it is the only town on this stretch of coast and the blue roofs of the harbour office and nearby apartment blocks are visible from 3M offshore. However, there are offlying dangers so it is best to start from ⊕387-Jard or identify the unlit SHM buoy that marks the start of the entry channel.

Jard-sur-Mer from southwest. The new visitors' pontoon is bottom left

From this buoy, it should be possible to identify two white beacons set in the sand dunes on 036°. Follow this transit towards the shore. The course appears to be quite a long way east of the harbour. This is necessary to avoid a shallow patch (dries 1.0m) southeast of the harbour.

Once the harbour opens, turn to port to enter. The transit is two red boards with a white stripe on 293° but it is sufficient to follow the line of the breakwater. There are also some beacons to indicate the deepest water.

By Night

Entry at night is not advisable as the harbour is unlit.

By GPS

⊕387-Jard, ⊕388-Jard 1, ⊕389-Jard 2

BERTHS AND ANCHORAGES

Jard-sur-Mer harbour

There is a new pontoon extending 75m from the Capitainerie and the southwest side of it is reserved for visitors. Alongside and 5m out from the pontoon a minimum depth of 1.2m at LW is maintained. But the fairway channel to this pontoon almost dries. Boats that can take the ground may dry out alongside the little quay on the outer breakwater, or borrow a mooring. It is also possible to anchor clear of the moorings but bow and stern anchors should be used and legs are obligatory.

⚓ Outside the harbour

Deep-keeled yachts can anchor outside in settled weather. The best spot is just south of where the two leading lines cross at neaps or further out at springs. This spot is untenable in any wind or swell from the west and it would be difficult to leave at night.

ASHORE IN JARD-SUR-MER

Water and electricity on the pontoon, showers, toilets and laundry at the capitainerie. There are cafés and restaurants round the harbour and modest shops and a bank in the village about 1km away. There are good beaches nearby.

⚓ Anse de Maupas, La Tranche-sur-Mer

This is a drying anchorage 1.75M to the east of Pointe du Grouin du Cou. Enter on a bearing of 335° on the end of the jetty used by tourist launches from St-Martin. The line starts about 0.5M east of the easternmost of two SCM buoys marking a shoal south of the jetty. Pick up one of the orange mooring buoys to the east of the jetty. It may be possible to remain afloat at neaps but the anchorage is exposed in winds from southwest to southeast and a swell comes round the point in westerlies.

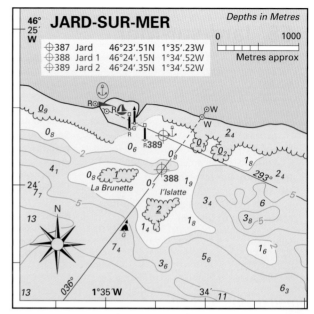

Jard-sur-Mer. Empty visitors' berths *P Taylor*

It is possible to dry out alongside the little quay on the outer breakwater *M&G Barron*

The entrance to Jard-sur-Mer harbour as the tide goes out *M&G Barron*

VII. Charente

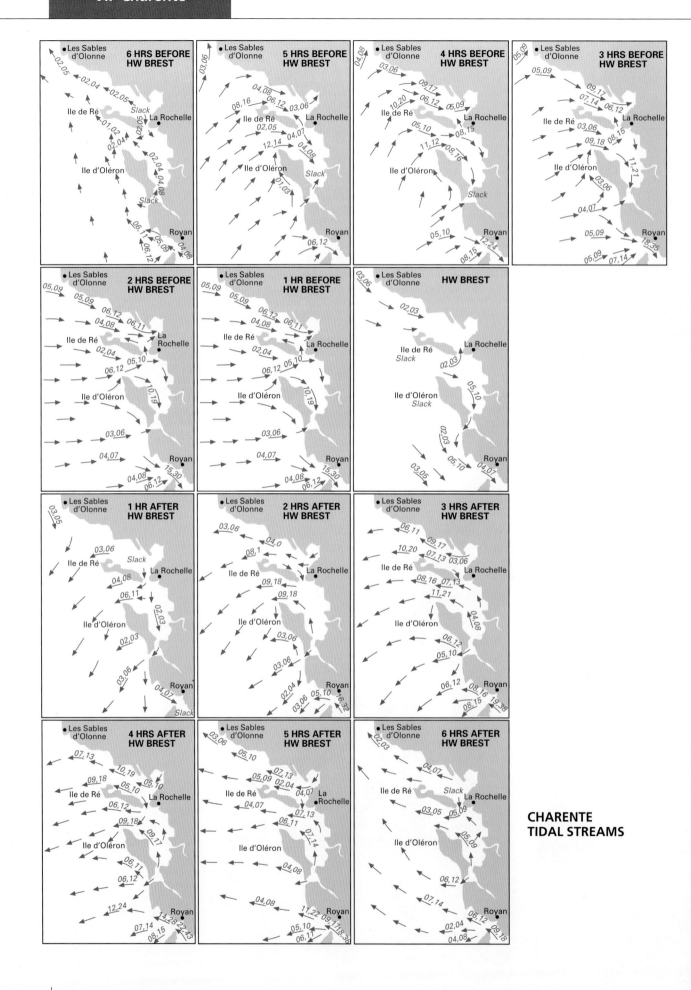

CHARENTE
TIDAL STREAMS

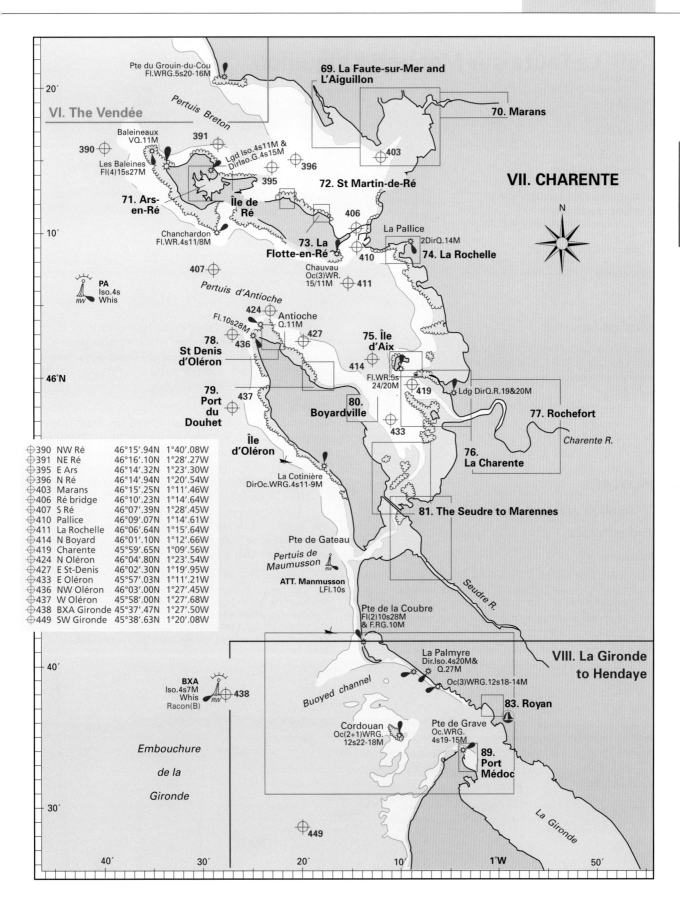

VI. The Vendée

Pte du Grouin-du-Cou
Fl.WRG.5s20-16M

Pertuis Breton

69. La Faute-sur-Mer and
L'Aiguillon

70. Marans

Baleineaux
VQ.11M

391

390

Les Baleines
Fl(4)15s27M

Lgd Iso.4s11M &
DirIso.G.4s15M

396

395

403

VII. CHARENTE

72. St Martin-de-Ré

71. Ars-
en-Ré

Île de
Ré

406

N

Chanchardon
Fl.WR.4s11/8M

73. La
Flotte-en-Ré

La Pallice
2DirQ.14M

74. La Rochelle

410

Chauvau
Oc(3)WR.
15/11M

411

PA
Iso.4s
RW Whis

Pertuis d'Antioche

407

424

Antioche
Q.11M

78.
St Denis
d'Oléron

Fl.10s28M

436

427

75. Île
d'Aix

414

79.
Port
du
Douhet

437

80.
Boyardville

Fl.WR.5s
24/20M

419

Ldg DirQ.R.19&20M

77. Rochefort

433

76.
La Charente

Charente R.

Île
d'Oléron

La Cotinière
DirOc.WRG.4s11-9M

81. The Seudre to Marennes

Pte de Gateau

Pertuis de
Maumusson
RW

ATT. Manmusson
LFl.10s

Seudre R.

Pte de la Coubre
Fl(2)10s28M
& F.RG.10M

VIII. La Gironde
to Hendaye

La Palmyre
Dir.Iso.4s20M&
Q.27M

Oc(3)WRG.12s18-14M

BXA
Iso.4s7M
Whis
RW Racon(B)

438

Buoyed channel

83. Royan

Pte de Grave
Oc.WRG.
4s19-15M

89.
Port
Médoc

Cordouan
Oc(2+1)WRG.
12s22-18M

Embouchure

de la

Gironde

La Gironde

449

390	NW Ré	46°15'.94N	1°40'.08W
391	NE Ré	46°16'.10N	1°28'.27W
395	E Ars	46°14'.32N	1°23'.30W
396	N Ré	46°14'.94N	1°20'.54W
403	Marans	46°15'.25N	1°11'.46W
406	Ré bridge	46°10'.23N	1°14'.64W
407	S Ré	46°07'.39N	1°28'.45W
410	Pallice	46°09'.07N	1°14'.61W
411	La Rochelle	46°06'.64N	1°15'.64W
414	N Boyard	46°01'.10N	1°12'.66W
419	Charente	45°59'.65N	1°09'.56W
424	N Oléron	46°04'.80N	1°23'.54W
427	E St-Denis	46°02'.30N	1°19'.95W
433	E Oléron	45°57'.03N	1°11'.21W
436	NW Oléron	46°03'.00N	1°27'.45W
437	W Oléron	45°58'.00N	1°27'.68W
438	BXA Gironde	45°37'.47N	1°27'.50W
449	SW Gironde	45°38'.63N	1°20'.08W

Key abbreviation

PdG Pointe de Grave

VII. CHARENTE

69 La Faute-sur-Mer and l'Aiguillon

Location
46°16'N 1°16'W

Shelter
Fair weather only

Hazards
Timber piles of mussel beds extend into channel

Depth restrictions
Approach dries 1.6m or more

Night entry Not recommended

HW time at St-Martin
Pointe de Grave HW+0005 neaps, –0030 springs

Mean height of tide (m)

	HWS	HWN	LWN	LWS
St-Martin	5.9	4.7	2.3	0.9

Tidal stream in approach
Flood – PdG HW–0530 to –0030 (1.3kns)
Slack – PdG HW–0030 to +0030
Ebb – PdG HW +0030 to +0530 (1.0kns)
Slack – PdG HW+0530 to –0530
1.5kns in river

Berthing
Drying jetty, moorings and anchorage. No visitor berths

Facilities Limited

Charts
BA 2999 (50)
SHOM 7404 (50)
Imray C41 (109)

Mud and mussels

The River Le Lay to La-Faute and L'Aiguillon is a genuine oyster river. The entrance dries 1.6m and at low water there is just a vast expanse of mud and salt grass.

A surprising number of yachts are based in the River Le Lay but a visitor will almost certainly have to take the ground in very soft mud, probably a long way from any facilities.

PILOTAGE

L'Aiguillon and La Faute-sur-Mer approach and entrance

Warning

Much of the shore is devoted to the culture of mussels. These are grown on substantial timber piles that cover at HW and are very dangerous. Yellow buoys or withies usually mark the mussel beds.

There is also a large rectangular mussel farm, 3x1M in area, in the middle of the Pertuis Breton. It is marked by four large Cardinal lightbuoys, one at each corner and a large yellow lightbuoy in the middle of each of the long sides.

By day

Approach only when the tide is well up. Start from a position about 0.3M west of Le Lay SCM. Head for the transformer, adjacent to a conspicuous barn, on a track of 035°. This course passes between No.1 and No.2 buoys.

After No.2 buoy, the channel swings steadily to port between oyster and mussel beds, until the river opens up and the distant town of L'Aiguillon, with the prominent water tower of Bel Air, can be seen ahead. From there, beacons mark the channel.

The River Le Lay and L'Aiguillon looking northeast. The river is shallow and the land is flat 'dry marsh'. Mussels are grown on substantial timber piles that cover at HW. Yellow buoys or withies usually mark the mussel beds
M&G Barron

L'Aiguillon *R Rundle*

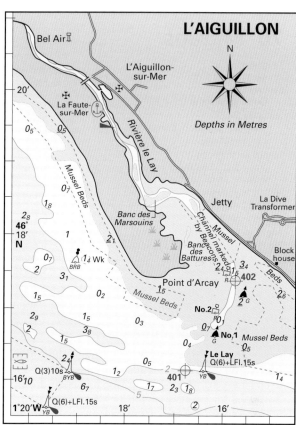

$\bigoplus$401 Faute   46°16'.14N 1°16'.68W
$\bigoplus$402 Faute 1 46°17'.37N 1°15'.85W

At Banc des Marsouins, the channel splits. Both channels are very narrow but the north one is preferred. The river then turns sharply to starboard and runs northwest to Faute-sur-Mar and L'Aiguillon.

By GPS

The entrance requires careful visual pilotage. The following waypoints may provide an indication of the route to the marked channel.

$\bigoplus$401-Faute, $\bigoplus$402-Faute 1

BERTHS AND ANCHORAGES

La Faute-sur-Mer

On the west bank about two-thirds of the way up to the bridge, is a landing slip marked by two posts with orange tops. Just upstream of the slip is the Yacht Club jetty (drying), where visitors may secure.

L'Aiguillon

Continuing up to L'Aiguillon, the river is full of fishing boat moorings and wooden jetties line the east bank. It may be possible to anchor or borrow a mooring in the pool below the bridge at L'Aiguillon. Depths are uncertain due to silting and the river can almost dry on any tide. Moorings are generally for shallow-draught fishing boats.

ASHORE IN L'AIGUILLON AND FAUTE-SUR-MER

There is a boat-yard and slipway but no fuel at L'Aiguillon. There are shops, cafés and restaurants in both L'Aiguillon and La Faute and a good beach at La Faute. There are markets in La Faute on Thursday and Sunday and in L'Aiguillon on Tuesday and Friday.

La Faute-sur-Mer mud berths *R Rundle*

L'Aiguillon oyster boats and yachts *R Rundle*

VII. CHARENTE

70 Marans

Location
46°17′N 1°10′W
Shelter
Good in Marans
Hazards
Shallow approach with strong streams; can be rough
Depth restrictions
Approach dries 0.1m
2.0m in canal to Marans
Brault lock times
Entry – Brault HW
Exit – Brault HW –0100
Night entry Not recommended
HW time at Brault lock
HW La Rochelle +0020
Mean height of tide (m)

	HWS	HWN	LWN	LWS
St-Martin	5.9	4.7	2.3	0.9

Tidal stream in approach
Flood – PdG HW–0530 to –0030 (1.3kns)
Slack – PdG HW–0030 to +0030
Ebb – PdG HW +0030 to +0530 (1.0kns)
Slack – PdG HW+0530 to –0530
4kns in river
Berthing Visitors' pontoon or Town quay
Facilities All facilities
Charts
BA 2999 (50)
SHOM 7404 (50)
Imray C41 (109)
Telephone
Lock ℡ 05 46 01 53 77

Gateway to the Marais Poitevin

The Marais Poitevin is a huge marshland conservation area that extends from the sea to Niort. The coastal part, west of Marans, has been drained to form the 'dry marsh' of flat fields and salt marsh. The 'wet marsh' extends from Marans to Niort and is a mass of canals that wind through the lush landscape.

In the 1920s and 30s a very large proportion of French cereal exports passed through Marans and many disused silos remain close to the harbour.

The 9M passage to Marans provides a wonderful opportunity to see the rich birdlife of the 'dry marsh' and, in Marans, it is possible to hire a canal boat to visit the 'wet marsh'. Marans is a pleasant market town where visiting boats are completely sheltered in an old canal.

PILOTAGE

Marans approach and entrance

Warning

Much of the shore is devoted to the culture of mussels. These are grown on substantial timber piles that cover at HW and are very dangerous. Yellow buoys or withies usually mark the mussel beds.

The lifting bridge and the Brault lock

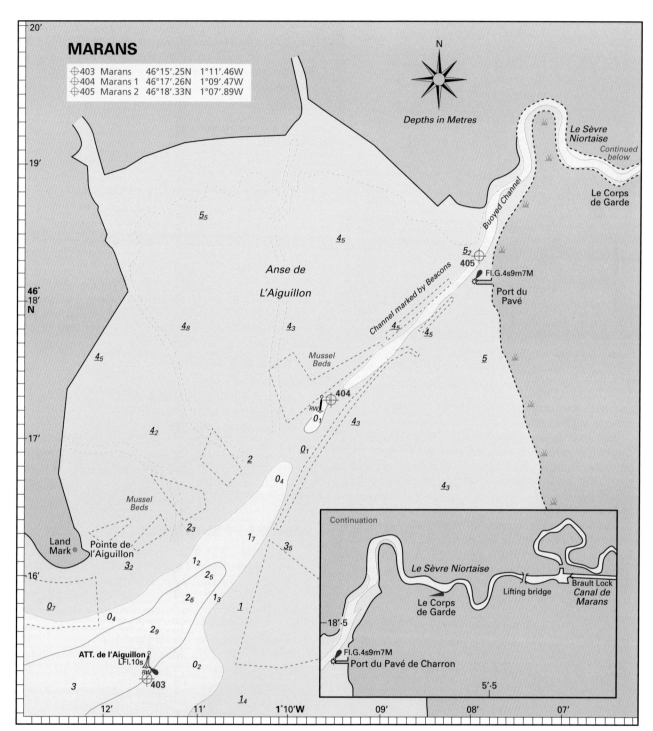

MARANS

⊕ 403	Marans	46°15′.25N	1°11′.46W
⊕ 404	Marans 1	46°17′.26N	1°09′.47W
⊕ 405	Marans 2	46°18′.33N	1°07′.89W

Depths in Metres

Anse de L'Aiguillon

Channel marked by Beacons

Buoyed Channel

Le Sèvre Niortaise

Continued below

Le Corps de Garde

Port du Pavé

Fl.G.4s9m7M

Mussel Beds

Mussel Beds

Land Mark

Pointe de l'Aiguillon

ATT. de l'Aiguillon
LFl.10s

Continuation

Le Sèvre Niortaise

Le Corps de Garde

Lifting bridge

Brault Lock
Canal de Marans

Fl.G.4s9m7M
Port du Pavé de Charron

VII. CHARENTE

If approaching from west, beware of the large rectangular mussel farm in the middle of the Pertuis Breton. *See page 230 under La Faute-sur-Mer and L'Aiguillon.*

Tidal strategy

Telephone the lock-keeper in good time to advise him of your arrival. The lock opens for entry at local HW, which is approximately 20 minutes after La Rochelle HW. The lifting bridge is 0.5M before the lock and about 5.5M from ATT. de l'Aiguillon SWM buoy so it is best to start well before La Rochelle HW and wait at the bridge. The tide will still be flooding quite strongly.

By day

Start at ATT. de l'Aiguillon SWM. Make good 035° for the second SWM. Try to hold the track accurately to avoid the mussel beds on either side. At the second SWM, follow the beacons on about 045° towards the SHM beacon on Port du Pavé jetty.

Beyond Port du Pavé, the river is constrained by banks. The plan indicates the deepest water but in general, stay in the middle but watch out for buoys that mark shoals on the bends.

The lifting bridge is about 3M beyond Port de Pavé. There are two waiting buoys on the starboard side before the bridge. Do not lie to these on a falling

Inside Brault lock with the swing bridge leading to the canal

tide with a strong west wind because they are very close to shallow water.

The lock-keeper operates the bridge using TV cameras to observe the road and river traffic. If boats are waiting, the bridge is opened so they can enter the lock at local HW. On the way back, remember that the departure opening is one hour before local HW.

The lock is enormous with gently sloping banks and a short pontoon on the port-hand side that can be used while the lock is operated. A swing road bridge, at the upper end of the lock, gives access to the Marans canal.

The attractive tree-lined canal runs straight for about 3M to Marans. Towards the end, it appears to come to a dead end, but the channel to Marans opens up to starboard, through a pair of permanently open lock gates.

By GPS

From the northwest use:

⊕396-N Ré

to avoid the mussel farm north of St-Martin.

Use:

⊕403-Marans, ⊕404-Marans 1, ⊕405-Marans 2

to cross the Anse l'Aiguillon and enter the river.

BERTHS AND ANCHORAGES

Marans Marina

Secure to new visitors' pontoon on the starboard side at the commencement of the mooring area or to the harbour wall or another yacht on the south side further on. There is 2.5m at the west end of the pontoon and 1.25m at the east end.

⚓ Anse de L'Aiguillon

Sheltered from northwest to northeast, it is possible to anchor between the two RW buoys. Go as far towards the second as depth permits.

⚓ Le Corps de Garde

Sufficient water to stay afloat at LW can usually be found in the region of Le Corps de Garde. This can be useful if lockng out of Marans in the late afternoon.

ASHORE IN MARANS

Marans has all marina facilities and is a popular place to over-winter. However, fuel is only available in cans from the garage by the supermarket.

The town has a good range of shops, cafés and restaurants. There is a covered market and an excellent supermarket on the main road out of town. Markets are held on Tuesday and Saturday.

Hire boats for the Marais Poitevin are found at the end of the marina, beyond the road bridge.

Marans visitors' pontoon looking downstream

Boats moored in the canal at Marans *M&G Barron*

71 Ars-en-Ré

Location
46°13'N 1°30'W

Shelter
Good in either marina

Hazards
Shifting very shallow approach. Easy to get neaped

Depth restrictions
Channel dries 3.4m
Marinas have 1.5m or more

Night entry Lit but not recommended

HW time: Pointe de Grave
HW+0005 neaps, –0030 springs

Mean height of tide (m)

	HWS	HWN	LWN	LWS
St-Martin	5.9	4.7	2.3	0.9

Tidal stream in approach
Slack – PdG HW–0030 to +0030
W – PdG HW+0030 to +0530
(1.2kns)
E – PdG HW+0530 to –0030
(1.3kns)

Berthing Two marinas

Facilities Marina facilities plus small town

Charts
BA 2999 (50)
SHOM 7404 (50), 7412 (15)
Imray C41 (large scale)

Radio VHF Ch 9

Telephone
Harbourmaster ✆ 05 46 29 25 10

Large drying natural harbour

Le Fier d'Ars is a large drying harbour on the northwest coast of Île de Ré. It is well sheltered and, despite only having access near HW, the two marinas have become the principal sailing centre for the island. The village is small but Ars-en-Ré is an excellent base for exploring the island by bicycle.

Le Fier d'Ars at low water looking north.
The moorings off Pointe du Fier are visible at the top of the picture. The marina is Bassin de la Criée. Note that the channel dries 3.4m where it narrows for the final approach

PILOTAGE

Le Fier d'Ars approach and entrance

Warning

The very shallow bar in the final approach (dries 3.4m) makes it extremely easy to get neaped. Occasionally the sluices are opened at LW to scour the channel. This is seldom done in season but when it occurs, access to the harbour is restricted.

By day

The easiest approach is to start from a position close north of Les Islattes NCM beacon tower. This is about 1M east of Pointe du Grouin.

VII. CHARENTE

Ars-en-Re leading light

The distinctive black-topped spire of Ars church on 231° is easier to see than the official leading marks on 232.5°
M&G Barron

Steer 268° towards the first SHM lightbuoy. (In 2009 the leading marks had been replaced by a small Dir.WRG light beacon which is quite difficult to see on the beach below the trees.) Le Banc du Bucheron tends to move south, so do not go too close to the SHM channel buoys and beacons as they may be off the line.

At the red beacon 0.25M east of Pointe du Fier turn to port and steer 231° for the black-topped Ars church spire. The official leading marks on 232° are not easy to see by day.

If proceeding to the harbour, follow the buoyed channel, which dries 3.4m.

By night

(See plan opposite).
Both transits are lit but night entry is not recommended for a first visit.

By GPS

The entrance shifts and the channel buoys are moved so the waypoints only provide an indication of the correct route.

From the west and northwest use:
⊕391-NE Ré, ⊕392-Ars, ⊕393-Ars 1, ⊕394-Ars 2

From the east use:
⊕395-E Ars, ⊕392-Ars, ⊕393-Ars 1, ⊕394-Ars 2

BERTHS AND ANCHORAGES

Bassin de la Criée

This is the outer locked marina and the gate opens local HW±0300. Time of access will depend on draught and height of tide. The height of tide over the sill is shown on boards inside and outside the gate.

It is close to the excellent daily market. It is quieter than Basin de la Prée and is probably the best and most comfortable base for exploring Île de Ré by bicycle. Visitors berth on the pontoon on the port side with larger yachts longer than 10m furthest from the entrance.

Bassin de la Prée

This is the inner harbour at Ars-en-Ré. It is in the centre of the attractive village and has a visitors' pontoon against the wall on the starboard side. The gate was inoperative in 2009 and apparently likely to remain so. The sill dries 3m and the time of access will depend on draught and the height of tide. There are drying berths immediately outside the gates to La Prée but they are mainly used by fishing boats.

The channel leading to the Bassin de La Prée with the difficult-to-see front leading mark on the right

The visitors' pontoon in the Bassin de la Criée

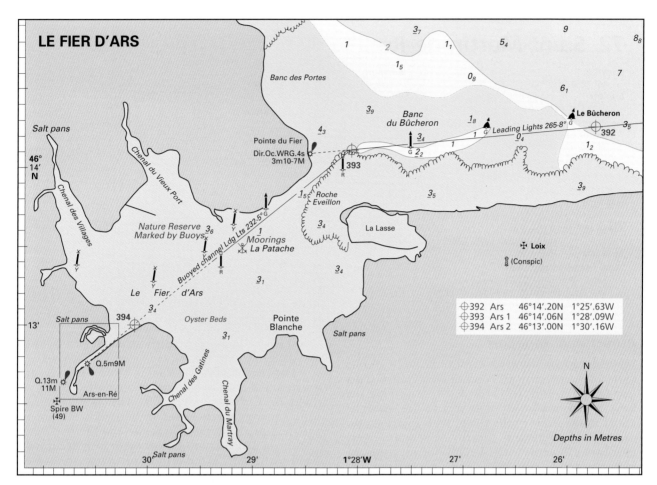

The waiting pontoon which dries

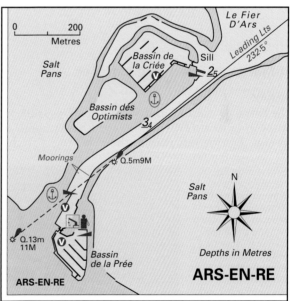

⚓ Les Portes

Sheltered from the southwest, there are visitors' buoys and an anchorage northeast of Les Portes.

⚓ Pointe du Fier

Sheltered except from the northeast, there are some drying moorings just outside the channel near Pointe du Fier. Anchoring is not allowed. There is an anchorage further east in a pool in the channel, however it is rather exposed and cannot be recommended.

ASHORE IN ARS-EN-RE

Ars-en-Ré has all the facilities of a small fishing, yachting and holiday town. There are basic marina facilities, including fuel at the entrance to the Bassin de La Prée. The small town is attractive and has shops, restaurants, cafés and, most important, bicycle hire. There is an excellent market every day during the season.

72 Saint-Martin-de-Ré

Location
46°12'N 1°22'W

Shelter
Good in wet dock

Depth restrictions
Entrance dries 1.5m
Wet dock has 3.0m

Other restrictions
Wet dock gets very crowded

Night entry Lit

HW time
PdG HW+0005 neaps, −0030 springs

Mean height of tide (m)

	HWS	HWN	LWN	LWS
St-Martin	5.9	4.7	2.3	0.9

Tidal stream in approach
Slack – PdG HW−0030 to +0030
W – PdG HW+0030 to +0530 (1.2kns)
E – PdG HW+0530 to −0030 (1.3kns)

Berthing
Drying harbour and wet dock

Facilities
All facilities in a very attractive town

Charts
BA 2999 (50)
SHOM 7404 (50), 7412 (15)
Imray C41 (large scale)

Radio VHF Ch 9. No Wi-Fi.

Telephone
Harbourmaster ☏ 05 46 09 26 69

Attractive historic port

Saint-Martin, on the north coast of Île de Ré, is one of the most attractive harbours in west France and a magnet for visitors. It is crowded in season but the lively atmosphere is part of its appeal. The yachts lie afloat in the heart of the town, with smart shops, cafés and restaurants nearby. Energetic crew members can explore the Vaubin fortifications or hire bicycles to tour the island. It was from the prison here that convicts used to be shipped out to the penal settlements in French Guiana.

PILOTAGE

St-Martin approach and entrance

By day

The entrance dries 1.6m so entry is only possible at neaps from local HW−0200 to +0130; a bit more at springs. During this period, the outer rocks to the west will be safely covered; those on the east will still be dangerous but are marked by a NCM beacon.

The harbour and Vaubin fortifications are distinctive. Start from a position about 1M away, with the harbour bearing 200°. Then approach with the square church tower in line with the green-topped pierhead marker at the end of the Grand Mole on 201°. Try to follow the transit accurately and particularly avoid drifting off course to the east by ensuring that the large, red-topped lighthouse is to the left of the church tower.

On arrival at the harbour, leave the wave breaker close to port and the mole head very close to starboard. The waiting pontoon in the outer harbour is to starboard and, beyond that, the channel to the dock gates is also to starboard.

Approaching from the east, keep well to the north of the NCM beacon on the Couronneau rocks and do not confuse the citadel, to the east, with St-Martin itself.

St-Martin-de-Ré looking northeast. When entering the harbour leave the wave breaker close to port and the mole head very close to starboard. Wait alongside the pontoon in the harbour for the lock to open. Once inside visitors raft in the north corner

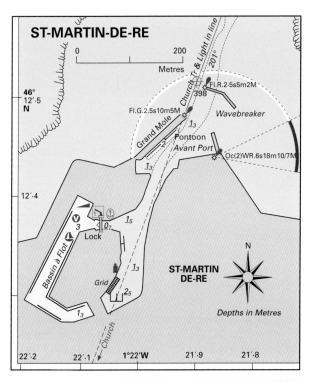

ST-MARTIN-DE-RE

⊕397 St-Martin   46°13′.31N 1°21′.46W
⊕398 St-Martin 1 46°12′.54N 1°21′.89W

By night

Approach in the white sector of St-Martin light bearing 200°. On close approach alter to starboard to bring the mole light onto 195° and enter leaving the light, marking the northwest end of the wave breaker, close to port and the mole light close to starboard.

By GPS

From the west or southwest use:

⊕391-NE Ré, ⊕395-E Ars, ⊕397-St-Martin, ⊕398-St-Martin 1

From Marans or the Ré bridge use:

⊕397-St-Martin, ⊕398-St-Martin 1

BERTHS AND ANCHORAGES

Outer harbour

In the summer months a long pontoon is arranged along the Grand Môle with a section dredged to 2m along its length. This is initially dredged 16m wide to allow boats to raft alongside the pontoon, but it quickly silts up with soft mud, into which the keels of deep-draught yachts sink. In northerly winds a swell enters round the wave breaker, causing the pontoon to pitch.

Drying harbour

There are quays on the east side that dry 1.5m. Vessels should not berth along the inner half of the west quay because there is a fuelling berth and a large grid.

Wet dock

The wet dock gates are opened about HW–0300 to +0230, less at neaps, between 0600 to 2300. Exact times are posted at the harbourmaster's office and other harbours in the area. The harbour staff take particulars as one enters.

To get a place inside, it is usually necessary to arrive early and wait in the outer harbour for the dock. Once inside, berth as directed. There is not much room and larger yachts are likely to be rafted alongside opposite the gate.

Rade de St-Martin

There are four white visitors' buoys off the entrance but they are subject to swell and tide. It is possible to anchor nearby.

ASHORE IN ST-MARTIN

The harbour has all facilities including a fuel berth on the W side of the drying harbour. The town is a sophisticated holiday resort with a good range of shops, cafés and restaurants. There is a market on Tuesday, Thursday and Saturday.

St-Martin-de-Ré lock gate

The waiting pontoon outside the lock gate

St-Martin-de-Ré entrance with green-topped pierhead light and church tower in line on 201°

VII. CHARENTE

73 La-Flotte-en-Ré

Location
46°11′N 1°19′W

Shelter
La Flotte, good except from N

Depth restrictions
La Flotte-en-Ré dries
Martray is shallow near the beach

Night entry La Flotte-en-Ré is lit

HW time
PdG HW neaps, –0030 springs

Mean height of tide (m)

	HWS	HWN	LWN	LWS
St-Martin	5.9	4.7	2.3	0.9

Tidal stream in approach
E – PdG HW–0530 to –0130 (0.9kns)
Slack – PdG –0130 to +0030
W – PdG HW+0030 to +0530 (0.9kns)
Slack – PdG HW +0530 to –0530

Berthing
Anchorages and drying
harbour

Facilities Limited

Charts
BA 2999 (50)
SHOM 7404 (50)
Imray C41 (large scale)

Radio VHF Ch 9

Telephone
La Flotte HM ☎ 05 46 09 67 66

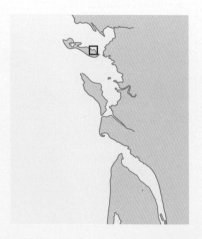

Attractive drying harbour

The drying harbour of La Flotte, 2M southeast of St-Martin, was once a fishing port, famous for its lobsters, shrimps and sole. Today it is a quiet, attractive leisure port with narrow streets, white painted houses and a beautiful church. The inner harbour is well sheltered so for shallow-draught boats and boats that can take the ground La Flotte provides a good alternative to the bustle of St-Martin. The outer harbour is exposed to the east and northeast and for deep keel yachts there are two visitors' berths which are dredged at the beginning

The attractive curved wall of the drying harbour at La-Flotte-en-Ré

of each season and where deep-keeled yachts are supposed to be able to lie afloat in a hole but the hole is reported to silt up with very soft mud quite soon after dredging.

PILOTAGE

La-Flotte-en-Ré approach and entrance

By day

La Flotte is easy to identify by the curved breakwater with the green-topped lighthouse on the end but the approach requires care. The channel through the sand dries 2.0m. On both sides are ledges of rock, and oyster beds marked by yellow beacons.

Start from a position about 1M offshore and steer 215° for the lighthouse on the end of the breakwater. A moiré fringe panel on a post to the left of the lighthouse will be visible day and night. This ingenious device displays vertical black and orange stripes on the correct course of 215° but, on incorrect courses, it changes to one or more arrowheads pointing in the direction to steer.

To enter the harbour, leave the breakwater head to starboard and steer for the narrow entrance between the jetty heads.

The lighthouse and moiré fringe panel at the end of the breakwater *M&G Barron*

By night

Approach on 215° in the white sector of the breakwater light.

By GPS

⊕399-La Flotte, ⊕400-La Flotte 1

BERTHS AND ANCHORAGES

Visitors' moorings

Deep-draught yachts can anchor or use the five white mooring buoys some 0.75M offshore north of the harbour in 2m.

Outer harbour

Visitors may use the outer sides of the hammerheads of the second and third pontoons (F and E) in from the outer breakwaterhead but only on the hammerhead of pontoon E will there be any chance of staying afloat in a keeled yacht. The outermost pontoon G is reserved for rescue craft etc.

Inner harbour

The inner harbour dries 2m. Pontoons for local boats are installed in the inner half of the basin. Space for visitors is limited but they may take the ground at the pontoon on the inner side of the Jetée Nord.

⚓ Anse du Martray (south coast)

Sheltered in light northwest to northeast wind, Anse du Martray is a sandy bay on the west end of the south coast. Start from a position 0.5M east of Chanchardon octagonal black-topped white tower. Steer 350° past the white mooring buoy into the bay. There are reefs less than 0.5M either side of the approach so it is important to hold the course fairly accurately. Anchor where depth permits but note that a deep-draught yacht will not be able to get very close to the beach. It is possible to land at the sea wall and walk to Ars-en-Ré through the salt pans or along the coast road to Martray.

⊕409-Martray 1 46°11'.56N 1°28'.02W

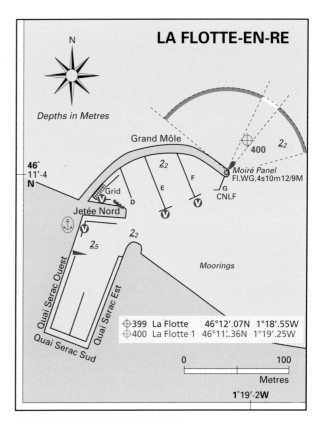

ASHORE IN LA FLOTTE

Water and electricity on the pontoons, showers and toilets ashore. There is a chandler and shops, cafés and restaurants in town. Markets are held every day. Fuel at St-Martin-de-Ré.

The visitors' berths on the outsides of the hammerheads

The inner harbour

VII. CHARENTE

74 La Rochelle

Location
46°09'N 1°10'W

Shelter Good

Depth restrictions
Approach old port 0.5m; Approach to Minimes 0.7m; Depth in old port 1.0m in very soft mud; Depth in Minimes 1.9m; Bassin à Flot 3.0m, sill 1.2m

Night entry Well lit

HW time
PdG HW +0015 neaps, –0030 springs

Mean height of tide (m)

	HWS	HWN	LWN	LWS
La Rochelle	6.0	4.9	2.4	0.9

Tidal stream in approach: Pointe de Grave
E – PdG HW–0530 to –0030 (1.9kns)
Slack PdG HW –0030 to +0030
W PdG HW+0030 to –0530 (2.3kns)

Berthing
Huge marina and old port

Facilities All facilities

Charts
BA 2999 (50), 2743 (15)
SHOM 7404 (50), 7413 (15)
Imray C41 (large scale)

Radio
Port des Minimes VHF Ch 9 (24H).
Wi-Fi available
La Rochelle VHF Ch 9
Wi-Fi available

Telephone
Minimes ☎ 05 46 44 41 20
La Rochelle HM ☎ 06 03 54 00 57

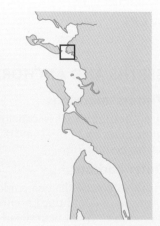

Fascinating historic city

La Rochelle has something for everyone. Elegant shops housed in some of France's finest historical arcaded buildings; a variety of museums; an ancient fortified port; dozens of cafés and restaurants as well as the best food market on this coast. In summer, street entertainers and musicians perform on the waterfront.

La Rochelle is so lively that wherever you moor expect to hear the sounds of music and of people enjoying themselves.

PILOTAGE

La Rochelle from the west or south

By day

Start from a position between Chauveau SCM buoy and Roche du Sud WCM buoy. Steer 059° towards the distinctive red Tour Richelieu and the two famous stone towers. The transit is two lighthouses in line on 059°. The front one is striped red and white; the rear one is white with a green top. They are very distinctive because they show bright white lights by day (Fl.4s) but these are quickly obscured when off the transit. Follow the transit to Tour Richelieu and follow the buoyed channel to the Vieux Port.

Port des Minimes is just past Tour Richelieu to starboard. The entrance is buoyed but be sure not to cut the corner; go all the way to the WCM buoy before turning into the channel.

By night

The leading lights on 059° make a night entrance very easy. However, note that north of the transit the stone towers may obscure the lights.

By GPS

From the west use:

⊕407-S Ré, ⊕411-La Rochelle, ⊕413-La Rochelle 2

Looking northwest. The red Richelieu tower is seen bottom left

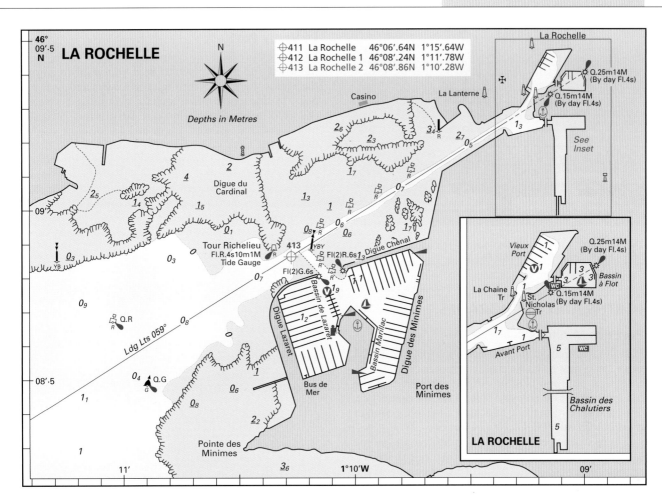

VII. CHARENTE

From the south use:

⊕412-La Rochelle 1, ⊕413-La Rochelle 2

To enter Minimes marina, turn to starboard 200m past Tour Richelieu. The WCM buoy and two PHM buoys are unlit, but there is normally plenty of background light.

La Rochelle via the Ré bridge

By day

The navigable part of the Ré bridge is clearly marked by buoys and on the pillars. The clearance is 30m. One arch is used for south-going boats and another for north-bound. After passing under the bridge, leave the outer breakwaters of the commercial harbour and the fishing harbour to port. Then follow the coastline, about 0.5M off, until the Tour Richelieu is sighted.

La Rochelle, Tour Richelieu is left to port on the approach

The final approach is the same as from the west or south. However, be sure to keep to the leading line for the final approach because there is a shallow patch just west of Tour Richelieu. The channel carries a minimum depth of 0.7m as far as Tour Richlieu and 0.5m into the Vieux Port.

By night

The navigable section of the bridge, the commercial harbour and the fishing harbour are all well lit. However, the shortcut inside Plateau du Lavardin is not lit.

By GPS

From the north via the Ré bridge use:

⊕406-Ré bridge, ⊕410-Pallice, ⊕412-La Rochelle 1, ⊕413-La Rochelle 2

This route has a least depth of 2.5m and passes close south of a shallow patch (dries 0.1m) near Pointe de Chef-de-Baie.

The fuel berth and the pontoon outside the harbourmaster's office at Minimes marina *M&G Barron*

BERTHS AND ANCHORAGES

Port des Minimes

Port des Minimes is a 3,000-berth marina about 1M from the centre of La Rochelle. It has 2m depth. The reception pontoon is opposite the entrance and the fuel pontoon is on the west side of the marina office. Tie up at reception to be allocated a berth or contact marina staff on VHF Ch 09 (24 hours).

There are excellent marina facilities and some local shops. It is a long walk to town but there is a regular water-bus from the southwest corner of the marina.

Le Vieux Port

Le Vieux Port is in the centre of the liveliest part of the town and is the place to be if you want to enjoy the atmosphere. Pass through the towers and bear to port. In times of conflict a chain was slung between the two towers to keep out marauding British privateers. The visitors' pontoons are straight ahead beyond the ferry pontoons. They only have depth of 1.0m but the mud is soft so deep-draught yachts remain upright. The pontoons have water and electricity and there are showers and toilets in the capitainerie by the lock gate into the Basin à Flot and at the Bassin des Chalutiers.

The Bassin à Flot

This may be preferable for boats over 12m, or for those staying a few days. The lock gate is to starboard just inside Le Vieux Port. The sill dries 1.2m and 3m depth is maintained in the basin. Access is from HW-0200 to HW+0030 by day. Call the harbourmaster to ask for space and for the lock gate to be opened.

Bassin des Chalutiers

The Bassin des Chalutiers is used for special events but, space permitting, it is also available for visitors. It is particularly suitable for larger boats and multihulls. It has 5m depth. Contact the harbourmaster to arrange for a berth and for the lifting bridge to be opened.

The Vieux Port and Bassin à Flot

The Bassin à Flot is approached from the Vieux Port. The picture also shows the lighthouses that form the leading line into La Rochelle *M&G Barron*

The lifting bridge into the Bassin des Chalutiers is to starboard just before the entrance to the Vieux Port. Access must be cleared with the harbourmaster before arrival *M&G Barron*

⚓ Anse l'Oubye

Sheltered from the west, there is a wide bay at the east end of Île de Ré, between Pointe de Chauveau and the bridge. Approach from the southeast and anchor in 2m on sand and mud or pick up one of the five free visitors' buoys.

ASHORE IN LA ROCHELLE

La Rochelle has every imaginable yachting facility. There are boat builders, chandlers, engineers and sail makers. Most major marine manufacturers have agencies.

In town there is so much to do that a guidebook or a visit to the tourist office (Le Gabut, south of the Bassin à Flot) is the best approach. Try to visit the museums early as they can become crowded later in the day.

The covered market is open every day and the street market fills the surrounding streets twice a week.

La Rochelle visitors' pontoons in the old harbour. The harbourmaster's office and showers are in the white house opposite

The Vieux Port at low water

75 Île d'Aix

Location
46°01′N 1°11′W
Shelter
Fair weather only
Depth restrictions
Visitors' buoys 2.0m
Night entry Approaches well lit
HW time
PdG HW +0015 neaps, −0045 springs
Mean height of tide (m)

	HWS	HWN	LWN	LWS
Île d'Aix	6.1	4.9	2.4	0.9

Tidal stream in approach
SE – PdG HW−0530 to +0030 (2.1kns)
Slack – PdG HW +0030 to +0130
NW – PdG HW+0130 to −0530 (1.7kns)

Berthing
Anchorages and visitors' buoys
Facilities
A few shops, restaurants and cafés
Charts
BA 3000(50), 2747 (20)
SHOM 7405 (50), 7415 (20)
Imray C41 (109)

Small island with history

Île d'Aix is a small island surrounded by beaches.

There are pretty white houses with multi-coloured hollyhocks, no cars, good walking or biking and two museums. It was here that Napoleon last stood on French soil before being transported to St-Helena.

The island is about 8M south of La Rochelle and is a good stopover on the way to Rochefort or a good day trip from La Rochelle. There are some visitors' buoys and several anchorages.

PILOTAGE

Île d'Aix approach and entrance

By day

The approach is simple from any direction. Avoid the reef, marked by two WCM beacons, that extends 0.5M to the northwest. Also avoid the oyster beds, marked by a yellow buoy, that extend 0.75M to the southeast.

By night

From the northwest, keep in the white sector of the Île d'Aix light until Chauveau light turns from red to white, bearing 342°. Steer 162° down this boundary, passing through the red sector of Île d'Aix light. When it turns white again, use the Charente leading lights bearing 115°. When Île d'Aix light bears north steer 020° and anchor in 3m, or pick up a mooring.

Île d'Aix from the southwest

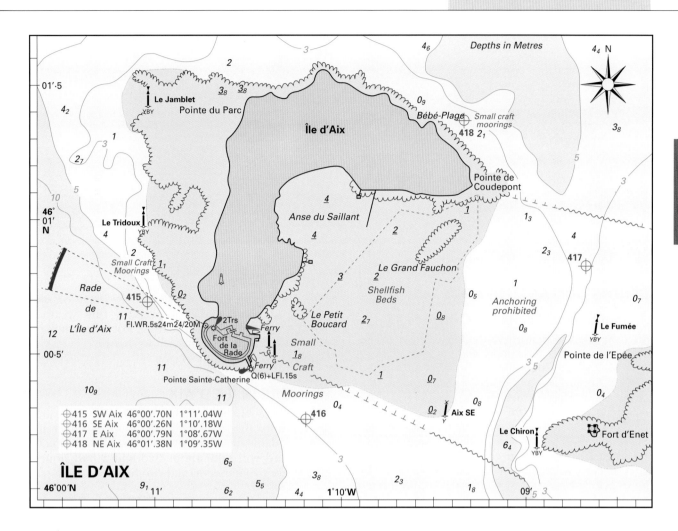

VII. CHARENTE

⊕415	SW Aix	46°00'.70N	1°11'.04W
⊕416	SE Aix	46°00'.26N	1°10'.18W
⊕417	E Aix	46°00'.79N	1°08'.67W
⊕418	NE Aix	46°01'.38N	1°09'.35W

ÎLE D'AIX

By GPS

Use: ⊕415-SW Aix or ⊕416-SE Aix or ⊕418-NE Aix as destination waypoints.

The passage E of Île d'Aix

By day

Fosse d'Enet is a narrow channel between Île d'Aix and the mainland.

Fort Boyard

From the north, leave the east point of the Île d'Aix at least 0.25M to starboard to avoid a rocky spur. Steer 195° toward the WCM beacon just west of the conspicuous Fort d'Enet. A yellow buoy marks the dangers southeast of Île d'Aix.

By GPS

From the north use:
⊕417-E Aix, ⊕419-Charente

Île d'Aix northwest from ferry pier to Anse du Saillant at LW

BERTHS AND ANCHORAGES

⚓ Southeast of Pointe Ste-Cathérine

Well sheltered from north and northwest with some shelter from other directions, there is an anchorage with four white visitors' buoys off the southeast tip of Île d'Aix in 2.4m and others with a dayglo green band which dry further in. Approach from the southeast and go in as far as depth allows. The mud is very soft so the holding is poor. The area is so well lit that it would be easy to leave at night and move to La Rochelle. Yachts that can take the ground can anchor close northeast of the Fort de la Rade by approaching close east of the ferry pier and leaving the two SHM beacons to starboard. However it would be wise to view the position of the oyster beds and other obsructions at LW beforehand.

⊕416-SE Aix 46°00'.26N 1°10'.18W

⚓ Northwest of Pointe Ste-Cathérine

Sheltered from the east and partially sheltered from the southeast, there is an anchorage with visitors' buoys northwest of Fort de la Rade.

⊕415-SW Aix 46°00'.70N 1°11'.04W

The visitors' moorings and beach northwest of Pointe Ste-Cathérine

⚓ Bébé-Plage

Sheltered from the southwest, Bébé-Plage off the northeast coast makes a pleasant fine weather anchorage. Night departure to La Rochelle would be very easy. There are some visitors' buoys.

⊕418-NE Aix 46°01'.38N 1°09'.35W

ASHORE IN ÎLE D'AIX

The village has modest shops and some cafés and restaurants. Bicycles and horse drawn carriages are also available for a tour of the island. A walk round the island will take about two and a half hours. There are two museums and two forts.

In Anse du Saillant, shellfish are raised on numerous wooden posts. These cover at high tide *M&G Barron*

76 River Charente

Location
45°59'N 1°07'W

Hazard
Dangerous bar at Fouras
Bore above Rochefort at big springs

Depth restrictions
Bar at entrance has 0.8m
River has 0.9m

Night entry Lit to Port-des-Barques

HW time Île d'Aix
PdG HW +0015 neaps, –0040 springs

HW time Rochefort
PdG HW +0035 neaps, –0010 springs

Mean height of tide (m)

	HWS	HWN	LWN	LWS
Île d'Aix	6.1	4.9	2.4	0.9
Rochefort	6.5	5.3	2.2	0.8

Tidal stream in river
Flood – PdG HW–0530 to +0030 (2.0kns)
Slack – PdG HW +0030 to +0130
Ebb – PdG HW+0130 to –0530 (2.0kns)
Stream can be 4.0kns in narrows

Berthing
Anchorages and visitors' buoys
Marina at Rochefort

Facilities
All facilities at Rochefort

Charts
BA 2747 (20)
SHOM 7415 (20)
Imray C41 (109)

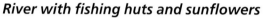

River with fishing huts and sunflowers

Despite its proximity to Rochefort, the Charente is completely rural with fishing huts and fields of sunflowers lining the banks. It is a very attractive river with masses of wildlife.

It is navigable for masted yachts for about 16M to Tonnay-Charente, about 3M beyond Rochefort. Motorboats can continue to Saintes, which is reported to be a delightful trip. Even quite large ships regularly make the passage to Rochefort and it is quite a surprise to be overtaken by a coaster in this idyllic rural setting.

Older charts show a lifting bridge below Rochefort. This has been removed and replaced by a bridge with 32m of headroom.

PILOTAGE

The Charente to Tonnay-Charente

Warning

There is a dangerous bar at the mouth of the river, near Fouras. Seas break heavily on the ebb in wind against tide conditions so it is best to cross the bar as close to HW as possible on the flood if the wind is from west or northwest.

By day

Start from a position south of Île d'Aix and close north of Les Palles NCM buoy. The first transit is on the land south of the town of Fouras. It is a very tall red-topped white lighthouse in line with a stubby red-topped white lighthouse on 115°. There is a tall radio mast nearby. The second transit is two lighthouses in Port-des-Barques in line on 135°. The rear lighthouse has a black, pointed roof and the front light is white with ears and a small black window.

Once the river has been entered it is generally sufficient to keep in midstream. There are beacons on the shore that provide a succession of transits. Each one carries a conspicuous letter, running from (T) at Port-des-Barques to (A), just below Rochefort. These are fun to follow but they are only really necessary for the coasters.

By night

The leading lines are lit as far as Port-des-Barques. Night passage beyond there is not permitted for small craft.

By GPS

The Charente requires visual pilotage; the following waypoints may help in the entrance.

⊕419-Charente, ⊕420-Charente 1, ⊕421-Charente 2, ⊕422-Charente 3, ⊕423-Charente 4

The low front lighthouse in Port-des-Barques in line with the taller black and white tower. Note the conspicuous white house on the right *M&G Barron*

The 'A' transit near Rochefort. The letter transits are really only for use by ships *M&G Barron*

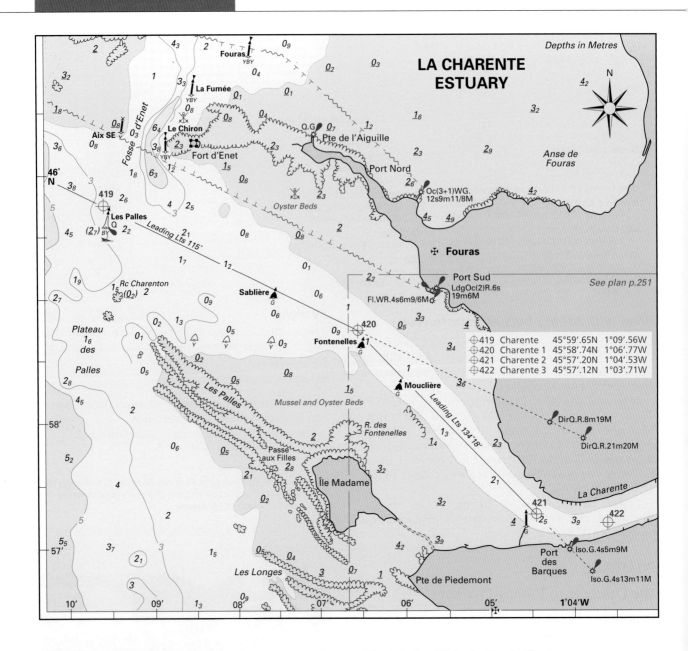

Depths in Metres

LA CHARENTE ESTUARY

	419	Charente	45°59'.65N	1°09'.56W
	420	Charente 1	45°58'.74N	1°06'.77W
	421	Charente 2	45°57'.20N	1°04'.53W
	422	Charente 3	45°57'.12N	1°03'.71W

BERTHS AND ANCHORAGES

Port-des-Barques

Sheltered from the northwest by a new jetty running north from the south shore there is now a visitors' pontoon with a fuel berth and also two visitors' mooring buoys in 2–3m. There are also two large white mooring buoys marked with a 'V' about 0.75M above Port-des Barques on the south side of the river with a landing slip close-by.

Soubise

Soubise has a visitors' pontoon and some visitors' moorings. Alternatively, anchor on the south side of the river as near to the bank as possible. Soubise is an attractive village with a boulangerie but no other shops. The supermarket is 20 minute walk. Frequent buses to Rochefort

The Yacht Club de Rochefort

The Yacht Club de Rochefort is on the east bank downstream of Soubise. It has landing facilities and a number of moorings along the opposite bank.

Rochefort

(See page 252).

Tonnay-Charente

Tonnay-Charente is 3M beyond Rochefort at the limit of masted navigation. It has a modern pontoon that may be available for visitors but the depth is unknown. There are shops, cafés and restaurants and a splendid, historic suspension bridge.

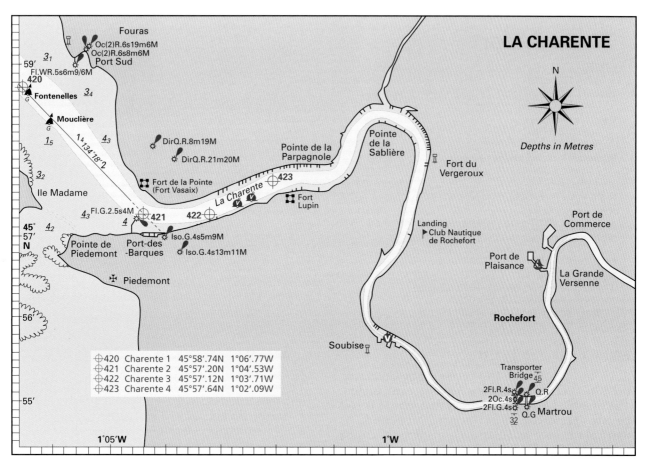

LA CHARENTE

N

Depths in Metres

Fouras
Oc(2)R.6s19m6M
Oc(2)R.6s8m6M
Port Sud
59′ 3_1
Fl.WR.5s6m9/6M
420
Fontenelles 3_4
Mouclière
1_5 1_4 134°18′.2 4_3
DirQ.R.8m19M
DirQ.R.21m20M
3_2
Ile Madame   Pointe de la Parpagnole
Pointe de la Sablière
Fort du Vergeroux
Fort de la Pointe (Fort Vasaix)   **423**
La Charente
4_3 Fl.G.2.5s4M   **421**   **422**
Fort Lupin
45° 4_2
57′ 4
N   Pointe de Piedemont   Port-des -Barques
Iso.G.4s5m9M
Iso.G.4s13m11M
Piedemont
Landing
Club Nautique de Rochefort
Port de Plaisance
Port de Commerce
La Grande Versenne
Rochefort
56′
Soubise
55′
⊕420   Charente 1   45°58′.74N   1°06′.77W
⊕421   Charente 2   45°57′.20N   1°04′.53W
⊕422   Charente 3   45°57′.12N   1°03′.71W
⊕423   Charente 4   45°57′.64N   1°02′.09W
Transporter Bridge 4_5
2Fl.R.4s   Q.R
2Oc.4s
2Fl.G.4s   Q.G   Martrou
3_2

1°05′W   **1°W**

VII. CHARENTE

River Charente transporter bridge with the new bridge behind it

A coaster coming downriver

77 Rochefort

Location
45°57′N 0°57′W

Shelter
Good in Rochefort marina

Depth restrictions
River has 0.8m
Marina has 1.8m or more

Rochefort lock and bridge opening
Rochefort HW−0015 to +0015
(but usually for longer)

Night entry Forbidden.

HW time Rochefort
PdG HW +0035 neaps, −0010 springs

Mean height of tide (m)

	HWS	HWN	LWN	LWS
Rochefort	6.5	5.3	2.2	0.8

Tidal stream in river
Flood – PdG HW−0530 to +0030 (2.0kns)
Slack – PdG HW+0030 to +0130
Ebb – PdG HW+0130 to −0530 (2.0kns)
Stream can be 4.0kns in narrows

Berthing
Marina at Rochefort

Facilities
Marina facilities, good shops,
restaurants and museums

Charts
BA 2748 (20)
SHOM 7415 (20)
Imray C41 (109)

Radio VHF Ch 9 Wi-Fi

Telephone
Harbourmaster ☎ 05 46 83 99 96
or ☎ 06 86 01 64 29

Historic naval shipyard

Rochefort is a delight. It was created by Colbert in the 17th century as a naval arsenal to rival Toulon. The dignified architecture from that period is still largely preserved. The original ropewalk is particularly fine and has been made into a rope museum. Alongside the museum in the old dock, craftsmen are building a replica of the 1779 frigate *L'Hermione* using traditional methods.

Rochefort has all the facilities of a regional centre, including excellent communications. This and the good facilities for yachtsmen, helpful marina staff and reasonable prices make it a good place to keep a yacht.

PILOTAGE

(See page 249).

BERTHS

Rochefort Port de Plaisance

The lock to the marina usually opens at about HW La Rochelle and remains open for between 30 and over 60 minutes. The exact times are given in a booklet *Le Guide de la Plaisance Rochefortaise* that is given away in port offices throughout the region. Alternatively call the port on ☎ 06 86 01 64 29 to find the lock times or to book a space.

The entrance to the marina requires a sharp turn to port just after the splendid 17th-century ropewalk. There is a waiting pontoon in the river outside and another at the entrance to the lock. The outside pontoon, which has access to the shore as well as water and electricity, may be used for up to 24 hours but rafting is not allowed. It dries at spring tides but has 2m at neaps and the bottom is soft mud.

When the lock opens, the two inner bridges open at the same time. Visitors are directed to a berth. Those staying longer than one night normally go into the second basin, Bassin Bougainville.

The berths are not well labelled and there is often a queue of boats entering when the lock opens, so manoeuvring can be interesting. It is best to leave as much space as possible behind the boat in front and be prepared to secure temporarily to the wall or another boat.

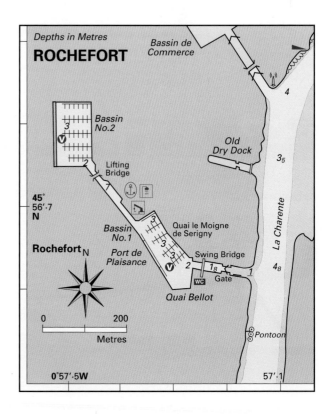

ASHORE IN ROCHEFORT

The marina has all facilities except a fuel berth. There are chandlers, engineers and repairs. The marina has a small crane for masting and mobile cranes are used for lift out. There is storage afloat and ashore.

Rochefort is a wealthy town with an excellent range of shops, cafés and restaurants. There is a supermarket upstream on the road by the river and an excellent street market in town on Tuesday, Thursday and Saturday. Car hire is by the marina and the railway station is within walking distance.

The ropewalk, maritime museum and dry-dock, where the replica frigate *L'Hermione* is being built, are all close to the marina and well worth visiting.

The old transporter bridge is a couple of miles south of the marina. It was restored in 1994 and takes cyclists and pedestrians across the river.

The entrance to the inner marina

The ropewalk

The River Charente and Rochefort looking north. The waiting pontoon in the river can be seen just downstream of the lock entrance. Bassin No.2 is entered through the narrow canal with a lifting bridge at the end

78 St-Denis-d'Oléron

Location
46°02′N 1°22′W

Shelter
Good in marina

Depth restrictions
Sill dries 1.5m
Waiting buoys 0.7m to 1.0m
Marina 1.5m to 2.5m but silts

Night entry Lit

HW time
PdG HW +0015 neaps, −0040 springs

Mean height of tide (m)

	HWS	HWN	LWN	LWS
Île d'Aix	6.5	5.3	2.2	0.8

Tidal stream in approach
E – PdG HW−0530 to −0030 (1.9kns)
Slack PdG HW−0030 to +0030
W – PdG HW+0030 to −0530 (2.3kns)

Berthing Marina

Fuel Marina entrance

Facilities
Limited repairs but good shops,
cafés and restaurants

Charts
BA 3000 (50)
SHOM 7405 (50)
Imray C41 (large scale)

Radio VHF Ch 9

Telephone
Harbourmaster ① 05 46 47 97 97

Friendly modern marina

St-Denis-d'Oléron, on the northeast tip of Île d'Oléron, makes a perfect base for exploring the north of the island. There are sheltered family beaches nearby and the wilder beaches of the windward west side are not far away. Île d'Oléron is particularly well set up for cyclists with many attractive cycle tracks away from roads and bikes can be hired near the marina.

The marina is modern and purpose built and offers good shelter and good facilities. The attractive village is about 0.25M away.

PILOTAGE

St-Denis approach and entrance

By day

Avoid the shoals north of the island and start the approach from a position quite well east of the town (⊕427-E St-Denis). Approach with the church spire in line with the green SHM beacon pole on 260°. In the final approach, leave the green beacon 100m to starboard and alter course to starboard to leave the red PHM beacon well to port. In the season the channel is marked with small red and green buoys.

By night

Start from a position about 2M north-northeast of the harbour. Approach in the narrow white sector of the directional light on 205°. On entering the white sector of the east breakwater light, alter to starboard to enter the marina. Leave the east breakwater 40m to starboard to avoid an outcrop of sand and stones encroaching on the channel.

By GPS

From the west and northwest use:

⊕424-N Oléron, ⊕425-St-Denis, ⊕426-St-Denis 1

From northeast and east use:

⊕425-St-Denis, ⊕426-St-Denis 1

From the southeast use:

⊕427-E St-Denis, ⊕426-St-Denis 1

This route passes over rocks that dry 0.6m but be careful not to stray further south because there are some much shallower rocks.

BERTHS

St-Denis Marina

The visitors' pontoon (A) is to port just beyond the fuel dock. There are finger berths on its north side and yachts over 10m berth alongside on the south side. The sill is 1.5m above CD and there is a tide guage on the west side of the entrance. At mid-tide there is 1.9m over the sill. The marina silts so note the depth at the sill on entering to be able to calculate the depth of water in the marina when the sill dries.

There are two waiting buoys 1M east-northeast of the entrance.

Pointe de Chassiron from the west with the lighthouse and Antioch beacon light tower in the distance

VII. CHARENTE

St-Denis d'Oléron looking south. The marina has been dug out of the sand and has a sill at the entrance. At low water the bay outside the marina dries

ASHORE IN ST-DENIS D'OLÉRON

The marina has a fuel berth at the entrance but there are no repair facilities on site. There are restaurants and a bike hire shop close to the marina. Further along is the village with shops, including a good supermarket and a daily market.

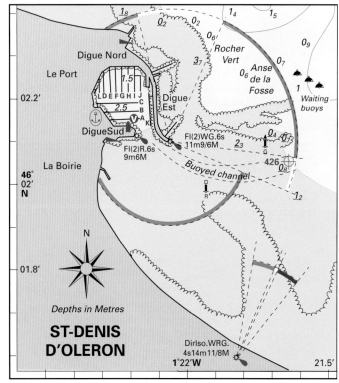

⊕425 St-Denis	46°03'.30N	1°20'.79W
⊕426 St Denis 1	46°02'.07N	1°21'.60W
⊕427 E St-Denis	46°02'.30N	1°19'.95W

St-Denis-d'Oléron from entrance, fuel berth and visitors' pontoon

79 Port du Douhet

Location
46°00'N 1°19'W

Shelter
Good in marina

Hazard
Overfalls in entrance in NE wind against ebb

Depth restrictions
Entrance dries 1.6m
Sill dries 1.8m
Visitors' pontoon 1.5m

Night entry Not lit

HW time
PdG HW +0015 neaps, −0045 springs

Mean height of tide (m)

	HWS	HWN	LWN	LWS
Île d'Aix	6.5	5.3	2.2	0.8

Tidal stream in approach
SE – PdG HW−0530 to +0030 (2.0kns)
Slack PdG HW+0030 to +0130
NW – PdG HW+0130 to −0530 (2.0kns)

Berthing Marina

Facilities Limited facilities

Charts
BA 3000 (50)
SHOM 7405 (50)
Imray C41 (large scale)

Radio VHF Ch 9

Telephone
Harbourmaster ☏ 05 46 76 71 13

Quiet marina with good beaches

Port du Douhet is about 3M southeast of St-Denis-d'Oléron. It is quiet, well sheltered and attractively set amongst pine trees. There are good beaches nearby but it is a long way from town.

PILOTAGE

Port du Douhet approach and entrance

Warning

The entrance is a narrow dredged channel across 0.5M of sand and rock that dries 1.6m or more. It must be positively identified before attempting an entrance. Note that the channel can be quite rough in north and east winds.

By day

Coming from the north, keep at least 2M offshore. Start the approach from Douhet NCM buoy (⊕428-Douhet). Steer 250° towards the marina and locate the red and green buoys that mark the channel. Follow the buoyed channel past two SHM beacons into the marina.

Once inside, turn sharply to port into the first basin. The visitors' pontoon is Pontoon D in 2.0m in the northwest of the basin. The southeast of the basin carries 1.5m.

Port du Douhet looking north.
Unlike the east coast of Île d'Oléron where mussel and oyster farming predominates, the west coast is mainly given over to tourism. The beaches are wonderful and there are miles of bicycle tracks

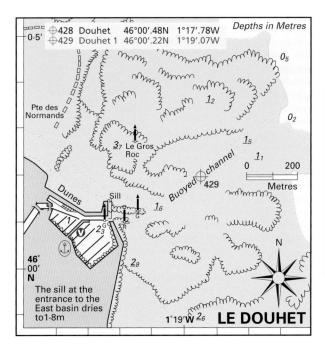

The visitors' pontoon on the starboard side in the east basin

The basin is accessible for a boat with a draught of 1.5m on a tide with a co-efficient of 80 HW –0300 to HW +0300.

By GPS

The channel into Douhet shifts so the following waypoints only provide an indication of the route:
⊕428-Douhet, ⊕429-Douhet 1

ASHORE IN LE DOUHET

Facilities include water and electricity on the pontoons, showers and toilets ashore, a boatbuilder and chandler but no fuel berth. There are a few small shops, including a baker and bike hire. Otherwise, the nearest shops are at La Brée les Bains (3km) or St-Georges d'Oléron (4km).

Douhet is well placed for visiting the safe family beaches and pine forests between Douhet and Boyardville.

VII. CHARENTE

The entrance at low water. Fort Boyard is on the horizon in the centre

Port du Douhet from seaward

80 Boyardville

Location
45°58'N 1°14'W
Shelter
Good in marina
Depth restrictions
Entrance dries 2.0m
Sill dries 1.8m
Visitors' pontoon 1.5m
Night entry partially lit
HW time
PdG HW +0015 neaps, –0040 springs
Mean height of tide (m)

	HWS	HWN	LWN	LWS
Île d'Aix	6.5	5.3	2.2	0.8

Tidal stream in approach
As Île d'Aix
2kns in river
Berthing Marina
Facilities All facilities but no fuel berth
Charts
BA 3000 (50)
SHOM 7405 (50)
Imray C41 (large scale)
Radio VHF Ch 9
Telephone
Harbourmaster ① 05 46 47 23 71

Small marina in a pleasant fishing town

Boyardville has a small marina in a locked basin accessed by tidal river. The basin is perfectly sheltered, in the centre of town, surrounded by shops and cafés. The ambience is pleasant but it does become busy in season.

On the weekend after 14 July a spectacular firework display takes place at Fort Boyard, 2M off the port. This can be watched from the beach, north of the town or from a boat at anchor off the beach.

The mussel bed in the Passage de l'Ouest

PILOTAGE

Boyardville approach and entrance

By day

Approaching from the north beware of a large mussel farm in the Passage de l'Ouest between Fort Boyard and Pte des Saumonards. It is marked by NCM and ECM lightbuoys.

Start from a position close to La Perrotine SHM buoy, which is about 2M south of the conspicuous Fort Boyard (*see photo on page 247*). Steer about 260° towards the breakwater and the second SHM buoy close to the breakwater. The channel shifts so watch the depth and be prepared to follow the deepest water. Once past the breakwater head, the best water is usually on the south side of the channel.

Boyardville marina and the river entrance looking northeast.
On the west side of the marina are a row of cafés and shops. The car park to the south is used for the market. The marshes are close by for walking or cycling and on Île d'Oléron a beach is never far away

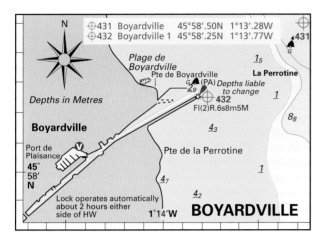

Boyardville harbour entrance

Continue into the river entrance and be prepared for a very sharp turn to starboard into the marina. When the turn comes it is important not to cut the corner: almost go past the entrance before turning.

The gates into the wet basin are automatically operated by the water level. They open approximately HW±0130 at neaps and HW±0300 at springs (24 hours). The sill dries 1.8m.

By night
The mole head is lit but night entry is not recommended.

By GPS
From the northwest use:

⊕430-W Boyard

⊕431-Boyardville, ⊕432-Boyardville 1

From the Charente or La Rochelle via Fosse d'Enet use:

⊕419-Charente, ⊕431-Boyardville, ⊕432-Boyardville 1

BERTHS AND ANCHORAGES

Port du Boyardville

Visitors berth on the pontoon to starboard of the entrance or on a pontoon berth as directed by the harbourmaster.

Drying out, alongside one of the quays in the river, may be possible but the bottom is uneven in places so check with the harbourmaster first.

Visitors' moorings

About 0.75M north-northwest of La Perrotine SHM buoy there are four white waiting buoys (marked PL29-32) and a large number of small craft moorings. Boyardville charges for their use and, in return, provides a taxi service to the beach. Alternatively, anchor nearby but note that the bottom shoals rapidly.

ASHORE IN BOYARDVILLE

The marina has all facilities but no fuel berth.

Boyardville is a small town with a full range of shops close to the marina. It is a good base for exploring the coast by bicycle. The Atlantic beaches are spectacular and run for miles along most of the west coast. The southeast coast is devoted to oyster and mussel farming, which is operated out of picturesque shacks in muddy creeks.

The lock gate is before the aluminium walkway and around the boats moored on the corner. Almost go past the entrance before turning *M&G Barron*

The entrance to the marina

The visitors' pontoon, to starboard

81 The Seudre to Marennes

Location
45°49′N 1°10′W

Shelter
Excellent in Marennes marina

Hazard
Pertuis Maumusson is not advised in any conditions

Depth restrictions
Entrance dries 1.0m
Marennes canal dries 2.5m

Height restriction
Road bridge 18m

Night entry Not lit

HW time La Cayenne (Seudre River)
Pointe de Grave HW +0030 neaps, −0015 springs

Mean height of tide (m)

	HWS	HWN	LWN	LWS
La Cayenne	5.6	4.6	2.4	1.0

Tidal stream in N approach
S – PdG HW−0530 to +0115 (2.1kns)
N – PdG HW+0115 to −0545 (1.7kns)
Complex at mouth of Seudre
4kns in Seudre

Berthing
Marina

Facilities
Basic facilities, good supermarket

Charts
BA 3000 (50)
SHOM 7405 (50), 7414 (25)

Telephone
Marennes marina ① 05 46 85 02 68

Oyster capital of France

Marennes is the centre of a huge area of marshes and tidal mud flats that stretch from Rochefort to Royan and include much of the east side of Île d'Oléron. The water is mostly shallow, the tides are strong and the area is dedicated to the culture of the renowned Marennes-Oléron oyster. Visiting boats are neither appropriate nor particularly welcome. Nevertheless, it is a fascinating area with outstanding seafood and can be visited in suitable conditions. There are several anchorages and a small marina at Marennes.

PILOTAGE

Pertuis de Maumusson

Warning

The Pertuis de Maumusson is the passage south of Île d'Oléron. It has a very dangerous bar that moves and may be shallower than shown on the chart. The strong tide over this bar combined with any onshore swell causes breaking seas even in good weather. Royan lifeboat coxswain advises visitors not to attempt the passage, even in perfect weather.

The Seudre River from the north

By day

The channel is intricate and the pilotage is mostly buoy hopping so an up to date version of the large-scale chart SHOM 7414 is recommended. Note that the direction of buoyage is from the south.

Start from a position close to ⊕433-E Oléron. Steer 157° with Marennes church spire in line with the Juliar ECM tower beacon. Leave Juliar beacon to starboard and continue on the same course using the Charret beacon (black rectangle with a white circle on a tall pole) in line with Marennes church, still on

River Seudre, La Cayenne and the Marennes Canal looking northwest.
The canal leads from La Cayenne to the small marina at Port de Marennes

VII. CHARENTE

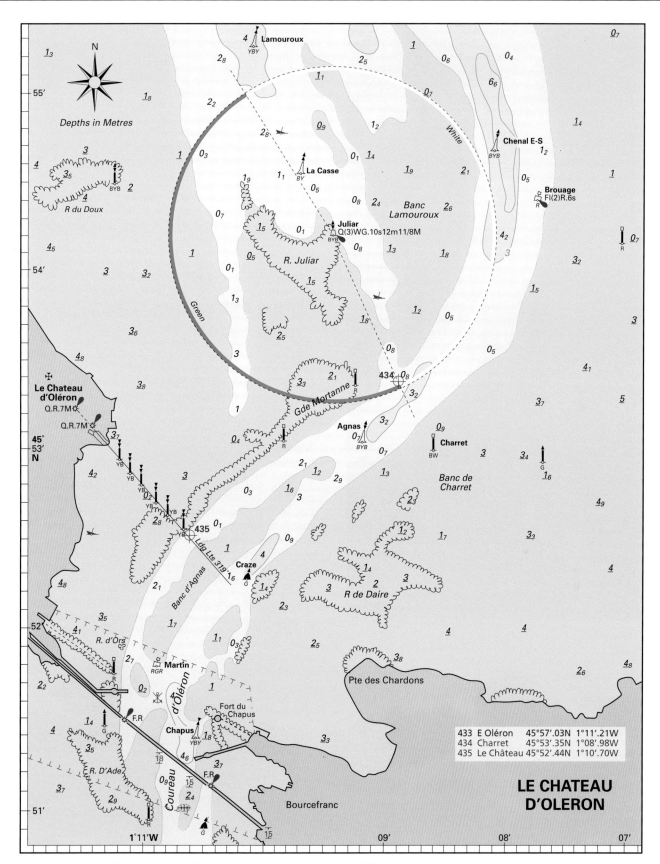

LE CHATEAU D'OLERON

433 E Oléron	45°57'.03N	1°11'.21W
434 Charret	45°53'.35N	1°08'.98W
435 Le Château	45°52'.44N	1°10'.70W

157°. About 0.5M from the Charret beacon (⊕434-Charret) turn to starboard and steer about 220° to leave Agnas ECM buoy to starboard and follow the buoys round the south side of Bank d'Agnas to the bridge.

The two preferred routes under the bridge (height 18m) are marked with either a red square or a green triangle on a white square. The southeast route is easier and has deeper water but is 3m lower. Pass under the bridge, taking care to avoid the wreck

Marennes

south of the bridge, and follow the buoys towards La Palette PHM buoy. When this buoy is abeam turn to port through 90° and steer 145° towards Soumaille northwest WCM buoy which is left close to port and so into the start of the River Seudre. Between La Palette PHM and Soumaille northwest WCM a bank which dries 0.7m will have been crossed so that an adequate rise of tide will be needed. Follow the buoys up the river and under the road bridge (height 18m above ML) to La Cayenne at the entrance to the Marennes canal. Beware that the sandbanks and buoyage are subject to change.

By GPS

The passage requires careful visual pilotage; the following waypoints may help in the approach to Charret beacon:

⊕433-E Oléron, ⊕434-Charret

BERTHS AND ANCHORAGES

⚓ La Cayenne

The best anchorages are near the disused ferry slips at La Cayenne (north bank) and at the entrance to La Tremblade canal about 0.5M upstream on the south bank. Anchor near the side of the river and land at the ferry slip. Above the entrance to the Tremblade canal is a wreck, marked by a green buoy.

Marennes

The entrance to the Marennes canal lies just downstream of the ferry pier. There is a shallow patch in the entrance marked by a PHM beacon with the best water on the starboard side. The perches marking the channel are high on the mud, and the best water lies roughly halfway between them. At the end of the canal is the wet basin, the gates of which open automatically at about HW±0100 at neaps and HW±0200 at springs but they only operate when the tidal co-efficient exceeds 50. A power cable (height 24m) crosses the canal below the gate and another (height 16m) crosses the dock. Both above ML.

Marennes canal downstream from lock *R Rundle*

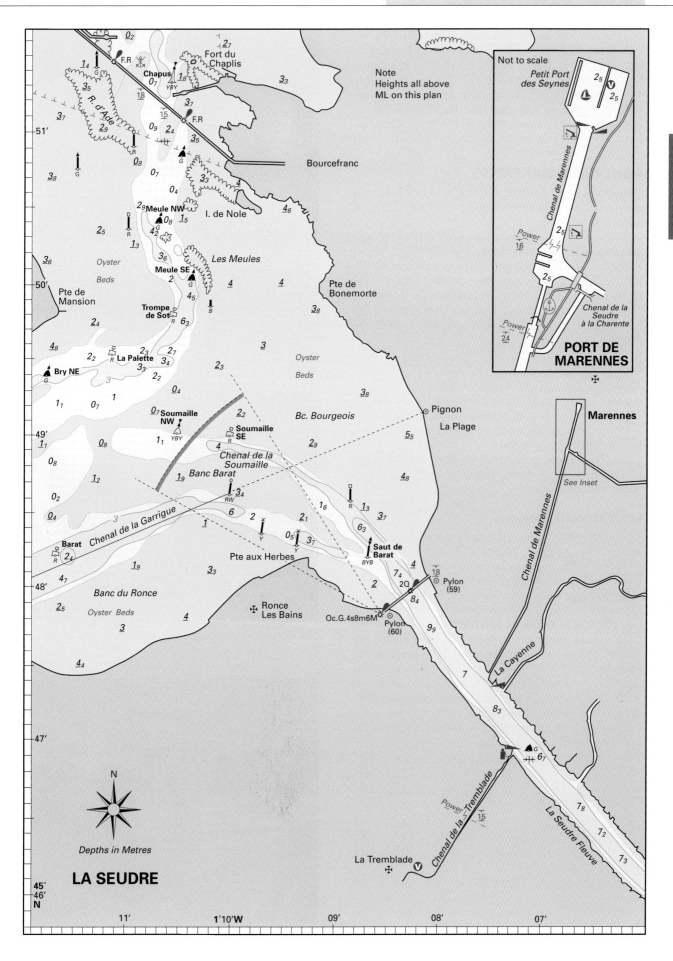

VII. CHARENTE

Not to scale

Petit Port des Seynes

PORT DE MARENNES

Chenal de Marennes

Power
16

Power
24

Chenal de la Seudre à la Charente

Marennes

See Inset

Note
Heights all above
ML on this plan

Bourcefranc

Fort du Chaplis

Chapus

R. d'Ade

Meule NW

I. de Nole

Les Meules

Meule SE

Pte de Mansion

Trompe de Sot

Oyster Beds

La Palette

Bry NE

Soumaille NW

Soumaille SE

Chenal de la Soumaille

Banc Barat

Pte de Bonemorte

Oyster Beds

Bc. Bourgeois

Pignon
La Plage

Barat

Chenal de la Garrigue

Pte aux Herbes

Banc du Ronce

Oyster Beds

Ronce Les Bains

Saut de Barat

Oc.G.4s8m6M

Pylon
(60)

Pylon
(59)

La Cayenne

La Seudre Fleuve

Power

Chenal de la Tremblade

La Tremblade

N

Depths in Metres

LA SEUDRE

45°
46'
N

11' 1°10'W 09' 08' 07'

51'

50'

49'

48'

47'

The marina is in an old dock. Visitors do occasionally arrive and yachts under 12m can be accommodated but it would be wise to telephone first or make contact on VHF Ch 09 before transiting the canal. There is a new marina building with showers, toilets and laundry. Repairs of all sorts can be undertaken through the harbourmaster. No fuel in the canal or the marina.

ASHORE IN MARENNES

Marennes has limited marina facilities but is charming and well-maintained and the town is attractive.

There is a good selection of shops, cafés and seafood restaurants as befits the oyster capital of Europe. A large hypermarket is at the rear of the post office a few minutes' walk through the municipal gardens. There are markets on Tuesdays, Thursdays and Saturdays. The fine church tower can be climbed to see the panoramic view over the marshes.

La Tremblade

There is a drying canal to Tremblade with a quay at the end of the canal beyond a power cable (height 15m), but there is very little room for visitors. It is very attractive with much oyster farming activity, but best visited by dinghy.

La Tremblade is a small market town with a boatyard, marine repair facilities and a range of shops and restaurants.

Le Château d'Oléron

This is an oyster port on the east coast of Oléron just before the bridge. Yachts are not particularly welcome at the moment but a new oyster harbour is being built just to the south so that there may be more room in the future. There are two pontoons in the avant port where a yacht drawing 1m would stay just afloat on a neap tide but otherwise a boat would have to take the ground. Approach from Mortanne Sud SCM beacon and make good 319° towards the leading lights. The rear light is a red-topped white light tower. The front light is a squat white tower with a red board above it but beware of oyster beds marked by rather insubstantial withies close to the channel. There are no specific facilities for yachts but the citadel is worth seeing.

⊕435-Le Château 45°52'·44N 1°10'·70W

The canal upstream from lock *R Rundle*

The entrance canal from marina *R Rundle*

Marennes Port de Plaisance *R Rundle*

VIII. The Gironde and Bassin d'Arcachon to Hendaye

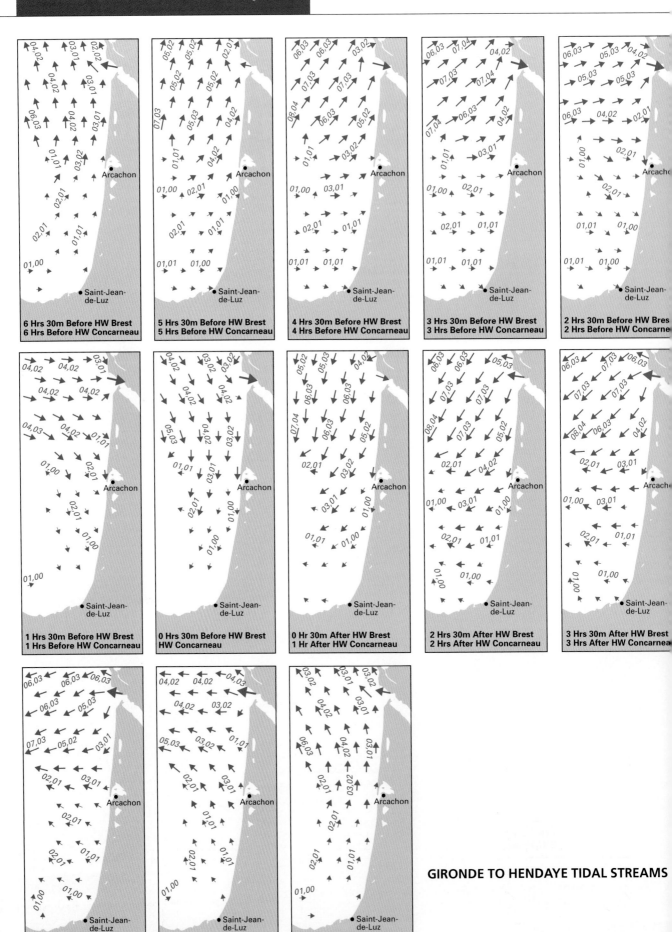

6 Hrs 30m Before HW Brest
6 Hrs Before HW Concarneau

5 Hrs 30m Before HW Brest
5 Hrs Before HW Concarneau

4 Hrs 30m Before HW Brest
4 Hrs Before HW Concarneau

3 Hrs 30m Before HW Brest
3 Hrs Before HW Concarneau

2 Hrs 30m Before HW Brest
2 Hrs Before HW Concarneau

1 Hrs 30m Before HW Brest
1 Hrs Before HW Concarneau

0 Hrs 30m Before HW Brest
HW Concarneau

0 Hr 30m After HW Brest
1 Hr After HW Concarneau

2 Hrs 30m After HW Brest
2 Hrs After HW Concarneau

3 Hrs 30m After HW Brest
3 Hrs After HW Concarneau

4 Hr 30m After HW Brest
4 Hr After HW Concarneau

5 Hr 30m After HW Brest
5 Hr After HW Concarneau

6 Hr 30m After HW Brest
6 Hr After HW Concarneau

GIRONDE TO HENDAYE TIDAL STREAMS

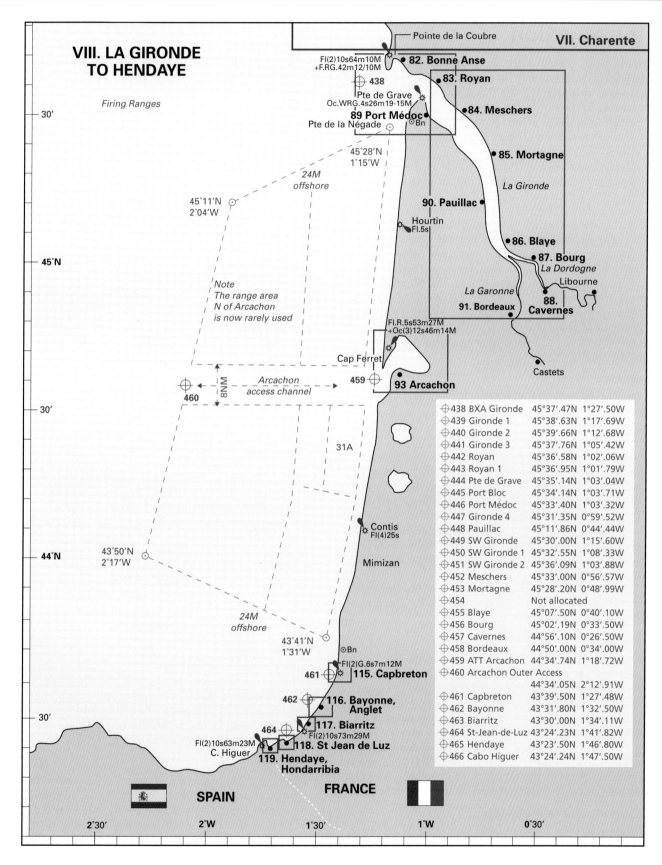

VIII. LA GIRONDE TO HENDAYE

VII. Charente

Firing Ranges

Pointe de la Coubre

Fl(2)10s64m10M +F.RG.42m12/10M

438

82. Bonne Anse

83. Royan

Pte de Grave Oc.WRG.4s26m19-15M

89 Port Médoc

Pte de la Négade

Bn

84. Meschers

45°28'N 1°15'W

85. Mortagne

24M offshore

La Gironde

45°11'N 2°04'W

90. Pauillac

Hourtin Fl.5s

Note
The range area
N of Arcachon
is now rarely used

86. Blaye

87. Bourg

La Dordogne

Libourne

La Garonne

88. Cavernes

91. Bordeaux

Castets

Fl.R.5s53m27M +Oc(3)12s46m14M

Cap Ferret

Arcachon access channel

459

93 Arcachon

460

31A

⊕438	BXA Gironde	45°37'.47N	1°27'.50W
⊕439	Gironde 1	45°38'.63N	1°17'.69W
⊕440	Gironde 2	45°39'.66N	1°12'.68W
⊕441	Gironde 3	45°37'.76N	1°05'.42W
⊕442	Royan	45°36'.58N	1°02'.06W
⊕443	Royan 1	45°36'.95N	1°01'.79W
⊕444	Pte de Grave	45°35'.14N	1°03'.04W
⊕445	Port Bloc	45°34'.14N	1°03'.71W
⊕446	Port Médoc	45°33'.40N	1°03'.32W
⊕447	Gironde 4	45°31'.35N	0°59'.52W
⊕448	Pauillac	45°11'.86N	0°44'.44W
⊕449	SW Gironde	45°30'.00N	1°15'.60W
⊕450	SW Gironde 1	45°32'.55N	1°08'.33W
⊕451	SW Gironde 2	45°36'.09N	1°03'.88W
⊕452	Meschers	45°33'.00N	0°56'.57W
⊕453	Mortagne	45°28'.20N	0°48'.99W
⊕454		Not allocated	
⊕455	Blaye	45°07'.50N	0°40'.10W
⊕456	Bourg	45°02'.19N	0°33'.50W
⊕457	Cavernes	44°56'.10N	0°26'.40W
⊕458	Bordeaux	44°50'.00N	0°34'.00W
⊕459	ATT Arcachon	44°34'.74N	1°18'.72W
⊕460	Arcachon Outer Access		
		44°34'.05N	2°12'.91W
⊕461	Capbreton	43°39'.50N	1°27'.48W
⊕462	Bayonne	43°31'.80N	1°32'.50W
⊕463	Biarritz	43°30'.00N	1°34'.11W
⊕464	St-Jean-de-Luz	43°24'.23N	1°41'.82W
⊕465	Hendaye	43°23'.50N	1°46'.80W
⊕466	Cabo Higuer	43°24'.24N	1°47'.50W

Contis Fl(4)25s

Mimizan

24M offshore

43°50'N 2°17'W

44°N

43°41'N 1°31'W

Bn

Fl(2)G.6s7m12M

461

115. Capbreton

462

116. Bayonne, Anglet

117. Biarritz

464

Fl(2)10s73m29M

118. St Jean de Luz

Fl(2)10s63m23M
C. Higuer

119. Hendaye, Hondarribia

SPAIN

FRANCE

VIII. THE GIRONDE AND BASSIN D'ARCACHON TO HENDAYE

2°30' 2°W 1°30' 1°W 0°30'

Key abbreviation

PdG   Pointe de Grave

Introduction

South of Île d'Oleron for the next 140 miles lies the largely featureless and flat pine-covered coast of Les Landes, only marked by the major estuary of the Gironde in the north, the large land-locked basin of Arcachon halfway down, and the four small ports in the southeast corner of the Bay, before the border with Spain is reached.

Unless proceeding up the Gironde to Bordeaux to enter the French canals, the temptation is to bypass this stretch of coast and sail direct to the north Spanish coast. This is a pity as the Arcachon basin is a fascinating area for the family holiday in a shoal draught or bilge keeled boat; there are excellent facilities for yachts both here, at Capbreton, Bayonne, St-Jean-de-Luz and Hendaye; tidal streams are no longer significant except in the river mouths or harbour entrances, the tidal range is much reduced and there are no dangers offshore. These ports all provide interesting and pleasant diversions on the outward or inward passage to the eastern end of the Spanish north coast.

Winds

Westerly winds are most frequent in the summer months in Biscay especially in July and August. In spring, early summer and late autumn winds between north and east occur more frequently. Most summer gales are associated with depressions passing to the north with backing winds followed by a veer to the northwest. The reputation of the Bay of Biscay as an area of strong gales and huge seas has not been borne out by the actual weather over the last few decades. Nevertheless muggy and thundery weather can produce unforecast severe local storms which are usually preceded by a sharp fall of the barometer.

In settled weather with high pressure holding over the area, land and sea breezes will set in which can strengthen to Force 5 or 6.

Visibility

Fog, of a thickness to reduce visibility to less than half a mile occurs less than one day in 20 but visibility of less than five miles due to mist or haze is more frequent in the summer. Reduced visibility is only likely to be of navigational significance in the Gironde and Arcachon approaches and estuaries.

The small amount of commercial, fishing and yacht traffic (except perhaps in the two areas above) does not present the threat in low visibility that is present in the more frequented waters further north.

Currents and tidal streams

There is a north-going current 5–6 miles off the coast of 0.5–1kn but this will increase after prolonged westerly gales. This starts as an east-going current along the Spanish coast turning northward to follow the coastline. A south-going countercurrent within a mile of the shore will often be found.

Tidal streams in the Gironde estuary are very strong and do not always follow the expected direction in the estuary. Out at sea tidal streams are very weak. In the other areas, tidal streams are only of significance in the rivers and entrances and these can be strong especially on the ebb. Details are in the appropriate port sections.

Swell

A feature of this part of the coast is swell which can appear without any warning, caused by a disturbance far away in the Atlantic. The French weather forecasts for shipping include forecasts of swell (la houle). As the coast is relatively steep-to and there are no off-lying shallows or dangers, swell only presents a problem entering or leaving harbours. It would be unwise to enter or leave the Gironde, Arcachon, Capbreton and Bayonne if there is any swell especially on the ebb. St-Jean-de-Luz and Rada de Higuer can be entered in these conditions provided the off-lying shallow patches are avoided.

Type of yacht

This stretch of coast accommodates all types of yacht, deep or shoal draught, mono or multihull. In the Gironde there is yacht or marina accommodation at the entrance, at Bordeaux and at two places in between. Yachts over about 15m length and 2.5m draught will not find an alongside berth between the harbours near the entrance to the Gironde and Bordeaux and would be limited to using one of the Lormont YC pontoons there. Similarly, larger yachts and big multihulls may find difficulties in the Capbreton, Anglet, Ciboure and Hendaye/Fuenterrabía marinas but in the latter two there are alternative anchorages, as there is at Arcachon. For yachts of about 12m in length and 2m draught or less there are few restrictions anywhere and for shoal draught or bilge keel yachts some of the smaller ports up the Gironde and Dordogne, and the many channels, small ports and the large sheltered expanse of the Arcachon basin all provide many cruising opportunities.

Fishing

Fishing activity in this area is confined to some netting in the Gironde, extensive oyster and shellfish beds in Bassin d'Arcachon and a few small boats working out of Capbreton, Bayonne and Biarritz. There are small fleets of middle water boats at St-Jean-de-Luz and Gurutzeaundi.

Laying up

Facilities for hauling out and laying up are available at Royan, Port Médoc, Port d'Arcachon, Capbreton, Anglet and Hendaye which, if used, would avoid a crossing of the Bay in spring to cruise the north Spanish coast.

Inland waterways

The rules and regulations for the French inland waterways apply to those entering the Canal Latéral à la Garonne above Castets. The minimum requirements for any vessel of less than 15m is that the helmsman should possess an RYA Helmsman's

An oyster port in the Arcachon Basin *R Rundle*

Overseas Certificate of Competence and that a current tax disc (*vignette*) is held. Details of the latter may be obtained from Voies Navigables de France, 175 rue Ludovic Boutleux, B.P. 820 62408, Béthune CEDEX. The French Government Tourist Office, 178 Piccadilly, London W1V0AL ② 0906 824 4123 can help further and will supply details of any closures (*chômages*).

Any boat drawing more than about 1.4m may have a problem in the summer months due to lack of water on this inland route. Enquiries should be made before lowering masts and committing to the transit.

The following references may be of further help:

Guides Vagnon (Les Editions du Plaisancier) Maps and text of waterways; English translation, Imray

Cartes Guides Fluviacarte Maps, Imray

Editions du Breil Maps, Imray

Euroregs for Inland Waterways, Adlard Coles Nautical

Inland Waterways of France, David Edwards-May, Imray

Waterway Routes through France, Map. Jane Cumberlidge, Imray

Through the French Canals, David Jefferson, Adlard Coles Nautical

Waypoints

For warnings and more information about the use of waypoints please see the *Introduction* on page 6. In this part of the book there are two types of waypoint:

1 Coastal waypoints

These indicate a clear track along the coast. Nevertheless, the waypoints and the tracks between them must be plotted and checked on an up-to-date chart before being used for navigation. And as the waypoints are according to WGS84 data do not forget to convert them before plotting on any chart using any other data.

2 Arrival waypoints

For individual ports or anchorages. They are placed at a safe distance from the destination at a point roughly where pilotage will take over from GPS navigation. Arrival waypoints are shown on the plan for each port or anchorage.

In a few instances an arrival waypoint may also serve as a coastal waypoint.

The waypoints given for the Gironde estuary south of Blaye and for the Garonne and Dordogne rivers are for planning purposes only.

Mortagne marina *P Taylor*

Search and Rescue

The Centres Régionaux Opérationels de Surveillance et de la Sauvetage (CROSS) are Maritime Rescue Co-ordination Centres (MRCC). The area from Pointe de Penmarc'h to the Spanish border is in the CROSS Etel area. Remote and linked sites include the following: Beg Meil, Saint-Julien, Piriac, Chemoulin, Saint-Sauveur, Les Baleines, Chassiron, Grave, Cap Ferret, Messanges and Socoa. CROSS Etel will respond to COSPAS/SARSAT emergency transmissions from EPIRBs, specialises in medical advice and is fully integrated into the DSC VHF and MF network. In an emergency CROSS Etel will respond either to a DSC activation on Ch 70 or Ch 16 or on MF. Details of the weather reports and navigational warnings broadcast from CROSS Etel and its remote stations are shown below.

Some harbourmasters require a form to be completed showing 'where from' and 'where bound'. This is passed to CROSS Etel who should be informed as soon as possible if plans change, otherwise a search may be started.

Radio services

There are no coastal radio stations except those which are part of the CROSS Etel Search and Rescue network and there are no radio beacons except aero radiobeacons.

CROSS Etel broadcasts weather bulletins at 0703, 0715, 0733, 0745, 0803LT and similarly in the evenings on VHF Ch 79 and 80.

Firing Ranges

Firing danger areas exist from Pointe de la Négade in the north to Capbreton in the south (*see plan*). They extend up to 35 miles offshore. Until recently there was a 3M-wide safety corridor between the range and the shore but this no longer exists and transit is only possible when the range is closed. The range is managed by Centre d'Essais des Landes (CEL) and the Range Control can be seen from the sea and is about 7M south of the LF buoy for Arcachon Basin.

Information on range activity is obtainable as follows:

☏ +33 (0)558 822 242/3 for 24 hr recorded message

☏ +33 (0)558 781 800 Monday–Thursday 0800–1700 and Friday 0800–1100 LT.

Information available via VHF Ch 16 from La Coubre, Cap Ferret and Socoa Coastguard Stations.

Or call them on VHF Ch 16, then Ch 06 or Ch 10.

These stations can give advance information of activity:

- CROSS Etel broadcasts at 1903 and 1933LT or ☏ +33 (0)297 553 535

- CEL broadcasts on VHF Ch 06 and Ch 10 at 0815 and 1615LT (Monday–Thursday) and at the same times on Friday only if the ranges are in use. Information is also available from CEL on request on the same VHF channels between 0800 and 1700 (Monday–Thursday and at the same times on Friday if the ranges are in use).

- Local NMs can be viewed at Arcachon Marina Office ☏ +33 (0)556 223 675 or Affaires Maritimes in Arcachon ☏ +33 (0)557 525 700.

Unless one is fluent in French the best option is to telephone CROSS Etel (where some English is spoken) before leaving port.

The range is patrolled by range craft when firings take place.

Meschers, cave houses in the cliff to the west of the town

The Gironde

Approaches to the Gironde Estuary

Location
45°38'N 01°28'W (BXA LF buoy)

Shelter
Very good in Royan and Port Médoc

Depth restrictions
11m minimum on leading lines
1.5m in Royan approach
3m in Port Médoc approach

Night entry
As by day. The Grande Passe de l'Ouest is extremely well lit but the buoys of the Passe Sud are not lit

Tidal information
As at Pointe de Grave (Pte de G)

Hazards
The tidal streams are very strong and do not always follow the line of the estuary in the mouth; constant checks are required to avoid being set off the intended track. Overfalls are severe and dangerous (5m). Do not attempt to enter the estuary in strong winds from the SW through W to N if there is any swell or on the ebb tide. If in doubt, stand off. Particular care is needed between Nos. 2A, 3, 4 and 5 entrance buoys where the channel is narrow and shoals quickly on either side. Only use the south channel in fine weather, good visibility and

favourable tidal conditions. Keep to the main channel unless indicated otherwise as there are a number of wrecks outside it. The sandbanks change their positions and depths during the winter storms and an up-to-date chart (BA 3058 or SHOM 7425) should be used and the latest *Notices to Mariners* consulted.

Wind effect on tidal level
Winds between S and NNW raise the water level up to 1m and advance the time of HW by up to 15 minutes. Winds from the N through E to S decrease the level by up to 0.3m and retard the time of HW by up to 15 minutes.

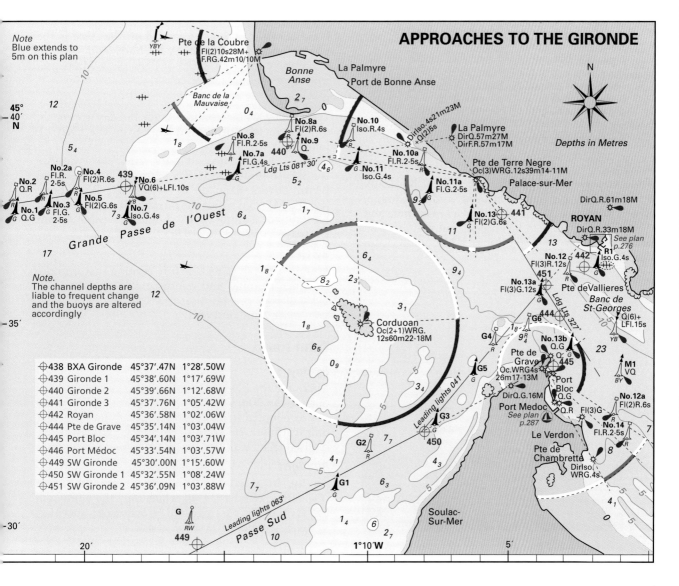

Tidal streams

The following is a simplification based on the times at Pointe de Grave:

	Flood begins	Spring rate knots	Ebb begins	Spring rate knots
BXA buoy	−0430	2.6	+0100	3.3
Off Royan	−0445	3.8	+0045	3.8
Off Mortagne	−0415	2.8	+0145	3.8
Pauillac	−0315	2.8	+0215	3.8
Bordeaux	−0115	2.8	+0315	3.8
Libourne	+0045	3.8	+0410	4.7

After Bordeaux there is no noticeable flood and the downward stream is significantly lessened.

Kilometre marks

They are on both banks and show the distance from Bordeaux (Pont de Pierre) and appear on all the charts. On the Dordogne they run from Libourne (0km) to Bourg (40km) and then revert to the Garonne distances.

Weather

On Ch 79
From Chassiron at 0703, 1533, 1903 LT in French
From Soulac at 0715, 1545, 1915 LT in French
Navtex from Corsen (A) (English) and (E) (French)
☏ 08 92 68 08 33 or VHF Ch 63 (recorded in French)

Charts

BA 3057 (50), 3058 (25), 3068, 3069 (various)
SHOM 7070 (167), 7426 (52), 7425 (25), 7427 (various)
Imray C41, C42

Radio

Port Control Bordeaux to BXA Ch 16 and 12 (24 hrs)
Radar guidance on Ch 12 on request
Gironde tide height Ch 17 (every 5 minutes)

Lifeboat

An all-weather lifeboat is maintained at Royan.

This extensive estuary leads to the city of Bordeaux and to the large rivers Garonne and Dordogne. Above Bordeaux the Canal Latéral à la Garonne and the Canal du Midi can be entered and may be used by craft smaller than 30m long, 5.25m wide, 1.4m deep and 3m high

Corduan lighthouse at the mouth of the Gironde

PILOTAGE

BXA LF buoy to Royan and Port Médoc

From BXA buoy and ⊕438 to R1 buoy and ⊕442 off Royan is 20M. Port Médoc is 2M further.

Grande Passe de l'Ouest

Tidal Strategy

Between No.3 and No.9 SHM buoys, wind against tide conditions generate very steep seas. In strong west winds against the ebb, the seas are dangerous and may break right across the channel.

Inward bound the best time to arrive at the entrance is at the commencement of the flood. Outward bound, Royan or Port Medoc should be left well before HW so as to be clear of the narrow part of the channel between buoys No.3 and No.9 before the ebb sets in.

In light weather, reliable auxiliary power is necessary to keep out of the breakers on the banks.

Approach from north

By day

Warning

It is essential to keep at least 5M off the coast in the later approach to the BXA LF buoy and ⊕438 to avoid the dangerous shoal of Banc de la Mauvaise. The corner should not be cut.

By night

The same warning applies. As for the day approach, do not cut the corner and start from the BXA LF buoy.

The lights are Pointe de la Coubre (Fl(2)10s64m28M & F.RG 42m; the northerly red sector covers Banc de la Mauvaise), BXA buoy (Iso.4s7M) from which the directional and intensified La Palmyré leading lights should be visible (Front Dir.Iso.4s21m20M, Rear Dir.Q.57m27M).

By GPS

Make ⊕438-BXA Gironde before turning east into the entrance channel and continue to ⊕439-Gironde 1, ⊕440-Gironde 2, ⊕441-Gironde 3, ⊕442-Royan or ⊕451-SW Gironde 2 and onwards.

From south

By day

Make for the BXA LF buoy on a track of 000° and outside the 20m line. This will clear all dangers. Do not be tempted to cut a corner through La Passe Sud unless the three conditions for its safe use are realised (See Passe Sud, Entrance below).

By night

As for by day. The lights of Pointe de Grave (Oc.WRG.4s26m19M) of which only the white will be visible in passing and Cordouan (Oc(2+1) WRG.12s60m22–18M) will assist.

By GPS

Make ⊕438-BXA Gironde before turning into the entrance channel.

Entrance

By day

From the BXA buoy (RW) make good a track of 081° until the entrance buoys or the Palmyre leading line can be picked out. Proceed down this line keeping between the buoys until between No.7a and No.9 SHM buoys the channel and leading line may be safely left, turning on to a track of about 110° to leave Nos.11 and 11a SHM buoys to port.

Pass No.13 SHM buoy close on either side. To proceed to Royan continue on a track of 105° towards R1 SHM buoy. Short of this buoy turn sharply to port on to 035° up the Royan entrance channel.

To proceed to Port Médoc or upriver, from No.13 buoy continue on about 140° down the line of SHM buoys past the Pte de Grave. At No.13b course may either be shaped for Port Médoc entrance, or continue upriver making about 145° to pick up the many subsequent lateral buoys.

By night

At the BXA LF buoy (Iso.4s) bring La Palmyre leading lights (Front Dir.Iso.4s Rear Dir.Q) into line on 081° and enter the channel between Nos.1 and 2 buoys (Q.G and Q.R). After No.7 buoy (Q(9)15s) the leading line and channel buoys diverge; for preference follow the former until No.9 NCM buoy (Q) is abeam to port when turn to a track of about 110° leaving No.11 (Iso.G.4s) and No.11a (Fl.G.2.5s) to port.

Pass No.13 buoy (Q) close on either side. To proceed to Royan continue on a track of 105° towards R1 buoy (Iso.G.4s). Just short of this buoy turn sharply to port on to 035° towards the jetty ends at Royan (Fl(2)R10s, Fl(3)R.12s).

To proceed to Port Médoc or upriver, from No.13 buoy (Fl(2)G6s) make 147° on a stern transit of Pointe de Terre-Nègre (Oc(3)WRG) and La Palmyre (DirF.R on the transit) of 327° leaving Nos.13a (Fl(3)G.12s) and 13b (Q.G) to starboard. At No.13b proceed as for *By day* above.

By GPS

From ⊕438-BXA Gironde use:

⊕439-Gironde 1, ⊕440-Gironde 2 and ⊕441-Gironde 3

Then if going to Royan:

⊕442-Royan

or if continuing up river:

⊕444-Pte de Grave, ⊕447-Gironde 4

or if to Port Médoc:

⊕444-Pte de Grave, ⊕446-Port Médoc

Note that between ⊕438-Gironde and ⊕439-Gironde 1 this route, although on the Ldg Line, leaves SCM buoy No.6 on the wrong side showing that the channel has moved so be careful to follow the buoyed channel.

Passe Sud (or Passe de Grave)

From the RW LF buoy G to Royan/Port Médoc and La Gironde

From the LF buoy it is 9M to Pointe de Grave and 11M to Royan.

From north

There is no advantage to be gained or reason to use this pass when approaching from the north.

From south

Make for the RW LF buoy (unlit) with a ball topmark by day; by night align the front Ldg LT (Dir.QG) with the rear Pte de Grave Lt (Oc.4s) to proceed up the line on 063°.

Entrance

By day
Warning

The minimum depth in the pass is 5m but this may vary. Entry should only be made in the absence of swell, the last quarter of the flood and good visibility.

Navigate to the southeast red and white LF buoy with a ball topmark and align the St-Nicolas (white tower) and Pointe de Grave (white tower with black corners and top) lighthouses on 063°. Proceed up this line towards ⊕450-SW Gironde 1 leaving G1 SHM buoy and G2 PHM buoy on either side. On reaching ⊕450-SW Gironde 1 (and before reaching G3 SHM buoy) turn on to 041° and align Le Chay (white tower, red top) and St-Pierre (red water tower just to the left of Royan church) on this bearing. On reaching G4 PHM move to starboard of the leading line to avoid Platin de Grave (dries) and leave G6 PHM buoy to port. Cross the estuary, passing No.13a SHM buoy and No.12 PHM buoy on either side to R1 SHM buoy (⊕442-Royan) whence it is 035° to Royan. Make sure Banc de St-Georges (0.4m) is left to starboard on this approach.

If going to Port Médoc or up river, leave the line in the vicinity of G4 PHM buoy to round Pointe de Grave which, except for a 1.2m patch just to the west of the short pier on the north side, is steep-to all the way round.

By night

The same *Warning* applies as by day but additionally all the buoys to Pointe de Grave are unlit. Make sure there is sufficient light to see them in time for avoidance.

By GPS

Use:

⊕449-SW Gironde, ⊕450-SW Gironde 1, ⊕451 SW Gironde 2 and ⊕442 Royan

but keep to starboard of this line after G4 buoy to avoid Platin de Grave (dries).

82 Bonne Anse

Location
45°42'N 12°00'W, 111km mark

Shelter
Good except in SW winds near HW

Depth restrictions
Dries 1.8m in approach
1–1.5m in marina

Night entry Not lit

Tidal Information
HW as for Pointe de Grave

Mean height of tide (m)

MHWS	MHWN	MLWN	MLWS
5.1	4.2	2.1	1.0

Tidal stream in approach
E – PdG HW–0440 to +0020 (2.5kns)

W – PdG HW+0050 to –0510
(4.2kns)

Berthing
On pontoons

Facilities
All but no fuel

Charts
BA 3057 (50), 3058 (25)
SHOM 7425 (25), 7426 (52)
Imray C41 (large scale) C42
(small scale)

Radio
VHF Ch 09

Telephone
☎ 05 46 22 44 31

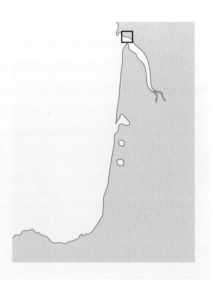

A small shallow marina in a wooded area near the mouth of the estuary

PILOTAGE

Approach and entrance

From the vicinity of No.10 buoy make good a northerly track in the last quarter of the flood to pick out the channel which runs close along the northeast shore (see photograph which shows this clearly). Care should be taken to keep to the southwest of the three groyne ends. This channel is sometimes buoyed in the season.

In the bay there are a number of oyster beds marked with the ubiquitous stakes which should be avoided; the bottom is flattish sand and mud.

The entrance is very narrow, marked by two spindly posts with sharp turn-in. There are crowded pontoons in the harbour in 1–1.5m with the deepest water at the ones on the southwest side.

Anchorage

Anchorage may be found in 1m to the west of the entrance.

ASHORE IN BONNE ANSE

The marina is close to the holiday village of La Palmyre with some shops and with excellent beaches and unspoilt pinewoods close by.

Bonne Anse looking NE near LW

83 Royan

Location
45°37'N 1°02'W

Arrival
⊕443-Royan 1 45°36'·95N 1°01'·79W

Shelter
Good in Royan Marina

Hazard
Gironde entrance dangerous in strong W wind or swell against ebb
Wreck with 3m over it 200m E of R1 buoy

Depth restrictions
Dredged channel 1.7m but less reported in 2009
Marina 2.5m

Night entry
Well lit

HW time Royan
As for Pointe de Grave

Mean height of tide (m)

MHWS	MHWN	MLWN	MLWS
5.1	4.2	2.1	1.0

Tidal stream in Gironde entrance
Flood – PdG HW–0445 to +0015 (1.3kns)
Ebb – PdG HW+0045 to –0515 (2.2kns)

Berthing
Alongside N side of reception pontoon or as directed in Marina

Facilities
All facilities. 26-tonne travel lift, 1.5 tonne crane

Charts
BA 3057 (50)
SHOM 7028 (50), 7425 (25)
Imray C41 (large scale) C42 (small scale)

Radio
Gironde tide height VHF Ch 17
Royan Marina VHF Ch 9, 16

Telephone
Royan Marina ✆ 05 46 38 72 22

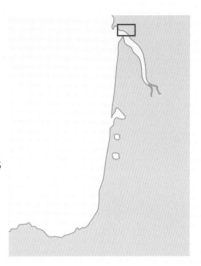

Royan marina looking west.
The fishing harbour is to port of the entrance. The harbourmaster's office and facilities are on the central spur opposite the entrance. The reception pontoon and fuel are on the north side of the spur and visitors moor to a long pontoon at the back of the spur

Holiday resort at the mouth of the Gironde

Royan was one of the most fashionable 19th century holiday resorts with magnificent hotels, casinos and villas. It was bombed flat by the British in April 1945 and has risen from the ruins around the Church of Notre Dame de Royan, of interesting modern design but which unfortunately is now badly affected by concrete cancer.

VIII. THE GIRONDE AND BASSIN D'ARCACHON TO HENDAYE

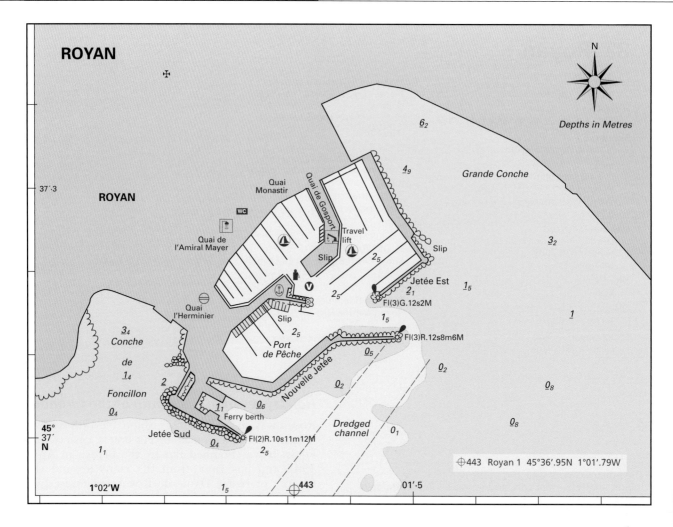

PILOTAGE

Tidal strategy

See page 271–273 under *Approaches to the Gironde* for information about entering and leaving the estuary but outward bound, Royan should be left well before HW so as to be clear of the narrow part of the channel between buoys No.9 and No.3 before the ebb sets in.

Beware that the entrance channel to Royan harbour can be quite shallow at LW springs and watch out for the frequent Port Bloc ferries arriving at and departing from their terminal close north of the entrance channel.

By day

From the northwest leave the main channel at No.13 buoy and continue on about 115° to R1 SHM buoy. Just before arriving at R1 SHM turn to port on to 035° and head for the harbour entrance. Leave the head of the Nouvelle Jetée breakwater close to port.

From the southeast beware of the shallow Banc de Saint-Georges (0.4m) and either navigate outside it by leaving No.12 PHM buoy to starboard and then altering on to 067° to R1 SHM buoy or pass inside the bank by leaving Ging Pointe de Suzac close to starboard and leaving R1 buoy to starboard on a course of 320° before heading for the harbour entrance on 035°.

By night

Make the R1 SHM buoy as by day but from the southeast it would be best to make the passage outside the Banc de Sainte-Georges. From R1 head for the east end of the south breakwater Fl(3)R.12s.

By GPS

From the west use:

⊕438-Gironde, ⊕439-Gironde 1, ⊕440-Gironde 2, ⊕441-Gironde 3, ⊕442-Royan, ⊕443-Royan1

but note that the Passe de l'Ouest moves so follow the buoyed channel.

BERTHS

Royan Marina

The reception berth is on the north side of the central spur to the left of the inner harbour entrance directly below the harbourmaster's office. Secure here and report to the helpful staff in the office unless met by the harbour launch in the entrance.

Pointe de Vallieres on which is the memorial to the Cockleshell Heroes

The old lighthouse at St-Georges-de-Didonne near the memorial

ASHORE IN ROYAN

Royan has all the facilities of a major marina including a fuel berth by the visitors' pontoon. It is a good place for de-masting prior to entering the Canal du Midi.

There are some shops, restaurants and cafés at the marina and plenty of shops in town. Royan has an interesting modern covered market.

There are few tourist attractions in the town since Royan is chiefly famous for its beaches, known locally as *conches*. Conche Foncillon is the small, family-friendly beach near the marina. The largest, longest and most famous beach is the Grande Conche.

History

A pleasant 2km walk for those interested in the history of the Second World War is to walk eastwards along the beach to Pointe de Vallières and view the memorial to the Cockleshell Heroes on the cliff edge near the disused lighthouse.

In December 1942 a daring operation by the Royal Marines code-named Operation Frankton was launched to disrupt the shipping using the docks in Bordeaux, which had been successfully breaking the Allied blockade.

Pointe de la Coubre lighthouse and the coastguard tower looking northeast

The entrance transit is the two lights at La Palmyre in line on 081°

VIII. THE GIRONDE AND BASSIN D'ARCACHON TO HENDAYE

Royan from Pointe de Vallieres with the modern church of Notre Dame in the middle

On a moonless night, five armed canoes known as cockles left their launch submarine HMS *Tuna* near the Cordouan light for the 60-mile journey in four stages upriver to Bordeaux; only two reached the docks. Limpet mines were successfully laid and exploded on five merchant ships and a patrol vessel, all of which settled on the bottom.

The two canoes escaped downriver and the four marines landed on the east bank where they split up to return to the UK with the help of the Resistance. Two were caught and shot by the Germans; the only two survivors of the original 10, Major Hasler and Marine Sparks, were back in England in April. (After the war Major Hasler initiated single-handed racing across the Atlantic in his junk-rigged folkboat *Jester* in which he invented servo pendulum type self-steering by windvane).

Leave the Nouvelle Jetée at Royan to port when entering the marina. Beyond is the wide curve of the Grande Conche beach

Memorial to the Cockleshell Heroes

Royan visitors' pontoon

84 Meschers

Location
45°33'·00N 00°57'·00W
89km mark

Arrival
⊕452-Meschers 45°33'·00N 00°56'·57W

Shelter
Good in the inner basin

Hazards
Strong cross set on approach

Depth Restriction
Dries 1.5m in approach channel
Dries 1.5–2m in outer basin
Sill dries 1.5m
2m in inner basin

Night Entry
Ldg Line lit

HW time
HW and LW as for Pointe de Grave

Mean Height of Tide

MHWS	MHWN	MLWN	MLWS
5.1	4.2	2.1	1.0

Tidal Streams
Flood PdG HW -0440 to +0030
Ebb PdG HW +0100 to -0520

Berthing
On pontoon ends in inner basin

Facilities
Water/electricity on pontoons
Showers/toilets/laundry ashore

Charts
BA 3057 (50), 3058 (25)
SHOM 7426 (50)
Imray C41 C42

Telephone
☎ 05 46 02 56 89 (Office hours)

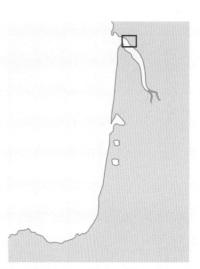

A small muddy harbour with marina in a locked inner basin

PILOTAGE

Approach

Identify the entrance from ⊕452 or from Talmont church 2M to the southeast close to the shore at the extremity of the same bay. The best time to enter is between HW–0200 and HW.

Entrance

Align the two white posts (F blue lights at night) on 352° and hold this line exactly between the port and starboard posts marking the outer end of the channel. There is a further SCM beacon to the east of these two posts which is left to starboard on the approach. The west side of the approach channel is marked with withies. There will be a strong cross stream at any time other than HW slack until within the inner channel.

Berthing

Reception pontoon with four drying berths on port side of entry channel.

If able to dry out, find a berth on the ends of A, B or C pontoons in the outer basin or on the northeast side just outside the lock.

The automatic lock opens HW ±0230 hours day and night and the sill dries 1.5m. There is reported to be 2m in the basin. Berth alongside end of pontoons E or F.

Anchorage

Outside to the east of the beacons in mud sounding in as far as possible out of the stream.

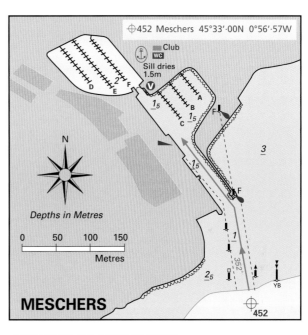

MESCHERS

ASHORE IN MESCHERS

Small restaurant and several shops. The nearest beach suitable for swimming is Plage des Nonnes half an hour walk to the northwest past man-made caves which have regular guided tours. Supermarket west of the church and markets on Tuesday, Wednesday, Friday and Saturday.

Meschers at low water

BOURG TO CAVERNES

457

27m

19m

20m

19m

Cavernes

La Dordogne

See plan p.284

27m

Bourg

456

The main channel in
La Dordogne from Bourg
upstream carries 2m+
to Libourne

La Garonne

N

Depths in Metres

◎ Pyramide de
Beaumont (66)

Port Maubert
F.R.9m5M
F.R.5m5M

Leading Lts 024.5

Valeyrac

Digue de

No.26
Fl.R.2.5s

No.27
Fl.G.
2.5s

No.24
Q.R.

No.25
Q.G.

No.22
Fl(2)R.6s

No.23
Fl(2)G.
6s

Banc de Richard

Pilet(4)

Mortagne

See plan p.282 ⚓ Sp (83)

453

No.20
Iso.R.4s

No.21
Iso.G.4s

La Gironde

◎ Pyramide de la Garde
(52)

No.18
Fl(2)R.
6s

No.19
Q.G.

16
Fl.R.2.5s

G
11

Tide gauge

(Disused)
Lt Ho
(17)

Oyster Beds

Mast 5 Wk
(14)

Banc des Marguerites

15
Iso.G.4s

447

Banc de Talais

Pte aux
Oiseaux

Oyster Beds

See plan p.279

1₈

452

Pte de
Meschers

(qp) (80)
(qp) (79)

(qp) (87)

Fl(2)6s

BRB

See plan p.271

◇ 442 Royan   45°36'.58N 1°02'.06W
◇ 444 Pte de Grave   45°35'.14N 1°03'.04W
◇ 445 Port Bloc   45°34'.14N 1°03'.71W
◇ 446 Port Médoc   45°33'.40N 1°03'.32W
◇ 447 Gironde 4   45°31'.35N 0°59'.52W
◇ 448 Pauillac   45°11'.86N 0°44'.44W
◇ 451 SW Gironde 2   45°36'.09N 1°03'.88W

ROYAN
Dir.Q.R.
33m18M
R11
Fl(2)R

Dir.Q.R.
Iso.G.4s
442

6

18

13

M1
V.Q.

12a
Fl(2)R.

14
Fl.R.

8₆
Fl.R.

Dir.Iso.WRG.
4s12-8M+
Fl.G.2.5s

Dir.Iso.WRG.
4s19-15M

Q(6)+
LFl.15s

23

23

13b
Q.G

13a
Fl(2)G.12s

12
Fl(3)R.12s

451

444
Q.
G

445
Iso.G.4s
Fl.G

6₈
Fl(3)G.2M
Fl.G.3M

446

Port
Médoc

Pte du Chay

Pte de Grave
Oc.WRG.4s19-15M

Port
Bloc

See plan

Dir.QG
22m16M

See plan
p.283

Ⅱ (43)
Ségonzac

Fort
(24)

BLAYE
455
Q(3)R.5s

Gasworks
Oil Refinery
Fl.G.4s

Ile Nouvelle

Fl.G.4s

Ile Verte
Q.G.4s

Fort Médoc

45°
30'
N

25'

280 ATLANTIC FRANCE

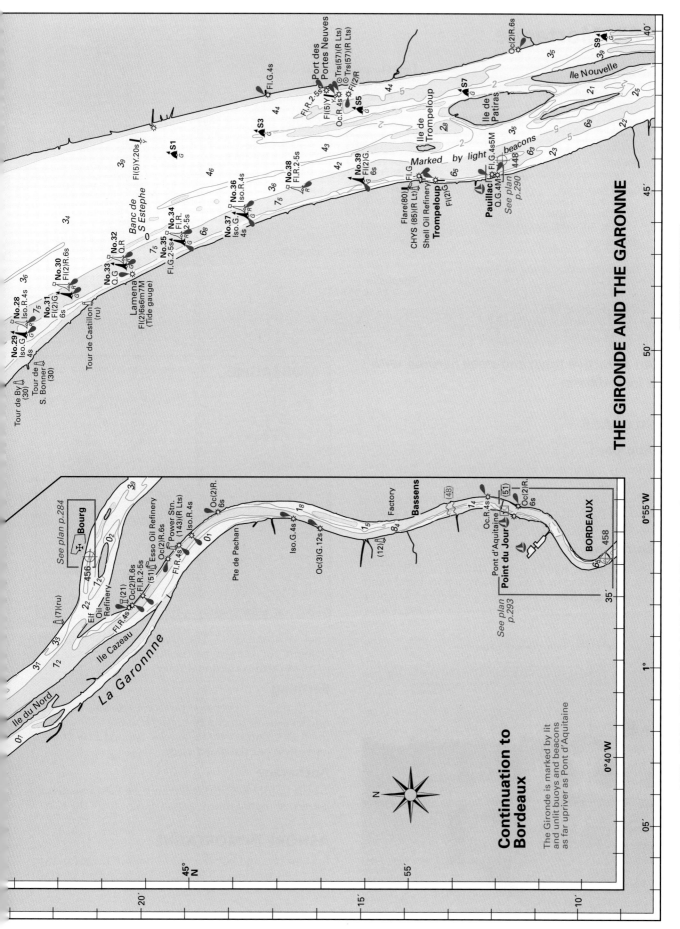

THE GIRONDE AND THE GARONNE

VIII.   THE GIRONDE AND BASSIN D'ARCACHON TO HENDAYE

85 Mortagne

Location
45°28'·00N 00°48'·00W
75km mark

Arrival
⊕453-Mortagne 45°28'·20N 00°48'·99W

Shelter
Good

Hazards
Strong cross set on approach

Depth Restriction
1.5–2.0m in approach
2m in outer basin
Up to 4m inside locked basin

Night Entry
Not lit

Tidal information: Pointe de Grave
HW +0018
LW +0030

Mean Height of Tide

MHWS	MHWN	MLWN	MLWS
5.3	4.3	1.7	0.5

Tidal Streams: Pointe de Grave
Flood HW -0415 to +0115
Ebb HW +0145 to -0445

Berthing
On pontoons in both basins

Facilities
All, but no laundry and no
travel-lift
Fuel from garage

Charts
BA 3068 (50)
SHOM 7427 (various)
Imray C41, C42

Radio
VHF Ch 09 from HW-0100 to
HW+0100

Telephone
☏ 05 46 90 63 15

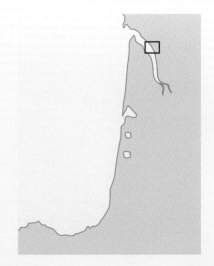

An attractive town and small harbour with a locked basin

PILOTAGE

Approach

There is a minimum of 4m in the approach to ⊕453 off the entrance whence the village of Mortagne can be seen on the hill above. Alternatively make good a track of 050° from main channel buoy No.22 until the entrance marks can be identified.

Entrance

The entrance marks are a destroyed port-hand beacon replaced by a WCM buoy, a port-hand main channel buoy (left to starboard on entering) and port and starboard markers. Pass between the latter on a

Mortagne marina from the lock gate

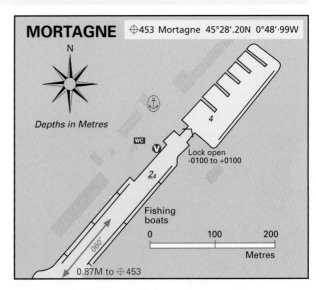

track of about 060°. The dredged channel is almost straight for 0.65M to the harbour entrance and marked by the occasional stake.

Berthing

There is a reception pontoon (dries) on the northwest side on entering. Berth on pontoons inside the lock in up to 4m. The lock is open HW±0100 regardless of tidal co-efficient.

Anchorage

To the southeast of the entrance as far in as depth allows, in mud. Quite exposed except from the east.

ASHORE IN MORTAGNE

Restaurants and bars on quay, shops in the attractive old town running up the hill. There is also a small boatyard.

86 Blaye

Location
45°07′·00N 00°40′·00W
37km mark

Arrival
⊕455-Blaye 45°07′·50N 00°40′·10

Shelter
Uncomfortable in SW winds

Hazard
Very strong currents at berths

Depth Restriction
None at pontoon
Small dinghy harbour dries

Night Entry
Q(3)R5s at N end of dinghy harbour
Lights on pontoon

Tidal Information
PdG HW +0140
PdG LW +0305

Mean Height of Tide (m)

MHWS	MHWN	MLWN	MLWS
5.2	4.1	0.8	0.3

Tidal Streams
Flood – PdG HW –0315 to +0245
Ebb – PdG HW +0315 to -0345

Berthing
On massive steel pontoon

Facilities
An active YC, otherwise few except shops

Charts
BA 3068 (50)
SHOM 7427 (various)

Radio
VHF Ch 12 with Bordeaux Port

Telephone
☎ 06 63 29 80 92

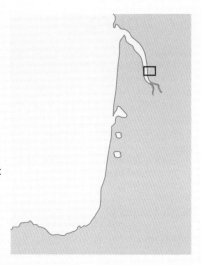

Historic town providing a fine-weather stop with good shopping

PILOTAGE

Approach

With a 2m draught, SHOM chart 7427 is essential to approach Blaye other than just before HW. With this available the channel to the east of Îles Patiras, Bouchard and Nouvelle can be used. Otherwise leave the main channel between Nos.52 and 52a PHM buoys, make good a track of 125° and leave the south end of Île Nouvelle 500m to port to head for ⊕455 or for the visitors' pontoon in front of the citadel.

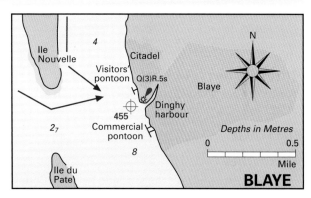

BLAYE

Berthing

There is little shelter from the west off Blaye and the ebb can run at up to 3.5 knots; it will be distinctly uncomfortable in these conditions but the yacht berths are on the inside of a very substantial pontoon which would provide some protection. However berthing when the ebb is running hard can be tricky with the very substantial walkway close downstream. It is best to berth on the downstream end of the pontoon if possible. The outside of the pontoon is used by commercial ships.

Facilities

Water and electricity are available on the pontoon which requires a code for access. A 2-pin plug is needed for an electrical connection. There is a telephone number posted on the pontoon for obtaining the code and for details on how to switch on the electrics. There is a large motorhome park close to the pontoon and we assumed that there were showers and toilets available there although we failed to find them.

ASHORE IN BLAYE

An important town with a small drying harbour only suitable for dinghies. The conspicuous and historic citadel is of much interest. There is a good range of restaurants and small shops.

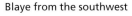

Blaye from the southwest

VIII. THE GIRONDE AND BASSIN D'ARCACHON TO HENDAYE

87 Bourg

Location
45°02'·00N 00°33'·00W
25km mark

Arrival
⊕456-Bourg 45°02'·19N 00°33'·50W

Shelter
Poor in W winds

Hazards
Strong W winds and ebb tide very uncomfortable
Large drying wreck outside W end of pontoon

Depth Restriction
1.7m on approach, +3m at pontoon

Night Entry
Unlit

Tidal information
PdG HW +0145
PdG LW +0300

Mean Height of Tide (m)

MHWS	MHWN	MLWN	MLWS
5.1	4.0	0.6	0.1

Tidal Streams
Flood PdG HW -0200 to +0245
Ebb PdG HW +0315 to -0230

Berthing
Visitors' berth on outside of W end of pontoon.
No rafting

Facilities
No electricity or water on pontoon. Fuel from garage

Charts
BA 3068 (50), 3069 (various)
SHOM 7427 (various)

Radio
Bordeaux Port Control on VHF Ch 12 in emergency

Telephone
① 05 57 68 40 06 (concierge)
① 05 57 68 31 72 (YC)

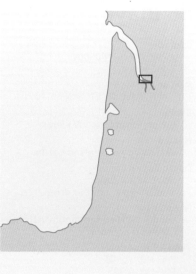

Attractive and historic town with a pontoon berth and some facilities ashore

PILOTAGE

Approaches

From downstream leave the Gironde by WCM buoy No.62 and head to port to enter the Dordogne, leaving Bec d'Ambès with its refineries and the Île d'Ambès with its drying shoal at the west end, to starboard. Avoid the long conspicuous drying wreck just to the south of the visitors' berths which are at the west end of the long pontoon. There is room to pass between the wreck and the shore if necessary.

Berthing

Doubling up on the pontoons is not allowed but yachts also berth on the inside where there appears to be plenty of water. If both sides are full there are no alternatives and anchoring off is not a happy option except at neaps and in fine weather. In 2009 the pontoons were somewhat dilapidated which

Bourg from south. It is high water and the wreck is hardly visible

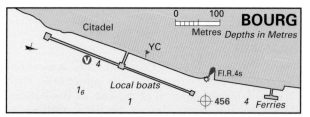

Bourg wreck and visitors' pontoon

suggests that they are at times exposed to violent motion. Water and electricity on quay. Code needed for access can be supplied at the swimming pool or at the campsite. Showers and toilets are available at both places.

ASHORE IN BOURG

An attractive old fortified town on the Dordogne just above the junction with the Garonne. Good restaurants and shops; there are two yacht clubs. The citadel is worth a visit.

88 Cavernes

Location
44°56'N 00°26'·3W

Arrival
⊕457-Cavernes 44°56'·10N 00°26'·50W

Shelter
Exposed to winds from NW and NE

Night Entry
Unlit

Tidal Information
HW PdG HW +0230
LW PdG LW +0345

Mean Height of Tide (m)

MHWS	MHWN	MLWN	MLWS
4.7	3.5	0.1	0.6

Tidal Streams: Pointe de Grave
Flood HW +0015 to +0330
Ebb HW +0400 to +0015

Berthing
Pontoon

Facilities
None

Charts
SHOM 7427 (only chart to show this part of river)

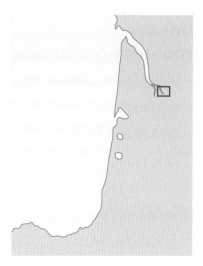

A very small village with a yacht pontoon

Cavernes is a small village on the south bank 16km above Bourg on the Dordogne. The river is buoyed occasionally but not lit. The depth in the channel is generally over 2m. The river is crossed by three electricity cables just above Bourg (height 27m) and three bridges (least height 19m above ML) below Cavernes.

It is a further 24km to Libourne but access is now not possible to masted craft due to a new low bridge (height 7m) just below Libourne.

The kilometre distances start at Libourne. Above this the Dordogne is tidal for 14 miles and navigable for 40 miles.

PILOTAGE

Approach

The passage is easy with or without SHOM chart 7427. Keep to the outside of the bends and follow the lateral buoyage. Cavernes is on the south bank on a left-hand bend just after the last bridge of three.

Berthing

There is a yacht pontoon off the village in 2m; water on the quay but nothing else.

Just above Cavernes on the opposite bank is a pontoon with water and electricity off the village of Asques, but there are no shops, restaurants or other facilities there either.

ASHORE AT CAVERNES

There is a restaurant but no shops. The nearest shop is at Saint-Loubés 1M to the south.

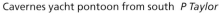

Cavernes yacht pontoon from south *P Taylor*

Minor harbours from Royan to Bordeaux
(distances from Bordeaux)

Port St-Georges de Didonne 96km

Port de Talmont 85km

Port des Monards 80km

Port de St-Sevrin d'Uzet 78km

Port Maubert 70km

Port de Conac 62km

Port de Vitrezay 60km

Port du Petit Vitrezay 59km

Port des Callognes 56km

Port des Portes Neuves 54km

Port de Freneau 50km

With the exception of the first, all these ports are muddy holes or river entrances which dry with few if any facilities. Some are marked on the approach with beacons and sometimes lights. Deep draught yachts are unlikely to want to use them and others only in an emergency and if the tide serves.

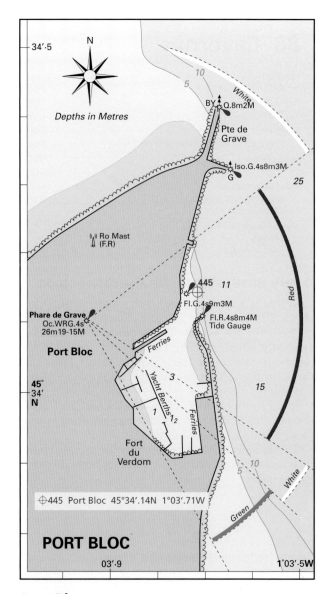

Port Bloc

⊕445 Port Bloc 45°34'.14N 1°03'.71W

Visiting yachts are not wanted or welcomed here and it is unlikely that there will be a vacant berth. In an emergency call on VHF Ch 09 before going in and keep clear of the ferries entering and leaving.

Port Bloc and Pointe de Grave looking north.
Port Médoc is just south of Port Bloc

89 Port Médoc

Location
45°34'·00N 01°04'·00W
94km mark

Arrival
⊕446-Médoc 45°33'·40N 1°03'·32W

Shelter
Excellent in marina

Hazards
Strong cross stream at entrance

Depth Restriction
3m at entrance
+2m over all marina

Night Entry
Lit

HW time
As for Pointe de Grave

Mean Height of Tide (m)

MHWS	MHWN	MLWN	MLWS
5.4	4.4	2.1	1.0

Tidal Streams
Flood PdG HW –0445 to +0100
Ebb PdG HW +0115 to –0445

Berthing
Finger pontoons

Facilities
All in marina but shops in village

Charts
BA 3057 (50), 3068 (50)
SHOM 7426 (52)
Imray C41, C42

Radio
VHF Ch 09

Telephone
✆ 05 56 09 69 15
Taxi ✆ 05 56 09 60 47

Huge modern marina with most facilities

PILOTAGE

Approach and entrance

Directions for the approach using Passe de l'Ouest or Passe Sud may be found on pages 271–273 *La Gironde approaches and estuary*. From SHM buoy No.13b (Q.G) or between it and the steep-to Pointe de Grave (Oc.G.4s) leave Port Bloc (Fl.G.4s and Iso.G.4s) to starboard and identify Port Médoc entrance 0.5M to the south or make for ⊕446.

Head for the entrance on a track of about 270° and round the east breakwaterhead to starboard allowing for a strong cross set until inside. The entrance has recently been modified to face southeast. The reception and fuel berth is now on the northernmost quay in front of the marina office.

Berthing

On fingers on pontoons, 25m maximum. There is a pontoon for multihulls on the south wall.

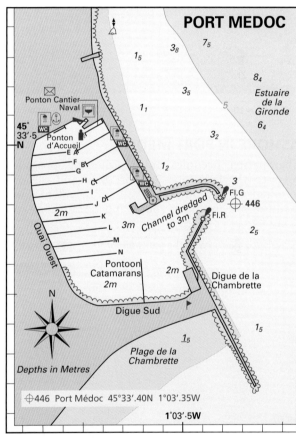

Port Médoc marina entrance

Port Médoc showing the new extension to north breakwater

ASHORE IN PORT MÉDOC

The marina occupies an unpromising position between the ferry port of Port Bloc and the oil terminal of Verdon. While all the usual marina facilities are installed, shops and restaurants are absent. However blocks of flats are planned and it is thought that shops will arrive with them. At present a taxi will be needed for serious provisioning from Soulac or the Port Bloc ferry to Royan is said to be convenient.

Port Médoc marina with the pontoon for multihulls viewed from the southeast

90 Pauillac

Location
45°12'·00N 00°45'·00W
47km mark

Arrival
⊕448-Pauillac 45°11'·86N 00°44'·44W

Shelter
Good in the marina

Hazards
The tidal stream sweeps through the marina so it is safer to enter or leave near slack water

Depth Restriction
1m in entrance, 4m at visitors' pontoons

Night Entry
Lit but not recommended

Tidal Information
PdG HW +0100
PdG LW +0150

Mean Height of Tide

MHWS	MHWN	MLWN	MLWS
5.5	4.4	1.1	0.5

Tidal Streams
Flood PdG HW –0315 to +0200
Ebb PdG HW +0215 to –0330

Berthing
Finger berths on pontoons

Facilities
All. 8-tonne crane and mast crane

Charts
BA 3068 (50)
SHOM 7427 (various)

Radio
VHF Ch 09 (office hours)

Telephone
☎ 05 56 59 12 16
Taxi ☎ 05 56 59 14 67

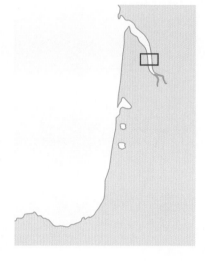

A useful halfway stop in good wine country

PILOTAGE

Approaches

From north

Pauillac and ⊕448 are 1.5M south of the conspicuous oil refinery at Trompeloup where a ship belonging to the Airbus consortium is frequently berthed. Leave the main channel at Nos.43 and 44 buoys (Fl(2)G. and Fl(2)R.) and head for the outer harbour wall (Fl.G.4s and Q.G).

From south

Leave the main channel at Nos.45 and 46 buoys (Iso.G and Fl.R) and head for the entrance.

Entrance

Entry and departure should only be attempted near slack water. The shuttering on the sides of the marina does not extend to the bottom and the

Pauillac from northwest. A suction dredger is to be seen working in the middle

VIII. THE GIRONDE AND BASSIN D'ARCACHON TO HENDAYE

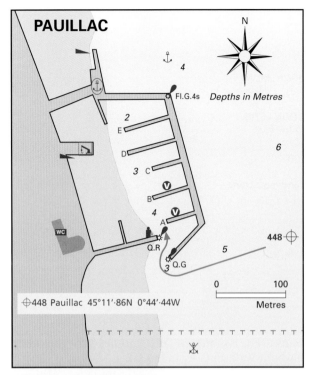

PAUILLAC

N

Depths in Metres

⊕448 Pauillac 45°11'·86N 0°44'·44W

0   100
Metres

stream flows through it. There is a white buoy with pick-up to the south of the marina to moor to while waiting.

There is reputed to be 3m in the entrance but in 2009 it was badly silted and it was impossible to enter or leave within two hours of low water. However a dredger was expected. Keep close to the east breakwater head when entering or leaving as the the mud shoals rapidly. There is reasonable light inside the marina but a night entry is not recommended unless it has been done before in daylight.

Berthing

The first two pontoons (A and B) ahead on entering are for visitors in depths up to 4m. They have fingers and haul-off lines.

Anchoring

Anchoring is prohibited for up to 500m south of the harbour due to cables. Either go beyond or anchor to the north off the slip to wait for the tide.

Mast stepping and unstepping

There is a 1-tonne crane on the end of the jetty in the northwest corner of the harbour. Yachts with shallow draught may be able to berth out of the stream on the north or south sides of the jetty at any state of the tide but deep-draught yachts will only be able to safely carry this out near HW slack lying alongside the outer end.

The harbourmaster and staff are helpful and obliging and sometimes make no charge, or only a nominal one, for this service. A *pourboire* is always appreciated.

ASHORE IN PAUILLAC

A useful yacht harbour halfway between Bordeaux and the sea in the centre of a famous wine growing region. Lifting or stepping masts is possible but only in safety near slack high water. There is no travel-lift but otherwise all the usual facilities including convenient shopping. The management is welcoming and friendly. English yachts have wintered afloat here.

La Maison du Tourisme et Les Vins de Médoc near the marina can arrange vineyard tours.

Travel

Rail and bus services to Bordeaux (50km) and Merignac airport with internal and some international flights.

The entrance to Pauillac marina. Mud builds up on the bank on the port side. Keep the outer breakwater close to starboard *M&G Barron*

Pauillac marina at LW looking upriver towards Bordeaux
M&G Barron

A ship transporting Airbus parts; berths just north of Pauillac

A floating hazard on La Gironde

Pauillac to Bordeaux

Approach

It is 47km between the two, and there should be no difficulty in navigating this wide and well marked and lit estuary with the use of the BA or SHOM charts and benefiting from the flood and ebb streams. Poor visibility in the area is infrequent.

The ebb increases in strength upriver and with much rain up-country can exceed 5kns, with the addition of a lot of debris including whole trees. Anchoring above Bec d'Ambès is not recommended and there are no safe or convenient stopping places for a yacht en route.

There is much commercial traffic in the river. Large ships unable to keep to the starboard side of the channel display a black ball forward and a red light by night and should be given right of way.

Lights

There are many lights and lit buoys marking the main channel up to Pont de Pierre at Bordeaux which are shown on the charts. In general white lights are leading marks, green are starboard-hand and red are port-hand buoys or marks when inbound.

Pauillac with marina on left

VIII. THE GIRONDE AND BASSIN D'ARCACHON TO HENDAYE

91 Bordeaux

Location
44°53'·00N 00°32'·00W

Arrival
⊕458-Bordeaux Pont de Pierre
44°50'·00N 00°34'·00W

Shelter
Good in old dock basin but streams are strong in river

Hazards
The ebb runs at 5kns and the flood at 3kns. Much debris comes down on the ebb.

Depth Restriction
+6m in channel
3m at Lormont pontoons
3m at waiting pontoon for basins
2.5m at Bègles pontoons

Height Restriction
St-Pierre bridge (clearance 4.2m above ML) and is the limit of navigation for masted vessels

Night Entry
Night movement not advised

Tidal Information
HW PdG +0215
LW PdG +0345

Mean Height of Tide

MHWS	MHWN	MLWN	MLWS
5.3	4.2	0.4	0.0

Tidal Streams
Flood PdG HW –0115 to +0315
Ebb PdG HW +0315 to –0130

Berthing
Pontoons at Lormont YC close to Pont d'Aquitaine
No.2 Basin through lock with waiting pontoon outside
Bègles Marina 4km upstream of Pont de Pierre

Facilities
Crane and water and electricity in No.2 Basin
Marine engineer in Basin No.2
Crane and water at Lormont YC
Minor facilities at Bègles Marina

Charts
BA 3069 (various)
SHOM 7427 (various)

Radio
Port Control VHF Ch 12 (24H)

Telephone
Lock-keeper for Basins ☏ 05 56 90 59 57
Lormont YC ☏ 05 56 31 50 10

Large industrial city in the centre of a famous wine growing region

BERTHING

It is not recommended that yachts berth on the walls on the west bank in the city which are high, rough and subject to strong streams.

Halte Nautique and Lormont Yacht Club

Just above and under Pont d'Aquitaine (clearance 51m) are three pontoons. On the west bank just above the bridge there is a small marina which is private and visitors are liable to be sent away. The pontoon above the bridge on the east side is for fishermen; the pontoon under the bridge may have a berth but the depths are not known. All pontoons have locked gates so a call ahead to Lormont YC is essential. They all have small cranes but it would be most unwise to rely on them to demast. This can only be done with certainty in Bordeaux in No.2 basin where a marine engineer has a mobile crane.

Nos 1 and 2 basins

Lock 20m wide, 4m deep.

The lock only opens at HW. Entry must be requested one hour before HW (30 minutes before HW on leaving) on Ch 12 or ☏ 05 56 90 59 57. There is a waiting pontoon in 3m outside.

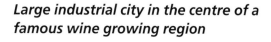
Pont d'Aquitaine from the north looking upstream

Lormont YC pontoons

The waiting pontoon outside the lock leading into the basins

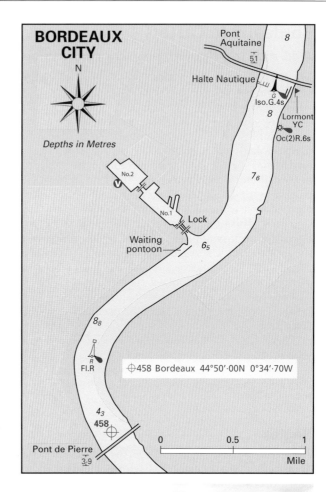

The lock into the basins with the bridge swung back

Pass through No.1 basin but stay in the middle as it is surprisingly shallow and, after passing through the lifting bridge between the two, select a berth as convenient in No.2. The northwest corner near the McDonalds is probably the best option.

ASHORE IN BORDEAUX

Bordeaux is a large and pleasant city in the centre of a renowned wine growing region. It is also a busy port and industrial centre and the passing yachtsman usually only sees the latter aspects. Both berths at Halte Nautique near Lormont and the basins have modest restaurants within walking distance. There is a floating restaurant in the southeast end of Basin No.1 and a McDonalds at the northwest end of Basin No.2. There are no toilets or showers and the whole place has a somewhat run-down aspect with the submarine pens opposite the yacht berths a grim reminder of the Second World War. In fact the McDonalds provides a useful facility as well as free Wi-Fi. In 2009 there was no harbourmaster and no charges. The excellent modern tram system stops near the lock and there is a bus which connects with the tram system near the McDonalds (closer).

There are many old and interesting buildings, churches, ruins and museums some dating from Roman times and the English occupation (1152–1453). Tours can be arranged through Syndicat d'Initiative, Allé de Tourney, 1 cours de 30 juillet who will supply maps and directions.

Bordeaux monument to Girondins

Travel

International airport at Merignac, bus and rail connections in all directions.

British Consul

At 353, Boulevard du Président Wilson, 30373 Bordeaux Cedex.
℡ 05 57 22 21 10.
Email postmaster.bordeaux@fco.gov.uk

Bordeaux waterfront

VIII. THE GIRONDE AND BASSIN D'ARCACHON TO HENDAYE

Bordeaux to Castets

A 40-mile trip through pleasant countryside

Masted navigation ceases at Pont de Pierre where the headroom is 4.2m above ML.

The many narrow arches of this bridge obstruct the flow on the flood and the ebb, causing an appreciable fall of water through the bridge and many violent eddies on the downstream side. These difficulties are only surmountable with a very powerful engine and normally the bridge must be passed with the current. Use one of the arches marked by a white disc but not one with a *No Entry* sign on it. This tidal barrier means that when coming downstream it is unlikely that the opening times of the lock to Nos 1 and 2 basins (shuts at HW) can be met. However, it is always worth a call on Ch 12 in plenty of time if entry looks a possibility.

The flood stream becomes negligible above the bridge and only causes a stand or diminution of the river flow.

There are three bridges above Pont de Pierre, all with greater headroom and larger arches.

There is a small marina on the west bank at Bègles above the third bridge and some 4km above Pont de Pierre.

Bègles

A small marina with 80 berths in 2.5m and arrangements for transients who are expected to berth on the outer pontoon particularly when the current is strong. This is in the full flow of the current and any debris coming down, so it is worth trying to get a berth inside when the current slackens.

Water and electricity on the pontoons; showers and toilets, fuel berth, boatyard, 9-tonne crane and chandler; shopping centre nearby.

Bègles is reasonably close to Merignac airport and is a possibility for changing crew.

VHF Ch 09, ☎ 05 5685 76 04 or 06 18 60 26 78 (weekday working hours).

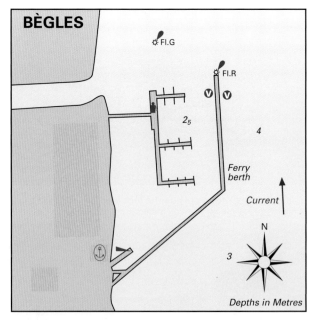

Castets

The first, largest and deepest lock of the Canal Latéral à la Garonne is here about 50km from Bordeaux. Approximately 1M short of the lock are some unmarked rocks which boats drawing 1.5m will hit before HW–0200. They are shown in the *Guide Chagnon* in a diagrammatic way but even if this is on board it would be wise to wait downstream at Langon until HW–0100 or later before proceeding. The locks will not open until just before HW anyway.

Approaching from downstream the right-hand lock is the one in use. There are vertical bars to secure warps to but they are widely spaced. Once through the lock, a narrow lake leads to the second lock with a 3.3m rise and warping bars. Both locks have keepers and open during working hours at HW. There is a shady, wooden quay on the south bank just through the second lock.

Bègles marina from east

92 Bassin d'Arcachon

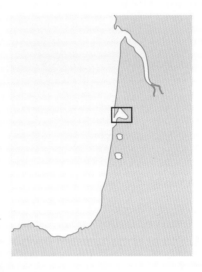

Location
44°35'N 01°18'W

Arrival
⊕459-ATT Arcachon 44°34'·74N 01°18'·72W
⊕460-Arcachon outer access 44°34'·05N
02°12'·91W

Shelter
Good inside Cap Ferret, none in approaches

Hazards
Dangerous entrance

Depth Restriction
3.7m at entrance to N channel
3–1.5m in Arcachon marina

Night Entry
Not lit

Tidal information
HW Cap Ferret PdG HW+0010
LW Cap Ferret PdG LW+0005
HW Arcachon Marina PdG HW+0020
LW Arcachon Marina PdG LW+0005

Mean Height of Tide (m)

MHWS	MHWN	MLWN	MLWS
4.1	3.3	1.3	0.5

Tidal Streams at Entrance
Flood PdG HW –0520 to –0115
Ebb PdG HW –0045 to –0550

Berthing
At pontoons in Arcachon
marina but various in small
ports

Facilities
Extensive

Charts
BA 2664 (200), 2750 (49)
SHOM 6766 (49)
Local (see below)

Radio
VHF Ch 09 for Arcachon
Marina
Cap Ferret VHF Ch 13/16 for
conditions at entrance

Telephone
Arcachon Marina ☎ 05 56
22 36 75
Cap Ferret ☎ 05 56 60 60 03

Lifeboat
A lifeboat is stationed at La
Vigne inside the entrance
on the inside of Cap Ferret

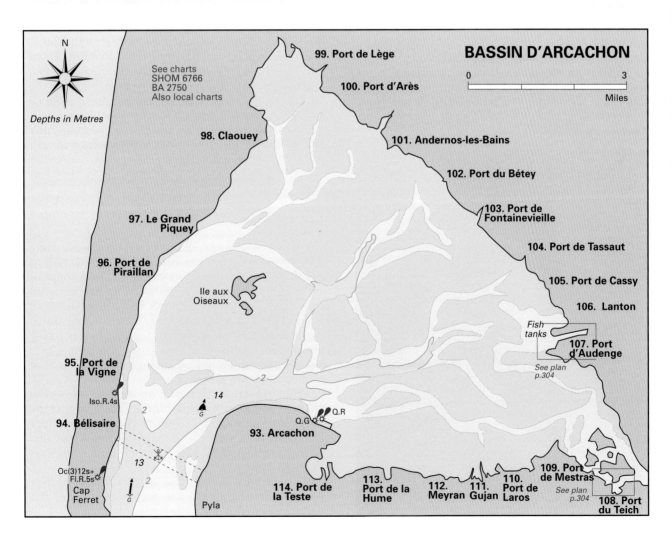

VIII. THE GIRONDE AND BASSIN D'ARCACHON TO HENDAYE

Arcachon Basin at low water

Extensive shallow basin with a large marina and many small harbours

No waypoints are given for ports inside the Bassin d'Arcachon.

Warning

The entrance channels are re-marked each year as they change in the winter storms but they may change after re-marking. Only enter between HW–0300 and HW+0100 and with less than 1m swell. Good visibility is also important as the buoys are far apart and unlike most French harbours there are no leading marks.

In the last 20 years the former South Channel has silted and is now closed with the buoyage removed whilst the North Channel has deepened to a least a depth of 3.9m to become the only access channel.

There is an air-to-air, air-to-sea and land-to-sea firing range on both sides of the entrance (*see page 270 in the Introduction to Section VIII*). It is unlikely

Cap Ferret looking north

that entry to Arcachon will be prevented by its activities but there may be some restriction from north or to the south.

In the basin green seaweed and pine needles may block engine filters.

Local charts

There are two local charts on a larger scale than SHOM 6766, produced by Feret et Fils from drawings by Jean-Marie Bouchet and available in local bookshops.

PILOTAGE

Approaches

From north

A featureless coast extends from the mouth of La Gironde along which the beacon at Pointe de la Négarde, Hourtin lighthouse, the beacon at La Grigne and Cap Ferret lighthouse are conspicuous. Do not cut the corner if entering Arcachon; head for the ATT ARC outer buoy and ⊕459 before turning in. The huge sand dune of Pyla (103m) is located 2M southeast of Cap Ferret and is a conspicuous feature.

The firing range area north of Arcachon is very seldom used but confirmation must be obtained (*See page 270*).

From south

From Capbreton a similar featureless coast stretches for 60M along which the Contis lighthouse, Bicarosse beacon and the firing range buildings stand out (*see page 270 for details of the firing range*). There may be a 3M wide safe passage between the shore and the range area but confirmation must be obtained. The 20m line provides a good danger limit from the shore which should be watched carefully when approaching the extended Arcachon shoals. The South Channel is closed.

Entrance

By North Channel (Chenal d'Accès)

It is advisable to enter from the vicinity of ⊕459 and the ATT ARC approach buoy (red buoy with white stripes and ball top, LFl.10s) during the last half of the flood. Follow the channel marked by a series of unlit red or green pillar buoys. The bar between Nos. 1N and 3N SHM buoys has a least depth of 3.7m. The channel leads northeast turning north towards Cap Ferret in the later stages. In any sea or swell there will be breakers on the sands on either side. Entry should not be attempted with a swell of more than 1m or on the ebb.

Once under the lee of Cap Ferret follow the channel round to the east for the final 5M past the piers and town of Arcachon to the marina. Older charts show a series of dangerous wrecks in this channel which have now been cleared to a least depth of 5m.

The entrance to Arcachon marina is marked by a large stone anchor on the port-hand side of the entrance and Q.R and Q.G lights.

Arachon entrance, the South Channel on the right is closed. The Banc d'Arquin in the middle is a nature reserve

Arcachon Basin *P Taylor*

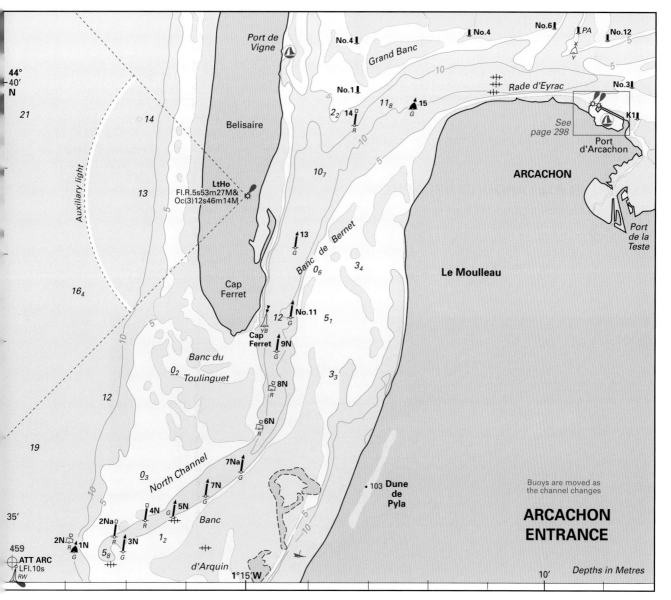

VIII. THE GIRONDE AND BASSIN D'ARCACHON TO HENDAYE

93 Port d'Arcachon

Large modern marina with all facilities close to town centre

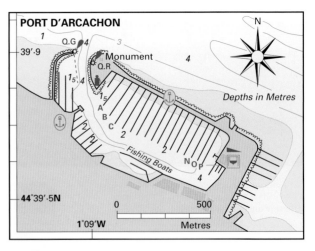

PILOTAGE

Entrance

There are port and starboard buoys indicating the channel to the entrance. It is 50m wide and leads in on 180°. Keep to the starboard hand on entry by the wavebreaker as there is a 1.5m patch by the fuel berth on the east side of the entrance. If this depth is no problem, go to the fuel berth to arrange a berth, or to pontoon A. The official reception berth is on the hammerhead on the starboard side after entering but it is a considerable walk to the harbour office from that side. The helpful marina office staff are English-speaking so that contact on VHF Ch 09 is easier.

Berthing

Try to negotiate a berth in the southwest corner, which shortens the walk to town considerably. Most pontoon berths on the northeast side of the harbour are in 2.5–1.5m. Maximum length 20m.

Anchorage

In 2m or more outside clear of moorings and the entrance.

ASHORE IN AND AROUND ARCACHON

A large modern seaside town with good shops, many restaurants and a casino with many beaches close by. The whole of the Bassin has been given over to the cultivation of oysters and shellfish since Roman times, and this is still the main industry. Yachting interests take second place to this.

Facilities

Everything expected in a large modern marina. The two travel-lifts (180- and 45-tonne), cranes (20-tonne), slips and workshops are in the southeast corner. Card operated fuel berth (24 hour). The marina office is in the middle of the northeast breakwater and the Yacht club at its southeast end.

Leisure

Europe's largest sand dune at Pyla by the entrance has a magnificent view from the top (103m) and a good beach at its foot. It is popular with hang gliders. Banc d'Arquin between the two channels in the approach to the Basin is a nature reserve but is often inundated or modified by the sea. Temporary buildings are put there in the season to illustrate the work of the reserve and ferries run there from Arcachon and Pyla. A visit to the Roman ruins can be rewarding. Devotees of Bernard Cornwell will recognise much of the area from *Sharpe's Siege*.

Travel

Good rail and bus services. The nearest major airport is at Merignac, Bordeaux (70km) but there are active grass airfields at Arcachon and Andernos.

Arcachon marina

94 –114 Small harbours around Bassin d'Arcachon

Many small harbours have been constructed round the sides of the basin in the easily worked sandy soil for the use of local boats and those who tend the shellfish beds. Although leisure craft have infiltrated many of the harbours, some are private and there is no room for visitors. A few retain some water behind sills but most dry to soft mud and are not suitable for deep draught boats without legs.

SHOM chart 6766, BA chart 2750 or the two large-scale charts available locally are essential to explore further than the main channels.

Brief details of these harbours are given below.

Warnings

Keep clear of the oyster beds, particularly between HW+0300 and HW–0300. They are marked with posts.

Green seaweed and pine needles may clog filters and logs.

PILOTAGE

The main channels usually have enough depth for small yachts even at LW springs (1–5m). The bottom is soft and sandy mud; the water is clear and the bottom can be seen. The channels are marked by beacons at all junctions and bear a letter and number as shown on SHOM 6766. The banks of the channels are marked by stakes on the 0m line.

It is advisable to explore on a rising tide and allow plenty of time to visit several harbours in search of a berth. Anchorages too are very congested now with moorings extending up to 300m from the shore. Streams in the larger channels can reach 6kns at springs.

Islands

Île aux Oiseaux in the centre of the Bassin is 0.75M long and 3m high and this and a smaller island nearby are the only islands of significance.

94 Bélisaire

Not a port but a long pier used by car ferries from Arcachon. There is a large area for moorings to the south of it and a good anchorage about 100m off the coast open to the southeast and south. There is a small village and shops nearby and a large water tower 600m south and 400m inland from the pier to which runs a pipe from Pyla on the opposite shore; anchoring is prohibited on either side of this pipe. The moorings extend south close to the shore to the spit running north from the east side of Cap Ferret.

95 Port de la Vigne

A medium-sized private yacht harbour with 270 berths on two pontoons; also two quays with pontoons. Only very short visits are allowed (i.e. to fuel), maximum length 8.5m but there are moorings and an anchorage to the south in up to 5m close to the beach. Red and green buoys and stakes mark the entrance and there is an Iso.R.4s light on the south of the entrance; 1m is reported in the entrance and inside. A partial barrier on the starboard hand breaks up any swell. There is a harbourmaster and a variety of facilities including fuel and water, restaurants and shops close to the harbour.

An all-weather lifeboat is moored off the entrance.

Port de la Vigne

Port de Piraillan

Warning

A bank with least depth of 0.8m lies 200m offshore for some distance north and south of the entrance. An approach from Bélisaire Pier keeping 100m offshore will avoid it.

96 Port de Piraillan

A small drying harbour for oyster and fishing boats with a large area of moorings and space for anchorage to the east. The harbour is in the form of a square with quays and quayed islands in the middle. The surrounding area is covered with pines.

97 Port le Grand Piquey

Not a port but an excellent anchorage and mooring area with a pier for landing and a slip. Depths up to 5m offshore but the streams in the channel run at up to 2.75 knots. Boatyard, mechanic, chandlery and shops in the village. Good fish restaurant.

Piraillan oyster village *R Rundle*

Port le Grand Piquey

Claouey

Port de Lège

98 Claouey

Not a harbour but a popular launching site with an anchorage and a large area of moorings which dry. Approach from south via beacons C1, C0 and B0. There is a large slip, *club nautique*, WCs, showers, boatyard, chandlery and shops in the village. Surrounded by pine trees.

99 Port de Lège

A small drying harbour for work boats. The approach is northwards from beacon B1; note that the last two miles are through a nature reserve and there is a fish farm to the east of the entrance. Entry is only possible at HW and there are two quays which dry out on soft mud. Water available and a shop nearby.

100 Port d'Arès

More a landing place than a yacht harbour, approached from beacon C8. It has a brick quay with firm sand alongside it. There is a water point on the quay and the *club nautique* has WCs and showers. There is a boatyard, mechanic and chandlery. Open to winds from the south sector.

Port d'Arès

VIII. THE GIRONDE AND BASSIN D'ARCACHON TO HENDAYE

Andernos-les-Bains

101 Andernos-les-Bains

A large harbour with 160 berths exclusively for fishing and oyster boats but there are drying moorings outside the harbour. Turn north into the channel at beacon D14. In the harbour there are waterpoints on the quays, a slip, mechanic, chandlery and shops nearby. The harbour and area outside is exposed to the southwest especially at HW.

There is a 300m pier between Andernos and Port du Bétey.

There is small airfield to the north of Andernos for light aircraft.

102 Port du Bétey

A small drying harbour entered from beacon D14 with a buoyed channel and 150 places for yachts and workboats. Yachts secure alongside quays or bows to the wall. Drying moorings outside but uncomfortable in a southwest wind. Facilities include water points, fuel nearby, two WCs and showers, a slip and shops at Andernos-les-Bains.

103 Port de Fontainevieille

A medium-sized drying yacht harbour entered via beacons E6 and E7 turning to port just before E8 out of the Tassaut channel. It has 200 berths (two for visitors) for yachts in a basin with pontoons. There is 1m in the entrance channel at half tide. Drying moorings outside the harbour. Facilities include water on the pontoons, pumped fuel, slip, restaurant, *club nautique* and a harbourmaster.

Port du Bétey showing the pier at Andernos-les-Bains

Port de Fontainevieille

Port de Tassaut

104 Port de Tassaut

A very small attractive harbour used by oyster boats. Enter via beacons E6, E7 and E8. The harbour dries and has 180 berths, a slip, water points and a landing place. There is a harbourmaster and a *club nautique*. Fuel nearby. Restaurants and shops in nearby village. There is a sailing school and moorings outside the entrance. A submerged wall to starboard on entry is marked by stakes.

105 Port de Cassy

An attractive medium-sized harbour for yachts with a few oyster boats. There is a winding entrance channel entered by beacon F3; a water tower to the north of the harbour helps identification. Quays and pontoons in three basins provide 225 berths (three

Yachts drying out at Cassy *R Rundle*

Port de Cassy

VIII. THE GIRONDE AND BASSIN D'ARCACHON TO HENDAYE

for visitors on a short pontoon in front of harbour office). The harbour dries to mud and sand and legs are obligatory if not of shallow draught. Good anchoring and beaching areas on either side of access channel. There are WCs, showers, water, a slip and crane plus a club nautique and shops in the village.

106 Lanton

Not a harbour but an area with fish farms and an estuary which might be suitable for further development.

107 Port d'Audenge

A medium-sized yacht and workboat harbour which has recently been enlarged. Workboats use the centre basin. For yachts there are 130 berths in the Nouveau Bassin (New Harbour on southeast side) and 85 berths in the Ancien Port (Old Harbour on northwest side). Maximum length 10m.

Enter down a long channel marked by beacons G4, G6 and G8 and stakes towards a tall, grey water tower. Enter at HW−0200 to HW+0200. The harbour dries at LW, soft sand and mud.

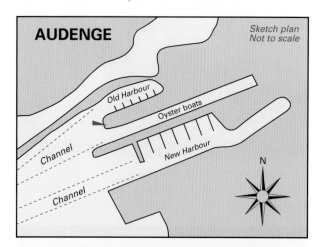

Port d'Audenge

There is a harbourmaster, water and electricity, two WCs and showers, fuel in the village, two fish restaurants and the usual shops in the large village of Audenge.

108 Port du Teich

A small drying harbour for yachts in the River L'Eyre on the south bank. Approach from the vicinity of K15 beacon. The entrance channel is buoyed and marked by perches further in. Boats moor to pontoons. Maximum 12m. Legs compulsory. Normal supplies from the village of Le Teich. Good fish restaurant.

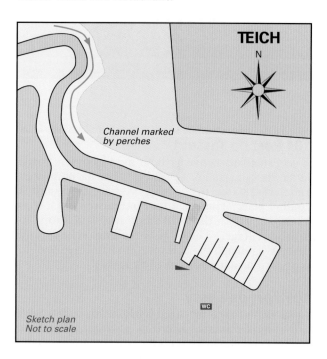

109, 110 and 111 Ports de Mestras, Larros and Gujan

Three medium-sized harbours side-by-side for fishermen and oyster farmers, with picturesque cottages lining the harbour walls. They all dry out at low water. Usual supplies from the large village of Gujan-Mestras. Larros has a large cross on its breakwater head. There is a local boat builder.

Worth a visit, but an empty berth is unlikely to be found. There is a good fish restaurant at Gujan.

112 Port de Meyran

A small harbour with drying berths each side used by oyster and fishing boats. Leave the main channel at beacon K5.

113 Port de la Hume

A medium-sized harbour for yachts, oyster and fishing boats. Leave the main channel at beacon K3, entrance channel marked by stakes and yellow buoys. It has quays and a pontoon in the east basin, a slip and a large restaurant specialising in fish dishes.

Ports de Mestras, Larros and Gujan

Port de la Hume

Port de Meyran

114 Port de la Teste

One of the larger harbours tucked behind Port d'Arcachon with a long and winding entrance channel from K1 beacon. Most of the berths are private and all dry to soft mud. Moor to a pontoon in west basin but priority is given to workboats. Fuel nearby and a good fish restaurant. Shops in La Teste village.

Port de la Teste

VIII. THE GIRONDE AND BASSIN D'ARCACHON TO HENDAYE

French Basque ports

115 Capbreton

Location
43°39'·00N 01°26'·00W

Arrival
⊕461-Capbreton 43°39'·50N 01°27'·48W

Shelter
Good once inside

Hazards
Le Fosse (or Le Gouf) de Capbreton, a deep submarine valley rising from 1300m, runs at right angles to the coast and ends 2M offshore.
Confused and breaking seas will be found here in heavy weather especially round the edges. Avoid it in these conditions.

Depth Restriction
Min 1.5m in the entrance
Max 2.4m in the marina

Night Entry
Lit but no Ldg Lts

Tidal Information: Pointe de Grave
HW PdG HW–0035
LW PdG LW–0035

Mean Height of Tide (m)

MHWS	MHWN	MLWN	MLWS
4.2	3.3	1.7	0.7

Tidal Streams
Up to 3kns in entrance,
1kn or less inside

Berthing
On pontoons. Max length 23m

Facilities
All, but a long walk to the shops

Charts
BA 1292 (175)
SHOM 6786 (130)
Imray C42 (has large scale sketch plan·

Radio
VHF Ch 09 (working hours)

Telephone
℡ 05 58 72 21 23

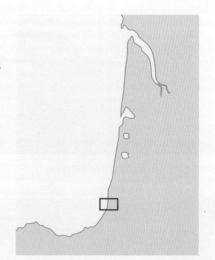

Holiday resort with a large marina but shallow entrance

PILOTAGE

Approaches

From north

A straight and featureless coastline with only Contis lighthouse breaking the monotony until the houses of Capbreton appear and the lighthouse at the end of the north breakwater can be identified. ⊕461 is off the entrance. *See page 270 regarding the firing ranges.*

From south

A similar featureless coastline from Bayonne northwards to ⊕461 when the breakwaters can be identified.

By night

The lights at Contis and Bayonne will assist and the 20m contour line provides a danger limit from the shore which is hazard-free in both directions. Otherwise it is GPS navigation in deep water.

Capbreton harbour entrance

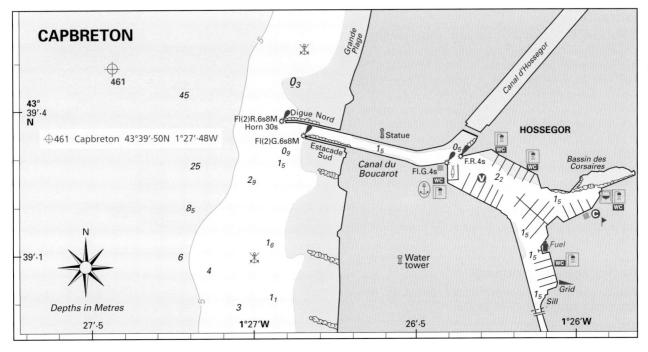

CAPBRETON

461

43°
39'·4
N

⊕461 Capbreton 43°39'·50N 1°27'·48W

45

25

8₅

6

4

N

Depths in Metres

27'·5

1°27'W

0₃

Grande Plage

Canal d'Hossegor

Fl(2)R.6s8M
Horn 30s
Digue Nord

Fl(2)G.6s8M
Estacade
Sud

0₉

1₅

2₉

1₆

1₁

3

5

Statue

1₅

Canal du Boucarot

Fl.G.4s

Water tower

26'·5

HOSSEGOR

0₅

F.R.4s

WC

WC

Bassin des Corsaires

V

2₂

WC

1₅

1₅

C

1₅

Fuel

WC

1₅

Grid

Sill

1°26'W

Capbreton Marina *P Taylor*

Capbreton Marina from the Capitainerie *R Rundle*

VIII. THE GIRONDE AND BASSIN D'ARCACHON TO HENDAYE

Entrance

This can be attempted at any time under fair conditions when draught permits (least depth 1.5m) but in any sea or swell only between HW–0200 and HW+0100. Do not enter if the waves break right across although they will usually be breaking at the sides. Best water is on the port side until the statue is abeam and then on the starboard side up to the marina entrance marked by two stone heads with light beacons.

The south breakwater has an underwater extension at its end for 30m which is awash at half tide.

At any time other than slack water be prepared for a cross set in or out of Canal d'Hossegor when entering the marina.

Anchorage and moorings

None, and anchorage is prohibited outside on either side of the entrance.

Berthing

The reception berth is pontoon B on the starboard side after entering but VHF Ch 09 is preferred. Do not berth on the hammerhead which is foul with old masonry at LW. Pontoon berths with fingers. Maximum length 23m. The marina is dredged to 1.5m but most of the outer part carries 2m. 60 visitors' berths.

ASHORE IN CAPBRETON

Capbreton is devoted primarily to the holidaymaker and to the yachtsman. There are only a few, small local fishing boats. There is an excellent yacht club with showers, bar and restaurant and adequate shops in Hossegor and Capbreton, although a good walk away. Hypermarket 300m east of bridge. There is a casino and fine bathing beaches close by. A dinghy trip up the Canal d'Hossegor (more a lake than a canal) and Lac Martin may amuse.

Capbreton marina visitors' pontoon is the second one
P Taylor

The entrance to the marina with the Capitainerie on the right *P Taylor*

Travel

Bus service in all directions; rail from Bayonne; airfield (mostly internal flights but some packages) at Biarritz (25km).

Repairs

30-tonne travel-lift, 1.5-tonne crane; small boatyard; chandlers; sailmaker.

Capbretton entrance channel *R Rundle*

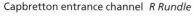

116 Bayonne and Anglet Marina

Location
43°42'·00N 01°32'·00W

Arrival
⊕462-Bayonne 43°31'·80N 01°32'·50W

Shelter
Good in Anglet

Hazards
Give way to merchant ships in entrance or channel.
Only attempy entrance from HW-0400 to HW+0100 in any sea or swell.

Depth Restriction
8.3m in entrance
2.5m in marina
5.3m in harbour channel

Night Entry
Well lit plus Ldg Lts

Tidal information
HW PdG HW–0032
LW PdG LW–0032

Mean Height of Tide (m)

MHWS	MHWN	MLWN	MLWS
4.2	3.3	1.7	0.7

Tidal Streams
Flood PdG HW –0550 to +0030
Ebb PdG HW +0100 to +0540

Berthing
On pontoons in Anglet
Possible alongside berth up-river

Facilities
All in Anglet. Shops 2km

Charts
BA 3640 (10)
SHOM 7440 (50)
Imray C42

Radio
Port Control VHF Ch 12, 16
Anglet marina VHF Ch 09 (working hours)
Wi-Fi

Telephone
Marina ☏ 05 59 63 05 45
Port ☏ 05 59 50 31 50

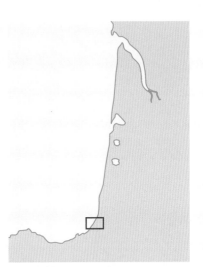

Historical town and commercial port with large marina accessible in most weathers

ASHORE IN BAYONNE

Four miles of estuary lead to the attractive old city. Most of the commerce and industry is concentrated on the north and east banks of the river at Boucau below the first bridge. The next bridge just below the cathedral is lower (5.2m) and restricts further navigation to small craft for another 40 miles to Pony.

A taxi or bus will be needed to reach the city from Anglet but it is worth the trip to see the 13th-century cathedral, Roman remains, two museums and the citadel. There are also good beaches to the north and south but sometimes heavy surf.

Anglet marina is well appointed and has all usual facilities including a 13-tonne travel-lift, crane and a welcoming yacht club. There are shops and restaurants within walking distance but the supermarket is 4km away.

History

The harbour and town were created by the Romans around 100 BC and many Roman remains including the foundations of Le Vieux Château can still be seen. Gascony (which includes Bayonne) became an English province in 1150AD and the English held it for 300 prosperous years. However, with their departure and the loss of trade with Britain, the river silted up and the town fell on hard times. The river was eventually dredged in the 18th century and the town prospered again with a free port and a large fishing fleet.

PILOTAGE

Approaches

From N

Head for ⊕462, the landfall buoy is about 0.75M north-northwest of it. The north breakwater end is conspicuous as are the warehouses and silos at Boucau.

From S

The low coastline is broken by the rocky outcrop of Pointe St-Martin and its lighthouse in front of Biarritz town. Head for ⊕462 and the breakwater end and buildings at Boucau will be identified.

By night

The lights of Pointe St-Martin, Capbreton and the landfall buoy (LFl.10s) will assist until the well lit entrance is identified.

Anglet Marina visitors' pontoon *P Taylor*

VIII. THE GIRONDE AND BASSIN D'ARCACHON TO HENDAYE

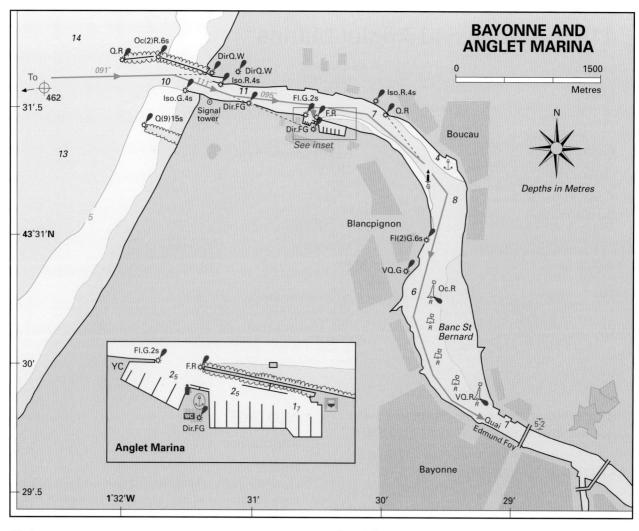

BAYONNE AND ANGLET MARINA

Entrance

By day and night

From ⊕462 align the first set of leading marks on 091° (both white lattice structures. *Front* – thin red vertical stripe on white ground, *Rear* – white vertical stripe on red ground and Q.W intense on line) and proceed on this line to leave the outer breakwater end 100m to port (Q.R). Before reaching the inner breakwater heads pick up the next leading line on 111° (*Front* – lattice structure, vertical green band on white ground DirF.G; *Rear* – DirF.G light in front of upper window of pagoda style building with sloping red roof which is the capitainerie) and pass through the inner entrance on this line. The inner entrance ends are lit by Iso.R and Iso.G both 4s. When the conspicuous port signal tower is abeam to starboard alter to about 095° to proceed up the centre of the channel. The entrance to the marina is marked on its west side by a white pylon, green top Fl.G.2s. The stream sets strongly across this entrance except for HW and LW slack. It is hardly necessary to stick to the next two leading lines if proceeding further upriver. Remain in the centre of the channel until Pointe de Blancpignon is passed, then favour the west bank and observe the lateral buoyage.

Berthing

In marina Up to 18m OA, dredged to 2.5m on pontoons with fingers. 60 visitors' berths. Visitors should call on VHF Ch 09 or telephone for a berth or go to the fuel berth which is at right angles to entrance and fine on the port bow on entry. The marina office is adjacent.

Upriver Berths near the city centre are now cut off by a bridge with 5.2m clearance. Just before this on the south bank Quai Edmund Foy may provide a temporary berth but the face is piled and is for commercial use. Foreign yachts will be chased away from the small naval base jetty on the west bank opposite Banc St-Bernard.

Anchorage

It is possible to anchor out of the main fairway in 2–4m, mud and sand but the streams run strongly especially on the ebb. Much debris comes down if the river is in spate. The anchorage shown off Boucau has good holding but is very noisy.

117 Biarritz

Arrival
  ⊕463-Biarritz 43°30′·00N 01°34′·11W

Tidal information, charts and weather
  As for Bayonne

Open anchorage for fair weather only

Still a fashionable watering-place but to the yachtsman only an open anchorage and tiny boat harbour not usable in any swell. A visit is only worthwhile in fair and settled weather

The town lies 3.5M south of Bayonne and 7M to the north-northeast of St-Jean-de-Luz.

Warning

The Plateau de St-Jean-de-Luz lies between 1.5–4 miles offshore with a minimum depth of 10m. The sea breaks over some of the rocky shallows in heavy weather or swell and should be avoided.

Depth restrictions

There is up to 1m in the approach to the tiny harbour which dries to 0.8m in the two basins; the third basin has a sill; the entrance is about 6m wide with a very sharp turn in to port. A dinghy can be left here.

Anchorage

As indicated on the plan in about 3m, adequate holding.

Ashore in Biarritz

The town has many better class restaurants, shops, casinos and places of amusement, most within reasonable walking distance of the harbour. Excellent beaches with supporting infrastructure. There are no facilities specifically for yachtsmen.

Travel

Medium-sized airport. Bus and rail connections in all directions.

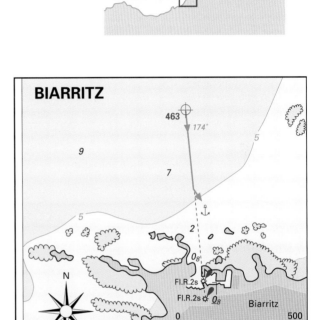

Biarritz. Port des
Pêcheurs entrance
R Rundle

118 St-Jean-de-Luz, Larraldénia and Socoa

Location
43°24'·00N 01°41'·00W

Arrival
⊕464-St-Jean-de-Luz 43°24'·23N 01°41'·82W

Shelter
Good in Larraldénia and Socoa;
Anchorage exposed in northerlies

Hazards
A number of off-lying banks break in heavy
weather. In these conditions only the Ldg
lines from ⊕464 should be used

Depth Restriction
Larraldénia 1m on approach
Socoa dries

Height Restriction
La Nivelle bridge has 1.9m clearance

Night Entry
Well-lit Ldg lines

Tidal Information
HW PdG HW–0042
LW PdG LW–0037

Mean Height of Tide

MHWS	MHWN	MLWN	MLWS
4.3	3.3	1.7	0.6

Tidal Streams
The flood (0.5kn) enters by the E entrance
and the ebb (1kn) exits by the W entrance
Flood PdG HW –0600 to –0030
Ebb PdG HW 0000 to +0530

Berthing
Pontoons at Larraldénia (8
visitors' max OA 15.99m)
Moorings afloat and drying
at Socoa
La Nivelle only for 8m OA
and lowering mast
Anchorage areas and some
moorings in bay

Facilities
All facilities

Charts
BA 3640 (10), 1292 (175)
SHOM 7440 (50)
Imray C42

Radio
Larraldénia VHF Ch 09
(working hours)

Telephone
Larraldénia ☎ 05 59 47 26 81
Socoa ☎ 05 59 47 26 81
Basque YC (Socoa) ☎ 05 59 47 18 31

Coastguard
There is a coastguard/signal station
in a tall white tower just to the S of
Socoa lighthouse
☎ 05 59 47 18 54

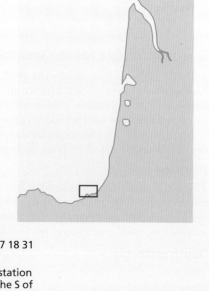

Large bay with seaside resorts and a small marina

PILOTAGE

Approaches

The directions below are given for heavy weather to avoid the shoal patches which have a least depth of 15m over them. In fine weather or little swell more direct lines may be taken.

From W

By day or night

A good offing should be maintained after Cabo Higuer to clear Les Briquets 1M off the conspicuous Pointe St-Anne. Proceed then outside the Belhara Perdun shoal to pick up the Socoa/Bordagain leading line 138° (*Front* – QWR, *Rear* – DirQW) to proceed to ⊕464, thence on the Sainte-Barbe leading line 101° (*Front* – DirOc(4)R.12s, *Rear* – DirOc(4)R.12s) transferring to the inner leading line 151° (*Front* – DirQ.G, *Rear* – DirQ.G) to pass through the west entrance. See *Appendix 1* for more details of these leading marks and lights.

From N

By day or night

Pick up the Socoa/Bordagain leading line and proceed down it to ⊕464 and thence as from west to pass through the west entrance.

From E or NE

By day

Follow the coast about 1M off and outside the 20m line inside the shoal patches until the Tour de Bordagain (tall stone tower on top of hill with trees round it) bears 193°. Keep on this bearing to pass through the east entrance. Do not cut the corner because of Les Esquilletac shoal.

By night

It would be prudent to proceed outside the shoals towards ⊕464 until the inner leading line (both Q.G) on 151° is identified and proceed down this through the west entrance.

Entrance

Larraldénia Marina is between two rocky training walls just southwest of the leading line. At night be careful not to go between the Finger Mole and the east training wall as the front leading light is well back. The entrance is dredged inside the wall-ends to 3m but it shoals to 1m outside. Delay entrance to HW if there is any swell as it can break right across. Once inside this entrance, the entrance to the marina will be fine on the port bow behind another wall running out from the west bank.

Berthing

Larraldénia Up to 16m in 3m on pontoons with fingers, eight for visitors. In the event of the marina being full, a berth in the fishing harbour on

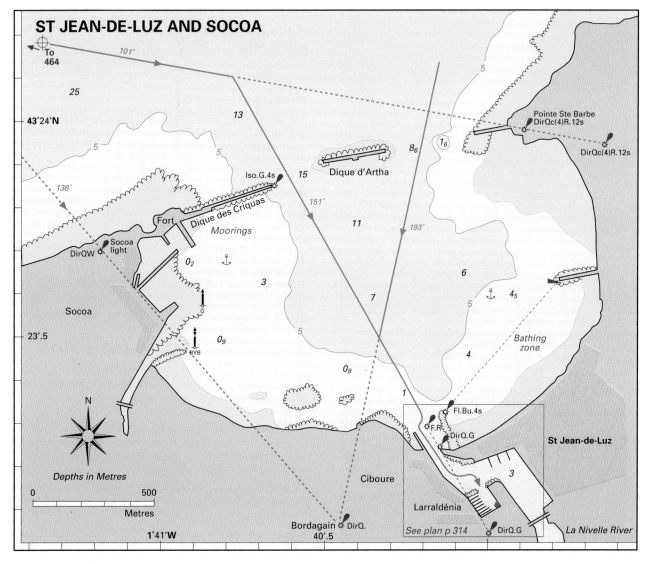

St-Jean de Luz entrance with the outer breakwater beyond *R Rundle*

VIII. THE GIRONDE AND BASSIN D'ARCACHON TO HENDAYE

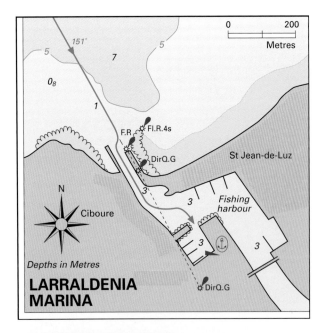

pontoons may be possible. As the marina is small an early arrival is advised.

Socoa Drying berths may be available in the harbour. Enquire at the yacht club.

Moorings

There are three visitors' moorings near the root of Digue des Criquas off Socoa in the middle of a number of private ones. Contact the YC if a private one is picked up.

Anchorages

The normal yacht anchorage is to the southwest of the west entrance and to the south of the moorings. Holding is doubtful and two anchors would be wise in heavy weather. Landing can be made just inside the Socoa harbour entrance.

An alternative anchorage is in the southeast corner of the bay clear of the bathing zone in 3m or more. There is a landing pier in the corner of the bay.

ASHORE IN ST-JEAN-DE-LUZ/SOCOA

St-Jean-de-Luz is a lively place with many amusements including a casino to entertain the tourists, of which there are many in August. There is a chandlery and basic services here but few repair facilities. Shops and restaurants in Ciboure.

Socoa has the very friendly Yacht Club Basque with restaurant and showers and there is also a diving club for those wanting any underwater work; a good selection of shops and restaurants. Fuel can be brought by camion around HW to an alongside berth ② 05 59 26 06 98.

Travel

Good rail and bus services in all directions. An airfield at Biarritz (15km) has some European flights; international flights from Fuenterrabía (10km) are via Madrid.

Larraldénia Marina *R Rundle*

St-Jean-de-Luz fishing harbour *R Rundle*

119 Hendaye and Hondarribia

Location
43°23'·00N 01°47'·00W

Arrival
⊕466-Cabo Higuer 43°24'·24N 01°47'·50W
⊕465-Hendaye 43°23'·50N 01°46'·80W

Shelter
Complete in both marinas

Hazards
River Bidasoa bar can break in a swell and on the ebb

Depth Restriction
1m on Rio Bidasoa bar
3m in Socoburu and Hondarribia

Night Entry
Well lit but no Leading Lights

Tidal Information
HW PdG HW–0040
LW PdG LW–0030

Mean Height of Tide

MHWS	MHWN	MLWN	MLWS
4.2	3.1	1.6	0.5

Tidal Streams
Not significant except in rio entrance where ebb can reach 5kns

Berthing
At pontoons in both marinas
Possible anchorages in main bay or in Baie de Chingoody

Facilities
All, in both marinas

Charts
BA 1157 (25), 1292 (175)
SHOM 6786 (130)
Imray C42

Radio
Hendaye VHF Ch 09 (24H)
Hondarribia VHF Ch 09 (24H)

Telephone
Socoburu ☎ 05 59 48 06 10
Hondarribia ☎ 943 641 711

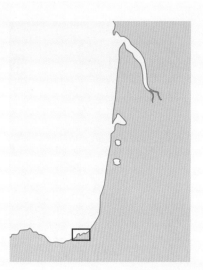

Two first-class marinas

The bay, estuary, harbours and Río Bidasoa lie between France and Spain. A large part of the bay is neutral area and the boundary between the two countries is complex (see BA chart 1181 for some details). There are two first-class marinas and plenty going on ashore. Hendaye is primarily a holiday resort whereas Hondarribia has more history.

PILOTAGE

Approaches

From west

By day or night

Navigate to the north of Cabo Higuer (Fl(2)10s23M) and enter the Baie de Fontarrabie leaving the headland 0.5M to starboard and the fishing port of Gurutzeaundi close to starboard. A track of 205° will then lead between the training wall heads of the Río Bidasoa (Fl(3)G.9s5M, LFl.R.10s5M). This track will leave Banc Iruarri (7.9m), on which the seas can break, 200m to port. Gurutzeaundi has Q(3)5s on its east corner and the entrance is marked by Fl(2)R.7s and Fl(2)G.7s lights.

From east

By day or night

Cabo Higuer lighthouse (Fl(2)10s23M) should be approached on a track of 240° or less to avoid Les Briquets rocks to the northeast of the bay. In heavy weather this should be reduced to 215° to avoid Banc Chicharvel (13m). When 0.5M from the headland proceed as above. Do not turn short if there is any sea or swell which may break on Banc Iruarri (7.9m).

Hondarribia from Hendaye

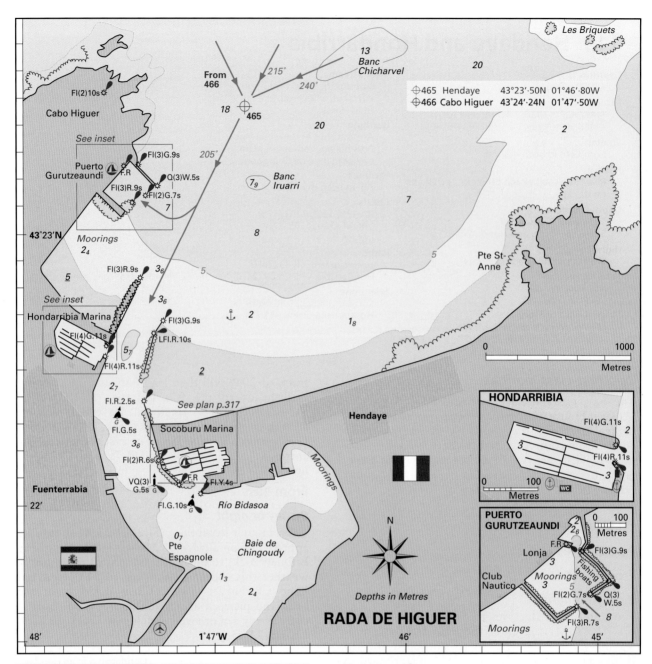

Les Briquets

13
Banc
Chicharvel

20

From 466

215°
240°

18   465

205°

20

⊕465	Hendaye	43°23'·50N 01°46'·80W
⊕466	Cabo Higuer	43°24'·24N 01°47'·50W

Fl(2)10s

Cabo Higuer

2

20

See inset

Puerto
Gurutzeaundi

Fl(3)G.9s
F.R
Q(3)W.5s
Fl(3)R.9s   Fl(2)G.7s

7₉   Banc
Iruarri

2

7

43°23'N

7

Moorings
2₄

8

5

Pte St-
Anne

5

See inset

Fl(3)R.9s   3₆

Hondarribia Marina

3₆

Fl(3)G.9s

2

Fl(4)G.11s

LFl.R.10s

1₈

Fl(4)R.11s

5₇

0   1000
Metres

2

2₇

Fl.R.2.5s

See plan p.317

Hendaye

G
Fl.G.5s

Socoburu Marina

3₆

HONDARRIBIA

Fl(2)R.6s

Fl(4)G.11s   2

VQ(3)
G.5s G

F.R   Fl.Y.4s

3

Fl(4)R.11s

Fuenterrabia

22'

Fl.G.10s G

Río Bidasoa

Moorings

0   100
Metres   WC

3

0₇
Pte
Espagnole

Baie de
Chingoudy

N

**PUERTO
GURUTZEAUNDI**   2₆   0   100
Metres

1₃

2₄

Depths in Metres

F.R
Lonja

Fl(3)G.9s

RADA DE HIGUER

Club
Nautico   Moorings
3   5

Fishing boats

48'   1°47'W   46'   Fl(2)G.7s   Q(3)
W.5s   8

Moorings   Fl(3)R.7s   45'

Hendaye visitors' pontoon for large yachts

From north

By day or night

A southerly course towards Cabo Higuer clears all dangers. The lighthouses of Cabo Higuer (Fl(2)10s23M) and Le Socoa (Q.WR.12M) assist. The houses of Hendaye above a long sandy beach stand out clearly.

By GPS

From west make:

⊕466-Cabo Higuer, ⊕465-Hendaye

From north and east go direct to:

⊕465-Hendaye

but from the east in heavy weather make sure Banc de Chicharvel (13m) is given good clearance by heading further out.

Puerto Gurutzeaundi (Spain)

This fishing harbour may be used as a refuge in the worst weather and sea conditions if the entrance to Río Bidasoa is impassable. The entrance is straightforward from an approach course of from 280° to 350° after taking particular care to avoid Banc Iruarri. Either anchor in the outer harbour, pick up a mooring or go alongside in the inner harbour which has a least depth of 2m.

Entrances to Rio Bidasoa

There is no bar and the least depth outside the ends of the Río Bidasoa training walls is 3.6m and it deepens inside to about 5m. The minimum depth of 3.6m is maintained right up to the Hendaye Marina entrance. However, do not enter if the seas are breaking across the entrance to the river. Go to Puerto Gurutzeaundi instead.

Hondarribia Marina (Spain)

Turn to starboard into the marina 400m up from the west training wall end. The entrance is marked by Fl(4)R.11s and Fl(4)G.11s on prominent pylons.

Socoburu Marina (France)

Continue up the río leaving a SHM buoy (Fl.G.5s) and a SHM beacon (VQ(3)G.5s) to starboard, follow the marina wall round to port at about 50m off passing a Fl(2)R.6s on its elbow and turn sharply to port into the entrance (F.R and Fl.Y.4s).

Berthing

Hondarribia Marina (Spain)

Reception berth is the first pontoon on the port side marked G and with a yellow light at its end. Maximum length 16m, depths 3m and 2m at finger pontoons. Office is in centre of southeast side.

Socoburu Marina (France)

The reception pontoon has finger berths in the northwest corner of the marina. Continue turning to port inside the entrance and go up the channel between the pontoon ends and turn to port to berth on this pontoon. Maximum length 20m, depths mostly 3m.

Moorings

There are many private moorings in Baie de Chingoody to the southeast of Socoburu. Ask at Socoburu office before picking one up.

Anchoring

Anchorage in 2–5m, mostly sand, is available anywhere in the main bay clear of any moorings but will be subject to swell.

The main sheltered anchorage is in the northeast corner of Baie de Chingoody clear of the moorings which are now extensive. To reach the anchoring area leave a SHM beacon (VQ(3)G.5s), the end of the airport runway and a SHM buoy (LFl.G.10s) all to the southwest of the marina breakwater to starboard. Keep a careful eye open for aircraft when passing the line of the runway and anchor well clear of it.

ASHORE IN HONDARRIBIA

The marina has all the facilities including a 36-tonne travel-lift and 5-tonne crane plus fuel (24 hours). Shops, *supermercados* and restaurants are a five minute walk away in the attractive old town of Fuenterrabía where Charles V's castle, Guadaloupe church, Mont Jaizkibel and Castillo San Telmo are worth a visit, and a wander round the old fortifications provides a pleasant interlude.

ASHORE IN HENDAYE

Socoburu has all the facilities of a first-class marina including a 30-tonne travel-lift, a secure laying up area and a welcoming yacht club. Hendaye is a popular family seaside resort with much activity in the season.

Travel

Locally there is a half-hourly bus service which runs between Hendaye and Fuenterrabía. Otherwise there are the usual bus services in all directions in France and Spain. The large railway station at Irun is 4km from Hondarribia and connects with the French and Spanish networks; the latter includes a slow line along the north coast to La Coruña.

The local airport at Fuenterrabía (also known as San Sebastián airport) services local flights and international flights via Madrid; Biarritz, 25km away, has the occasional charter and international flight, otherwise connects with Paris.

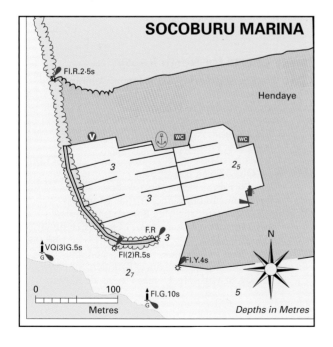

SOCOBURU MARINA

Hendaye

Fl.R.2·5s

VQ(3)G.5s
F.R
Fl(2)R.5s
Fl.Y.4s
Fl.G.10s

0   100
Metres   Depths in Metres

Appendix

1. CHARTS AND BOOKS

Obtaining Charts

Up-to-date information on British Admiralty chart coverage for Atlantic France is available at
www.ukho.gov.uk
where full details of chart schemes, titles and scales are given.

French (SHOM – Service Hydrographique et Océanographique de la Marine) charts, which offer more comprehensive coverage are listed at
www.shom.fr

Note that SHOM chart numbers change and the SHOM website should be checked for the latest details.

Up-to-date lists of sales agents for SHOM are available on the websites.

Imray Laurie Norie and Wilson, the publishers of *Atlantic France*, are sales agents for UKHO charts and publications which may be ordered through
www.imray.com

Imrays are able to help with enquiries and supply French charts.

Chart agents

Before departure

British Admiralty and Spanish charts from
Imray Laurie Norie & Wilson Ltd,
Wych House, The Broadway, St Ives,
Cambs PE27 5BT
☎ 01480 462114, *Fax* 01480 496109
www.imray.com.

Planning charts – North to South

	BA	SHOM	Scale
Île d'Ouessant to Pointe de Penmarc'h	2643	(NA)	1:200,000
Pointe de Penmarc'h to Île d'Yeu	2646	(NA)	1:200,000
Île d' Yeu to Pointe de La Coubre	2663	(7069)	1:200,000
Pointe de la Coubre to Pointe d'Arcachon	2664	(7070)	1:200,000

Passage charts – North to South

	BA	SHOM	Scale
Goulet de Brest to Portsall	2356	(7149)	1:50,000
to Chaussée de Sein	2350	(7172)	1:50,000
Chaussée de Sein to Pointe de Penmarc'h	2819	(7147)	1:50,000
Pointe de Penmarc'h to Pointe de Trevignon	2820	(7146)	1:50,000
Île de Penfret to Plateaux des Birvideaux	2821	(7031)	1:50,000
Île de Groix to Belle-Île	2822	(7032)	1:50,000
Quiberon to Croisic	2823	(7033)	1:50,000
Approaches to La Loire	2986	(7395)	1:50,000
Pointe de St-Gildas to Goulet de Fromentine	2981	(7394)	1:50,000
Les Sables d'Olonne to Île de Ré	2998	(7403)	1:50,000
Pointe du Grouin du Cou to Pointe de Chassiron	2999	(7404)	1:50,000
La Rochelle to Pointe de la Coubre	3000	(7405)	1:50,000
Approaches to La Gironde	3057	(7426)	1:50,000
La Gironde	3068/3069	(NA)	1:50,000

Large scale charts – North to South

	BA	SHOM	Scale
Chenal du Four	3345	(NA)	1:25,000
Approaches to Brest	3427	(7401)	1:22,500
Rade de Brest	3429	(7400)	1:22,500
Baie de Douarnenez	2349	(7121)	1:30,000
Raz de Sein	2348	(7423)	1:20,000
Harbours of the W Coast of France	3640	(NA)	Various
Loctudy to Concarneau	3641	(NA)	1:20,000
Cours de l'Odet – De Bénodet à Quimper	NA	(6679)	1:20,000
Îles de Glénan, partie Sud	NA	(6648)	1:20,000
Ports et mouillages en Bretagne Sud	NA	(7138)	Various
Île de Groix	NA	(7139)	1:20,000
Passes et Rade de Lorient	304	(7140)	1:10,000
Belle-Île	NA	(7142)	1:25,000
Abords des Îles de Houat et de Hoëdic	2835	(7143)	1:20,000
Golfe de Morbihan	2371		1:25,000
La Baie de Pont-Mahé to Piriac-sur-Mer	NA	(7136)	1:15,000
La Turballe to Pornichet	NA	(7145)	1:25,000
Île d'Yeu	NA	(7410)	1:20,000
La Charente Île d'Aix to Tonnay-Charente	2747	(7415)	1:20,000

Imray Charts for North Biscay

C18 **Western Approaches to the English Channel and Biscay** 1:1,000,000
C35 **Baie de Morlaix to L'Aber-Ildut**
Plans Approaches to L'Aber-Wrac'h and L'Aber-Benoît, Argenton, Port du Pontusval, Moguériec, Portsall, L'Aber-Ildut, Port de Morlaix 1:75,000
C36 **Île d'Ouessant to Raz de Sein**
Plans Port du Conquet, Port de Brest and Marina du Moulin Blanc, Port de Morgat, Port de Camaret-sur-Mer, Baie de Lampaul (Ouessant), Port Douarnenez, l'Elorn (Continuation to Landerneau) 1:80,000
C37 **Raz de Sein to Bénodet**
Plans Lesconil, La Guilvinec, Bénodet, Audierne, Loctudy, St-Guénole, L'Odet Fleuve, Île de Sein 1:80,000

C38 **Anse de Bénodet to Presqu'île de Quiberon**
   Plans Port-La-Forêt, Concarneau, Lorient,
   Lorient Yacht Harbour, Port Tudy, Étel,
   Brigneau & Merrien, Port Manech, Doëlan,
   Îles de Glénan (North)   1:80,000
C39 **Lorient to Le Croisic**
   Plans Sauzon, Le Palais, Port Haliguen,
   La Trinité-sur-Mer, Port de Crouesty,
   Piriac-sur-Mer, La Turballe, Le Croisic, Baie de
   Pouliguen
   Inset Continuation of la Vilaine   1:80,000
C40 **Le Croisic to Les Sables d'Olonne**
   Plans Joinville, Pornic, St-Nazaire,
   Goulet de Fromentine, St-Gilles-Croix de Vie,
   Les Sables d'Olonne, Le Croisic,
   L'Herbaudière   1:109,000
C41 **Les Sables d'Olonne to La Gironde**
   Plans Jard-sur-Mer, Bourgenay, Ars-en-Ré,
   St-Martin-de-Ré, La Flotte-en-Ré, Rochefort, Douhet,
   St-Denis d'Oléron, Rade de Pallice, Boyardville, La
   Rochelle and Port des Minimes, Royan   1:109,400
C42 **La Rochelle to Santander including the entrance to
   the Gironde, the Approach to Arcachon and the
   Basque ports.**
   Plans Approach to Arcachon, Capbreton, Rada de
   Higuer, Getaria, Zumaia, Abra de Bilbao, Santoña,
   Santander   1:350,000

2. ⊕ WAYPOINTS

All waypoints are based on the WGS 84 datum. While every
effort has been taken to ensure their accuracy, no liability can
be accepted for any errors.

⊕	*WP Name*	*Latitude*	*Longitude*
I. Finisterre			
A	Libenter	48°37'.40N	4°38'.70W
B	Malouine	48°38'.00N	4°36'.30W
C	Basse Portsall	48°36'.60N	4°46'.00W
1	Le Four	48°31'.36N	4°49'.38W
2	NW Four	48°29'.63N	4°52'.08W
3	NW Aber Ildut	48°29'.37N	4°49'.68W
4	Aber Ildut	48°28'.09N	4°48'.14W
5	Aber Ildut 1	48°28'.20N	4°46'.65W
6	Aber Ildut 2	48°28'.21N	4°45'.83W
7	Porspaul	48°26'.58N	4°48'.08W
8	Porspaul 1	48°26'.61N	4°47'.26W
9	Luronne	48°27'.18N	4°54'.80W
10	Valbelle	48°26'.39N	4°50'.16W
11	Plâtresses	48°25'.22N	4°52'.15W
12	Corsen	48°24'.30N	4°48'.91W
13	Porsmoguer	48°24'.09N	4°46'.78W
14	Taboga	48°23'.18N	4°48'.27W
15	St-Pierre	48°23'.13N	4°49'.01W
16	Porz-Illien	48°22'.95N	4°46'.18W
17	L'Ilette	48°22'.37N	4°47'.37W
18	Blanc Sablons	48°22'.27N	4°46'.27W
19	Vinotière	48°21'.94N	4°48'.67W
20	Kermorven	48°21'.86N	4°47'.72W
21	Le Conquet	48°21'.60N	4°47'.11W
22	Fourmi	48°19'.25N	4°47'.85W
23	St-Mathieu	48°18'.98N	4°46'.97W
24	Martel	48°18'.72N	4°42'.33W
25	Bertheaume	48°20'.38N	4°41'.58W
26	Ste-Anne	48°21'.53N	4°32'.88W
27	Pénoupèle	48°21'.41N	4°30'.51W
28	Elorn	48°22'.42N	4°27'.28W
29	Moulin Blanc	48°22'.79N	4°25'.86W

⊕	*WP Name*	*Latitude*	*Longitude*
30	Moulin Blanc 1	48°23'.22N	4°25'.78W
31	Kéralliou	48°23'.16N	4°24'.83W
32	Camfrout	48°23'.55N	4°23'.00W
33	Île Ronde	48°19'.21N	4°27'.96W
34	Auberlac'h	48°19'.55N	4°25'.48W
35	La Chèvre	48°19'.41N	4°21'.89W
36	Tinduff	48°20'.27N	4°21'.85W
37	Daoulas	48°19'.99N	4°19'.57W
38	Bindy	48°18'.69N	4°20'.64W
39	Aulne	48°18'.33N	4°22'.17W
40	Hôpital	48°18'.63N	4°18'.72W
41	Le Fret	48°17'.12N	4°30'.17W
42	Roscanvel	48°19'.41N	4°31'.58W
43	Roscanvel 1	48°18'.81N	4°32'.62W
44	Espagnols	48°20'.76N	4°31'.62W
45	Robert	48°20'.41N	4°33'.40W
46	Kerviniou	48°19'.59N	4°34'.90W
47	Capucins	48°19'.10N	4°35'.17W
48	Camaret	48°17'.44N	4°36'.08W
49	Camaret 1	48°16'.92N	4°35'.19W
50	N Toulinguet	48°16'.94N	4°38'.08W
51	S Toulinguet	48°16'.13N	4°38'.20W
52	Tas de Pois	48°14'.82N	4°38'.40W
53	Pen-Hir	48°15'.45N	4°36'.97W
54	Dinan	48°15'.04N	4°33'.87W
55	Vandrée	48°15'.22N	4°48'.55W
56	Basse du Lis	48°12'.99N	4°44'.58W
57	Bouc	48°11'.51N	4°37'.51W
58	SW Chèvre	48°09'.64N	4°34'.78W
59	Basse Vielle	48°08'.12N	4°35'.28W
60	S Chèvre	48°08'.44N	4°32'.58W
61	SE Chèvre	48°09'.43N	4°32'.32W
62	St-Nicolas	48°10'.74N	4°32'.20W
63	St-Norgard	48°11'.77N	4°30'.92W
64	Morgat	48°13'.39N	4°29'.18W
65	Île de l'Aber	48°13'.42N	4°25'.81W
66	Verrès	48°12'.56N	4°25'.90W
67	Douarnenez	48°06'.82N	4°21'.24W
68	Douarnenez 1	48°06'.14N	4°20'.44W
69	Coulinec	48°06'.32N	4°21'.05W
70	Jument	48°06'.62N	4°24'.88W
71	Porz Péron	48°05'.38N	4°29'.35W
72	Duellou	48°05'.37N	4°35'.83W
73	Basse Jaune	48°05'.01N	4°42'.44W
74	Van	48°04'.06N	4°44'.58W
75	E Tévennec	48°03'.90N	4°46'.25W
76	Trépassés	48°03'.07N	4°44'.19W
77	Trépassés 1	48°02'.87N	4°42'.78W
78	NE Raz	48°02'.91N	4°46'.26W
79	Not allocated		
80	Raz	48°02'.37N	4°45'.86W
81	W Tévennec	48°04'.29N	4°50'.47W
82	N Sein	48°03'.68N	4°50'.70W
83	Vouzerez	48°02'.61N	4°50'.89W
84	Men Brial	48°02'.36N	4°50'.85W
85	NE Sein	48°03'.30N	4°49'.45W
86	Nerroth	48°02'.61N	4°50'.47W
87	E Sein	48°02'.61N	4°48'.57W
88	Ganaloc	48°02'.61N	4°51'.57W
89	SE Raz	48°01'.83N	4°45'.78W
90	Koummoudog	48°01'.50N	4°43'.31W
91	Fuenteun-Aod	48°01'.54N	4°41'.60W
92	Anse du Loc'h	48°01'.44N	4°38'.29W
93	Cabestan	48°00'.56N	4°35'.91W
94	W Gamelle	47°59'.54N	4°33'.00W
95	Ste-Evette	48°00'.31N	4°32'.87W
96	Audierne	48°00'.50N	4°32'.41W

⊕	WP Name	Latitude	Longitude
97	NE Gamelle	48°00'.07N	4°32'.05W
98	E Gamelle	47°59'.46N	4°31'.55W
99	Pors-Poulhan	47°59'.00N	4°27'.80W
100	St-Guénolé	47°48'.80N	4°24'.20W
101	St-Guénolé 1	47°48'.41N	4°23'.33W
102	St-Guénolé 2	47°48'.59N	4°22'.99W

II. Benodet Bay

103	Eckmühl	47°46'.81N	4°23'.88W
104	Penmarc'h	47°45'.94N	4°25'.08W
105	Guilvinec	47°45'.79N	4°20'.33W
106	Guilvinec 1	47°46'.72N	4°18'.28W
107	Guilvinec 2	47°47'.16N	4°17'.60W
108	Guilvinec 3	47°47'.41N	4°17'.22W
109	Spineg	47°45'.08N	4°18'.89W
110	S Guilvinec	47°45'.42N	4°17'.28W
111	Lesconil	47°47'.62N	4°12'.51W
112	Lesconil 1	47°47'.73N	4°12'.21W
113	Karreg Kreiz	47°46'.01N	4°10'.84W
114	Boulanger	47°47'.33N	4°08'.98W
115	Roustolou	47°46'.48N	4°06'.86W
116	Malvic	47°48'.51N	4°06'.88W
117	Bilien	47°49'.10N	4°07'.95W
118	Loctudy	47°49'.70N	4°07'.58W
119	Loctudy 1	47°50'.08N	4°09'.21W
120	Loctudy 2	47°50'.20N	4°09'.70W
121	Loctudy 3	47°50'.19N	4°10'.21W
122	Bénodet	47°51'.55N	4°06'.42W
123	Bénodet 1	47°52'.19N	4°06'.66W
124	Astrolabe	47°47'.84N	4°04'.48W
125	La Voleuse	47°49'.32N	4°03'.15W
126	Mousterlin	47°48'.56N	4°02'.48WI
127	Men Vras	47°49'.62N	4°01'.56W
128	Porceaux	47°45'.84N	3°59'.73W
129	La Pie	47°43'.94N	3°59'.74W
130	Bananec	47°43'.24N	3°59'.10W
131	Chambre	47°43'.20N	3°59'.56W
132	N Penfret	47°43'.94N	3°56'.91W
133	W Penfret	47°43'.06N	3°57'.93W
134	E Penfret	47°43'.07N	3°56'.83W
135	Ruolh	47°40'.97N	3°54'.89W
136	Ruolh 1	47°41'.14N	3°56'.36W
137	S Glénan	47°38'.52N	4°01'.37W
138	Brilimec	47°39'.14N	3°59'.64W
139	Brilimec 1	47°42'.04N	3°57'.90W
140	Brilimec 2	47°42'.46N	3°58'.62W
141	Bluiniers	47°43'.23N	4°04'.12W
142	Broc'h	47°43'.26N	4°01'.38W
143	SE Beg-Meil	47°50'.73N	3°57'.23W
144	Laouen Pod	47°51'.22N	3°57'.96W
145	Beg Meil	47°51'.87N	3°58'.53W
146	Cap Coz	47°52'.81N	3°58'.80W
147	La-Forêt	47°53'.39N	3°58'.18W
148	Vas Hir	47°51'.67N	3°56'.66W
149	Concarneau	47°51'.35N	3°55'.73W
150	Concarneau 1	47°51'.84N	3°55'.34W
151	Kersos	47°51'.83N	3°54'.72W
152	Kersos 1	47°51'.56N	3°54'.46W
153	Concarneau 2	47°51'.99N	3°54'.76W
154	Concarneau 3	47°52'.22N	3°54'.76W
155	Pouldohan	47°50'.47N	3°54'.96W
156	Pouldohan 1	47°50'.81N	3°54'.08W
157	An Houarnou	47°49'.70N	3°55'·46W
158	W Trévignon	47°46'.94N	3°54'.08W
159	SW Trévignon	47°46'.40N	3°52'.56W

⊕	WP Name	Latitude	Longitude

III. Groix and The Rias

160	E Glénan	47°42'.54N	3°49'.50W
161	SE Trévignon	47°45'.74N	3°49'.75W
162	Kersidan	47°46'.93N	3°49'.53W
163	Kersidan 1	47°47'.62N	3°49'.45W
164	Île Verte	47°45'.98N	3°48'.14W
165	Raguénez	47°46'.70N	3°47'.71W
166	Aven & Belon	47°47'.66N	3°43'.91W
167	Port Manec'h	47°48'.10N	3°44'.26W
168	Belon	47°48'.37N	3°43'.31W
169	W Brigneau	47°46'.08N	3°40'.09W
170	Brigneau	47°46'.31N	3°39'.71W
171	Brigneau 1	47°46'.76N	3°40'.09W
172	Merrien	47°46'.20N	3°39'.06W
173	Merrien 1	47°46'.60N	3°39'.02W
174	Doëlan	47°45'.70N	3°36'.75W
175	Doëlan 1	47°46'.14N	3°36'.57W
176	Pouldu	47°45'.17N	3°32'.44W
177	Pouldu 1	47°45'.74N	3°32'.20W
178	Kerroc'h	47°41'.66N	3°28'.09W
179	Kerroc'h 1	47°42'.18N	3°28'.09W
180	Pérello	47°41'.69N	3°26'.40W
181	Loméner	47°41'.29N	3°25'.58W
182	Loméner 1	47°41'.99N	3°25'.63W
183	W Lorient	47°40'.81N	3°24'.85W
184	Lorient	47°41'.93N	3°22'.30W
185	Lorient 1	47°42'.30N	3°22'.13W
186	Larmor Plage	47°42'.29N	3°22'.74W
187	S Lorient	47°40'.67N	3°22'·35W
188	Locmalo	47°41'·67N	3°22'·20W
189	Cabon	47°42'.10N	3°21'.58W
190	Souris	47°42'.20N	3°21'.57W
191	Cochon	47°42'·87N	3°21'.89W
192	Kernével	47°43'·36N	3°21'·95W
193	Pen Mané	47°44'.24N	3°20'.96W
194	Commerce	47°44'.56N	3°20'.92W
195	Port Louis	47°42'.78N	3°21'.45W
196	Anéno	47°43'.18N	3°21'.41W
197	Locmiquélic	47°43'.53N	3°21'.12W
198	Blavet	47°44'.29N	3°20'.17W
199	Port Tudy	47°38'.96N	3°26'.46W
200	Mélite	47°38'.94N	3°25'.38W
201	Pte de la Croix	47°38'.14N	3°24'.87W
202	Cougy	47°37'.96N	3°23'.77W
203	SE Chats	47°35'.64N	3°23'.42W
204	Les Chats	47°36'.09N	3°25'.08W
205	Locmaria	47°36'.54N	3°26'.19W
206	Locmaria 1	47°37'.36N	3°26'.39W
207	St-Nicolas	47°37'.74N	3°29'.59W
208	Etel	47°38'.03N	3°13'.04W
209	Etel 1	47°38'.65N	3°12'.70W
210	Chiviguete	47°35'.29N	3°13'.93W
211	W Birvideaux	47°29'.14N	3°18'.91W
212	S Birvideaux	47°27'.44N	3°17'.48W

IV. Quiberon Bay

213	SW Quiberon	47°27'.82N	3°08'.35W
214	Port Maria	47°27'.84N	3°07'.43W
215	Port Maria 1	47°28'.49N	3°07'.32W
216	Poulains	47°23'.94N	3°14'.88W
217	Sauzon	47°22'.80N	3°12'.81W
218	Sauzon 1	47°22'.61N	3°12'.95W
219	Port Jean	47°21'.94N	3°11'.29W
220	Taillefer	47°22'.03N	3°09'.28W
221	Le Palais	47°20'.84N	3°08'.98W
222	Salio	47°19'.84N	3°08'.19W

⊕	WP Name	Latitude	Longitude
223	Yorc'h	47°19'.65N	3°07'.23W
224	Port Maria Bl	47°17'.56N	3°04'.38W
225	Pouldon	47°17'.29N	3°08'.58W
226	Herlin	47°17'.94N	3°10'.39W
227	Kerel	47°17'.79N	3°12'.22W
228	Goulphar	47°17'.51N	3°14'.10W
229	Goulphar 1	47°17'.99N	3°13'.92W
230	Goulphar 2	47°18'.11N	3°13'.72W
231	Stêr-Wenn	47°22'.62N	3°15'.82W
232	Stêr-Wenn 1	47°22'.40N	3°15'.15W
233	S Goué Vas	47°25'.44N	3°04'.87W
234	E Goué Vas	47°26'.28N	3°03'.98W
235	Teignouse	47°27'.54N	3°02'.30W
236	E Teignouse	47°27'.02N	3°01'.26W
237	S Beniguet	47°23'.67N	3°00'.70W
238	Rouleau	47°23'.79N	3°00'.36W
239	Béniguet	47°23'.79N	2°59'.62W
240	N Béniguet	47°24'.55N	2°59'.97W
241	Portz Ler	47°24'.02N	2°59'.26W
242	Hastellic	47°23'.89N	2°58'.74W
243	Portz Navallo	47°23'.76N	2°58'.42W
244	St-Gildas	47°23'.61N	2°57'.26W
245	Er Jeneteu	47°23'.94N	2°56'.51W
246	En Tal	47°23'.61N	2°56'.08W
247	Er Yoc'h	47°23'.27N	2°56'.08W
248	E Houat	47°23'.19N	2°55'.17W
249	Gourhed	47°23'.17N	2°56'.99W
250	Houteliguet	47°22'.54N	2°56'.48W
251	Beg Pell	47°22'.03N	2°56'.63W
252	SE Houat	47°21'.52N	2°56'.08W
253	Chevaux	47°21'.65N	2°58'.23W
254	Gadoérec	47°22'.24N	2°57'.68W
255	Chubéguez	47°22'.64N	2°57'.68W
256	Salus	47°22'.81N	2°57'.50W
257	SW Houat	47°22'.52N	2°59'.08W
258	S Soeurs	47°20'.15N	2°55'.36W
259	N Soeurs	47°21'.22N	2°54'.82W
260	NW Hoedic	47°21'.38N	2°53'.50W
261	Argol	47°20'.74N	2°52'.50W
262	N Hoëdic	47°21'.14N	2°52'.25W
263	NE Hoëdic	47°21'.25N	2°51'.58W
264	Gurannic'h	47°20'.79N	2°50'.41W
265	Lannegui	47°20'.30N	2°51'.16W
266	Lannegui 1	47°20'.35N	2°51'.67W
267	SE Hoëdic	47°18'.74N	2°50'.34W
268	Madavoar	47°19'.62N	2°51'.47W
269	La Croix	47°19'.91N	2°52'.08W
270	S Hoëdic	47°18'.80N	2°53'.06W
271	Haliguen	47°29'.39N	3°05'.88W
272	Orange	47°31'.32N	3°07'.37W
273	Colomban	47°33'.79N	3°05'.93W
274	W Carnac	47°33'.86N	3°04'.40W
275	E Carnac	47°33'.92N	3°03'.32W
276	Trinité	47°33'.48N	3°00'.46W
277	Trinité 1	47°34'.90N	3°00'.95W
278	E Trinité	47°32'.59N	2°59'.86W
279	Philibert	47°33'.27N	2°58'.94W
280	Philibert 1	47°33'.76N	2°58'.90W
281	Meaban	47°31'.20N	2°57'.86W
282	SW Crouesty	47°30'.68N	2°55'.32W
283	Crouesty	47°32'.19N	2°54'.77W
284	NE Crouesty	47°32'.51N	2°55'.28W
285	Kerpenhir	47°33'.21N	2°55'.27W
286	Grégan	47°33'.74N	2°55'.04W
287	Huernic	47°34'.87N	2°56'.02W
288	Creizig	47°34'.92N	2°52'.01W
289	Fogeo	47°32'.04N	2°53'.26W

⊕	WP Name	Latitude	Longitude
290	Cornault	47°30'.86N	2°51'.37W
291	Chimère	47°28'.76N	2°54'.08W
292	Recherche	47°25'.73N	2°47'.58W

V. The Vilaine and The Loire

⊕	WP Name	Latitude	Longitude
293	St-Jacques	47°28'.09N	2°47'.38W
294	St-Jacques 1	47°28'.97N	2°47'.08W
295	Suscinio	47°28'.63N	2°43'.78W
296	Suscinio 1	47°29'.94N	2°43'.38W
297	Pénerf	47°28'.94N	2°38'.91W
298	Pénerf 1	47°30'.01N	2°38'.88W
299	E Pénerf	47°29'.11N	2°38'.48W
300	E Pénerf 1	47°29'.89N	2°38'.63W
301	Accroche	47°28'.96N	2°33'.88W
302	Accroche 1	47°30'.37N	2°31'.27W
303	W Varlingue	47°28'.31N	2°31'.98W
304	W Varlingue 1	47°30'.37N	2°30'.53W
305	Varlingue	47°28'.23N	2°31'.26W
306	Varlingue 1	47°30'.37N	2°29'.92W
307	Vilaine	47°30'.36N	2°28'.68W
308	Mine d'Or	47°28'.16N	2°29'.87W
309	Mesquer	47°25'.59N	2°29'.88W
310	Mesquer 1	47°25'.44N	2°28'.20W
311	Dumet	47°24'.77N	2°36'.94W
312	Piriac	47°23'·89N	2°32'·26W
313	Piriac 1	47°23'.17N	2°32'.66W
314	Rohtrès	47°24'·22N	2°33'·60W
315	Bayonnelles	47°22'·56N	2°35'.38W
316	Turballe	47°20'.54N	2°31'.63W
317	Turballe 1	47°20'.60N	2°30'.91W
318	Turballe 2	47°20'.70N	2°30'.88W
319	N Croisic	47°19'.43N	2°31'.98W
320	Croisic	47°18'.80N	2°31'.57W
321	Croisic 1	47°18'.25N	2°31'.11W
322	W Croisic	47°18'.11N	2°34'.76W
323	SW Croisic	47°17'.07N	2°33'.28W
324	Basse Capella	47°15'.64N	2°42'.39W
325	Batz	47°15'.65N	2°29'.48W
326	W Pornichet	47°15'.14N	2°25'.08W
327	Pouliguen	47°15'.21N	2°24'.28W
328	Pouliguen 1	47°15'.54N	2°24'.23W
329	Pouliguen 2	47°16'.06N	2°24'.93W
330	Pornichet	47°15'.50N	2°21'.19W
331	SW Pornichet	47°14'.13N	2°22'.63W
332	Banche	47°09'.94N	2°28'.58W
333	N Lambarde	47°11'.34N	2°21'.65W
334	SW Lambarde	47°10'.33N	2°23'.28W
335	Charpentier	47°12'.62N	2°19'.13W
336	Loire	47°11'.24N	2°17'.73W
337	Loire 1	47°13'.76N	2°16'.00W
338	Trébézy	47°14'.88N	2°15'.33W
339	St-Nazaire	47°15'.72N	2°12'.06W
340	St-Gildas	47°08'.74N	2°14'.78W
341	St-Gildas 1	47°08'.42N	2°14'.58W
342	W St-Gildas	47°07'.89N	2°16'.21W
343	S St-Gildas	47°07'.34N	2°14'.81W
344	Pornic	47°06'.35N	2°07'.08W
345	Pilier	47°03'.52N	2°22'.86W
346	N Herbaudière	47°03'.94N	2°17'.39W
347	Herbaudière	47°02'.69N	2°17'.62W
348	Herbaudière 1	47°02'.36N	2°17'.69W
349	Herbaudière 2	47°01'.67N	2°17'.83W
350	W Herbaudière	47°01'.22N	2°20'.33W
351	Pères	47°03'.39N	2°14'.37W
352	Chaise	47°00'.59N	2°12'.84W
353	Noirmoutier	46°59'.37N	2°12'.80W
354	Réaumur	46°57'.44N	2°24'.38W

APPENDIX

⊕	WP Name	Latitude	Longitude
355	Morin	46°55'.93N	2°20'.54W
356	Morin 1	46°58'.70N	2°17'.98W

VI. The Vendée

⊕	WP Name	Latitude	Longitude
357	Boeufs	46°55'.04N	2°28'.16W
358	Fromentine	46°52'.84N	2°12'.73W
359	Fromentine 1	46°53'.51N	2°09'.65W
360	Fromentine 2	46°53'.54N	2°08'.80W
361	NW Yeu	46°44'.60N	2°24'.00W
362	Broches	46°44'.27N	2°24'.41W
363	Broches 1	46°43'.85N	2°23'.50W
364	Joinville	46°44'.22N	2°20'.23W
365	Joinville 1	46°43'.77N	2°20'.76W
366	E Joinville	46°43'.34N	2°18'.00W
367	E Yeu	46°41'.25N	2°16'.00W
368	SE Yeu	46°40'.95N	2°17'.18W
369	Vieilles	46°41'.17N	2°18'.30W
370	Vieilles 1	46°41'.53N	2°18'.70W
371	S Yeu	46°40'.85N	2°20'.00W
372	Meule	46°41'.19N	2°20'.91W
373	Meule 1	46°41'.49N	2°20'.78W
374	SW Yeu	46°41'.74N	2°23'.10W
375	W Yeu	46°43'.00N	2°26'.00W
376	St-Gilles	46°40'.82N	1°58'.18W
377	St-Gilles 1	46°41'.44N	1°57'.32W
378	SE St-Gilles	46°40'.80N	1°56'.82W
379	Barge	46°28'.88N	1°50'.66W
380	W Sables	46°28'.49N	1°47'.25W
381	Sables	46°28'.90N	1°46'.86W
382	Sables 1	46°29'.26N	1°47'.37W
383	Sables 2	46°29'.51N	1°47'.61W
384	E Sables	46°28'.00N	1°45'.78W
385	Bourgenay	46°25'.22N	1°41'.99W
386	Bourgenay 1	46°26'.27N	1°40'.71W
387	Jard	46°23'.51N	1°35'.23W
388	Jard 1	46°24'.15N	1°34'.52W
389	Jard 2	46°24'.35N	1°34'.52W

VII. Charente

⊕	WP Name	Latitude	Longitude
390	NW Ré	46°15'.94N	1°40'.08W
391	NE Ré	46°16'.10N	1°28'.27W
392	Ars	46°14'.20N	1°25'.63W
393	Ars 1	46°14'.06N	1°28'.09W
394	Ars 2	46°13'.00N	1°30'.16W
395	E Ars	46°14'.32N	1°23'.30W
396	N Ré	46°14'.94N	1°20'.54W
397	St-Martin	46°13'.31N	1°21'.46W
398	St-Martin 1	46°12'.54N	1°21'.89W
399	La Flotte	46°12'.07N	1°18'.55W
400	La Flotte 1	46°11'.36N	1°19'.25W
401	Faute	46°16'.14N	1°16'.68W
402	Faute 1	46°17'.37N	1°15'.85W
403	Marans	46°15'.25N	1°11'.46W
404	Marans 1	46°17'.26N	1°09'.47W
405	Marans 2	46°18'.33N	1°07'.89W
406	Ré bridge	46°10'.23N	1°14'.64W
407	S Ré	46°07'.39N	1°28'.45W
408	Martray	46°09'.72N	1°27'.48W
409	Martray 1	46°11'.56N	1°28'.02W
410	Pallice	46°09'.07N	1°14'.61W
411	La Rochelle	46°06'.64N	1°15'.64W
412	La Rochelle 1	46°08'.24N	1°11'.78W
413	La Rochelle 2	46°08'.86N	1°10'.28W
414	N Boyard	46°01'.10N	1°12'.66W
415	SW Aix	46°00'.70N	1°11'.04W
416	SE Aix	46°00'.26N	1°10'.18W
417	E Aix	46°00'.79N	1°08'.67W

⊕	WP Name	Latitude	Longitude
418	NE Aix	46°01'.38N	1°09'.35W
419	Charente	45°59'.65N	1°09'.56W
420	Charente 1	45°58'.74N	1°06'.77W
421	Charente 2	45°57'.20N	1°04'.53W
422	Charente 3	45°57'.12N	1°03'.71W
423	Charente 4	45°57'.64N	1°02'.09W
424	N Oléron	46°04'.80N	1°23'.54W
425	St-Denis	46°03'.30N	1°20'.79W
426	St-Denis 1	46°02'.07N	1°21'.60W
427	E St-Denis	46°02'.30N	1°19'.95W
428	Douhet	46°00'.48N	1°17'.78W
429	Douhet 1	46°00'.22N	1°19'.07W
430	W Boyard	46°00'.22N	1°15'.00W
431	Boyardville	45°58'.50N	1°13'.28W
432	Boyardville 1	45°58'.25N	1°13'.77W
433	E Oléron	45°57'.03N	1°11'.21W
434	Charret	45°53'.35N	1°08'.98W
435	Le Château	45°52'.44N	1°10'.70W
436	NW Oléron	46°03'.00N	1°27'.45W
437	W Oléron	45°58'.00N	1°27'.68W

VIII. The Gironde and Basin d'Arcachon to Hendaye

⊕	WP Name	Latitude	Longitude
438	BXA Gironde	45°37'.47N	1°27'.50W
439	Gironde 1	45°38'.63N	1°17'.69W
440	Gironde 2	45°39'.66N	1°12'.68W
441	Gironde 3	45°37'.76N	1°05'.42W
442	Royan	45°36'.58N	1°02'.06W
443	Royan 1	45°36'.95N	1°01'.79W
444	Pte de Grave	45°35'.14N	1°03'.04W
445	Port Bloc	45°34'.14N	1°03'.71W
446	Port Médoc	45°33'.40N	1°03'.32W
447	Gironde 4	45°31'.35N	0°59'.52W
448	Pauillac	45°11'.86N	0°44'.44W
449	SW Gironde	45°30'.00N	1°15'.60W
450	SW Gironde 1	45°32'.55N	1°08'.33W
451	SW Gironde 2	45°36'.09N	1°03'.88W
452	Meschers	45°33'.00N	0°56'.57W
453	Mortagne	45°28'.20N	0°48'.99W
454	Not allocated		
455	Blaye	45°07'.50N	0°40'.10W
456	Bourg	45°02'.19N	0°33'.50W
457	Cavernes	44°56'.10N	0°26'.50W
458	Bordeaux	44°50'.00N	0°34'.00W
459	ATT Arcachon	44°34'.74N	1°18'.72W
460	Arcachon Outer Access	44°34'.05N	2°12'.91W
461	Capbreton	43°39'.50N	1°27'.48W
462	Bayonne	43°31'.80N	1°32'.50W
463	Biarritz	43°30'.00N	1°34'.11W
464	St-Jean-de-Luz	43°24'.23N	1°41'.82W
465	Hendaye	43°23'.50N	1°46'.80W
466	Cabo Higuer	43°24'.24N	1°47'.50W

3. LIGHTS

I FINISTERRE

Le Corréjou
  Lizen-Ven-Ouest Buoy VQ(9)W.10s5m. W Cardinal
  Île Vierge Fl.W.5s77m27M Grey tower. Horn 60s.

1 L'Aberwrac'h

  Ldg Lts. 100°
  Front **Île Wrac'h** Q.R.20m7M. White square tower, orange top, dwelling
  Rear **Lanvaon** Q.W.55m12M. White square tower, orange triangle. Intense 090° to N side 110°. Synchronised with front.
  N.Breakwater. Dir. 128° Dir.Oc.WRG.6s5m13/11M. White structure. 126°-G-127°-W-129°-R-130°
  Breac'h Ver Fl(2)G.6m3M. Starboard beacon tower.

2 Chenal du Four

A **Le Four** 48°31'·4N 4°48'·3W Fl(5)15s28m22M Horn(3+2)60s Grey tower
   Ldg Lts 158·5°
B *Front* **Kermorvan** 48°21'·7N 4°47'·4W Fl.5s20m22M Horn 60s White square tower
C *Rear* **Saint Mathieu** 48°19'·8N 4°46'·3W Fl.15s56m29M & DirF.54m28M 157·5°-intens-159·5° White tower, red top
D **Plâtresses N buoy** FlG2.5s. 48° 26'·61N 04° 50'·73W
E **Valbelle buoy (port)** 48°26'·4N 4°50'·0W Fl(2)R.6s5M
F **Plâtresses SE buoy** Fl(2)G6s 48° 25'·96N 04° 50'·52W
G **Basse St-Paul buoy (port)** 48°24'·8N 4°49'·2W Oc(2)R.6s

  Chenal de la Helle

  Ldg Lts 138°
  Front **Kermorvan** 48°21'·7N 4°47'·4W Fl.5s20m22M Horn 60s White square tower
  Rear **Lochrist** 48°20'·6N 4°45'·6W DirOc(3)12s49m22M 135°-intens-140° Octagonal white tower, red top
  Le Faix 48°25'·7N 4°53'·9W VQ.16m8M Tower (N card)
  Le Stiff 48°28'·5N 5°03'·4W Fl(2)R.20s85m24M Two white towers, side by side
  Pourceaux buoy (NCM) 48°24'·0N 4°51'·3W Q
  Both channels
  Corsen 48°24'·9N 4°47'·6W DirQ.WRG.33m12-8M 008°-R-012°-W-015°-G-021° White hut
  La Grande Vinotière 48°21'·9N 4°48'·4W LFl.R.10s12m5M Octagonal red tower
  Le Rouget buoy (starboard) 48°22'·1N 4°48'·9W Fl.G.4s
  St-Mathieu Q.WRG.26m12–8M 085°-G-107°-W-116°-R-134°
  White tower
  Tournant et Lochrist buoy (port) 48°20'·6N 4°48'·1W Iso.R.4s
  Les Vieux Moines 48°19'·3N 4°46'·6W Fl.R.4s16m5M 280°-vis-133° Octagonal red tower

S Approaches Chenel de Four

  Leading lights 007°
  Front **Kermorvan** 48°21'·7N 4°47'·4W Fl.5s20m22M Horn 60s White square tower
  Rear **Trézien** 48°25'·4N 4°46'·7W DirOc(2)6s84m20M 003°-intens-011° Grey tower, white towards south

3 Goulet de Brest

  Pointe du Petit Minou 48°20'·2N 4°36'·9W Fl(2)WR.6s32m19/15M Horn 60s shore-R-252°-W-260°-R-307°-W(unintens)-015°-W-065·5° 070·5°-W-shore Grey round tower, W on SW side, red top
  Ldg Lts 068°
  Front **Pte de Petit Minou.** DirQ.30m23M 067·3°-intens-068·8° Same structure
  Pointe du Portzic 48°21'·5N 4°32'·1W Oc(2)WR.12s56m19/15M 219°-R-259°-W-338°-R-000°-W-065·5° 070·5°-W-219° 041°-vis-069° when W of Goulet Grey 8-sided tower

Ldg Lts 068°
  Rear **Pte du Portzic** DirQ.54m22M 065°-intens-071° Same structure
  Auxillary DirQ(6)+LFl.15s54m23M 045°-intens-050° Same structure
  Basse du Charles Martel buoy (port) 48°18'·9N 4°42'·2W Fl(4)R.15s
  Fillettes buoy (WCM) 48°19'·8N 4°35'·7W VQ(9)10s
  Roche Mengam 48°20'·3N 4°34'·6W Fl(3)WR.12s10m9/6M 034°-R-054°-W-034° Black tower, red band.

7 Brest

  L'Elorn river
  Pénoupèle buoy (port) 48°21'·5N 4°30'·5W Fl(3)R.12s
  Naval Base
  Ldg Lts 334°
  Front Dir.Q.WRG.24m9/6M. 334° -G-342° -W-346° -R-024°
  Rear Dir.Q.W.32m9M On château ramparts
  Main entrance. W head. Oc(2)G.6s8m6M Synchronised
  E head Oc(2)R.6s8m6M Synchronised
  R2 buoy (port) 48°22'·1N 4°28'·7W Fl(2)R.6s
  R1 buoy (starboard) 48°21'·8N 4°28'·3W Fl.G.4s
  R4 buoy (port) 48°22'·2N 4°28'·1W LFl.R.10s
  R3 buoy (NCM) 48°22'·5N 4°28'·1W Q(6)+LFl.15s
  (to be left to port)
  Beacon 48°22'·7N 4°26·5W Fl(4)R.15s2M red pile
  Moulin Blanc buoy (port) 48°22'·8N 4°26'·0W Fl(3)R.12s
  Starboard and port buoys MB1 Fl.G.2s MB2 Fl.R.2s
  Marina entrance beacons Fl.G.2s & Fl.R.2s &
  MBA Beacon ECM 48°23'·5N 4°25'·8W Q(3)10s E card beacon

8 Camaret-sur-Mer

  North mole head 48°16'·9N 4°35'·3W Iso.WG.4s7m12/9M135°-W-182°-G-027° White pylon, green top
  South mole head 48°16'·6N 4°35'·3W Fl(2)R.6s9m5M Red pylon

9 The Crozon Peninsula

  Pointe du Toulinguet 48°16'·8N 4°37'·7W Oc(3)WR.12s49m15/11M shore-W-028°-R-090°-W-shore White square tower on building
  Pointe du Petit Minou 48°20'·2N 4°36'·9W Fl(2)WR.6s32m19/15M shore-R-252°-W-260°-R-307°-W(unintens)-015°-W-065·5°, 070·5°-W-shore Grey round tower white on SW side, red top
  Pointe du Portzic 48°21'·5N 4°32'·1W Oc(2)WR.12s56m19/15M 219°-R-259°-W-338°-R-000°-W-065·5°, 070·5°-W-219° Grey 8-sided tower
  Le Bouc buoy (WCM) 48°11'·5N 4°37'·4W Q(9)15s

10 Morgat

  Basse Vieille buoy (IDM) 48°08'·2N 4°35'·8W Fl(2)6s8m7M
  Pointe du Millier 48°05'·9N 4°27'·9W Oc(2)WRG.6s34m16-11M 080°-G-087°-W-113°-R-120°-W-129°-G-148°-W-251°-R-258° White house
  Pointe de Morgat 48°13'·2N 4°29'·8W Oc(4)WRG.12s77m15-10M shore-W-281°-G-301°-W-021°-R-043° White square tower, red top, white house
  Morgat buoy (port) 48°13'·6N 4°29'·7W 48°13'·7N 4°29'·6W Fl.R.4s
  Entrance between wave-breakers
  Port Fl.R.4s
  Starboard Fl.G.4s

11 Douarnenez

  Île Tristan 48°06'·1N 4°20'·3W Oc(3)WR.12s35m13/10M shore-W-138°-R-153°-W-shore Grey tower, white band, black top
  Pointe Biron head 48°06'·1N 4°20'·5W Q.G.6m6M White column, green top
  Port-Rhu Dir Lt 48°05'·4N 4°19·8W DirFl(5)WRG.20s16m5-4M 154°-G-156°-W-158°-R-160° Lantern on bridge
  Barrage Ls 48°05'·7N 4°20·1W Fl.G.5s & Fl.R.5s either side of gate.

12 Île de Sein

Île de Sein, main Lt 48°02′·6N 4°52′·1W Fl(4)25s49m29M White tower, black top
Same tower Dir.Q.WRG 8/6M 267° -G-269° -W-271° -R-275°
Men Brial 48°02′·3N 4°51′·0W Oc(2)WRG.6s16m12–7M 149°-G-186°-W-192°-R-221°-W-227°-G-254° Green and white tower
Cornoc an Ar Braden buoy (starboard) 48°03′·2N 4°50′·9W Fl.G.4s
Tévennec 48°04′·3N 4°47′·8W Q.WR.28m9/6M 090°-W-345°-R-090° White tower and dwelling
DirFl.4s24m12M 324°-intens-332° same structure
Le Chat 48°01′·4N 4°48′·9W Fl(2)WRG.6s27m9-6M 096°-G-215°-W-230°-R-271°-G-286°-R-096° S card tower

13 Raz du Sein

Tévennec 48°04′·3N 4°47′·8W Q.WR.28m9/6M 090°-W-345°-R-090° White tower and dwelling
DirFl.4s24m12M 324°-intens-332° same structure
La Vieille 48°02′·4N 4°45′·4W Oc(2+1)WRG.12s33m18-13M Horn(2+1)60s 290°-W-298°-R-325°-W-355°-G-017°-W-035°-G-105°-W-123°-R-158°-W-205° Grey square tower, black top
La Plate 48°02′·4N 4°45′·6W VQ(9)10s19m8M W card tower

14 Sainte Evette

A **Pointe de Lervilly** 48°00′·0N 4°33′·9W Fl(3)WR.12s20m14/11M 236°-W-269°-R-294°-W-087°-R-109° White round tower, red top
B **Jetée de Ste-Evette head** 48°00′·3N 4°33′·1W Oc(2)R.6s2m7M Red column
Passe de l'Est. Ldg Lts 331°
C *Front* Jetée de Raoulic head 48°00′·5N 4°32′·5W Fl(3)WG.12s11m14/9M shore-W-034°-G-shore, but may show W 037°-055° White tower
D *Rear* Kergadec 48°01′·0N 4°32′·8W DirQ.WRG.43m12/9M 321°-intens-341°White 8-sided tower, red top
E **Pors Poulhan W side of entrance** 47°59′·1N 4°27′·9W Q.R.14m6M White square tower, red top

15 Audierne

As 13 Sainte Evette.

II BENODET BAY

16 Pointe de Penmarc'h

A **Eckmühl** 47°47′·9N 4°22′·4W Fl.5s60m23M Horn60s Grey 8-sided tower
B **Men Hir** 47°47′·7N 4°24′·0W Fl(2)WG.6s19m7/4M 135°-G-315°-W-135° White tower, black band
C **Locarec** 47°47′·3N 4°20′·3W Iso.WRG.4s11m9/6M 063°-G-068°-R-271°-W-285°-R-298°-G-340°-R-063° Metal column on rock
D **Lost Moan** 47°47′·0N 4°16′·8W Fl(3)WRG.12s8m9/6M 327°-R-014°-G-065°-R-140°-W-160°-R-268°-W-273°-G-317°-W-327° White tower, red top
E **Cap Caval buoy (WCM)** 47°46′·5N 4°22′·7W Q(9)15s Whis
F **Spinec buoy (SCM)** 46°45′·2N 4°18′·9W Q(6)+LFl.15s Whis
G **Karreg Kreiz (ECM)** 47°46′·0N 4°11′·4W Q(3)10s Whis

17 Le Guilvinec

A **Névez buoy (starboard)** 47°45′·8N 4°20′·1W Fl.G.2·5s
B **Spinec Buoy (SCM)** 46°45′·2N 4°18′·9W Q(6)+LFl.15s Whis
C **Locarec** 47°47′·3N 4°20′·3W Iso.WRG.4s11m9/6M 063°-G-068°-R-271°-W-285°-R-298°-G-340°-R-063° Metal column on rock
Ldg Lts 053° Synchronised
D *Front* 47°47′·4N 4°17′·1W Q.7m8M 233°-vis-066° White pylon on starboard mole spur
Middle 210m from *front* Q.WG.12m14/11M 006°-W-293°-G-006° Red square on white column
Rear 1085m from *front* DirQ.26m8M 051·5°-vis-054·5° Red square on white tower, red stripe

E **Capelan buoy (starboard)** 47°47′·1N 4°17′·6W Fl(2)G.6s
F **S mole head** 47°47′·5N 4°17′·2W Fl.G.4s5m6M Round white hut, green top

18 Lesconil

A **Karreg Kreiz (ECM)** 47°46′·0N 4°11′·4W Q(3)10s
B **Men-ar-Groas** 47°47′·8N 4°12′·7W Fl(3)WRG.12s14m10-7M 268°-G-313°-W-333°-R-050° White tower, green top
C **E breakwater head** 47°47′·7N 4°12′·7W Q.G.5m5M Green tower
D **S breakwater head** 47°47′·7N 4°12′·7W Oc.R.4s5m6M White pylon, red top

19 Loctudy

A **Pointe de Langoz** 47°49′·9N 4°09′·6W Fl(4)WRG.12s12m15-11M 115°-W-257°-G-284°-W-295°-R-318°-W-328°-R-025° White tower, red top
B **Île aux Moutons** 47°46′·5N 4°01′·7W Iso.WRG.2s18m15-11M 035°-W-050°-G-063°-W-081°-R-141°-W-292°-R-035° White tower and dwelling
C **Pte de Combrit** *Front* 47°51′·9N 4°06′·8W Oc(2)WR.6s19m12-9M 325°-W-017°-R-325° White square tower grey corners
D *Rear* Pyramide 340m from *front* Oc(2+1)12s48m11M White tower, green top
E **Bilien buoy (ECM)** 47°49′·1N 4°08′·1W VQ(3)5s Whis
F **Karek-Saoz** 47°50′·0N 4°09′·4W Fl.R.2.5s3m1M Red truncated tower
G **Le Blas** 47°50′·3N 4°10′·2W Fl(4)G.15s5m1M Green truncated column

20 Bénodet and Sainte Marine

A **Pointe de Langoz** 47°49′·9N 4°09′·6W Fl(4)WRG.12s12m15-11M 115°-W-257°-G-284°-W-295°-R-318°-W-328°-R-025° White tower, red top
B **Île aux Moutons** 47°46′·5N 4°01′·7W Iso.WRG.2s18m15-11M 035°-W-050°-G-063°-W-081°-R-141°-W-292°-R-035° White tower and dwelling
C **Pte de Combrit** *Front* 47°51′·9N 4°06′·8W Oc(3+1)WR.12s19m12-9M 325°-W-017°-R-325° White square tower grey corners
D *Rear* Pyramide 340m from *front* Oc(2+1)12s48m11M White tower, green top
Ldg Lts 345·5°
F *Front* Pte du Coq 47°52′·3N 4°06′·7W DirOc(2+1)G.12s11m17M 345°-intens-347°White round tower, vertical green stripe
Rear Pyramide 1180m from *front*. Oc(2+1)12s48m11M White tower, green top
G **Pte du Toulgoët** 47°52′·3N 4°06′·9W Fl.R.2.5s2m1M Red mast

21 River Odet

22 Îles de Glénan

A **Île aux Moutons** 47°46′·5N 4°01′·7W Iso.WRG.2s18m15-11M 035°-W-050°-G-063°-W-081°-R-141°-W-292°-R-035° White tower and dwelling
B **Penfret** 47°43′·3N 3°57′·2W Fl.R.5s36m21M White square tower, red top
Auxiliary light Q.W.34m12M 295°-vis-315° Same structure
C **La Pie** 47°43′·8N 3°59′·8W Fl(2)6s9m3M Isolated danger beacon

23 Port-La-Fôret

A **Cap-Coz (west) mole head** 47°53′·5N 3°58′·3W Fl(2)WRG.6s5m7-5M shore-R-335°-G-340°-W-346°-R-shore Red lantern on grey post, white hut
B **Kerleven (east) mole head** 47°53′·6N 3°58′·4W Fl.G.4s8m1M Green lantern on grey mast, white hut
C **Marina mole head** 47°53′·9N 3°58′·6W Iso.G.4s5m1M Green lantern on grey mast, white hut
D **Buoys marking entrance of channel** Fl(2)G.2·5s & port Fl.R.2·5s

24 Concarneau

A **Le Cochon** 47°51′·5N 3°55′·5W Fl(3)WRG.12s5m9–6M 048°-G-205°-R-352°-W-048° Green tower

B **Basse du Chenal buoy (port)** 47°51'·6N 3°55'·6W Q.R
C **Men Fall buoy (starboard)** 47°51'·8N 3°55'·3W Fl.G.4s
  Ldg Lts 028·5°
D **La Croix** *Front* 47°52'·2N 3°55'·1W Q.W14m13M 006·5°-
  vis-093° Red and white tower
E *Rear* Beuzec 47°53'·4N 3°54'·0W 1·34M from *front*
  DirQ.87m23M 026·5°-intens-030·5° Belfry
F **Lanriec** 47°52'·0N 3°54'·6W Q.G.13m8M 063°-vis-078°
  Green window in white gable
G **La Médée** 47°52'·1N 3°54'·8W Fl(3)R.12s9m4M Red tower
H **Ville-Close** 47°52'·3N 3°54'·7W QWR.4m9-6M 209°-R-
  354°-W-007°-R-018° Red tower below wall of
  La Ville Close
I **East side (No. 1) Beacon** 47°52'·2N 3°54'·6W Fl.G.4s4m5M
  Green round tower
J **Entrance to Marina** 47°52'·2N 3°54'·7W Fl(4)R.15s3m1M
  Red post on N end of wavebreaker

III GROIX AND THE RIAS

25 The Aven River and Port Manec'h
A **Port Manec'h (Pointe de Beg-ar-Véchen)** 47°48'·0N
  3°44'·4W Oc(4)WRG.12s38m10-7M 050°-W(unintens)-
  140°-W-296°-G-303°-W-311°-R-328°-W-050° Obscd by
  Pointe de Beg-Moreg when bearing less than 299° White
  and red tower

26 River Belon

27 Merrien
A **Brigneau mole head** 47°46'·9N 3°40'·2W
  Oc(2)WRG.6s7m12-9M 280°-G-329°-W-339°-R-034° White
  column, red top
B **Merrien** 47°47'·1N 3°39'·0W Q.R.26m7M 004°-vis-009°
  White square tower, red top

28 Doëlan
  Ldg Lts 013.8°
A *Front* 47°46'·5N 3°36'·5W Oc(3)WG.12s20m13/10M shore-
  305°-G-314°-W-shore White tower, green band and top
B *Rear* 47°46'·5N 3°36'·3W 326m from *front* Oc(3)R.27m9M
  White tower, red band and top

29 Le Pouldhu

30 Lomçner
A **Anse de Stole** 47°42'·3N 3°25'·6W DirQ.WRG.13m10–8M
  349·2°-G-355·2°-W-359·2°-R-005·2° White tower, red top
B **Kerroc'h** 47°42'·0N 3°27'·7W Oc(2)WRG.6s22m11-8M
  096·5°-R-112·5°-G-132°-R-302°-W-096·5° White truncated
  tower, red top

31 Lorient
Passe de l'Ouest
  Ldg Lts 057°
A *Front* Les Soeurs 47°42'·1N 3°21'·8W DirQ.11m13M
  042·5°-intens-058·5° Red tower, white bands
B *Rear* Port Louis 47°42'·4N 3°21'·3W 740m from *front*
  DirQ.22m18M White daymark on building, red bands
C **Les Trois Pierres** 47°41'·5N 3°22'·5W Q.RG.11m6M 060°-G-
  196°-R-002° Black tower, white bands
Entrance
  Île Saint-Michel Ldg Lts 016·5°
F *Front* 47°43'·5N 3°21'·6W DirQ.G.8m13M 014·5°-intens-
  017·5° Grey tower, green top
G *Rear* 47°43'·7N 3°21'·5W 306m from *front*
  DirQ.G.14m13M 014·5°-intens-017·5° Synchronised with
  front grey tower, green top
H **La Citadelle** 47°42'·6N 3°21'·9W Oc.G.4s6m6M 012°-vis-
  192° Green concrete tower
I **La Petite Jument** 47°42'·6N 3°22'·1W Oc.R.4s5m6M 182°-
  vis-024° Red concrete tower
K **Le Cochon** 47°42'·8N 3°22'·0W Fl.R.4s5m5M Red tower,
  green band

Harbour
  Kéroman Submarine Base Ldg Lts 350°
L *Front* 47°43'·6N 3°22'·0W DirOc(2)R.6s25m15M Red
  house, white bands
M *Rear* 91m from *Front* DirOc(2)R.6s31m15M 349°-intens-
  351° Synchronised with *front* Red and white topmark on
  grey pylon, red top
  Kernével Ldg Lts 217°
N *Front* 47°43'·0N 3°22'·3W DirQ.R.10m15M 215°-intens-
  219° Red truncated cone on red and white metal
  framework tower
O *Rear* 47°42'·9N 3°22'·4W DirQ.R.18m15M 215°-intens-
  219° White square tower, red top
P **Pte de L'Espérance** 47°44'·5N 3°20'·76W DirQ.WRG.8m10-
  8M 034·2°-G-036·7°-W-037·2°-R-047·2° (White sector
  covers Kernével Ldg Lts 14, 15) White tower, green top
Q **Fishing harbour entrance, E side** 47°43'·6N 3°21'·9W
  Fl.RG.4s7m6M 000°-G-235°-R-000° White truncated
  tower, green top
R **Pengarne** 47°43'·9N 3°21'·2W Fl.G.2·5s3m3M Green
  tower
S **Ro Ro terminal jetty head** 47°44'·4N 3°21'·0W Q.R.7m2M
  Red structure
Kernével
T **South basin, E Breakwater head** 47°43'·2N 3°21'·9W
  Fl.Y.2·5s4m2M
U **North basin entrance E side (buoy)** 47°43'·5N 3°22'·0W
  Fl.Y.2·5s Conical yellow buoy, can topmark
V **North basin entrance W side (buoy)** 47°43'·5N 3°22'·0W
  Fl(4)Y.15s Conical yellow buoy, triangle topmark
Locmiquélic (Ste-Catherine)
W **Breakwater head (S side of entrance)** 47°43'·6N 3°21'·0W
  Q.G.5m2M Green post
X **N side (buoy)** 47°43'·5N 3°21'·1W Q.R Red can buoy, can
  topmark
Port de Commerce
Y **Entrance, S side (No.8 buoy)** 47°44'·6N 3°21'·0W Fl.R.2·5s
  Red can buoy, can topmark

32 Port Louis and Locmalo
A **Île aux Souris** 47°42'·2N 3°21'·5W DirQ.WG.6m3/2M
  041·5°-W-043·5°-G-041·5° Green framework tower
B **Port Louis jetty** 47°42'·7N 3°21'·37W Fl.G.2·5s7m4M 043°-
  vis-301° White tower, green top

33 Port Tudy
A **East mole head** 47°38'·7N 3°26'·8W Fl(2)R.6s11m7M 112°-
  vis-226° White round tower, red top
B **North mole head** 47°38'·7N 3°26'·7W Iso.G.4s12m7M
  White tower, green top

34 Locmaria
A **Pen Men** 47°38'·9N 3°30'·5W Fl(4)25s60m29M 309°-vis-
  275° White square tower, black top
B **Pointe des Chats** 47°37'·2N 3°25'·3W Fl.R.5s16m19M
  White square tower and dwelling
C **Les Chats buoy (SCM)** 47°35'·7N 3°23'·6W Q(6)+LFl.15s
D **Pointe de la Croix** 47°38'·0N 3°25'·0W Oc.WR.4s16m12-
  9M 169°-W-336°-R-345°-W-353° White pedestal, red
  lantern

35 Etel
A **Plateau des Brivideaux** 47°29'·1N 3°17'·5W
  Fl(2)6s24m10M Black tower, red bands
B **West side of entrance** 47°38'·7N 3°12'·9W
  Oc(2)WRG.6s13m9-6M 022°-W-064°-R-123°-W-330°-G-
  022° Red metal framework tower
C **Epi de Plouhinec head** 47°38'·7N 3°12'·8W Fl.R.2·5s7m2M
  Red structure

IV QUIBERON BAY

36 Sauzon
A **West jetty** 47°22'·4N 3°13'·1W Q.G.9m5M 194°-vis-045° White tower, green top
B **NW jetty head** 47°22'·5N 3°13'·1W Fl.G.4s8m8M White tower, green top
C **SE jetty head** 47°22'·4N 3°13'·1W Fl.R.4s8m8M White truncated tower, red top

37 Le Palais
A **South jetty head** 47°20'·8N 3°09'·1W Q.R.11m7M White round tower, red lantern
B **North jetty head** 47°20'·8N 3°09'·1W Q.G.11m7M White tower, green top

38 Belle-Île Anchorages
A **Goulphar** 47°18'·6N 3°13'·7W Fl(2)10s87m27M Grey tower, red lamp
B **Pointe des Poulains** 47°23'·3N 3°15'·2W Fl.5s34m23M White square tower and dwelling, red lamp
C **Pointe de Kerdonis** 47°18'·6N 3°03'·6W Fl(3).15s49m15M White square tower, red top and white dwelling

39 Teignouse Passage
A **Port Maria main light** 47°28'·8N 3°07'·5W Q.WRG.28m14-10M 246°-W-297°-G-340°-W-017°-R-051°-W-081°-G-098°-W-143° Obscured 252°-291°(39°) White tower, green lantern
B **La Teignouse** 47°27'·5N 3°02'·8W Fl.WR.4s20m15/11M 033°-W-039°-R-033° White round tower, red top
C **Goué Vaz Sud buoy (SCM)** 47°25'·8N 3°04'·9W Q(6)+LFl.15s Whis
D **Basse du Milieu buoy (starboard)** 47°25'·9N 3°04'·1W Fl(2)G.6s9m2M Green triangle on green HFPB
E **Goué Vaz E buoy (port)** 47°26'·2N 3°04'·3W Fl(3)R.12s
F **NE Teignouse buoy (starboard)** 47°26'·6N 3°01'·9W Fl(3)G.12s
G **Basse Nouvelle buoy (port)** 47°27'·0N 3°02'·0W Fl.R.2·5s
H **Port Haliguen, E breakwater head** 47°29'·3N 3°06'·0W Oc(2)WR.6s10m11-8M 233°-W-240·5°-R-299°-W-306°-R-233° White tower, red top

40 Île Houat
A **Port St-Gildas N mole** 47°23'·6N 2°57'·3W Fl(2)WG.6s8m9-6M 168°-W-198°-G-210°-W-240°-G-168° White tower, green top

41 Île Hoëdic
A **Port de l'Argol breakwater head** 47°20'·7N 2°52'·6W Fl.WG.4s10m9-6M 143°-W-163°-G-183°-W-194°-G-143° White tower, green top
B **Grouguéguez (Les Grands Cardinaux)** 47°19'·3N 2°50'·1W Fl(4)15s28m13M Red tower, white band

42 Port Haliguen
A **Port Maria main Lt** 47°28'·8N 3°07'·5W Q.WRG.28m14-10M 246°-W-252°, 291°-W-297°-G-340°-W-017°-R-051°-W-081°-G-098°-W-143° White tower, green lantern
B **Marina, new breakwater head** 47°29'·3N 3°06'·0W Oc(2)WR.6s10m11-8M 233°-W-240·5°-R-299°-W-306°-R-233° White tower, red top
C **Old breakwater elbow** 47°29'·3N 3°06'·0W Fl.R.4s10m5M 322°-vis-206° White tower, red top
D **NW mole head** 47°29'·4N 3°06'·1W Fl.G.2·5s9m6M White column, green top
E **Pier head** 49°29'·3N 3°06'·0W Fl.Vi.2·5s5m Purple column

43 La Trinité
La Trinité Ldg Lts 347°
A *Front* 47°34'·1N 3°00'·4W Q.WRG.11m10-7M 321°-G-345°-W-013·5°-R-080° White tower, green top
B *Rear* 560m from *front* Q.21m13M 337°-intens-357° Synchronised with *front* White round tower, green top
C **La Trinité-sur-mer Dir Lt** 347° 47°35'·0N 3°01'·0W DirOc.WRG.4s9m13-11M 345°-G-346°-W-348°-R-349° White tower
D **Le Petit Trého buoy (port)** 47°33'·5N 3°00'·7W Fl(4)R.15s

E **S pier head** 47°35'·1N 3°01'·5W Oc(2)WR.6s6m9/6M 090°-R-293·5°-W-300·5°-R-329° White tower, red top
F **Marina pierhead** 47°35'·3N 3°01'·5W Iso.R.4s8m5M White framework tower, red top

44 River Auray
A **Port Navalo** 47°32'·9N 2°55'·1W Oc(3)WRG.12s32m15-11M 155°-W-220°, 317°-G-359°-W-015°-R-105° White tower and dwelling
B **Le Grand Mouton beacon (starboard)** 47°33'·7N 2°54'·9W Q.G.4m2M Green tripod
C **Grégan** 47°33'·9N 2°55'·1W Q(6)+LFl.15s3m7M Black beacon, yellow top

45 Vannes
As 44 The Auray River and Auray

46 Port du Crouesty

47 Morbihan Anchorages

V THE VILAINE AND THE LOIRE

48 Pénerf
A **Le Pignon** 47°30'·0N 2°38'·9W Fl(3)WR.12s6m9-6M 028·5°-R-167°-W-175°-R-349·5°-W-028·5° Red square on tower

49 The Vilaine to Arzal
A **Basse de Kervoyal** 47°30'·4N 2°32'·6W DirQ.WR.7m6-4M 269°-W-271°-R-269° S card beacon tower
B **Basse Bertrand** 47°31'·1N 2°30'·7W Iso.WG.4s6m9-6M 040°-W-054°-G-227°-W-234°-G-040° Green tower
C **Penlan** 47°31'·0N 2°30'·1W Oc(2)WRG.6s26m14-11M 292·5°-R-025°-G-052°-W-060°-R-138°-G-180° White tower, red bands
D **Pointe du Scal** 47°29'·7N 2°26'·8W Q.G.8m4M White square tower, green top

50 La Roche Bernard and Foleux

51 Redon

52 Piriac-sur-Mer
A **Inner Mole Head** 47°22'·9N 2°32'·7W Oc(2)WRG.6s8m10-7M 066°-R-148°-G-194°-W-201°-R-221° White column
B **East Breakwater head** 47°23'·0N 2°32'·7W Fl.R.4s5m5M White structure, red top

53 La Turballe
A **Jetée de Garlahy (W breakwater head)** 47°20'·7N 2°30'·9W Fl(4)WR.12s13m10-7M 060°-R-315°-W-060° White pylon, red top
Ldg Lts 006·5°
B *Front* 47°20'·8N 2°30'·9W DirIso.R.4s11m3M 004°-intens-009° Metal mast, orange top
C *Rear* 280m from *front* DirIso.R.4s19m3M 004°-intens-009° Metal mast, orange top

54 Le Croisic
A **Jetée du Tréhic head** 47°18'·5N 2°31'·4W Iso.WG.4s12m14-11M 042°-G-093°-W-145°-G-345° Grey tower, green top
B **Basse Hergo tower** 47°18'·6N 2°31'·7W Fl.G.2·5s5m2M Green beacon tower
First Ldg Lts 156°
C *Front* 47°18'·0N 2°31'·0W DirQ.10m13M 154°-intens-158° Orange topmark on white metal framework tower
D *Rear* 116m from *front* DirQ.14m13M 154°-intens-158° Synchronised with *front* Orange topmark on white metal framework tower
Second Ldg Lts 174°
E *Front* 47°18'·1N 2°31'·1W DirQ.G.5m8M 171°-vis-177° Yellow can topmark, green stripe on green and white pylon
F *Rear* 48m from *front* DirQ.G.8m8M 171°-vis-177° Yellow can topmark, green stripe on green and white pylon
G **Le Grand Mabon** 47°18'·0N 2°31'·0W Fl(3)R.12s6m2M Red framework structure and pedestal

Third Ldg lights 134·7°
H *Front* 47°17'·9N 2°30'·8W DirQ.R.6m8M 125·5°-intens-143·5° Red and white chequered rectangle on white pylon, red top
I *Rear* 52m from *front* DirQ.R.10m8M 125·5°-intens-143·5° Synchronised with *front* Red and white chequered rectangle on pylon, on fish market roof

55 Le Pouliguen
A **Les Guérandaises buoy** 47°15'·0N 2°24'·3W Fl.G.2·5s Starboard-hand pillar buoy
B **Penchâteau buoy** 47°15'·2N 2°24'·4W Fl.R.2·5s Port-hand pillar buoy
C **Petits Impairs** 47°16'·0N 2°24'·6W Fl(2)G.6s6m2M Green triangle on tower
D **Le Pouliguen, S jetty** 47°16'·4N 2°25'·4W Q.R.13m9M 171°-vis-081° White column, red lantern

56 Pornichet
A **Les Guérandaises buoy** 47°15'·0N 2°24'·3W Fl.G.2·5s Starboard-hand pillar buoy
B **Penchâteau buoy** 47°15'·2N 2°24'·4W Fl.R.2·5s Port-hand pillar buoy
C **Pornichet, S breakwater head** 47°15'·5N 2°21'·2W Iso.WRG.4s11m10/7M 303°-G-081°-W-084°-R-180° White tower
D **Pornichet entrance west** 47°15'·5N 2°21'·1W Q.G.3m1M
E **Pornichet entrance east** 47°15'·5N 2°21'·1W Q.R.4m1M

57 Saint-Nazaire and Nantes
A **La Banche** 47°10'·6N 2°28'·1W Fl(2)WR.6s22m15-11M 266°-R-280°-W-266° Black tower, white bands
B **Île du Pilier** 47°02'·6N 2°21'·6W Fl(3)20s33m29M Grey pyramidal tower
 Auxiliary light Q.R.10m11M 321°-vis-034° same structure
C **Le Grand Charpentier** 47°12'·8N 2°19'·2W Q.WRG.22m14-10M 020°-G-054°-W-062°-R-092°-W-111°-R-310°-W-020° Grey tower, green lantern
D **Pointe de St-Gildas** 47°08'·2N 2°14'·8W Q.WRG.20m14-10M 264°-R-308°-G-078°-W-088°-R-174°-W-180°-G-264° Column on white house, green top
E **Pointe d'Aiguillon** 47°14'·5N 2°15'·8W Oc(3)WR.12s27m13-10M 207°-R-233°-W-293°, 297°-W-300°-R-327°-W-023°-R-069° White tower
 Ldg lights 025·5°
F *Front* 47°15'·2N 2°15'·0W DirQ.6m22M 024·7°-intens-026·2° White column on dolphin
G *Rear* 0.75M from *front* DirQ.36m24M 024°-intens-027° Synchronised with *front*, shown throughout 24 hours Black square, white stripe on metal tower
H **Villè-es-Martin, jetty head** 47°15'·3N 2°13'·7W Fl(2)6s10m10M White tower, red top
I **Morées** 47°15'·0N 2°13'·0W Fl(3)WR.12s12m6-4M 058°-W-224°, 300°-R-058° Green truncated tower
J **St-Nazaire, W Jetty** 47°16'·0N 2°12'·3W Oc(4)R.12s11m8M White tower, red top
K **St-Nazaire E Jetty** 47°16'·0N 2°12'·1W Oc(4)G.12s11m11M White tower, green top
M **Basse Nazaire Sud buoy** 47°16'·2N 2°11'·6W Q(6)+LFl.15s S card pillar buoy
N **Old mole head** 47°16'·3N 2°11'·8W Q(3)10s18m11M White tower, red top

58 Saint-Gildas
A **Pointe de St-Gildas** 47°08'·2N 2°14'·8W Q.WRG.20m14-10M 264°-R-308°-G-078°-W-088°-R-174°-W-180°-G-264° Column on white house, green top
B **Breakwater head** 47°08'·5N 2°14'·7W Fl(2)G.6s3M Metal post

59 Pornic
A **Pointe de St-Gildas** 47°08'·2N 2°14'·8W Q.WRG.20m14-10M 264°-R-308°-G-078°-W-088°-R-174°-W-180°-G-264° Column on white house, green top
B **Pointe de Noëveillard** 47°06'·6N 2°06'·9W Oc(4)WRG.12s22m13-9M shore-G-051°-W-079°-R-shore White square tower, green top, white dwelling

C **Marina elbow** 47°06'·4N 2°07'·0W Fl.2.5s4m3M Grey structure
D **Marina entrance, S side** 47°06'·5N 2°06'·7W Fl(2)R.6s4m2M Black column, red top
E **Marina entrance, N side** 47°06'·5N 2°06'·7W Fl(2).G.6s4m2M Black column, green top
F **Fairway buoy** 47°06'·5N 2°06'·6W LFl.10s Red and white buoy

VI THE VENDÉE

60 Herbaudière
A **Île du Pilier** 47°02'·6N 2°21'·6W Fl(3)20s33m29M Grey pyramidal tower
 Auxiliary Lt Q.R.10m11M 321°-vis-034° same structure
B **Basse du Martroger** 47°02'·6N 2°17'·1W Q.WRG.11m9-6M 033°-G-055°-W-060°-R-095°-G-124°-W-153°-R-201°-W-240°-R-033° N card beacon tower
C **Passe de la Grise** SCM 47°01'·7N 2°20'·0W Q(6)+LFl.15s
D **Pierre Moine** 47°03'·4N 2°12'·4W Fl(2)6s14m7M Isolated danger tower
 L'Herbaudière
I **West jetty** 47°01'·6N 2°17'·9W Oc(2+1)WG.12s9m10/7M 187·5°-W-190°-G-187·5° White column and hut, green top
 Ldg Lts 187·5°
J *Front* 47°01'·6N 2°17'·9W Q.5m7M 098°-vis-278° Grey mast
K *Rear* 310m from *front* Q.21m7M 098°-vis-278°Grey mast
L. **East jetty head** 47°01'·7N 2°17'·7W Fl(2)R.6s8m4M Red tripod

61 Noirmoutier Anchorages
A **Pointe du Devin (Port Morin)** 46°59'·1N 2°17'·6W Oc(4)WRG.12s10m11-8M 314°-G-028°-W-035°-R-134° White column and hut, green top
B **Basse du Martroger** 47°02'·6N 2°17'·1W Q.WRG.11m9-6M 033°-G-055°-W-060°-R-095°-G-124°-W-153°-R-201°-W-240°-R-033° N card beacon tower
C **Pierre Moine** 47°03'·4N 2°12'·4W Fl(2)6s14m7M Isolated danger tower
D **Pointe des Dames** 47°00'·7N 2°13'·3W Oc(3)WRG.12s34m19-15M 016·5°-G-057°-R-124°-G-165°-W-191°-R-267°-W-357°-R-016·5° White square tower
E **Port de Noirmoutier jetty** 46°59'·3N 2°13'·1W Oc(2)R.6s6m6M White column, red top.

62 Fromentine

63 Port-Joinville
A **Petite Foule (main light)** 46°43'·1N 2°23'·0W Fl.5s56m24M Square white tower green lantern
B **Les Chiens Perrins** 46°43'·6N 2°24'·6W Q(9)WG.15s16m7-4M 330°-G-350°-W-200° W card beacon tower
C **Pointe des Corbeaux** 46°41'·4N 2°17'·1W Fl(2+1)R.15s25m20M White square tower, red top
D **Port Joinville NW jetty head** 46°43'·8N 2°20'·8W Oc(3)WG.12s10m11-8M shore-G-150°-W-232°-G-279°-W-285°-G-shore White octagonal tower, green top
 Quai du Canada Ldg Lts 219°
F *Front* 46°43'·6N 2°21'·0W Q.R.11m6M 169°-vis-269° Pylon
G *Rear* 85m from *front* Q.R.16m6M 169°-vis-269° Pylon

64 Port de la Meule
A **Port de la Meule** 46°41'·7N 2°20'·8W Oc.WRG.4s9m9-6M 007·5°-G-018°-W-027·5°-R-041·5° Grey square tower, red top

65 Saint-Gilles-Croix-de-Vie
A **Pointe de Grosse Terre** 46°41'·5N 1°57'·9W Fl(4)WR.12s25m18-15M 290°-R-339°-W-125°-R-145° White truncated conical tower
 Ldg Lts 043·7°
B *Front* 46°41'·9N 1°56'·7W Q.7m15M 033·5°-intens-053·5° White square tower, red top
C *Rear* 260m from *front* Q.28m15M 033·5°-intens-053·5° Synchronised with *front* White square tower, red top
D **Pill'Hours buoy** (SCM) 46°41'·0N 1°58'·1W Q(6)+ LFl.15s

E **NW jetty head** 46°41'·6N 1°57'·2W Fl.R.4s8m6M Red column on white hut

F **SE jetty head** 46°41'·5N 1°57'·3W Fl.G.4s8m6M White structure, green top

66 Les Sables d'Olonne

A **L'Armandèche** 46°29'·4N 1°48'·3W Fl(2+1)15s42m24M 295°-vis-130° White 6-sided tower, red top

B **Les Barges** 46°29'·7N 1°50'·5W Fl(2)R.10s25m13M Grey tower

C **Petite Barge buoy** (SCM) 46°28'·9N 1°50'·6W Q(6)+LFl.15s3M Whis
   Passe du SW Ldg Lts 032·5°

D *Front* 46°29'·4N 1°46'·4W Iso.4s12m16M Shown throughout 24hrs Metal mast

E *Rear* 330m from *front* Iso.4s33m16M Shown throughout 24hrs White square masonry tower

F **Nouch Sud buoy (SCM)** 46°28'·6N 1°47'·4W Q(6)+LFl.15s
   Passe du SE Ldg Lts 320°

G *Front* Jetée des Sables 46°29'·4N 1°47'·5W Q.G.11m8M White tower, green top

H *Rear* Tour d'Arundel 465m from *front* Q.33m12M Large grey square tower surmounted by white turret

I **Jetée Saint Nicolas head** 46°29'·2N 1°47'·5W Q.R.16m8M 143°-vis-094° White tower, red top
   Entrance Ldg Lts 328·1°

J *Front* 46°29'·7N 1°47'·8W Iso.R.4s6m9M Red square on white hut

K *Rear* 65m from *front* DirIso.R.4s9m9M 324°-vis-330° Red square on white hut

67 Bourgenay

A **Fairway buoy** 46°25'·3N 1°41'·9W LFl.10s Red and white striped pillar buoy
   Ldg Lts 040°

B *Front* 46°26'·4N 1°40'·6W Q.G.9m7M 020°-vis-060° Green rectangle on white tower

C *Rear* 162m from *front* Q.G.19m7M 010°-vis-070° Green rectangle on white tower

D **W breakwater head** 46°26'·3N 1°40'·5W Fl.R.4s8m9M Red structure

68 Jard-Sur-Mer

VII CHARENTE

69 La Faute-Sur-Mer and L'Aiguillon

70 Marans

71 Ars-en-Ré

A **Pointe du Grouin du Cou (mainland)** 46°20'·7N 1°27'·8W Fl.WRG.5s29m20-16M 034°-R-061°-W-117°-G-138°-W-034° White 8-sided tower, black lantern

B **Les Baleineaux** 46°15'·8N 1°35'·2W VQ.23m7M Pink tower, red top

C **Les Baleines** 46°14'·6N 1°33'·7W Fl(4)15s53m27M Grey 8-sided tower, red lantern
   Le Fier d'Ars Dir.Oc.WRG.4s10M/7M. 275·5°-G-267·5°-W-268·5°-R-274.5°

Ars-en-Ré
Ldg Lts 232·5°

F *Front* 46°12'·8N 1°30'·6W Q.5m9M White rectangular hut, red lantern

G *Rear* 370m from *front* Q.13m11M 142°-vis-322° Black rectangle on white framework tower, green top

72 Saint-Martin-de-Ré

A **Ramparts E of entrance** 46°12'·4N 1°21'·9W Oc(2)WR.6s18m10-7M shore-W-245°-R-281°-shore White tower, red top

B **Mole head** 46°12'·5N 1°21'·9W Fl.G.2.5s10m5M White tripod, green top

C **W end of breakwater** 46°12'·5N 1°21'·9W Fl.R.2·5s5m2M White post, red top

73 La-Flotte-en-Ré

A **La Flotte-en-Ré** 46°11'·3N 1°19'·3W Fl.WG.4s10m12-9M 130°-G-205°-W-220°-G-257° Moiré effect Dir Lt 212·5° White round tower, green top

74 La Rochelle

A **Le Lavardin** 46°08'·1N 1°14'·5W Fl(2)WG.6s14m11-8M 160°-G-169°-W-160° Black tower, red band

B **Tour Richelieu** 46°08'·9N 1°10'·4W Fl.R.4s10m7M Red 8-sided tower
   Ldg Lts 059°

C *Front* 46°09'·4N 1°09'·2W DirQ.15m14M 056°-intens-062°Red round tower, white bands (By day Fl.4s)

D *Rear* 235m from *front* Q.25m14M 044°-vis-074°, 061°-obscd-065° Synchronised with *front* White 8-sided tower, green top (By day Fl.4s)

E **Port de Minimes W mole head** 46°08'·9N 1°10'·1W Fl(2)G.6s9m5M White tower, green top

F **Port de Minimes E mole head** 46°08'·9N 1°10'·0W Fl(2)R.6s6m5M White tower, red top

75 Île d'Aix

A **Chauveau (SE of Île de Ré)** 46°08'·0N 1°16'·4W Oc(3)WR.12s27m15-11M 057°-W-094°-R-104°-W-342°-R-057° White round tower, red top

B **Fort Boyard** 46°00'·0N 1°12'·9W Q(9)15s Fort

C **Île d'Aix** 46°00'·6N 1°10'·7W Fl.WR.5s24m24-20M 103°-R-118°-W-103° Two white round towers, red tops

La Charente river entrance Ldg Lts 115°

D *Front* 45°58'·0N 1°04'·4W DirQ.R.8m19M 113°-intens-117° White square tower, red top

E *Rear* 600m from *front* DirQ.R.21m20M 113°-intens-117° White square tower, red top
   Auxiliary Q.R.21m8M same structure

76 River Charente

Ldg Lts 115°

D *Front* 45°58'·0N 1°04'·4W DirQ.R.8m19M 113°-intens-117° White square tower, red top

E *Rear* 600m from *front* DirQ.R.21m20M 113°-intens-117° White square tower, red top
   Auxiliary Q.R.21m8M same structure
   Port-des-Barques Ldg Lts 134·3°

C *Front* 45°57'·0N 1°04'·2W Iso.G.4s5m9M125°-intens-145° White square tower

D *Rear* 490m from *front* Iso.G.4s13m11M 125°-intens-145° Synchronised with *front* White square tower with black band on W side

77 Rochefort

78 St-Denis-d'Oléron

A **Pointe de Chassiron** 46°02'·8N 1°24'·7W Fl.10s50m28M White round tower, black bands

B **Rocher d'Antioche** 46°03·9'N 1°24'·7W Q.20m11M NCM tower, surrounded by above-water wrecks.

St-Denis

C **Dir Ldg Lt 205°** 46°01'·6N 1°22'·0W Dir Iso.WRG.4s14m11-8M 190°-G-204°-W-206°-R-220° White concrete mast

D **East breakwater head** 46°02'·1N 1°22'·1W Fl(2)WG.6s11m9-6M 205°-G-277°-W-292°-G-165° Square masonry hut with pole

E **South breakwater head** 46°02'·1N 1°22'·2W Fl(2)R.6s3m6M Square masonry hut

79 Port Du Douhet

80 Boyardville

A **La Perrotine Mole head** 45°58'·2N 1°13'·9W Fl(2)R.6s8m5M White metal framework tower, red top

81 The Seudre to Marennes

A **Tourelle Juliar** 45°54'·2N 1°09'·4W Q(3)WG.10s12m11-8M 147°-W-336°-G-147° E card beacon tower

Le Château Ldg Lts 319°

B *Front* 45°53'·1N 1°11'·4W Q.R.11m7M 191°-vis-087° Red rectangle on low white tower

C *Rear* 240m from *front* Q.R.24m7M Synchronised with *front* White tower, red top

VIII THE GIRONDE

The Entrance to The Gironde

A **La Coubre** 45°41'·80N 1°14'·00W Fl(2)10s64m28M Auxiliary F.R.G.42m10M White truncated tower, red top

B **La Palmyre** Ldg Lts 081·5° Front 45°39'·56N 1°08'·77W Dir.Iso.4s21m20M White pylon on dolphin

C Common Rear 45°39'·72N 1°07'·25W Dir.Q.57m27M Grey radar tower
   Auxiliary Lt Dir.F.R.57m27M

D **Terre-Nègre** Ldg Lts 327·3° Front 45°38'·77N 1°06'·38W Oc(3)WRG.12s39m18/14M

E **Cordouan** 45°35'·20N 1°10'·40W Oc(2+1)WRG.12s60m22/18M

F **1st Ldg Lts 063°** Front 45°33'·73N 1°05'·01W Dir.Q.G.22m16M
   Rear 0·84M from front 45°34'·11N 1°03'·95W Oc.WRG.4s26m17/13M

G **Ldg Lts 041°** Front Le Chay 45°37'·31N 1°02'·43W Dir.Q.R.33m18M White tower, red top
   Rear 0·97M from front 45°38'·04N 1°01'·52W Dir.Q.R.61m18M Red water tower

The Gironde

A **Royan Jetée Sud**. Head 45°37'·00N 1°01'·80W Fl(2)R.10s11m12M White tower red brickwork base

B **Pointe de Grave**. Jetée Nord. Head 45°34'·40N 1°03'·70W Q.W.9m2M ↕ on yellow beacon, black top
   Spur 45°34'·32N 1°03'·64W Iso.G.4s8m3M Green ▲ on green beacon

C **Pointe de la Chambrette** 45°31'·92N 1°02'·12W Dir.Iso.WRG.4s4m12/8M Two platforms on white dolphin, black top, white bands base

D **Laména** 45°20'·10N 0°47'·80W Fl(2)6s6m7M Dolphin

E **Vitrezay** 45°19'·60N 0°43'·10W Fl(2)R.6s6m6M White column red top

F **Pauillac-Trompeloup** 45°13'·60N 0°44'·70W Fl.G.4s17m5M White pylon green top

G **Pauillac Marina Breakwater** 45°12'·00N 0°44'·60W Fl.G.4s7m5M Green mast

H **Blaye**. N Quay. Head 45°07'·50N 0°39'·90W Q(3)R.5s6m3M Red mast

I **Bec d'Ambès** 45°02'·53N 0°36'·47W Q.G.7m4M White pylon, green top

The Atlantic Coast

A **Hourtin** 45°08'·50N 1°09'·70W Fl.5s55m23M Red square brick tower, grey top

B **Cap Ferret** 44°38'·70N 1°15'·10W Fl.R.5s53m27M White truncated tower, red top
   Auxiliary Lt Oc(3)12s46m14M

C **ATT-ARC** 44°34'·05N 1°18'·71W LFl.W.10s5M • on red buoy, white stripes

D **Contis** 44°05'·70N 1°19'·20W Fl(4)25s50m23M White round tower black diagonal stripes

The Basque ports:

Capbreton

A **Capbreton. Digue Nord**. Head 43°39'·36N 1°26'·90W Fl(2)R.6s13m8M White square tower, red top

B **Estacade Sud (South Pier)** 43°39'·34N 1°26'·86W Fl(2)G.6s9m8M White metal tube, green top

Bayonne

A **Digue Jean Lesbordes**. Head 43°31'·89N 1°31'·99W Q.R.12m8M White square tower, red top

B **Boucau** Ldg Lts 090° Front 43°31'·82N 1°31'·23W Dir.Q.7m19M White pylon, red top
   Rear 43°31'·82N 1°31'·04W Dir.Q.16m19M

C **N Jetty Head** 43°31'·82N 1°31'·42W Iso.R.4s12m8M White pylon, red top

D **S Jetty Head** 43°31'·74N 1°31'·47W Iso.G.4s9m9M White square tower, green top

E **Digue Sud** 43°31'·53N 1°31'·74W Q(9)15s15m7M Yellow pylon, black band

F **Entrance Ldg Lts 111·5°** Front 43°31'·63N 1°30'·93W Dir.Q.G.7m13M White hut, green band
   Rear 43°31'·60N 1°30'·82W Dir.Q.G.10m13M White square tower, green bands

G **Training wall. Nord**. W end 43°31'·77N 1°31'·24W Fl(2)R.6s10m8M White tower, red top

H **Sud. E End** 43°31'·63N 1°30'·89W Q.G.7m8M White column, green top

I **Forges de l'Adour** Ldg Lts 322·4° Front 43°31'·62N 1°29'·92W Dir.Q.R.15m8M White pylon, red top
   Rear 43°31'·68N 1°29'·98W Dir.Q.R.22m13M Pylon

J **Blancpignon**. Quai Edouard-Castel 43°30'·94N 1°29'·60W Fl(2)G.6s8m6M Green metal column on white base

K **Pont de L'Aveugle**. Dir Lt 172·5° 43°30'·06N 1°29'·53W Dir.Q.WRG.8m10/7M Metal column

L **Pointe Saint-Martin** 43°29'·63N 1°33'·23W Fl(2)10s73m27M White truncated tower, black top

Biarritz

A **Ldg Lts 174°** Front 43°29'·02N 1°33'·96W Fl.R.2·5s7m3M White metal mast
   Rear 83m from front 43°28'·97N 1°33'·95W Fl.R.2·5s19m3M White metal mast

B **Guéthary. Ldg Lts 123°**. Front 43°25'·60N 1°36'·50W Q.R.11m6M Red top on white mast
   Rear 43°25'·60N 1°36'·50W Q.R.33m6M White tower

St-Jean-De-Luz

A **Sainte-Barbe** Ldg Lts 101° Front 43°23'·96N 1°39'·87W Oc(4)R.12s30m18M White ▲ on white hut
   Rear 43°23'·93N 1°39'·62W Oc(4)R.12s47m18M Black ▲ on white square tower

B **Entrance Ldg Lts 150·6°** Front 43°23'·26N 1°40'·13W Dir.Q.G.18m17M White pyramidal tower, red stripe
   Rear 43°23'·06N 1°39'·99W Dir.Q.G.27m17M White pyramidal tower, green stripe

C **Digue des Criquas. Head** 43°23'·84N 1°40'·66W Iso.G.4s11m6M Green square tower

D **Passe D'Illarguita** Ldg Lts 138·4° Front 43°23'·70N 1°41'·19W Q.WR.36m12/8M White square tower, black stripe
   Rear 0·77M from front 43°23'·13N 1°40'·49W Dir.Q.67m20M White pylon, black bands

Hendaye

A **Hendaye. Épi Socoburu**. Head 43°22'·67N 1°47'·23W LFl.R.10s8m5M White column, red top

B **Training Wall. Head** 43°22'·83N 1°47'·34W Fl(3)G.9s9m5M Green tower

C **N breakwater. Corner** 43°23'·17N 1°47'·29W Q(3)W.5s13m3M ↕ on black post, yellow band on stone column

D **Cabo Higuer** 43°23'·52N 1°47'·52W Fl(2)W.10s63m23M White square tower, red cupola

APPENDIX

Index